Artificial Intelligence
and the Future of Testing

Artificial Intelligence and the Future of Testing

Edited by

Roy Freedle
Educational Testing Service

Psychology Press
Taylor & Francis Group
New York London

First Published by
Lawrence Erlbaum Associates, Inc., Publishers
365 Broadway
Hillsdale, New Jersey 07642

Transferred to Digital Printing 2009 by Psychology Press
270 Madison Ave, New York NY 10016
27 Church Road, Hove, East Sussex, BN3 2FA

Library of Congress Cataloging-in-Publication Data

Artificial intelligence and the future of testing / edited by Roy
   Freedle.
        p.   cm.
   Includes bibliographical references.
   ISBN 0-8058-0117-0
   1. Educational tests and measurements — United States — Congresses.
   2. Artificial intelligence — Educational applications — Congresses.
   3. Computer-assisted instruction — United States — Congresses.
   I. Freedle, Roy O.
   LB3051.A755   1990
   371.2'6'0973 — dc20   90-31396
                                                             CIP

*To Elizabeth Winifred White, who stimulated
my intellectual, aesthetic, and spiritual
quest 41 years ago—with affection.*

Contents

Preface

Funds were made available by ETS's Senior Vice President Robert Solomon (now ex officio) for conducting a conference to explore how current fields of AI might contribute to ETS's plans to automate one or more of its testing activities. Towards this end, experts in several AI specialties were brought together with ETS researchers and test developers for 2 days to hear and discuss 12 papers that were written with testing issues in mind. In addition to these 12 papers, two discussants were asked to give their critiques of the conference.

Of these 14 presentations, 11 reached the final-draft stage and these have been included in this volume. To these, two additional documents have been added. Prior to the conference proceedings, I sent a paper to each conference participant to raise what I thought might be interesting topics for discussion. The first chapter of this volume, with minor alterations, represents this preconference material; it provides a convenient overview of the wide variety of topics that the conference was intended to survey. In addition to this opening chapter, I have added a final contribution by Randy Bennett and colleagues in order to illustrate the type of AI activity that is currently being supported at ETS; it is a collaborative effort between several ETS researchers and AI experts at Yale University.

Each author was asked first to survey his area of expertise and, whenever possible, to include some comments on how his or her field might impinge upon testing issues. By and large, all authors commented on how their field may impinge on testing.

A brief overview of all the chapters will help to contextualize additional comments that I wish to make below:

The opening chapter by Freedle used the topic outline of the three-volume *Handbook of Artificial Intelligence* (Barr & Feigenbaum, 1981, 1982; Cohen & Feigenbaum, 1982) to speculate about possible uses each AI specialty might have for a wide number of testing activities. Issues such as parsing, text generation, understanding spoken language, search routines, automatic programming, semantic network models of memory, automatic deduction, vision, learning and inductive inference, planning and problem solving, robotics, and so forth were taken up in turn. Suggestions for what types of testing formats might be pursued were considered along with suggestions for emphasizing a developmental perspective in theory building. Problems such as the scoring open-ended (constructed) response formats and the incorporation of spatial/visual ability estimates in our testing activities were also addressed.

The next two chapters (by Ager and by Milson, Lewis, & Anderson) cover the area of mathematic tutors. The chapter by Ager surveys the VALID and EXCHECK instruction systems for symbolic logic and set theory. For numerous reasons, Ager favors an instructional system that eschews development of a formal model of the learner. Ager further considers several types of testing situations that might be suitable for achievement and diagnostic testing, especially for mathematical and logical reasoning.

The chapter by Milson, Lewis, and Anderson surveys a general methodology for the design of intelligent tutoring systems. They apply the ACT methodology (see Anderson, 1983) to the domain of algebra by building an intelligent tutoring system for a high school algebra class. Part of such intelligent tutoring systems is the development of a formal model of the student learner for the domain at hand. The application to testing issues is obvious inasmuch as part of the process of instruction (via the AI tutor) is evaluation of what the student knows at each step of the learning process.

The next two chapters (by Pinker and by Kitchen) deal with the broad areas of graph comprehension and computer vision. The chapter by Pinker presents a theory of graph comprehension. Pinker develops his theory in part to help explain why the presentation of information in pictorial form (whether it is by line or bar graphs, Venn diagrams, tree structures, and so forth) is a preferred means of information presentation. The relevance for test situations should be obvious—many quantitative items are presented with visual diagrams to help state the problem; furthermore, instructions for producing written essays for evaluation are sometimes accompanied by tables and/or graphs to stimulate a student's written productions. A cognitive theory of what types of graph structures are easier to process than others should be very useful for test developers; this is true whether the test is presented via a computer terminal or by conventional paper-and-pencil methods.

The chapter by Kitchen is a survey of selected issues in computer vision.

This chapter deals, among other things, with such practical issues as the automatic reading (with or without comprehension) of, say, a student's handwritten essay. Clearly, AI vision potentially has great practical import for handling some of the data-management tasks of a testing organization.

The next two chapters deal broadly with the issues of student reasoning and the human accessing of relevant information. The first, by Burstein and Adelson, deals with a theory of analogical learning. Such a theory which seeks to explain how explanations presented as analogies are applied by students who are learning about new content domains should be of value in developing a more detailed model of the student as learning in some of the AI tutorial programs such as were presented by Milson, Lewis, and Anderson in Chapter 3. Incidentally, this chapter by Burstein and Adelson, along with their citations of the work of Carbonell (1983, 1986), can be viewed as AI's answer to the developmental issue that I raised in the introductory chapter.

The chapter by Ross deals with the accessing and use of relevant information from memory for problem solving. Ross, in part, considers the implications of his work from the perspective of individual differences. He points out that for a restricted domain, learners of different ability levels can vary in when and how they notice relevant information. From this, he speculates about how one might measure such variation within a testing situation. This illustrates, for test developers, how close attention to cognitive processes can generate new testing formats in order to measure the underlying processes. The suggestion is a general one and could be applied presumably to automated testing as well as conventional paper-and-pencil methods.

The chapter by Adelson deals with modeling software design within a general problem-space architecture. Adelson presents data that illustrate how within an open-ended response format (constructed responses) people can solve design problems; here the design problem deals with constructing a computer mail message system (also see connection with Bennett and colleagues' chapter on the AI evaluation of open-ended solutions to math problems).

The next chapter by Rau deals with memory organization and retrieval. Although Ross's chapter deals with data concerning human retrieval of relevant information in memory, Rau deals with the AI perspective for similar problems. Rau's key assumptions are that memory organization is hierarchical, categorical, continuous, associative, procedural, and distributed. In terms of testing applications, one again can see that if Rau's characterization of memory is correct, this places limits on the types of learner model that might be envisioned in, say, AI tutorial systems.

The chapter by Jacobs deals with natural language systems. He points out that although natural language systems for restricted domains is already a reality, robust programs for comprehending freeform text (as, for example, in analyzing a student's essay) are still wanting. Jacobs indicates that two problems need to be addressed: Computer programs need to be equipped with a core of knowledge that applies across domains, and, programs are needed that integrate linguistic and conceptual processes.

The next two chapters are selective critical commentaries by two emminent AI researchers: Saul Amarel and Aravind Joshi. Both commentaries bring to bear a rich historical perspective and make numerous suggestions about the possibilities of applying AI to the domain of testing activities. A developmental perspective is evident in Amarel's chapter, especially his comments concerning the shift from a single problem-solving episode to a focus on a history of problem-solving episodes. Also, the movement from simple "toy-problems" to dealing with the complexities of the real world (as in analyzing natural text) reflects a developmental perspective.

The final chapter by Bennett, Gong, Kershaw, Rock, Soloway, and Macalalad represents an application of AI to the scoring of open-ended response formats produced by people writing their solution to computer programming problems. The first four of these authors are ETS researchers; the latter two are AI experts from Yale. This type of collaborative research represents a good division of labor and a prototype of how ETS might be able to move quickly ahead in applying AI knowledge to testing issues.

SOME PHILOSOPHICAL ISSUES REGARDING AI AND EDUCATION

At this point I would like to step outside the framework of the conference to point out some potential dangers that I feel are implicit in wedding AI to testing as well as instructional activities.

We are at an exciting juncture in applying AI to testing activities. But, any intelligent person is surely aware how easily an overreliance on technology for solving educational or social problems can lead to a worsening of such ills. This danger is especially acute, it seems to me, given the overemphasis in Western education on the development of technologically useful skills, especially the verbal, quantitative, and more recently, the reasoning skills. These skills are important, to be sure; but so are the abilities to create paintings, poetry, and to form emotional bonds with excellent teachers who in turn can inspire students towards one career or another. These other abilities bring life to an otherwise barren experience.

In short, the human element is easily misplaced in current Western educational settings, even though that element is admittedly still present. However, it is present not because it is explicitly honored as a crucial ingredient in developing a student's motivation to learn and a motivation to serve society in a positive (less self-seeking) manner, but because it is a holdover from earlier more humanistic and less frantic times when teachers had the leisure to be concerned about each student and when people felt confident in a stable future.

This overemphasis on left-hemisphere (and frontal cortext) functions in education coupled with a devaluation of the teacher's input in learning (i.e., a devaluation stemming from society's belief that only indifferent, causal mechanisms truly matter) can lead to a disruption of the real goal of education, to teach not only useful economic skills but to inspire good citizenship and an appreciation of the aesthetic realm of life (which, I believe, in the long run is what really matters).

I would like to feel that this new beginning represented by the wedding of AI and educational testing can represent a positive force in our culture. One possible way in which this is likely to occur within a technological-educational setting is by recognizing that the student is a complex biological system (a feeling system, not only a thinking rational system) and so is not just an assembly of disconnected skills, abilities, and strategies to be separately measured and categorized.

By a series of steps, I can envision that AI modeling of the human can gradually incorporate not only the base-level skills and abilities (such as the motoric, the visual, the cognitive, the auditory, etc.) but also can expand this into a more general systems' model so as to include awareness of the emotional and motivational goals of the individual, the impact of varying situational settings, the changing social values, and so forth. Indeed, as Amarel (this volume) has pointed out, AI naturally seems to move into these more complex real-life modelling situations. So, a general systems' approach to modelling the whole individual within an extended cultural framework does not seem so unlikely a goal as it might at first reading. So, two directions within AI seems likely to me. One is the increased specialization that is currently so evident in AI (e.g., with vision research pursuing its separate goals apart from, say, the cognitive-linguistic goals represented in the natural language camp). But, another direction that seems inevitable would be represented by an integrative general biological systems' approach such as has been proposed by J. Miller (1978).

As I see it, this latter systems approach can be modelled (and the behaviors studied in large simulations) using a pastiche of current AI models as a starting point and broadening them to reflect the integrated nature of the human, including the need for being inspired, for being motivated and goal-oriented in terms of a career, being motivated to contribute something positive to the society at hand, and having the need to feel creative at some level, however small. The need for such integrative AI systems will become increasingly important as new applications in real-world settings become more pressing. I feel that AI will be the natural place to model these many facets of the human, and will, through computer simulations, allow for the exploration of this new integration of knowledge leading to a ecologically balanced biological system's framework.

I would like to see future conferences direct their attention to the development of an integrated biological system's perspective of the student, teacher, industry, and society at large. In this way, I believe, AI coupled with testing and assessment truly can become a powerful tool in building a more viable society.

Roy Freedle
Princeton, New Jersey

REFERENCES

Anderson, J. R. (1983). *The architecture of cognition.* Cambridge, MA: Harvard University Press.

Barr, A., & Feigenbaum, E. A. (1981). *Handbook of artificial intelligence* (Vol. 1). Los Altos, CA: W. Kaufman.

Barr, A., & Feigenbaum, E. A. (1982). *Handbook of artificial intelligence* (Vol. 2). Los Altos, CA: W. Kaufman.

Carbonell, J. G. (1983). Learning by analogy: Formulating and generalizing plans from past experience. In R. S. Michalski, J. G. Carbonell, & T. M. Mitchell (Eds.), *Machine learning: An artificial intelligence approach.* Palo Alto, CA: Tiaoga.

Carbonell, J. (1986). Derivational analogy: A theory of reconstructive problem solving and expertise acquisition. In R. S. Michalski, J. G. Carbonell, & T. M. Mitchell (Eds.), *Machine learning* (Vol. 2). Los Altos, CA: Morgan Kaufman.

Cohen, & Feigenbaum, E. A. (1982). *Handbook of artificial intelligence* (Vol. 3). Los Altos, CA: W. Kaufman.

Miller, J. G. (1978). *Living systems.* New York: McGraw-Hill.

1 Artificial Intelligence and Its Implications for the Future of ETS's Tests

Roy Freedle
Educational Testing Service

GENERAL INTRODUCTION

A quick overview of AI research and its possible relevance to ETS activities (e.g., test assembly of current multiple-choice tests, automatic analysis of constructed responses, design of new test instruments, such as evaluation of student's ability to reason about mathematical proofs, image processing of tests, graphs, and other student documents) are considered in this chapter. Some particular issues that we will consider in greater detail are:

1. Issues of improving old ways of testing using multiple-choice tests (e.g., automatic analysis of the structure and content of, say, inference items used in reading-comprehension passages).
2. The issue of automatically *generating* multiple-choice items such as analogies. Using AI to bring critical elements together (see comments later in this chapter on a natural flow of cognitive-linguistic research which leads to many, but maybe not all, of the critical ingredients for automatically writing such items).
3. The issue of adding a new measure somewhere between multiple-choice and totally constructed responses (e.g., math cloze-elide for proofs; see examples later in this chapter).
4. The issue of scoring totally constructed responses.
5. A loose critique of AI and its relevance to ETS testing: for example, the need to examine in detail the topic of explicitly modeling errors in AI—this seems to be avoided in the rush to get something that works approximately like a proficient adult. But, if true, this glosses

over the really hard part that is of great interest to ETS: namely, how to detect and correct errors in performance. If AI programs focus on production of correct responses their products will be of less interest to ETS. Hence part of this conference will hopefully focus on the possibility of modeling the developmental aspects of human performance, where errors in approximating the adult model are explicitly formulated in the AI programming and in the knowledge-representation problem. By refocusing in this way, those AI people interested in such an approach would provide programs of greater value to test construction, especially of the open-ended variety.

Outline of AI with a Running Commentary on its General Relevance for ETS's Plans for Testing and Evaluation in the 21st Century

While we are scanning several major areas of AI research, we will focus on those topics that appear to have the greatest potential for ETS tests (with respect to either modifying or improving current multiple-choice tests and/or with respect to designing future instruments which might emphasize constructed responses in order to broaden the range of skills and knowledge which might be emphasized in tomorrow's classrooms).

The three-volume *Handbook of Artificial Intelligence*, edited by Barr and Feigenbaum (1981, 1982; Vols. 1 & 2) and Cohen and Feigenbaum (1982; Vol. 3), has been the source of this outline. The running commentary which accompanies this outline represents *solely the opinions of the author and should not be construed to reflect official ETS policy regarding current or future testing activities.*

Natural-language Analysis

The topics of greatest concern to AI are: (1) Machine translation from one language to another. This is an old discipline in AI; it does not seem to have any obvious applications for ETS testing. (2) Study of grammars. There are many approaches to writing grammars; work is still going on in this realm and about five new grammars are currently being investigated. This work may or may not be important to ETS. That is, the exact approach taken to represent syntactical structure and the ways to compute these structures may not be directly relevant to ETS issues of assessing language ability. However, if we study the ways to *reason* about language (as a mastery skill which native adult language users are assumed to have), then this work might become more important to us. (3) Parsing. This is definitely of importance to ETS. Some parsing routines, such as Augmented Transition Networks (ATN), are widely used to represent efficiently and quickly the underlying structure of sentences. ETS probably will need some parsing routines which will work on PCs so that teachers can be advised on their use for essay analysis or for comparison of different classrooms texts (to see how complex the language is across different texts). Alternatively, if ETS offers a service to teachers—to analyze student essays that are stored on a disk and transmitted to ETS via a modem, then ETS perhaps can uniformly apply a more powerful ATN program and offer guidelines (of a diagnostic type) to each student on a regular basis (say, this service would be provided every 4 months to different school systems; each of ETS's regional centers could also have their own ATN programs to make this service more efficient across regions of the country). (4) Text generation. There are numerous AI researchers who have explored how to write software that will be able to answer questions about a text in natural-sounding English. Other researchers have explored how to write stories automatically using AI methods. This work probably has implications for ETS, inasmuch as the knowledge that is represented in these programs should be applied to assess the quality of written stories or essays that students might be asked to compose. This information would be used in conjunction with the parsing programs (ATN) described herein.

Understanding Spoken Language

This effort of AI has tremendous potential for assessment (and strong implications for the practical world of business). If AI research makes significant headway in how to process the natural flow of speech automatically as it is used in its everyday environment, ETS would be able to use this product to score automatically the teaching ability of teachers for different subject matters, the speaking ability of students, the writing of research reports by ETS staff (without the need for extensive typing pools). However, judging by the field's current limitations—its inability to process only several hundred words, the need to have clear separation between the spoken words (this is very unnatural), and the need for prior training with a given speaker's voice (the speaker must repeat several times a long list of words so that the computer program can internalize the idiosyncrasies of each speaker), it seems that much work still must be done to make this educationally and commercially viable. However, recent developments in parallel distributed processing (Rumelhart & McClelland, 1986) may dramatically alter this state of affairs in the near future.

Search Routines

This is a large field of study with many useful techniques to offer. This field may be of value to ETS, inasmuch as programs have been written, for example, to prove mathematical theorems automatically.

In applications to proof theory in mathematics, one requests that the program find a path that will determine whether a given starting state (a theorem) can be linked to a final state (a statement which proves or disproves the theorem).

This is similar to many kinds of problem-solving situations. The problem is the starting state, and the solution is a series of steps that ends by showing that a resolution to the problem exists or not.

This AI specialty also deals with ways to query efficiently a data bank to retrieve information on some particular subject (e.g., a library literature search probably uses some of these techniques). One might offer a service at ETS to search through an educational data bank to look for such miscellaneous categories as:

1. Teachers qualified to teach a particular course and currently available for consultation,
2. Professors who report that they are experts in a given field and are available for consultation 1 day a week,
3. Software programs which are classified by the variety of tasks they can perform (that have educational import), and so on.

In terms of developing a test for evaluating the competence of programmers in AI, this specialty would probably be a good source for generating problem settings requiring constructed responses or multiple-choice items.

Knowledge Representation

Barr and Feigenbaum (1982) list the following types of representations: logic, procedural representations, semantic networks, production systems, direct (analogical) representations, semantic primitives, frames and scripts. This part of AI is much too technical to convey here; the interested reader will want to refer to Barr and Feigenbaum (1982) for details.

Applications of AI (Primarily Expert-systems)

(1) Medicine.   The following programs are listed by Barr and Feigenbaum: MYCIN, CASNET, INTERNIST, IRIS, EXPERT, digitalis therapy adviser, and present illness program.

Since expert systems have been widely written about, I won't attempt to outline the contents of these expert systems. An ETS research program that emphasizes the acquisition of *mastery* for a given content area might want to verify some of the cognitive implications of mastering the use of knowledge in an expert system. Based on early work by Fleishman and Hempel (1955), one would expect a battery of paper-and-pencil cognitive tests to correlate around zero with the *final* proficiency of initially naïve people who are learning how to apply the knowledge contained in the expert system. Although the Fleishman–Hempel study would seem to suggest otherwise, it might be interesting, in the short run, to conduct some on-site studies that try to identify those characteristics of naïve people that will allow them to become "masters" in applying the expert-system knowledge.

(2) Expert systems in education (special AI tutors).   Since I reviewed this from the ETS perspective in an earlier (Freedle, 1985) report it will not be repeated here. However, later in this report we make particular recommendations concerning the use of one of Suppes's logic tutors, which is currently used at Stanford University.

(3) Expert systems in science.   Several systems are listed: programs in chemistry (chemical analysis and organic synthesis), including TEIRE-SIAS, DENDRAL, CONGEN, Meta-DENDRAL, CRYSALIS. Other scientific applications: MACSYMA, data-base management, PROSPEC-TOR.

All of these are too specific and too complex to be summarized here.

(4) Automatic programming.   This is an extremely interesting specialty in AI. Problems in how to get a computer to write the software for another computer (or for itself), given very general suggestions of the kinds of problem/solutions one is interested in, are considered here. Basically, if one can apply one of the mathematical proof programs to the problem at hand, one can generate directly from the sequence of statements in the proof a software program that will solve a particular problem involving the "theorem" proven by the proof program.

While it appears that not too much progress has been made in this realm (except for the astounding result that many famous mathematical theorems can be generated *de novo* from very simple assumptions) it might be a very good area to develop items which are intended to assess a student's programming skills. Barr and Feigenbaum (1982) list the following programs that have studied different aspects of automatic programming: PSI, CHI, SAFE, PECOS, DEDALUS, NLPQ, LIBRA, protosystem I, and the Programmer's Apprentice.

Models of Cognition

The following general topics are considered in the handbook:

Semantic Network Models of Memory. The general problem solver (e.g., Newell & Simon's work) is considered here as are Anderson and Bower's ideas on memory representation using the programs ACT HAM; other programs include EPAM MEMOD and the use of belief systems.

Automatic Deduction. This deals with mathematical proofs (also see the relevance of automated math proof theory to automated software development). Topics of interest here include nonmonotonic logics and logic programming.

Vision. This is a very specialized topic and inlcudes material that at first seems to be very remote to ETS interests. One AI approach is to tackle how one can efficiently recognize a variety of geometrical configurations (such as two-dimensional renderings of boxes, with or without boxtops, and other geometrical shapes). While not directly tied to AI work, ETS may need to consider how to process information automatically in a photo or in a variety of line drawings in order to quantify (or objectify) the *complexity* of photos and diagrams in test questions. Also the ability of programs to rotate images might prove useful in creating new item types that involve dynamic visual abilities such as the ability to tell when two objects will collide, given their original trajectories (which then get occluded somewhere on the viewing screen); a student would press a button at a point in time when he or she thought the two objects would collide. Also the ability to tell which of 2 (or *n*) figures are identical under rotation could be investigated (one could supplement this approach by allowing the student to select cues to help in making a decision; e.g., a quantification of "cues" might consist of the number of degrees that the student had to rotate an object along each plane before he or she was willing to say whether the two figures were identical). Numerous other visual tasks of a nonstatic nature can be invented. Presumably there are fields of education that depend more strongly on mastery of visual skills than other fields (e.g., algebraic geometry, architecture, graphic design, etc.).

Learning and Inductive Inference

This includes a study of AI approaches to modeling the games of chess and checkers, which have been prominently featured in the popular press. Other topics considered by Cohen and Feigenbaum include: learning by taking advice, as opposed to learning from examples—where the computer program is doing the "learning." It would seem that such topics may be of value to help build diagnostic instruments that make recommendations for how to teach concepts that a student is having trouble with.

Special attention probably should be paid to some of the special programs in this section. HACKER, for example, is intended to be a model of the process of *acquiring programming skills* even though a robot is doing the learning. There may be important clues here as to what aspects of programming skills should be assessed should ETS consider developing such a test.

Planning and Problem Solving

Since ETS has become increasingly interested in the assessment of reasoning skills (e.g., the College Board's Project Equality and GRE's analytical reasoning section), there are probably aspects of AI's approach to planning and problem-solving skills that will prove useful to ETS.

Cohen and Feigenbaum define problem solving as a process in which a sequence of actions is developed to achieve some goal. Planning, to them, means deciding upon a course of action prior to initiating the actions. A plan might consist of an unordered list of goals or it might consist of an ordered set of goals (first do this, then do that, etc.). In a sense most of the AI literature can be subsumed under this broad concept of problem solving. It should be a rich source for designing other test instruments which form a unique reasoning factor distinct from the typical verbal and quantitative factors typically found in factor analyses of the SAT and GRE.

Robotics

Oddly enough, the handbook deals only sporadically with the topic of robotics. In the last few years Carnegie–Mellon University has developed what appears to be an extensive set of studies on the automation of movement, such as walking, running, galloping, and grasping objects with an artificial hand. One might develop an ETS test which seeks to explore how well students can extrapolate from a given list of programmed conditions whether a program will function the way it is intended to—in terms of achieving a balanced model of a horse in motion, for example. If the program fails to achieve balance one might want to examine how the student would modify the program (which parameters will be altered and by how much) so that the perceived failure will be overcome, if possible.

In addition, I know informally that work has been progressing on the use of computers to help some handicapped people walk (a computer synchronizes the muscle movements and apparently sends electrical signals to each muscle to make it contract or relax so that the handicapped person can walk or climb a set of stairs).

The work of Ward and Frederiksen on students' generation of scientific hypotheses might be fruitfully extended to cover *specific topics of ongoing AI work* where graduate students (and professors) must examine what seems to have gone wrong in a program (here, one involving coordinating motor movements) and see what hypotheses they generate to overcome the failure and how they implement that altered hypothesis by program modifications. By studying cognitive hypothesis formation in true-to-life situations (in a real scientific laboratory with true scientific models at stake) one might be able to generate useful ETS tests that will interest graduate schools across a variety of scientific and/or humanistic disciplines.

Haptic Sense (Touch)

It also seems odd that the handbook does not deal with simulations of ability to describe and recognize objects as a function of their shape, size, texture, weight (kinesthetic sense), and so on. At several places in the handbook, the sense of touch is dismissed as an inefficient way to process information (however, I think readers would like to see a separate treatment of this in order to decide for themselves whether further work is warranted). While the sense of touch is undoubtedly valuable in some professions (e.g., pilots need levers of different shapes and textures to help make quick discriminations in carrying out maneuvers: often there is not time to scan all the instruments to be sure one has grabbed the right set of controls) it is not clear whether ETS should be interested in this.

Miscellaneous Comments Concerning Related AI Work that Touches on Some of the Issues Raised in the Foregoing AI Outline

A recent report of mine (Freedle, 1988) shows that even fairly elementary programs in LISP can be quite useful in efficiently and quickly scoring some aspects of open-ended constructed responses (sentence-combining responses, in this case).

Other ETS programs might try to examine which aspects of constructed responses might be assigned to AI programming—I'm thinking here of such "routine" corrections as punctuation in essays, subject–verb agreement, use of a vs. an, and so on. It should be quite easy to program other aspects that are known to correlate with the quality of most essays; for example, mere length of essay is often the best predictor of essay quality (quality being determined by a holistic score which has been assigned based on a subjective judgment). Other simple predictors are number of paragraphs used in the essay, use of "fronted" structures to begin sentences and paragraphs (e.g., some examples of frontings would be adverbials of time and place "at noon we . . . ; in the beginning they . . . ; when we get home we will . . . ."; other frontings would be the use of clefts "there are many . . . ; It is true that . . ."; use of coordinators which begin independent clauses [such as "And then he said . . . .; But I said . . . ."]). Approximately 30% to 40% of the variance of holistic scores can be accounted for by such predictors (see Freedle, Fine, & Fellbaum, 1981); and all of these should be very easy to program. A teacher might speed up the grading of essays (which have been typed by the students into a computer) by first roughly sorting the students' essays into probable high-quality, medium-quality, and low-quality batches by use of such a program.

Suggested Ways in which AI Fits into 1 Type of Cognitive Research Program at ETS

There is a natural flow of cognitive research on test content and test processes into math models of the processes; and from this detailed understanding there is a natural movement into automatic generation of new test-item exemplars (of the same type as studied) using AI techniques.

Not all of AI need be used to make this cycle of research and T.D. (test development) profitable to ETS. It may be sufficient to generate partly good items which can then be modified by human intervention prior to evaluation of the items (prior to pretesting).

Examples. C. Fellbaum and I have done some cognitive/linguistic analyses of TOEFL's aural Sentence Comprehension items (Freedle & Fellbaum, 1987). One hundred items were analyzed into some of their linguistic components, such as phonemes and graphemes (the sentences were aurally presented, hence the phoneme analysis; the multiple-choice options had to be read, hence the grapheme analysis), morphemes, exact lexical repetitions, and other linguistic categories.

These linguistic categories were related to item difficulty by regression analysis. This isolated three important predictors of item difficulty. One of these predictors seemed to be best described as reflecting a cognitive strategy in choosing a response option.

Additional analyses were informally conducted on whether the type of sentence structure (33 different sentence types were used in this Sentence Comprehension task) also contributed to item difficulty. Two types were found to be reliably related to the easy end of the spectrum while two other types were related to the difficult end of the spectrum.

Using various aspects of these empirical findings, a math model (a modified two-dimensional-choice model similar to Luce's 1959 models) was fitted to the data. This predicted quite well the proportion of time each response option was selected for every test item (100 items times four response options = 400 predicted probabilities). This process was repeated for four other ability groups; in all, 400 × 5 = 2000 probabilities were predicted quite well using a few parameters.

The next logical step (this was never undertaken) would be to take all the detailed information learned up to this point concerning sentence comprehension to see whether new items could be written of a specified level of difficulty; ideally one would like to automate as many of these steps in the production of new items as possible (perhaps using LISP programming techniques).

Second Example. I have also finished analyzing the content and psycholinguistic characteristics of SAT analogies. I am able to predict (via regression methods) about 35% of the variance of item difficulty for 600 disclosed analogies. Also Kostin and I (see Freedle & Kostin, 1986) are able to account for differential ethnic responses to these items (based on analysis of 240 items for which ethnic deviancies scores were calculated).

Regression analyses have isolated about six variables which consistently account for item difficulty and/or ethnic deviancies.

A math model showing how these selected variables combine to yield the exact proportion with which each response option will be chosen has yet to be done.

The automatic assembling of new items from word-pairs which have already been classified according to their semantic features would be a logical next step in this development. While a visiting scholar at ETS, Roger Chaffin (personal communication) began to implement an automatic program for assembling analogies which predicted their a priori difficulty.

Third Example. Irene Kostin and I have begun to investigate the cognitive/linguistic characteristics of antonyms, sentence completions, and reading-comprehension items (primarily using the SAT, although we have a fairly large sample of these item types for the GRE as well). The analysis of these item types has proceeded as for the analogies; we have developed other psycholinguistic measures of these items, related these measures to ethnic deviancies as well as item difficulty indices. We have isolated several major predictors of difficulty. Next we plan to construct a mathematical model showing the proportion of time each response alternative will be chosen for each item (if possible); we will then try to simulate these results using an AI program which will assemble new items (or will reassemble parts of old items) and will predict the difficulty of each new item. Finally, we hope to validate how well these new items actually perform by administering these new items to student examinees.

Defining the Intersection of AI and ETS Interests. In the past ETS was primarily concerned, it seems, with rapid assessment of human skills using restricted formats; just the formal language mode was assumed to be important, and just the restricted multiple-choice format was considered feasible for large-scale testing efforts. Less formal language registers were probably considered inappropriate to classroom language learning and constructed responses were either too expensive to evaluate or it was assumed that the information obtained from constructed responses was not substantially different from those obtained from multiple-choice formats.

With the new technology that AI makes available and with classroom teachers now expressing a need for evaluating such crucial skills as writing, ETS is becoming increasingly interested in evaluating open-ended constructed responses (especially writing skills); furthermore, many of these constructed responses can be associated with a broader set of educational purposes in mind, from college admission and placement decisions to teacher aids for diagnosing student problems.

This new interest in evaluating individual differences using constructed response formats presents a challenge for ETS with respect to cost of scoring, speed of scoring (get results back soon enough to be useful to clients), reliability of scores, predictive validity in a variety of settings, and so on. Each of these variants might require innovation in testing procedures.

Previously, ETS's attention was with how many multiple-choice items a student got correct; its interest now is becoming focused on why people make errors, how to score partly correct answers (as can easily happen in constructed responses), how to diagnosis student misconceptions and poor strategies? That is to say, a cognitive theory of error was missing, and error, in some vague sense promoted by classical test theory, was thought of as a probability-driven "guessing" factor which did not require further cognitive investigation. However, even within the context of multiple-choice testing formats, the problem of selecting distractors for items implicitly poses the problem of how rationally to select or generate distractors so that some people will be "fooled" into confusing it with the true "correct" answer—that is, such a concern implicitly poses the need for a cognitive understanding of how people arrive at answers in testing situations—how they solve the "problem" posed by a test item to find the "best" answer and reject the "not-so-good" alternatives. Certainly, in order to explore the diagnostic implications of the old as well as the new test scores, one must pursue and answer such questions.

With a renewed focus on evaluating constructed test responses, the need for a cognitive theory of error has become increasingly important. Psychometricians are incompletely trained to merge statistical, content-free theory with cognitive and linguistic theories of how people set up mental routines or cognitive procedures for solving problems.

I say all this for several reasons. AI is currently struggling to find ways to mimic "correct" or highly mastered behavior, be it human or animal behavior (as in the masterfully choreographed movements of a prancing horse, something currently of interest at Carnegie–Mellon). That is, AI is interested in doing things as efficiently as *practiced* humans can do them. Seeing things as practiced adult humans would see (and interpret) visual input, understanding language (meaningfully and correctly) the way practiced adult humans understand and use language, moving about by robots with the same grace as an mature animal might.

This is all well and good, but as already mentioned, work at ATS is becoming increasingly concerned with understanding how to score *approximately* correct constructed responses and automatically recognizing *grossly incorrect* ones as well.

There is some work in AI on detecting semantic *errors* and in detecting "broken-syntax," but in general the AI programs seem to be written to reflect well-practiced, high-quality behavior, rather than early acquisition of vision, audition, and movement—that is, there is typically no developmental analysis in AI involving gradual approximations to correct responses. Hence AI does not try to focus on the detection of typical errors in vision or audition (or on clumsy movements); instead it focuses on smooth adult performance as the goal of AI. This may *not* be a good strategy for constructing viable AI models of behavior—to model the final behavior directly *without an understanding or representation of how one developmentally achieved the adult behavior.*

The AI models do not explicitly allow for the regular occurrence of error in normal human behavior (and the various nuances of error that continually occur in walking, minor stumbling, slips of the tongue, hesitations, false starts, sudden changes in topic, avoidance of some topics, shifting of language modes when certain topics and situations arise; e.g., discussion of dating in a men's dorm, as opposed to discussion of mores of dating by the same people in a classroom on sociology).

Error detection, error correction (which is relevant to diagnostic testing), and error grading and evaluation is a large part of evaluating constructed responses (in Sentence Combining it is the scoring of errors that is expensive and time consuming, the scoring of correct responses is relatively easy and efficient; see my report, Freedle, 1988).

This conference between AI and ETS personnel might therefore have as one of its themes: *building AI theory for modeling incorrect and correct behavior* preferably using a developmental learning perspective. The many subtopics would include an account of, for example, correct speech, building AI theory for realistically modeling clumsy and smooth motor skills, models of expert and novice skills and expert/novice knowledge representations. (e.g., when do naïve lay beliefs get modified to reflect the "better" representation that an expert has; when does even the expert fall back into a naïve layperson's knowledge representation even within his or her own specialty?).

AI people might contend it is hard enough to build a model of the correct behavior. But since their goal is to mimic real human behavior (error and all)—developmental and sustained skill levels included—this conference hopefully will promote work in the direction that ETS might see some direct applications for its current concerns; such as grading (automatically whenever possible) the new array of constructed responses which might be elicited from diagnostic tests, or automatically grading essays for such programs as TOEFL, GRE, and College Board.

By extending the interest and focus of AI researchers in this way, ETS would benefit, but so will the AI researchers. As I see it now, one purpose of this conference can be to explore what AI can say about human errors in vision and audition (speech recognition); reading printed and hand-written words; recognizing correct story formats and poor formats, good planning ability (reasoning skills), and errors in implementing a plan, and so on.

Additional Comments

If one examines samples of various kinds of student essays one finds that most are ill formed in some ways. But AI does not currently focus on the frequent occurrence of ill-formed structures from real people; they tend to select highly edited materials that are "perfect" models, probably under the assumption that AI programs will be simplified if the correct behavior alone is modeled first. However, has anyone really tested such an assumption? Isn't knowing what kinds of error are frequently made (in vision, say) an important aspect of correct modeling? Might it be the case that the best AI program and the simpler AI program might be one that tries to model simultaneously correct and incorrect patterns? Since both behaviors stem from the same visual system (as expectant input; that is, human vision is not just neural wiring; its thresholds are altered by cognitive expectations, so errors are also influenced by this interaction of expectation and visual sensory inputs). AI people might be making the same kinds of erroneous (and mechanistic) generalizations that early psychologists made: that the organism is a "passive machine" that takes sensory input, finds a template matching the input (from memory), and makes some reflexive (or learned) response to the stimulus.

Psychology itself does not have a clear focus on how "error" in all behaviors occurs—what constitutes "error" seems to change by situation and can vary with the rigor or attitude of some external observer. Psychology still tends to look at behavior as a "given" without a sense that every behavior (be it vision, audition, social, linguistic, *ever greater responsibility*, being in charge of computer complexes, for example, that control manufacturing, publishing, agricultural planning, food preparation, computerized skyscrapers, and so on, all areas crucial to support the life functions of a society.

Need for New Definitions of Semantic Similarity

Similarity is needed to define *degree* of success of a constructed response.

Similarity is needed to define degree of pull of a distractor away from the correct response (in multiple-choice formats).

Something akin to similarity is also needed to define the seriousness of an error—how far from the goal does a given error make one? (this would be helpful to quantify the importance of giving "hints" to students in solving problems).

When AI programs make errors (as they do), are these errors like human errors? Can their similarity to humans be measured?

In finding the *route* to a solution in AI search routines, is this the most obvious way of defining psychological similarity (by a measure of "closeness" to the goal?)

In an earlier report (Freedle, 1984), I suggested various ways in which AI and ETS interests might overlap. One issue especially, that of *semantic similarity* (as just suggested) needs to be thoroughly explored by both AI problem-solving-oriented, etc.) changes by situation, by the participant structure, by shifts in purpose (goal), by prior contextual effects, and so on. These are serious limitations which are characteristic of a static "trait" approach for explaining behavior—this static approach has only partly been mitigated within a framework of multitrait, multimethod experimental designs. What is typically left out of such designs is a developmental, longitudinal approach in real-life contexts; also left out is a long-range sample of continuous behavior. Instead we focus on short-range behavior, usually requiring a discrete response, and within that domain, usually requiring a multiple-choice discrete response from a nonrepresentative well-structured problem set.

Although we have so drastically limited what and how we sample by way of behavior, we have the audacity to feel comfortable about the small number of factors that are found when we analyze the responses collected from these very limited domains. If we are to suggest that the AI researchers open up their domains of behavior modeling, I think we should expect that psychologists do the same. This is not just for the sake of completeness, it is for the sake of answering the new external demands (from industry and education) for a more complex system of evaluation that is truer to life's complexities. Tests of *reasoning and creativity* (especially under conditions of stress) *are needed and are crucial because the students will move into jobs of* researchers and ETS personnel in some joint enterprise. More specific ideas for this exploration will be the topic of another progress report.

Anticipated Problems in Defining Similarity in the Face of Possible Contextual Effects within an Item (a priori Definitions of Similarity and Counterexamples to their Usefulness)

Suppose we wanted to define the similarity of two array of numbers. Naïvely one might suppose that the similarity between two numbers can be established apart from knowing how these two numbers are used in any context (we shall call this the decontextualized notion of "similarity"). We shall show that this probably won't work.

Let the two array of numbers by 12345 and 54321. These numbers are *not* close in a sequential sense. They are, however, close in the sense that one is the mirror image of the other. Thus we can easily imagine one type of item which induces us to define numerical similarity emphasizing the sequential aspect while another item might induce us to perceive the mirror image as also important to numerical similarity judgments.

Some Suggestions for Generating New Items Requiring Either Open-ended (Constructed) Responses or for Modifying Existing Multiple-choice Formats to Get at New Skills

For Constructed Responses. (1) For linguistic responses—as in writing essays, or generating hypotheses concerning scientific reasoning from empirical facts. (2) Or for free symbolic responses as in writing or typing a statement in the proof of some theorem or the answer to some algebra problems.

Suggestions for Retaining Old Multiple-choice Formats, but Adding New Item Types to Assess Additional Skills

Reading comprehension items (as currently constituted) are known to be among the best predictors of first-year graduate student grades (for the GRE test). Currently, reading comprehension item subtypes consist of checking for student ability to find specific information from a text, or to make a global judgment about an author's purpose or goal or attitude as reflected in the text (this can be called a inference which requires retrieving relevant global world-knowledge to make such a judgment), and inferences which relate more specifically to claims made in the text itself (still requiring retrieval of some world-knowledge, but usually of a less global nature than judgments of an author's purpose or attitude would require).

Recent work in text analysis suggests that one can improve considerably in developing a scoring system which will reliably tap more levels of inference than is currently the case. Some inferences are tangential to the main purpose of a text; other inferences are crucial to a text's purpose. Some inferences use information from two previous text propositions. Other inferences require integration of more propositions; this can be *quantified* in advance given a prior analysis of the text structure. Currently such inference items as are written are not quantified by item writers—the technology for this did not yet exist. Now there is reason to believe that a procedure for quantifying these inferences exists and some aspects of it have been automated (some of Carl Frederiksen's recent work at McGill University).

Because reading comprehension items already are the best predictors of first-year graduate performance (and probably of first-year college performance as well, although this has not been specifically demonstrated) it seems likely that one should invest some research into *augmenting* the types of inference items that are written. One should also separately score these different subtypes of inferences to see if each subtype is differentially predictive of first-year graduate (undergraduate) performance.

Because schools are increasingly interested in testing and evaluating the reasoning ability of students (reasoning being the key factor in improving a student's level of mastery of any given area of study, especially the sciences and perhaps also valuable in the arts and humanities), and because specific kinds of text inferences should be closely allied with reasoning skills, it would seem wise to invest funds to expand (within the multiple-choice format) other types of text inferences to assess reading comprehension better as an important measure of reasoning.

Implications of Suppes's Mathematical "Parser" for Correcting Constructed Student Proofs On-line

Suppes for several years has used a computing system to teach students basic logic. The system is very flexible and can catch errors in student's logical reasoning, especially in constructing a sequence of responses needed to prove a theorem. One should be able to adapt one's system (which takes some practice to familiarize oneself with how to signal the program concerning some desired step in a proof) in order to create a new item type: GRE test of mathematical reasoning, say.

This could be done more easily without extensive practice by using the following format:

Create redundant steps in a proof (the student must detect redundancies); create erroneous steps in a proof (concomitant with redundancies for some problems); the student must detect erroneous steps; create a missing slot; the student must construct a response to fit the missing information required to complete some proof; this could occur early or late in the steps of some proof.

Thus instead of having a student create an entire proof (which might only be possible with extensive training in how to use Suppes's program), we tentatively suggest adapting the program so that the student must detect errors of commission, errors of redundancy, and/or fill in critical steps (errors of omission) in some proof.

The program would be needed to evaluate automatically the student's constructed information (and so this type of problem would have to be administered on-line).

The important point is that such programs are already in use; ETS should consider how to adapt this technology for purposes of large-scale testing and evaluation of higher-order mathematical reasoning. That is, the type of problem solving involved in proving a theorem is surely a different order of magnitude from learning how to add numbers. One can be done by rote (with or without understanding of addition), but proofs can only be done by *understanding* what is involved in proving a mathematical hypothesis.

Comments on Need for Tests of Spatial/visual Ability

We have briefly commented upon some uses of AI work on automatic visual processing and testing. Here I would like to expand upon this topic since some recent work of Kosslyn (1986) has appeared.

While it is probably not at all certain whether there is a close relationship between actual perceptual-visual skills (based on old measures of visual capability in the laboratory and via paper-and-pencil methods) and a person's ability to reason and think in visual imagery, some of the recent results of Kosslyn point out the possibility of a rich connection between visual imagery ability and problem-solving ability Students kept an hourly diary of mental images that occurred to them. (Often other sensory images were combined with the visual including smell, taste, sound, and/or touch.) Six types of mental images occurred. The most common (about 33%) used images to *help solve a problem or make a decision*. If this can be verified, it suggests that ETS might consider using visual tests and/or visual imagery tests (hopefully of a more objective nature than self-report) as indirect measures of *individual differences in problem-solving ability*. That is, not only is there a quite reasonable connection of visual skills with such specialties as architecture and mathematical geometry, but there may be a pervasive use of mental-visual imagery in many problem-solving situations if Kosslyn's results are confirmed.

Some of the decision making that the students engaged in were quite ordinary (choosing what clothes to wear, choosing what to eat, etc.). But the ordinariness of these decisions and the apparent need for visual imagery to help solve these everyday problems does not necessarily mean that similar imagery would not be used in solving less ordinary problems (such as solving the problem of composing an essay on the threat of a greenhouse effect; perhaps some topics lend themselves more to visual imagery than others). This is a matter to be studied.

In addition about 25% of the images were used to help understand a verbal description. Thus a student's ability to read and understand a descriptive passage might well be a function of his or her ability to form visual images.

The images also functioned in a large number of cases to help *motivate* the student to perform some task; that is, the student had learned to create images that would provide the self-motivation for wanting to go ahead with some previously onerous task. Thus such imagery might well be correlated with individual differences in study habits and rate of learning.

Imagery was also used prior to constructing a verbal production of some event. Thus imagery might function not only for language reception skills (reading comprehension has been cited) but language production skills as well.

Kosslyn has suggested that imagery skills can be improved through training.

REFERENCES

Barr, A., & Feigenbaum, E. A. (1981). *Handbook of artificial intelligence* (Vol. 1). Los Altos, CA: W. Kaufmann.

Barr, A., & Feigenbaum, E. A. (1982). *Handbook of artificial intelligence* (Vol. 2). Los Altos, CA: W. Kaufmann.

Cohen, P. R., & Feigenbaum, E. A. (1982) *Handbook of artificial intelligence* (Vol. 3). Los Altos, CA: W. Kaufmann.

Fleishman, E. A., & Hempel, W. E., Jr. (1955). The relation between abilities and improvement with practice in a visual discrimination task. *J. Experimental Psychology, 49,* 301–312.

Freedle, R. (1984). *A state of the art survey of artificial intelligence and its applications to the analysis and production of verbal test items. Final Report.* Princeton, NJ: Educational Testing Service.

Freedle, R. (1985). *Implications of language programs in artificial intelligence for testing issues: With special attention to use of tutoring programs in education. Final Report.* Princeton, NJ: Educational Testing Service.

Freedle, R. (1988). A semi-automatic procedure for scoring protocols resulting from a free-response sentence-combining writing task. *Machine-Mediated Learning, 2,* 309–319.

Freedle, R., & Fellbaum, C. (1987). An exploratory study of the relative difficulty of TOEFL's listening comprehension items. In R. Freedle & R. Duran (Eds.), *Cognitive and linguistic analyses of test performance.* Norwood, NJ: Ablex.

Freedle, R., Fine, J., & Fellbaum, C. (1981). Some discourse features which predict good and bad essay ratings. Paper presented at the Annual Roundtable on Language and Linguistics, held at Georgetown University, Washington, DC.

Freedle, R., & Kostin, I. (1988). *Relationship between item characteristics and an index of differential item functioning (DIF) for the four GRE verbal item types.* (ETS Research Report No. 88-29.) Princeton, NJ: Educational Testing Service.

Kosslyn, S. (1986). *Visual cognition.* Cambridge, MA: MIT.

Luce, R. D. (1959). *Individual choice behavior.* New York: Wiley.

Rumelhart, D. E., & McClelland, J. L. (1986). Parallel distributed processing (Vol. 1). Cambridge, MA: MIT Press.

2 From Interactive Instruction to Interactive Testing

Tryg A. Ager
Institute for Mathematical Studies in the Social Sciences
Stanford University

During the past two decades, Suppes and coworkers have produced several computer-assisted instruction (CAI) systems that are based on the ideas of interactive proof checking and interactive theorem proving (Suppes, 1981a). The main examples are a course in symbolic logic, the VALID program, and a course in axiomatic set theory, the EXCHECK system. Both courses cover material normally included in one-semester college courses, and in each the computer bears the main burden of instruction. The logic course has been in continuous operation at Stanford since 1972 where about 3,100 students have taken it. Since 1982, when VALID was rewritten in a portable language, it has been used at about 25 other institutions. The set theory program, EXCHECK, has run each academic quarter since 1974. Set theory is an advanced undergraduate and graduate-level subject, and in total, about 300 students have taken it at Stanford. EXCHECK has not been transported elsewhere.

Currently, we are developing a similar comprehensive system for computer-based instruction in first-year calculus (Suppes et al., 1987). This system will support the interactive construction of the equational derivations used for calculus problem solving, and as an additional optional component, use interactive theorem proving to enable students to prove the main theorems of elementary real analysis that form the foundations of calculus.

The VALID program, with 15 years of continuous instructional use, and the 13-year-old EXCHECK system provide a wealth of real examples of effective instructional strategies and in data collected over the years, an important resource for studying the behavior of students who are solving real problems while taking a standard college course for credit in an on-line, open-ended situation. Furthermore, since both VALID and EX-CHECK, as well as the current work on the calculus instructional system, can justifiably be viewed as incorporating substantial knowledge of a subject matter and embodying significant intelligence about problem solutions, the question of the relevance of these instructional techniques to future kinds of intelligent on-line testing naturally arises. This is a reasonable question because CAI, more than many other kinds of instruction, already has a close relationship to testing since every response by a student in a CAI situation is, or easily could be, subject to some kind of analysis or scoring. Therefore, it should come as no surprise that many ideas from testing theory have been borrowed or adapted by CAI systems, especially those classified as "intelligent." This indebtedness of CAI to testing theory provides a view of ideas shared by testing and CAI that contrasts rather sharply to the tutoring techniques used in VALID and EXCHECK.

CAI'S DEBT TO TESTING THEORY

There is an important commonsense distinction between instruction and testing. The purpose of instruction is to teach a skill, or to produce knowledge of a domain, or to induce understanding of ideas and concepts. The purpose of testing is to evaluate, verify, or measure someone's skills, aptitudes, knowledge, or comprehension. Teaching and instruction try to change the learner; testing gauges or measures the learner. While the purposes of instructions and testing clearly differ, the methodologies may not. Many testing methodologies, both formal and informal, can be usefully applied as part of instruction. For example, no one would teach elementary algebra without giving quizzes to help ensure that students are learning the basic rules. Mastery learning, exploratory learning, and traditional computer-managed instruction all use standard testing techniques as an essential component of their instructional method. Some CAI methodologies, and especially some of the main approaches to intelligent tutoring, are strongly related to testing methods. I will discuss three different exemplifications of this relationship, both to bring out the influence of testing theory and to lay groundwork for distinguishing the VALID and EX-CHECK systems from other kinds of intelligent CAI.

Use of Item Response Analysis

An interesting example of adapting testing methods to instruction is traditional computer-assisted instruction, which is characterized by extensive use of multiple-choice, question–answer dialogues. These interactive dialogues are descendants of programmed learning modules. Historically, the programmed learning approach was not wedded to a particular technology, and in fact workbook, radio, and television formats have all been tried. It turned out that programmed learning was especially well matched to interactive computing, and in that respect, it is one of the foundations of traditional CAI. And because testing theory had data and analytical tools for determining the discriminating effects of items, traditional CAI could make good use of item-response analysis in a framework that combined presentation of material with continuous evaluation or testing of students. Continuous testing became a powerful technique that obviously could be used to evaluate student performance. More importantly, the sampling could be used to modulate the instructional content, level, and pace, thereby adapting the tools of testing to individualize instruction.

At its best, traditional CAI applies an instructionally oriented set of criteria for item analysis in order to maximize student achievement over the long run. The objective of testing, on the contrary, is to get accurate discriminations in a short time with a limited set of items. No one would say that a CAI course in fifth-grade arithmetic should be designed to preserve a random distribution of arithmetic skills among the fifth graders. The instructional purpose is to design a sequence of items that can bring the most students to or beyond grade level 5, that is, to increase similarities among the students. The testing purpose is to detect, classify, and diagnose differences. It is a nontrivial exercise, however, to convert the theory of how test items discriminate students into a theory of how to use continuously accumulating data to modulate learning and maximize achievement. One way is the technology of adaptive CAI, where the testing data control the sequencing of material to the student. The curriculum is presented in an amount and an order that depends on how the student does on carefully selected test items.

It is clear also that the relationship between instruction and testing is a two-way street with respect to the use of item analysis. The idea of individualizing instruction can be transposed to the concept of adaptive testing where continuous sampling modulates the test itself in order to obtain more precise or informative measurements for a given amount of test time.

Use of Diagnostic Testing

Some key literature on intelligent CAI can usefully be viewed as an attempt to borrow and extend diagnostic testing methodologies for the sake of instruction. To the extent that it constitutes a proposal for intelligent computer-assisted instruction, the work on BUGGY (Brown & Burton, 1978; Burton, 1982) where a marvelous network of subtraction "bugs" was discovered, clearly presupposes that detailed diagnostic testing is relevant to the teaching of subtraction skills. It is an application of the commonsense idea that if we know what is wrong we can try to fix it, to a situation where the analysis of what could be wrong is unexpectedly complex. Sleeman's work (1982) on students' mistakes in algebra ("mal-rules") also takes this approach. But although algebra is more complicated than subtraction, Sleeman's analysis is not as fine-grained as Brown and Burton's analysis of subtraction. In both cases, however, the instructional strategy is based on detailed systematic models of possible errors, diagnostics to detect occurrences of the individual errors, and instructional decision making to present exercises that are intended to correct erroneous operations by students. The difference I want to emphasize here is that the remediation is done with respect to the topology of a skill rather than with respect to interrelationships of content.

There are, of course, many instructional strategies that are driven by diagnostics, but the examples cited here are generally regarded as paradigms of applications of artificial intelligence to instruction. In particular, the complexity of these diagnostic models of skills is one of the main reasons tutoring that uses them is called intelligent. Metaphorically speaking, the detailed model of the possible errors, miscues, or bugs in exercising a skill means the program "understands" the skill it is trying to teach.

But this work on subtraction and algebra, however strongly motivated by diagnostic testing and detailed modeling of skills, runs counter to common sense, especially when the actual complexity of serious, college-level reasoning is taken into account. For subjects such as calculus or predicate logic, which are orders of magnitude more complex than column subtraction, an approach that requires detailed diagnostic testing and a complete skill model is impractical if not impossible.

The point I want to make is not that diagnostics are not useful in instruction, but that the detailed, elaborate diagnosis of cognitive errors, which is identified with Brown and Burton's and Sleeman's approach to intelligent tutoring, currently does not hold much promise as an extensible instructional strategy, say to language teaching, where student errors are both formal and semantic, or as mentioned, to advanced mathematical and logical subjects where individual errors have deep and subtle semantical aspects as well as being formally complex. By the same token, returning this methodology to testing theory would seem to have practical difficulties because the granularity of the diagnosis provided by such elaborate and detailed models may be inappropriate in the overall framework and mission of standardized testing.

Testing as Profiling

If we see diagnostic testing as influencing an approach to instruction where a local skill is modeled in extensive detail, we can also see a related strand of testing as influencing an approach where the problem-solver is modeled and the instructional process is partly driven by a model of the student's plans or goals. In the diagnostic skill-modeling approach, the learning is modulated by an abstract, learner-independent model of the skill being taught. Subtraction, as a skill, has the same components for everyone, but individuals have different "bugs." The profiling approach seems to advocate modeling an individual's solution path and therefore would seem to be a learner-dependent kind of modeling.

Whereas Sleeman and Brown and Burton test for conceptual "bugs," Goldstein (1982) has tried to probe for data from which to construct a different kind of model that represents the student's plans and strategies rather than a network of skills. Goldstein emphasizes his intent to model the learner rather than domain expertise, and justifies it with an explicit principle of teaching (p. 67): "To offer appropriate technical advice, a teacher must model the student." So if the teacher is a computer, then we need a software student model, according to Goldstein. A model of a student qua problem solver is prima facie, an entirely different idea than a model of a skill. If we consider the vast literature on psychological testing, personality inventories, and intellectual profiles, we might think these techniques can help us build a model of a student that can be used to make individualized instructional decisions. But in its application to intelligent tutoring, there is less here than meets the eye. What normally happens is that a skill model is built and the problem's goal is to bring it about that the student satisfies every criterion in the skill model. The BIP program, which taught introductory programming in BASIC, worked in this way, and although different students traversed the course on different paths, the interdependencies defined for the subject matter completely determined the student's degrees of freedom, not, as might be expected from the phrase "model the student" an inventory or profile of individual students with respect to the different ways they approached programming tasks (Westcourt, Beard, & Barr, 1981).

Goldstein's idea for modeling students was to construct a "genetic graph" that represented the student's evolving formulation of the rules of the WUMPUS cave or network exploration game. It is clearly a subjective model. What, then, is the relation between the subjective, learner-dependent model and the objective, learner-independent game or procedural skill? We can easily see that the more accurate the learner model, misconceptions and all, becomes the more difficult it is to relate it to the objective procedural skill. Both Goldstein and Brown and Burton share a principle that a student model, no matter how flawed, and a domain model are isomorphic. Brown and Burton map subtraction bugs to subtraction subskills. Goldstein conjectures a developmental mechanism of refinement, generalization, simplification, and so on, to explain how the novice becomes skilled and maps student behavior to this mechanism. The difficulty with Goldstein's way is that we get the mapping at the cost of a psychologistic theory of mathematical subject matter.

Goldstein came closer than BIP to actually modeling an individual's own plan or goal, but that is because it is fair to assume that a WUMPUS player is trying to win and is applying a strategy. The relevance of this to actual academic subjects, which as wholes are far too complex to be learnable under some determinate unified strategy, is that certain "set-pieces" such as truth tables or simple logical proofs might be pursued along the lines Goldstein illustrated with the WUMPUS coach. But for complicated academic subject matters such as calculus, we have a long way to go before we can even understand what individual students have in mind, especially if they are making mistakes.

Thus although the belief that testing can tell us interesting things about individuals appears to be influential in the CAI literature, in fact most programs that attempt to model the student actually conform with the converse of Goldstein's maxim, namely, "To receive appropriate technical advice, a student must fit the computer's model of a solution." Indeed, this is a good description of the approach of Anderson's group at Carnegie Mellon, where the working assumption is that a student problem solver can be represented as a set of production rules, and intelligent tutoring consists of the fact that both the computer and, in an operational sense of the term, also the student can "execute" these rules. Anderson's approach, however, does not seem to be indebted to testing theory in any clear way. Instead, its roots are in cognitive science, linguistics, and formal grammars. Yet this approach must walk the same fine line of trying to gain a psychological model of the student without losing the correct and complete formalization of the subject matter that makes open-ended tutoring possible.

There are three strands in the development of CAI that seem to me to be indebted in detail or in spirit to testing theory: (1) CAI that individualizes instruction based on determinations of content mastery clearly owes a debt to item-response analysis and the principle that individual item responses indicate content mastery in an objective, learner-independent sense. (2) CAI that measures students against detailed skill models owes a debt to diagnostic testing and to the principle that conceptual skills can be decomposed into determinate and learner-independent topologies. (3) CAI that tries to model student plans or strategies clearly has ideological ties to the principle that response sampling can support inferences to learner-dependent problem solving strategies.

Alternatively, one might describe these three approaches as different ideas about where the "intelligence" of intelligent CAI resides. There is a school that thinks it lies in the organization of the content of the course. There is a school that thinks it lies in learner-independent skill models. And there is a school that thinks it lies in learner-dependent representations of strategies.

ANOTHER APPROACH

The design of the VALID and EXCHECK systems, which emphasize interactive proof construction, theorem proving, and mathematical reasoning, does not borrow heavily from any of the testing methodologies described herein, nor does it fit cleanly into any of the three CAI methodologies surveyed. VALID and EXCHECK do not use refined item-analysis methods to design the curriculum or to pace the students. Nor do they use highly specific probes to detect buggy mental skills. Nor do they profile students to build overall, individualized models of plans and goals for problem solving in symbolic logic and set theory.

Instead, these systems, which are effective in actual practice, are based on quite a different kind of instructional strategy. I will explain this idea metaphorically at first, then show how the metaphor directly applies to the cases at hand. Suppes (1981b, 1984) and Goldstein and Carr (1977) use the idea of a coach, in the familiar sense of an athletic or music coach, to characterize some components of computer-assisted instruction. In that vein, I want to identify several aspects of coaching present in VALID and EXCHECK.

First, a coach's job is to train his charges in basic skills, sharpen those skills through practice, consolidate basic skills into relevant chunks of action (e.g., producing vibrato on a cello, "kicking" at the finish of a long-distance run, proving a theorem by proving two easier lemmas, etc.). Each coaching domain has its own set of appropriate skills and levels of consolidation. For example, both physical therapists and track coaches coach running, but at entirely different levels of consolidation and skill.

Second coaching at any interesting level of sophistication in real activity is done in media res. A batting coach can recommend an adjustment in stance without involved reductionistic analysis of skeletal structure, center of effort, forces, and motion. Several years ago, the coach of the Minnesota Vikings football team was widely criticized and lost his job because he imposed an ineffective and presumptuous regime of "getting in shape" on experienced, professional athletes. The team rebounded when the previous coach returned from retirement and applied a more appropriate coaching strategy. Similarly, one would not expect to find a masters' class in cello spending all its time on first-position scales, nor a beginners' class spending most of its time on interpretation or attack.

Third, a coach's fundamental task is developmental. Coaches take some-one's "raw talent" and through practice and training refine the talent within the structure of the activity and where appropriate, push the limits, as has happened in the past decade in men's competitive ice-skating. Coaching at the upper extreme of the developmental spectrum can hardly be char-acterized as the coach knowing more than the player, or vice versa, let alone either having a detailed local or global model of the activity. At best, these coaches must advise, encourage, and support their charges based on partial information; yet the best individual performers usually have coaches, and the relationship at high levels of skill is interactive and (not always in a polite way in athletics) cooperative.

Finally, although a good coach is an expert in the field, all coaches admit that there is always more to learn, especially in endeavors combining skilled action with aspects involving creativity in strategy or interpretation. It must, therefore, be emphasized that actual coaching frequently is successful, not because of the completeness of coaching knowledge, but because of the way the knowledge is used. Good coaching gets to the heart of the matter; it does not depend on knowing everything, but it does depend on knowing the right things. This point needs to be emphasized here, because most CAI coaches are omniscient with respect to the subject matter, be it WUM-PUS, How the West was Won, or subtraction. Real coaches work in sit-uations where highly consolidated skills are exercised in an open-ended way within an artistic or athletic or other competitive domain. It is not omniscience or completeness, but rather the pragmatic relevance of inter-ventions and advice that characterizes effective coaching of skilled activity.

There are, of course, many kinds of coaches and coaching. I have tried to argue by way of examples that effective coaching of a complex skill is not conveniently reduced to knowing success or failure on individual com-ponents of the skill (item analysis) or knowing in detail how the skill is performed at a sophisticated level (skill modeling) or having a complete model of how one intends to perform the skill (strategy modeling). This argument by reference to examples also brings out the point that as the complexity of the skill increases and we place the skill in a developmental context, the characterization of coaching by any single paradigm becomes less and less plausible. These ideas about coaching apply quite directly to the VALID and EXCHECK systems.

First, the systems use skill building and skill consolidation. Instead of reducing an intuitively basic skill such as subtraction or transitivity of im-plication to a subskill network and diagnosing bugs, VALID and EX-CHECK take the straightforward approach that the relevant basic skills for symbolic logic can be acquired by practice, and the instructional goal is not merely to practice basic skills interactively, but also to consolidate them into an ability to generate solutions to complicated problems and proofs of nontrivial theorems. The emphasis is always on progress and consolidation rather than intensive diagnosis and remediation of errors. Thus an instructional goal is to get students working at a level of consolidated skills rather than to diagnose why they are not.

Second, symbolic logic, calculus, and set theory are well-defined subjects already organized in ways that promote skill acquisition and consolidation. VALID and EXCHECK are intended to cover all the material of a standard course. Thus the changing scope and increasing complexity of the material work against having elaborate, specialized coaching tools applicable only to fragments of the course. Fortunately, the systematic organization of the subjects supports a pragmatic style of coaching.

Third, these systems explicitly take into account the cooperative character of coaching sophisticated skills. On the student's side there is freedom to try novel solutions to the many different kinds of open-ended exercises; the coaching side constrains such novelty according to the rules of the problem domain. It is an interactive partnership where strategical and tactical decisions are the student's responsibility, and consistency checking is the coach's job.

Finally, the principle of pragmatic relevance is the key to understanding VALID and EXCHECK as coaches. Both systems use a system of error detection and warnings as the fundamental mode of coaching. Actual usage over many years by many students shows that this method is pragmatically effective for the subjects being taught.

For the most part, VALID and EXCHECK use an uncomplicated, practical and for the subject, a natural approach to coaching that relies on a representation of the student's work that monitors its consistency and conformity with the rules of inference of logic and set theory. The tools the student uses to construct derivations are themselves demonstrably consistent operations on the representation of the problem solution. So, student operations can always be evaluated rigorously in the underlying implementation of the theory. Unlike the other systems we have surveyed, VALID and EXCHECK are built around the formalizable core of the subject matter. This is their distinguishing feature and the reason they can be comprehensive without being either inordinately complex internally or tedious and mistargeted for the college-level student.

Now, returning to the main question of this conference, whether there is anything in VALID and EXCHECK that testing theory or future testing methodologies can borrow, I think there is. I have tried to indicate that unlike much intelligent CAI, the instructional methodologies of VALID and EXCHECK have not been motivated by ideas borrowed from testing theory in the first place. Nor are the design considerations drawn from off-the-shelf learning theories. Therefore, what VALID and EXCHECK have to offer will not be old wine in new bottles.

EXAMPLE FROM PROPOSITIONAL LOGIC:
INTERACTIVE DEDUCTION

Having established a background, let us turn to several detailed examples of the interactive deductive environments in VALID and EXCHECK. Additional details about VALID and a comparison with other programs that teach logic is in Ager (1984); Blaine (1981) explains the workings of EXCHECK. The principle feature of all the examples is the interactive construction of sustained deductive arguments. In this chapter I have chosen examples that lead into discussions of empirical studies by various IMSSS researchers of actual student usage of the systems. The studies give detailed clues about what the IMSSS style of interactive instruction has to offer to testing. I want to emphasize that data collection and analysis of real students routinely using the VALID and EXCHECK systems to take college courses for credit has been one of Suppes's main research themes.

Proofs in propositional logic are relatively simple. The following examples clearly show the style of student interaction with the VALID proof checker. Student commands are in underscored italics. I have added annotations in italics to help you follow the proof. The computer typed the rest. The program checks each command for correctness, and detects when the student reaches the required goal. At that point, the proof is reprinted in cleaned-up form with the command dialogue removed and extraneous lines pruned.

Remarks on Propositional Logic Derivations.

Figs. 2.1–2.4 show how students use the interactive proof checker. Figs. 2.1 and 2.2 show the construction and summary of a proof of exercise 408.8. Figs. 2.3 and 2.4 show a completely different derivation for the same problem, illustrating the open-ended nature of the VALID proof checker. For each of the more than 600 derivation-type exercises in VALID, multiple solutions are possible. The following particular points are important:

1. Students seldom type in formulas. Instead they use a command language to direct the checker to make a certain step of inference. This interface is conceptually demanding in that it requires students to have knowledge of the available commands, of which at this stage there are more than 20, and to formulate a plan for the derivation. Trial and error is not a useful strategy.

2. Erroneous commands are rejected with error messages. The system only checks whether the proposed step is valid. It does not model student skills or strategies in any way. Instead it is building up the student's solution as a proof-theoretical object. Two effects of this methodology are that any derivation is always in a formally valid state,

```
408.8   Commutation Rules:  Practice with CQ, CC, and CD
DERIVE:  R < - > W & U

P                       (1)     U & W < - > NOT NOT R
* wp r          introduce a working premise
WP                      (2)     R                               (2)
* 2 dnn         apply double negation rule
2 DNN                   (3)     NOT NOT R                       (2)
* 3 1 rqr       replace equivalents
3,1 RQR                 (4)     U & W                           (2)
* 4 cc          commute conjuncts
4 CC                    (5)     W & U                           (2)
* 2 5 cp        conditional proof
2,5 CP                  (6)     R - > W & U
* wp w&u        introduce a working premise
WP                      (7)     W & U                           (7)
* 7 cc          commute conjuncts
7 CC                    (8)     U & W                           (7)
* 1 8 rqr       replace equivalents
You need a biconditional or universally quantified biconditional
as the second premise for RQR.
* 8 1 rq        replace (tried wrong rule above)
8,1 RQ                  (9)     NOT NOT R                       (7)
* 9 dnp         remove double negation
9 DNP                   (10)    R                               (7)
* 7 10 cp       conditional proof
7,10 CP                 (11)    W & U - > R
* 6 11 lb       law of the biconditional
6,11 LB                 (12)    R < - > W & U
```

FIG. 2.1.   Propositional logic derivation: Construction (method 1).

```
408.8   Commutation Rules:  Practice with CQ, CC. and CD
DERIVE:  R < - > W & U

P               (1)     U & W < - > NOT NOT R
WP              (2)     R                               (2)
2 DNN           (3)     NOT NOT R                       (2)
3,1 RQR         (4)     U & W                           (2)
4 CC            (5)     W & U                           (2)
2,5 CP          (6)     R - > W & U
WP              (7)     W & U                           (7)
7 CC            (8)     U & W                           (7)
8,1 RQ          (9)     NOT NOT R                       (7)
9 DNP           (10)    R                               (7)
7,10 CP         (11)    W & U - > R
6,11 LB         (12)    R < - > W & U

    Strategy:           Constructive.  Prove each component conditional.
                        Combine them.
```

FIG. 2.2.   Propositional logic derivation: Summary (method 1).

```
408.8   Commutation Rules:  Practice with CQ, CC, and CD
DERIVE:  R < - > W & U

P                              (1)    U & W < - > NOT NOT R
* wp r
WP                             (2)    R                                    (2)
* 2 dnn
2 DNN                          (3)    NOT NOT R                            (2)
* 2 3 cp
2,3 CP                         (4)    R - > NOT NOT R
* wp not not r
WP                             (5)    NOT NOT R                            (5)
* 5 dnn
5 DNN                          (6)    NOT NOT NOT NOT R                    (5)
* 6 del        deletes line 6
* 5 dnp
5 DNP                          (6)    R                                    (5)
* 5 6 cp
5,6 CP                         (7)    NOT NOT R - > R
* 4 7 lb
4,7 LB                         (8)    R < - > NOT NOT R
* 8 1 rqr
8,1 RQR                        (9)    R < - > U & W
* 9 cc
9 CC                           (10)   R < - > W & U
```

FIG. 2.3.   Propositional logic derivation: Construction (method 2).

```
408.8   Commutation Rules:  Practice with CQ, CC, and CD
DERIVE:  R < - > W & U

P               (1)    U & W < - > NOT NOT R
WP              (2)    R                              (2)
2 DNN           (3)    NOT NOT R                      (2)
2,3 CP          (4)    R - > NOT NOT R
WP              (5)    NOT NOT R                      (5)
5 DNP           (6)    R                              (5)
5,6 CP          (7)    NOT NOT R - > R
4,7 LB          (8)    R < - > NOT NOT R
8,1 RQR         (9)    R < - > U & W
9 CC            (10)   R < - > W & U

    Strategy:        Prove   R < - > NOT NOT R  as a lemma.
                     Replace   NOT NOT R  in the premise.
                     Commute conjunction directly.
```

FIG. 2.4.   Propositional logic derivation: Summary (method 2).

and that much information about the logical structure of the solution is available for tutorial interchanges, even though the program does not automatically generate a solution to the problem.

3. Theoretically, there is an infinite number of solutions to each problem. The programs presently do not rank or otherwise evaluate the "quality" of a solution. The reader might find it interesting to ponder whether one of the two solutions to 408.8 is "better" than the other.

Empirical Study

Moloney (1981) reports a study done in 1970 of Stanford students taking a precursor of the VALID instructional program as part of the regular Stanford logic course. The study attempts to classify problems in quantifier-free elementary logic according to difficulty and to correlate variables describing student behavior with variables describing the structure of problems. Student behavioral variables included total time on the proof, latency per line, number of error messages produced, and number of lines in the student's proof. The key structural variables were the length of a "standard proof" or "expert's solution," the number of uses of key rules, such as conditional proof, reductio ad absurdum, and modus ponens, and finally the number of uses of axioms and theorems. The behavioral variable that was correlated most strongly with "difficult" problems was the time or latency per line.

Moloney concluded that while latency per line and a structural concept of difficulty of problems were related, the regression model that established this correlation did not provide a model of dynamic problem-solving behavior of the student. Moloney, however, established the validity of a difficulty measure that was derived from the structure of the problem and a "standard solution" to it.

EXAMPLE FROM INTEGER ARITHMETIC: AXIOMATIC SYSTEMS

Moloney's study included proofs in propositional logic, but also took into account another segment of the VALID curriculum, namely, proofs in what is called "integer arithmetic" in the present curriculum. Integer arithmetic is a quantifier-free presentation of the theory of an ordered field. The new characteristic of these proofs is that they require the use of axioms and previously proved theorems. This step from propositional logic to a detailed, real mathematical theory illustrates very clearly the ideas of skill consolidation and development mentioned in the earlier discussion of the coaching metaphor.

The proofs of a theorem in integer arithmetic in Figs. 2.5–2.7 illustrate uses of axioms to establish simple theorems. I have chosen elementary examples that emphasize direct proofs from axioms. The curriculum, however, contains theorems whose proofs are much more complicated, requiring 15 or more steps typically. But even this simple example shows, again, that interestingly different solutions to one problem are possible. The strategy used in Figs. 2.5 and 2.6 differs remarkably from that used in Figs. 2.7 and 2.8, although both approaches use the same two axioms.

Remarks on Integer Arithmetic Examples

Integer arithmetic problems move from a natural deduction system for logic to an axiomatic formulation, a transition not frequently done at all in many logic textbooks. The following points are important.

1. The rules that use axioms smooth out the choosing of instances, and as shown in the Replace Equals steps that use an axiom, the relevant instance of the axiom is chosen automatically. That is, we presume the student sees the substitution under which the axiom applies, so we find the substitution instance internally. This illustrates how VALID is supportive of naturalness and skill consolidation.

2. Students are encouraged to prove and store their own sets of useful theorems. There is a wide range of behavior that has not yet been systematically studied: Which and how many theorems are stored? How often do students recognize that their stored theorems may be useful and try to use them? We know from inspection of data that students store from none to more than 100 theorems on their private

---

PROVE: $3+X+(-X) = 3$

* ax z	*Start by introducing the zero axiom*
AXIOM Z: $X+0 = X$	
Substitute for X (X): * 3	
AXIOM Z	(1) $3+0 = 3$
* ax ai	*introduce the additive inverse axiom*
AXIOM AI: $X+(-X) = 0$	
Substitute for X (X): *x	
AXIOM AI	(2) $X+(-X) = 0$
* 1 2 rer	*replace equals by equals*
1,2 RER	(3) $3+X+(-X) = 3$

FIG. 2.5. Integer arithmetic proof: Construction (method 1).

```
PROVE:  3 + X + (−X) = 3

AXIOM Z          (1)    3 + 0 = 3
AXIOM AI         (2)    X + (−X) = 0
1,2 RER          (3)    3 + X + (−X) = 3

   Strategy:           Prove from axioms directly
                       Combine additive inverse and zero axioms.
```

FIG. 2.6. Integer arithmetic proof: Summary (method 1).

```
PROVE:  3 + X + (−X) = 3

* li 3 + (x + (-x))  introduce an identity
LI               (1)    3 + X + (−X) = 3 + X + (−X)
* 1 re 2 ax ai
1RE2             (2)    3 + X + (−X) = 3 + 0
* 2 re ax z
2RE              (3)    3 + X + (−X) = 3
```

FIG. 2.7. Integer arithmetic proof: Construction (method 2).

```
PROVE:  3 + X + (−X) = 3

LI               (1)    3 + X + (−X) = 3 + X + (−X)
1 RE2 using ax AI (2)   3 + X + (−X) = 3 + 0
2 RE  using ax AZ (3)   3 + X + (−X) = 3

   Strategy:           Start with an identity
                       Simplify using additive inverse and zero axioms
```

FIG. 2.8. Integer arithmetic proof: Summary (method 2).

theorem lists. Those who use stored theorems often produce very elegant proofs of the difficult theorems in integer arithmetic.

3. The integer arithmetic lessons provide an algebra laboratory, since in the last lesson, students are given axioms for a commutative group, then discuss possible effects of dropping the commutative axiom, and finally prove a number of theorems for noncommutative groups.

Empirical Study

Working from Moloney's classification scheme, Kane (1981) studied about 2,900 student proofs of theorems in integer arithmetic. Kane's purpose was to analyze their diversity. He devised a proof classification system that takes account of five degrees of similarity, ranging from loosely similar (proofs are similar if they use the same rules) to completely identical. He then analyzed the relationship between the "difficulty" of proofs, using Moloney's difficulty measures, and the occurrence of different student solutions. Kane drew the general conclusion that variations in proofs can be predicted from the structure of the "standard" or "expert" solution to a problem. In particular, from the length and the independence of one step from another in the standard proof, one can predict differences in the order of steps. Also, from the number of theorems or from the number of axioms and rules of inference available, one can predict the amount of variation in student solutions. Kane's discussion does not give examples of how this predictability works in specific cases. He gives no examples of a particular problem and a description of a particular outcome or what that outcome means in terms of instructional design. However, we can see that Moloney's and Kane's approaches are suggestive in terms of designing open-ended problems that have predictably diverse sets of correct solutions.

Observations on Modeling the Student

Neither Moloney nor Kane really addresses cognitive questions regarding student proofs. Both imply that it should and perhaps could be done. But even in a simple theory such as propositional logic, students will solve the same problem differently. We shall see that such diversity of student solutions to on-line exercises is a pervasive and fundamental fact that pertains to every example that follows. This simple fact that different students do the same task differently raises an important point regarding expectations we might place on an intelligent tutoring system: Can it pick up on what the student is intending to do and help him or her with that task? Propositional logic is a decidable theory, and many people have written advice givers based on one or another of the constructive decision procedures that give a procedure for finding a proof of any valid propositional logic sentence. It seems obviously desirable to write an advice giver that decides if the goal is provable from the student's initial steps, finds a proof, and coaches the student along.

But if, as is usually the case in logic exercises, the conclusion does follow from the given premises, then no matter what steps the student has done, the decision algorithm can compute a proof. But what guarantees that the generated proof is relevant to what the student has in mind? And if we take student steps into account, which steps should they be? It is one thing to find a proof automatically of a logically true sentence. It is quite another to diagnose where the student is or what he is up to. One lesson of these examples regarding modeling the student is that automated provers don't imply interactive tutors. Another lesson is a clear counterexample to the claim that intelligent tutors or computer coaches must model the student. It is plain that if a computer coach can rigorously, naturally, and within the accepted limitations of the subject, take a student through an investigation of the differences between commutative and noncummutative groups yet not have a model of the student, it is not necessary to have a model of the student.

The second sort of data pervading these examples is that students spend different amounts of time to do the same things in an open-ended environment. Most students complete the assigned work in the VALID course in between 60 and 80 hours of work at the terminal. The range, however, is from under 40 hours to more than 150. This degree of variance extends to time spent on individual lessons. The data are consistent from year to year at Stanford.

In the examples from propositional logic and integer arithmetic where the task is to construct derivations, we have seen that a diversity of solutions and differences in time spent are the prominent features of student behavior in open-ended, on-line logic instruction.

TRANSITION STATES: LOGICAL
OR MATHEMATICAL JUDGMENT

In addition to straightforward derivation problems, the VALID curriculum contains several exercise types that depend fundamentally on students making overall decisions about which formal methodology applies to a problem. In logic, it is common to ask students to decide whether a given argument, presented in English, is valid or invalid. The problem involves a translation step and then application of either a proof or refutation procedure. In propositional logic, the refutation procedure is by a counterexample, using familiar truth table methods. In predicate logic, the procedure is more complex. To refute a first-order argument, students must find an interpretation in integer arithmetic where the premises and denial of the conclusion map to theorems of integer arithmetic.

Fig. 2.9 is a flow chart for the derive-counterexample problems in first-order logic. Students are free to move back and forth along the vertical links. Activity within the derivation environment is similar to the examples already shown, except that quantifier rules are available.

Remarks on Derive or Interpret Problems

This type of exercise adds a new component to the skills built up in the VALID course, namely, mathematical judgment. These problems embed the interactive proof-checking apparatus in a structure where the transition

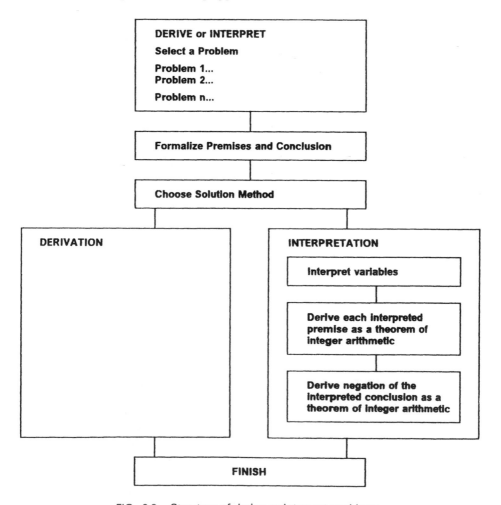

FIG. 2.9. Structure of derive or interpret problems.

from one method of attack to another, or from one problem to another is presumably motivated by judgment rather than the success or failure of any particular step of inference. The following points are important:

1. A goal of this kind of exercise is to encourage students to make informed, top-level judgments of validity or invalidity. We have not, however, tried to capture their judgments as explicit mental representations or tried to record their reasons for making a transition. These protocols would be extremely interesting.

2. The flow of control is up to the student, who can switch between derivation to refutation methods ad lib, alter the interpretation, or even defer the problem and select another to work on. The main constraint is that formalization must be completed before evaluation of validity can begin. Nothing is done explicitly to control student transitions within the structure of the derive or refute problems.

3. The method of refutation is conceptually very sophisticated. It is, in fact, the technique of a relative consistency proof. If a student grasps fundamental ideas about mappings, straightforward use of model theoretical techniques is possible. There is no study, however, of how individual students understand the construction of a mapping between first-order formulas and integer arithmetic formulas.

Empirical Study

Larsen (1981) did a preliminary model of student's transition behavior in 450 instances of 10 different derive-or-refute exercises where the original argument was invalid. Given that a student is in the interpretation state, the next transitions could be to try a derivation, try a revised interpretation, or finish. Since all problems in her study were invalid, however, the only transition for a student in a derivation state is to the interpretation state. She modeled the flow chart as a first-order Markov chain, and reported two interesting results: Students who initially decide that the argument is invalid have a 50% chance of finishing the problem with their original interpretation. The second result was that for students who made three transitions, the third state was a good predictor of alterations from then on. That is, a student who is doing an interpretation by state 3 has a 56% estimated probability of changing the interpretation on the next transition and a 25% probability of finishing the problem with that interpretation. A student trying a derivation (remember these are problems that have no derivations!) by state 3 has a 54% estimated probability of settling into an interpretation to interpretation transition pattern on the next state change. Of the 450 solutions, 88% were completed with eight or fewer transitions; 61% of the solutions used three or fewer transitions.

Larsen also considered the length of time students stayed in a state, but because the time they were in a state was strongly influenced by the fact that response time on the computer system was inconsistent and extremely variable, she did not find clear patterns of transition models of student behavior when time was taken into account. But it is clear that such data would be interesting when latencies accurately reflect student behavior. We have an adage that computer-assisted instruction, if nothing else, should run at the speed of thought. Larsen's study of time transitions suffered because of a ploddingly slow system.

Observations

Larsen's study used an older version of VALID which had a very user-unfriendly interface to derivation-refutation problems. It was especially difficult to revise an interpretation. Secondly, Larsen did not examine in detail the revisions made to interpretations in interpretation-to-interpretation transitions. Nor did she look at other variables such as how long the futile derivation had become. Nor was the overall complexity of the transition matrix taken into account. Besides switching from derive to interpret and finish, students could defer the problem and try another or log out altogether.

Nevertheless, the fundamental quality of problem solving in this basic approach of measuring transition probabilities highlights the diversity among solutions and although results are inconclusive, the possible role of time as a significant variable. And it shows a third aspect of the instructional method in VALID: Open-ended exercises can require the student to exercise mathematical judgment.

EXAMPLE OF FINDING-AXIOMS: MATHEMATICAL CONJECTURE

VALID has one other exercise type that I would like to discuss. This is by far the most complex type of problem in the course. Based on an idea of R. L. Moore and modified for interactive use in VALID, there are seven "finding-axioms" exercises, of which the following is the simplest. The purpose is to axiomatize a set of formulas. Fig. 2.10 shows how the problem is presented and Fig. 2.11 shows an initial choice of axioms. There is great flexibility in approaching the problem since it is not required that a full set of three axioms be chosen immediately, and the axiom selection may be revised at any time.

430.1   Exercise 1 on Finding Axioms

Choose three of the six statements as axioms. Prove the other three.

For intuitive purposes, you may interpret X LEQ Y as 'X is less than or equal to Y'.

    1. X LEQ X

    2. X LEQ Y & Y LEQ X −> X = Y

    3. X LEQ Y & Y LEQ Z −> X LEQ Z

    4. X LEQ Y & Y LEQ Z & Z LEQ Z1 −> X LEQ Z1

    5. X LEQ Y OR Y LEQ X

    6. NOT (X = Y) −> X LEQ Y OR Y LEQ X

Choose 3 formulas as axioms and prove the rest as theorems.

Select axioms by typing AXIOM <number list>. Or CHECK
* *axiom 2 3 5*

FIG. 2.10.   Finding axioms problem.

FINDING AXIOMS: Prove these theorems from your choice of axioms.

1   **X LEQ X**

4   **X LEQ Y & Y LEQ Z & Z LEQ Z1 −> X LEQ Z1**

6   **NOT (X = Y) −> X LEQ Y OR Y LEQ X**

Type the number of the formula you wish to prove as a theorem.
* *6*

FIG. 2.11.   Derivation tasks after selecting axioms.

Fig. 2.12 shows the detailed proof of Theorem 6, one of the three tasks necessary to complete the problem. Notice that the student generated seven lines in the deduction, of which only three were necessary. This can be interpreted as being on the wrong track and recovering. In the construction, lines 3, 6, and 7 are the solution, but line 3 is clearly in an off-the-track segment. The complexity of student behavior in open-ended problems is brought out by this example.

DERIVE: NOT X = Y -> X LEQ Y V Y LEQ X

* report axioms
2 AXIOM   X LEQ Y & Y LEQ X -> X = Y
3 AXIOM   X LEQ Y & Y LEQ Z -> X LEQ Z
5 AXIOM   X LEQ Y OR Y LEQ X
* axiom 2
AXIOM 2: X LEQ Y & Y LEQ X -> X = Y
Substitute for X (X): *
Substitute for Y (Y): *
AXIOM 2   (1) X LEQ Y & Y LEQ X -> X = Y
* 1 cop
1COP   (2) NOT X = Y -> NOT (X LEQ Y & Y LEQ X)
* hyp
HYP   (3) NOT X = Y   (3)
* 2 3 aa
2,3AA   (4) NOT (X LEQ Y & Y LEQ X)   (3)
* 4 dm
4 DM   (5) NOT X LEQ Y V NOT Y LEQ X   (3)
* axiom 5
AXIOM 5: X LEQ Y V Y LEQ X
Substitute for X (X): *
Substitute for Y (Y): *
AXIOM 5   (6) X LEQ Y V Y LEQ X
* 3 6 cp
3,6 CP   (7) NOT X = Y -> X LEQ Y V Y LEQ X

430.1   Exercise 1 on Finding Axioms
DERIVE: NOT X = Y -> X LEQ Y V Y LEQ X

HYP   (1) NOT X = Y   (1)
AXIOM 5   (2) X LEQ Y V Y LEQ X
1,2 CP   (3) NOT X = Y -> X LEQ Y V Y LEQ X

You have finished this proof. Press ENTER to go on.

FIG. 2.12. Proof construction and summary for Theorem 6.

Remarks on Finding-axioms Exercises

In addition to all the previous comments on diversity, time, and state transition, the following remarks apply to finding-axioms problems.

1. It is clear that the task here is to put forward a reasonable conjecture about how to systematize a body of mathematical propositions and rigorously prove that the systematization satisfies some mathematical criterion, in this case derivability from a set of axioms.

2. Not only are there completely different ways to do the systematization, but there are completely different schemes for top-level classification of the components of the problem. In the given example, depending on one's mathematical background, one might try to think of a model, say natural numbers, or look at it as a syntactical puzzle, or analyze it in terms of prior knowledge of the properties of relations. At a more behavioral level, there are many different orders in which the work may be done, and certain incorrect axiomatizations may be pursued at length, say when there are a dozen or more formulas to axiomatize. The situations that trigger revision of a choice of axioms are extremely interesting from a psychological point of view.

Empirical Study

Goldberg and Suppes (1972) studied student results of finding-axioms problems at a time when the only on-line component to the exercise was typing in the various proofs of the theorems. Thus all that was available was the bottom-line choices students made for axioms in any given problem. They found that in an exercise approximately the same as the example, only two different solutions were found by 11 students. Their sample included both gifted junior high school students and college students. The disparity in age and mathematical maturity was apparent in the data they gathered.

Data for Stanford students during spring 1987 for the exercise used as the example here show that 51 students found only two different solutions (8 chose 2, 4, and 5 as axioms and 43 chose 2, 3, and 5 as axioms). This example is simple; its purpose is to teach students how to do finding-axioms problems. The second finding-axioms exercise required selecting 10 axioms from 14 formulas, and showed great diversity. The 51 students found 16 different solutions. One solution was found by 16 students; none of the other 15 solutions was used by more than 5 students. The third exercise required selecting 3 axioms from 7 formulas. There were 6 different solutions by the 51 students. The fourth finding-axioms exercise required selecting 6 axioms from 11 formulas and produced 20 different solutions by 50 students. Again 1 solution was used by 15 students, 1 by 8 students, and the rest by 4 or fewer students each.

The data about different choices of axioms are only one layer of the complexity, since there are usually many ways to derive the required theorems from the given axioms. Thus in finding-axioms exercise 1, where there are only two reasonable sets of axioms, we nevertheless see diversity in the ways and order students who chose formulas 2, 3, and 5 as axioms proved formulas 1, 4, and 6 from them.

Finally, this diversity reflects only the bottom-line answers to finding-axioms exercises. We did not gather detailed data about the transition patterns of students as they made and altered their choices of axioms. It should be clear that detailed flight recorders or instrumentation of such open-ended, problem-solving environments used by large numbers of students can contribute to our understanding of how problem solving proceeds in a CAI environment.

EXAMPLE FROM EXCHECK: WRITING ELEGANT PROOFS

The preceding examples already show the great complexity and variety of on-line problem solving in logic and mathematics. But all these examples are with very simple logical theories. What happens to the important factors of diversity, time, transition, and top-level strategies when the theories considered are mathematically sophisticated? Data from the student use of the EXCHECK interactive theorem prover can help us understand such questions.

The following two examples give an idea of the more complex interaction and more powerful rules in EXCHECK. Interactions between the program and the student are represented in italics, with student input underlined. Fig. 2.13 shows the details of how a student interacts with EXCHECK as a proof is being developed. Notice that the powerful rules require specification of several parameters. Fig. 2.14 is a completed proof of a different theorem that shows the concise, cleaned-up summary of the proof the student constructed.

In operational details the EXCHECK system is quite similar to VALID. Students issue commands and the computer performs the inference if it can determine that the inference is valid. The difference lies in:

1. The greater power and higher level of the inference rules available. EXCHECK has the following decision procedures: For inferences depending on propositional logic, there is a TAUTOLOGY command. For inferences in class logic, a decidable system, there is a BOOLE command that verifies or rejects in one step assertions of class logic. TEQ does the same for assertions whose validity depends only on tautology and the properties of equality.

Theorem 2.4.2 (A A,B,C)(A ⊆ B & B ⊆ C → A ⊆ C)

* *hyp*

Hyp   (1)   **A ⊆ B & B ⊆ C**

* *1 simp*

Occurrences (1) * *1*

1 Simp   (2)   **A ⊆ B**

* *definition* <name> * *subset*

                          (A B,C)(B ⊆ C iff (A x)(x ∈ B → x ∈ C)

                          Do you want to specify? (yes) * *y*

                          Variables (B,C) * *B C*

                          Substitute for B? (B) * *A*

                          Substitute for C? (C) * *B*

Definition Subset   (3)   **A ⊆ B iff (A x)(x ∈ A → x ∈ B)**

* *2 3 implies*

2 Implies using 3   (4)   **(A x)(x ∈ A → x ∈ B)**

* *us*

                    Substitute for x? (x) * *x*

4 US   (5)   **x ∈ A → x ∈ B**

* *5 hyp*

5 HYP   (6)   **x ∈ A**

* *5 6 aa*

5 6 AA   (7)   **x ∈ B**

* *1 7 verify (8) x ∈ C*

                    using * *definition* <name> *subset*

1 7 Verify   (8)   **x ∈ C**

* *6 8 CP*

6 8 CP   (9)   **x ∈ A → x ∈ C**

* *ug*

                    Generalize? (x) * *x*

9 UG   (10)   **(A x)(x ∈ A → x ∈ C)**

* *10 establish (11) A subset C*

                    using * *definition* <name> *subset*

Establish   (11)   **A ⊆ C**

* *qed*

FIG. 2.13. Proof of Theorem 2.4.2 in EXCHECK: Construction.

Theorem 2.4.5 (A B,C)(B ⊂ C → C ¬⊆ B)

Assume	(1)	B ⊂ C
Assume	(2)	C ⊆ B

1 Eliminate using definition proper subset

	(3)	B ⊆ C and B ≠ C
2 3 Establish	(4)	B = C
2 3 4 Contradiction	(5)	C ¬⊆ B
1 5 CP	(6)	If B ⊂ C then C ¬⊆ B
6 UG	(7)	(A B,C)(B ⊂ C → C ¬⊆ B)

FIG. 2.14.   Proof of Theorem 2.4.5 in EXCHECK: Summary.

2.   For inferences not contained in a decidable fragment, EXCHECK provides several powerful inference procedures: VERIFY, IMPLIES, and CONTRADICTION. VERIFY is a rule that uses a resolution theorem prover to try to validate a student's claim that one formula follows from others. Students may cite a combination of previous lines, axioms, theorems, and definitions when calling VERIFY. Since first-order logic is not decidable, the result of a call to the VERIFY rule is either validation of the student's claim or a report that VERIFY cannot justify the inference. Whereas TAUTOLOGY and BOOLE, when passed an invalid inference, can actually construct counterexamples and show the student why the inference is invalid, VERIFY can only run out its allotted CPU time before returning with the message that it could not find a proof. While VERIFY is powerful, a greater burden is on the student to formulate correct inferences because VERIFY cannot explain why a conclusion does not follow. IMPLIES simplifies the application of universally quantified theorems to particular cases. CONTRADICTION is an alternate interface to the resolution theorem prover.

3.   In set theory, a great deal of nonlogical domain knowledge is required to do the proofs. This includes understanding the axioms of set theory, the use of sorted variables, and familiarity with the definitions and accumulation of theorems as the course develops. The ESTABLISH rule (Blaine 1981) was an attempt to deal with this extensive domain knowledge by using expert-system techniques to decompose problems and anticipate the next step, based on the structure of the problem itself and the data base of axioms, theorems, and definitions. The advice that the ESTABLISH rule gives, however, is not diagnostic in the sense of explaining student errors.

4. Finally, the complexity of set theory requires a great deal of machinery for natural input and output of formulas. One of Suppes and Blaine's goals in EXCHECK was to make the interaction natural in the sense that the proofs were of about the same granularity as proofs in a treatise on set theory. So the program tries to suppress trivial details and encourage students to use the powerful rules. It also means that much work was done on finding effective ways to review interactive proofs in progress, and summarize them when they are finished.

Empirical Studies

The EXCHECK curriculum in set theory requires students to prove between 25 and 45 theorems. Suppes and Sheehan (1981a, 1981b) did an extensive study of nearly 1,500 student proofs. They were looking for models or dimensions of comparison that could characterize the mechanism of developing a proof. The analysis is lengthy and sophisticated; I will only summarize the conclusions here.

Since the construction of a proof is a sequence of applications of rules of inference, it was natural to study the observed sequences of rule use and try to find a probabilistic model for them. Analysis showed that neither a deterministic model, in which there was a dependence of a given command on one or more previous commands, nor a geometrical distribution model, where there is no dependence on prior rules, explained the data. Suppes and Sheehan summarize as follows:

> As the data analysis shows, there is little hope of a deterministic model reflecting all the complexities of student-constructed proofs. It is important to note that this complexity is at the level of the validity of a proof, not how the proof is found. An analysis of the conversational aspects of the proof and the student search for particular steps he uses is an even more probabilistic matter as far as the current data go. It thus seems, in any near future, totally hopeless to us to propose a deterministic model of how students find or organize what they have found as a proof into a valid proof acceptable to the program. (1981a, p. 33)

Considering proofs as wholes and comparing the lengths of proofs of the same theorem showed a distribution of lengths that clusters around the mean length. This fact supports the idea that proof construction is a probabilistic process, which is complicated in the EXCHECK environment by the structure of the theorems themselves, the multiple and overlapping proof tools available to students, and individual differences among students in attacking problems or consolidating and applying what they have learned.

The studies of EXCHECK proofs are important because they show how complex on-line open-ended problem solving is, and show how difficult it would be to "grade" such solutions if they were regarded as test items.

TOWARD INTELLIGENT INTERACTIVE TESTING

I have described an approach to intelligent CAI used in the VALID and EXCHECK systems that is characterized by: (1) The internals of the programs are implementations of consistent proof-theoretical systems of inference. (2) The curriculum is organized in a way that promotes skill building and consolidation. (3) Coaching is based on early error detection and keeping the student's solution in a proof-theoretically consistent state. Coaching is driven by the internal representation of the properties of the problem domain and the state of the student's solution rather than by comparison of student solution with either generated or stored solutions. (4) Within the bounds of consistency, students have control of their solution paths. This results in a diversity of solutions, which, as the subject matter becomes complex, defies a deterministic analysis.

What, then, can the testing community gather from these programs? Because the problems of diversity and complexity of solutions is so apparent, the first thing that can be given to testing is a program of research to investigate in more detail and across a broader spectrum the following kinds of questions pertaining to the actual behavior of students who are solving problems on-line.

Requirement for a Taxonomy of Problems and Solutions

Both the problems and the solutions in VALID and EXCHECK are formal objects. Logical theory has a clear method for classifying both formulas and proofs for its own purposes, but we lack a classification that is useful for characterizing and explaining the diversity of student solutions to complex problems that is appropriate for either instructional or testing uses. In discussing Goldstein's ideas about modeling students for the purposes of coaching, I pointed out that there is an inherent dilemma in intelligent CAI: If you try to model the student and map that to content, there is a risk of psychologizing the content. If on the other hand you model the content, it is difficult to map it to students' plans (including misconceptions). One hopes there is a principle of symmetry such as Brown and Burton's isomorphism of "bugs" and subtraction subskills, but Suppes and Sheehan's work shows that it will not be easy to find such a principle for logical and mathematical deductions.

Significance of Time as a Variable

Many of the studies looked at solutions to problems dynamically, and data already indicate substantial individual differences with respect to latencies at all levels of the VALID and EXCHECK curricula. It would appear that in interactive, time-constrained testing using open-response items, the time spent on a problem would be significant because it is relevant to distinguishing among the student who solved a problem quickly (found it easy?), one who lagged (found it hard?), and one who solved it in distinct episodes.

The Significance of Transition States and Solution Paths

One valuable feature of the VALID and EXCHECK pragmatic method of coaching is that students are not held by the hand, so we can get good observations of intense floundering by serious problem solvers who are truly in difficulty. Protocol analysis from confused human subjects is difficult and time consuming. Full instrumentation of VALID and EXCHECK can show exactly what happens when a student flounders. But the patterns of this behavior have not been studied at all for the problems in VALID and EXCHECK. In a testing situation, recognition of floundering would be extremely valuable both from a scoring point of view and from an adaptive testing point of view. The student who flounders is different from one who is meticulous or slow, but both might have the same time on task.

The solution paths of successful students are also of interest and are good starting points for stochastic models of certain classes of problem solutions. As has already been indicated in the discussion of sample problems, a solution path is related to making of strategical and tactical judgments about how a problem can be solved.

Understanding Intensely Interactive Problem-solving Environments

The differences computers make in problem solving are in the nature and frequency of feedback to the student. It may have seemed that the VALID and EXCHECK systems are primitive in their approaches to coaching. But considering that both programs can tell a student, instantly, what is right or wrong about any of hundreds of individual logical and mathematical operations, the coaching is effective and appropriate in the context. The coaching is also low-profile in that messages generated by errors the student already knows about, such as typing mistakes or self-diagnosed errors, are not disruptive. Metaphorically, it's the difference between one coach yelling "kick" to a runner finishing a mile race and another pulling the runner onto a remedial track to find out why he didn't kick. We would also expect that interventions appropriate for an instructional context would not necessarily carry over to an interactive testing context.

Intense interactive environments also have effects of their own that shape problem solving. With respect to the diversity of student solutions, some effects are surely related to response time and the command options available in the computational environment. For example, in EXCHECK the VERIFY rule tends to take a "long" time before a result is returned, whereas primitive rules return "immediately." It is not unreasonable to believe some people prefer several immediate feedback points to a riskier and longer call to VERIFY in order to get to the same place in a derivation.

We have to take the effects of the interactive environment into account in the analysis and interpretation of data generated by on-line problem solvers. This is important for both testing and instruction. But much literature on CAI has not done a scientific analysis of the effects of the medium at the fine-grained level of problem solving behavior.

In discussing the applicability of VALID and EXCHECK to future kinds of testing, my main theme is that before we can make that transition we need to find analytical tools to cope with the data that on-line problem solving generates. We do not have discrete "right–wrong" answers to problems. In fact under the VALID and EXCHECK model, there can be only three bottom-line states for a problem: (1) Finished correctly; (2) Started and in a consistent state; (3) Not started. There is no "wrong" category. So if VALID and EXCHECK became on-line testing tools, scorers would have the misleadingly attractive situation of a set of test papers, "with no wrong answers."

A PROPOSAL TO INTEGRATE TEACHING
AND TESTING

I would like to close with a radical suggestion about how to integrate interactive instruction and one kind of competency testing. Both VALID and EXCHECK cover a complete course. So does the calculus system we are building. Unlike symbolic logic and set theory, there are agreed-upon criteria for evaluating competence in calculus, including the Advanced Placement test. Currently the Advanced Placement evaluation is based on less than a half-day's work by a student, but can have an enormous impact on that student's standing upon entry to college.

But if the majority of the student's problem solving in calculus occurred in an on-line interactive tutoring framework and suitable methods for evaluating student data were available, certification and instruction would be the same process from the student's point of view. So in a sense, one path from interactive instruction to interactive testing leads to the disappearance of the latter.

ACKNOWLEDGMENT

Research on the VALID and EXCHECK systems was partly supported by National Science Foundation Grants EPP-74-15016-A01, SED-74-15016-A03 and SED-77-096998 and by the Fund for Improvement of Postsecondary Education Grant G00-780-3800. Research on the calculus instructional system is supported by NSF Grant MDR-85-50596.

REFERENCES

Ager, T. (1984). Computation in the philosophy curriculum. *Computers and the Humanities 18,* 145–156.

Blaine, L. (1981). Programs for structured proofs. In P. Suppes (Ed.), *University-level computer-assisted instruction at Stanford: 1968–1980* (pp. 81–119). Stanford, CA: Stanford University, Institute for Mathematical Studies in the Social Sciences.

Brown, J. S., & Burton, R. R. (1978). Diagnostic models for procedural bugs in basic mathematical skills. *Cognitive Science 2,* 155–192.

Burton, R. R. (1982). Diagnosing bugs in a simple procedural skill. In D. Sleeman & J. S. Brown (Eds.), *Intelligent tutoring systems* (pp. 157–184). New York: Academic Press.

Goldberg, A., & Suppes, P. (1972). A computer-assisted instruction program for exercises on finding axioms. *Educational Studies in Mathematics 4,* 429–449.

Goldstein, I. P. (1982). The genetic graph: A representation for the evolution of procedural knowledge. In D. Sleeman & J. S. Brown (Eds.), *Intelligent tutoring systems* (pp. 51–78). New York: Academic Press.

Goldstein, I. P., & Carr, B. (1977). The computer as coach: An athletic paradigm for intellectual education. *Proceedings of the annual conference, Association for Computing Machinery,* Seattle, October, pp. 227–233.

Kane, M. T. (1981). The diversity in samples of student proofs as a function of problem characteristics: The 1970 Stanford CAI logic curriculum. In P. Suppes (Ed.), *University-level computer-assisted instruction at Stanford: 1968–1980* (pp. 251–276). Stanford, CA: Stanford University, Institute for Mathematical Studies in the Social Sciences.

Larsen, I. B. (1981). Stochastic models for student behavior in deciding and proving that an argument is invalid. In P. Suppes (Ed.), *University-level computer-assisted instruction at Stanford: 1968–1980* (pp. 237–249). Stanford, CA: Stanford University, Institute for Mathematical Studies in the Social Sciences.

Moloney, J. M. (1981). An investigation of college-student performance on the 1970 Stanford CAI curriculum. In P. Suppes (Ed.), *University-level computer-assisted instruction at Stanford: 1968–1980* (pp. 277–300). Stanford, CA: Stanford University, Institute for Mathematical Studies in the Social Sciences.

Sleeman, D. (1982). Assessing aspects of competence in basic algebra. In D. Sleeman & J. S. Brown (Eds.), *Intelligent tutoring systems* (pp. 185–200). New York: Academic Press.

Sleeman, D., & Brown, J. S. (Eds.). (1982). *Intelligent tutoring systems.* New York: Academic Press.

Suppes, P. (Ed.). (1981a). *University-level computer-assisted instruction at Stanford: 1968–1980.* Stanford, CA: Stanford University, Institute for Mathematical Studies in the Social Sciences.

Suppes, P. (1981b). Future educational uses of interactive theorem proving. In P. Suppes (Ed.), *University-level computer-assisted instruction at Stanford: 1968–1980* (pp. 165–182). Stanford, CA: Stanford University, Institute for Mathematical Studies in the Social Sciences.

Suppes, P. (1984). The next generation of interactive theorem provers. In R. E. Shostak (Ed.), 7th international conference on Automated Deduction, Napa, CA, May 14–16 (pp. 303–315). *Lecture Notes in Computer Science 170.* New York: Springer-Verlag.

Suppes, P., Ager, T., Berg, P., Chauqui, R., Graham, W., Maas, R., & Takahashi, S. (1987). *Applications of computer technology to pre-college calculus: First annual report,* (Tech. Rep. 310, Psychology and Education Series). Stanford, CA: Institute for Mathematical Studies in the Social Sciences.

Suppes, P., & Sheehan, J. (1981a). CAI course in axiomatic set theory. In P. Suppes (Ed.), *University-level computer-assisted instruction at Stanford: 1968–1980* (pp. 3–80). Stanford, CA: Stanford University, Institute for Mathematical Studies in the Social Sciences.

Suppes, P., & Sheehan, J. (1981b). CAI course in logic. In P. Suppes (Ed.), *University-level computer-assisted instruction at Stanford: 1968–1980* (pp. 193–226). Stanford, CA: Stanford University, Institute for Mathematical Studies in the Social Sciences.

Westcourt, K. T., Beard, M., & Barr, A. (1981). Curriculum information networks for CAI: Research on testing and evaluation by simulation. In P. Suppes (Ed.), *University-level computer-assisted instruction at Stanford: 1968–1980* (pp. 817–840). Stanford, CA: Stanford University, Institute for Mathematical Studies in the Social Sciences.

3

The Teacher's Apprentice Project: Building an Algebra Tutor

Robert Milson
McGill University

Matthew W. Lewis
The RAND Corporation

John R. Anderson
Carnegie Mellon University

The Advanced Computer-Tutoring Project has been working on the development of intelligent computer-based tutors for mathematics and computer programming. The first tutoring systems constructed were a tutor for high school geometry (Anderson, Boyle, & Yost, 1985) and a tutor for introductory LISP programming (Anderson & Reiser, 1985). The theoretical foundation for the design came from the ACT* theory of skill acquisition (Anderson 1983). The experience gained by the construction and evaluation of these systems resulted in a general methodology for the design of intelligent tutors. A summary of ACT*, the tutor design guidelines, and the LISP and geometry tutors is given in Anderson, Boyle, Corbett, and Lewis (in press).

The ACT approach to computer-tutoring research is based on the finding that private human tutors are far more effective than typical classroom instruction (Bloom, 1984). The observation is supported by the ACT* theory, which predicts that skills can be acquired only through practice. The advantage of a private tutor is the opportunity for learning in the context of practice, something conventional classroom instruction cannot offer. Thus, an effective computer tutor should teach students by helping them practice problem solving.

All ACT systems are built using a design methodology known as model tracing. A computer model, or simulation, of the student generates solution paths for problems and the human learner's progress and errors are traced in reference to the model's solutions. Students solve problems in a computerized work environment. The tutor follows the student's solution attempts, and interrupts when the student makes mistakes or asks for help. A model-tracing tutor consists of three subsystems:

- The *tutoring interface* is a computerized problem-solving environment suitable for the domain being tutored.
- The *student model* is a computer simulation of problem solving that allows the tutor to interpret student activity in the interface.
- The *tutorial module* is a set of rules and heuristics on how to guide the student through a problem.

The algebra tutor, developed and implemented on Xerox 1109 Dandetigers, is an application of the ACT design methodology to the domain of introductory algebra (high school Algebra I). Designing an interface is the first step in building a new tutoring system. A concrete interface formalizes the tutor's domain by allowing a problem solution to be formulated as a sequence of primitive interface operations. The first section of this chapter describes the algebra tutor's interface and the psychological principles that guided its design. We describe the tutor's interface first, because the discussion of the other components can then utilize concrete examples of the algebra tutor's problem-solving structure. The second section describes how the algebra system simulates both correct and buggy algebraic problem solving. The next section discusses which tutorial strategies maximize student learning and how such tutorial strategies are implementated within the context of the algebra tutor.

Along with the implementation of an algebra tutor, our project is pursuing the more ambitious goal of designing of tutoring architecture that can be applied in different domains of high school mathematics. The focus of our approach is to select an interface and a tutoring strategy that are as domain-independent as possible. The task of extending the tutor to a new domain is thereby reduced to creating a new student model. The penultimate section of this chapter discusses this aspect of our work.

The final section describes evaluation of the algebra system and documents some success in using the system to teach equation solving to students.

THE INTERFACE

The interface of a tutoring system is a structured problem-solving environment for the particular skill being tutored. A computer implementation of a problem-solving environment requires a formal definition of the problem-solving process. Such a formalization must not be oversimplified: It has to be able to express a solution process that has the features of a human-generated solution. For instance, defining the algebraic problem-solving process as a series of equation transformations is inadequate. Such a formalization is too coarse because considerable computation (working with fractions and signed numbers) goes on within each equation transformation and the novice will need to take these smaller steps explicitly. In addition, the equation transformation formalism is superficial because it does not reflect the fact that people use strategic plans to guide their choice of transformations.

The ACT* theory indicates human problem solving is organized around a hierarchical representation of the current goals. Therefore, an important pedagogical task is to communicate the domain's goal structure to the student. A tutoring system can facilitate this objective by implicitly incorporating the problem-solving structure into the structure of the interface. Consider the example of the ACT Geometry Tutor. Instead of representing a proof in the conventional two-column format, the Geometry Tutor uses a proof graph. The graph implicitly emphasizes the premise–conclusion relationship between proof statements (see Fig. 3.1).

The algebra tutor's interface structures problem solving by identifying problem-solving goals with operators. An operator can be thought of as a nondeterministic functional subroutine. It takes arguments, performs an evaluation, and returns a result. The arguments and results can be numbers, expressions, or equations. Table 3.1 shows three examples of operator application. The evaluation of an operator is done by evaluating a sequence of simpler suboperators. Table 3.2 shows the decomposition of the strategic operator that moves all the variable terms to one side of an equation. This operator, abbreviated MoveVarTerms, takes two arguments: the solution variable and the equation, and requires three substeps for evaluation.

Fig. 3.2 shows a snapshot of the Algebra Tutor interface. The student's work is displayed in the history window (long window on the left). The tutor gives the student messages via the black window in the upper right. Immediately below the message window is a calculation window, used by the student to do difficult numerical computations. The interface draws a frame around each operator. Suboperators are indicated by stacked frames. The "operator imbedded within operator" format is a graphic analog to the mental structure of algebraic problem solving. Algebraic manipulation is essentially the execution of procedures that transform symbolic formulas. Complicated algebraic procedures are the cumulative result of simpler procedures. It is this character of the algebraic domain that we have attempted to capture with the interface's graphic representation.

The student manages the interface via two input mechanisms: the goalpad and the keypad (see Fig. 3.3). The goalpad allows the student to select an operator. The keypad is used to input operator arguments and results. The cycle of student/interface interaction begins with the student selecting an operator from the goalpad. Next, the operator's argument(s) are entered via the keypad. After the arguments have been entered the student has a choice. He or she can either enter the result of the selected operator or

	STATEMENT	REASON
(1)	∠XEJ ≅ ∠XEK	*Given*
(2)	∠XEJ ≅ ∠YEJ	*Given*
(3)	∠EXJ ≅ ∠YXK	*Given*
(4)	JK *bisects* ∠XJY	*Given*
(5)	∠EJX ≅ ∠EJY	*Definition of Bisector* (4)
(6)	XE ≅ XE	*Reflexive*
(7)	△EJX ≅ △EKX	*ASA* (1)(5)(3)
(8)	JE ≅ JE	*Reflexive*
(9)	△EJX ≅ △EJY	*ASA* (2)(8)(5)
(10)	△EJY ≅ △EKX	*Transitivity* (7)(9)

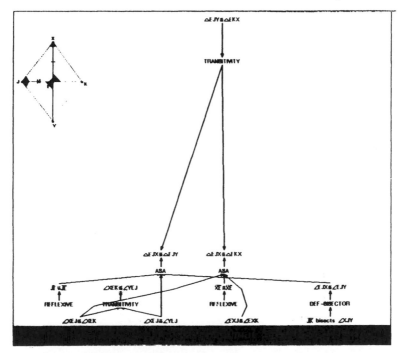

FIG. 3.1. A screen image from the ACT Geometry Tutor showing a completed proof that a student has constructed in a proof-graph form.

select another operator. If an operator is selected, it is treated as a subgoal and is placed within a subframe. After evaluating a number of suboperators (the scheme is recursive and any of the suboperators can have sub-suboperators) the student mouses the result box of the original operator to indicate that he or she is finished with the evaluation. The cycle is completed by entering the result via the keypad. Fig. 3.4 shows a sequence of student inputs and the resulting state of the interface.

Our second guideline for interface design is derived from the observation that there are limitations to a student's working memory. Decreasing the

TABLE 3.1
Examples of Operator Application

Operator		Result
ADD {5, 10}	→	15
Solve {3X + 5 = 6, X}	→	X = 1/3
CollectConstants {3X + 5 − 5 = 6 − 5}	→	3X = 6 − 5
	→	3X + 5 − 5 = 1
	→	3X = 1

The ADD operator has 2 arguments and corresponds to the goal of adding numbers.

The SOLVE operator has 2 arguments and corresponds to the goal of solving an equation for a given variable.

The COLLECTCONSTANTS operator has 1 argument and corresponds to the goal of collecting constants. Unlike the ADD and SOLVE operators, COLLECTCONSTANTS is nondeterministic, i.e., there is more than 1 correct way to evaluate it.

number of details that demand the student's attention will reduce the load on working memory and consequently will reduce the number of student errors. Therefore, the tutoring interface should manage all nonessential features of the problem-solving process independently of the student and make all essential problem features highly visible and organized.

The algebra tutor's interface reduces working memory demands on the student in several ways. The frame-based graphic format organizes the problem goal stack. After completing a substep the student need not reconstruct the context for that substep; the context is clearly visible via the organization of operator frames. The student does not need to expend mental resources on determining how his or her latest action fits into the overall scheme of the problem's solution.

Another feature of the interface facilitates the input of algebraic strings. A student can point to any expression on the screen and with a single mouse click enter it as the desired argument or result. This feature reduces copying errors and minimizes the effort required for the incidental task of generating algebraic expressions.

TABLE 3.2
Decomposition of the Strategic Operator

Goal:	MoveVarTerms {X, 18 − 3X = X}		
Substep1:	AdditiveInverse {−3X}	→	3X
Substep2:	AddToEquation {18 − 3X = X, 3X}	→	18 − 3X + 3X = X + 3X
Substep3:	CollectLikeTerms		
	{X, 18 − 3X + 3X = X + 3X}	→	18 = 4X
Result:	18 = 4X		

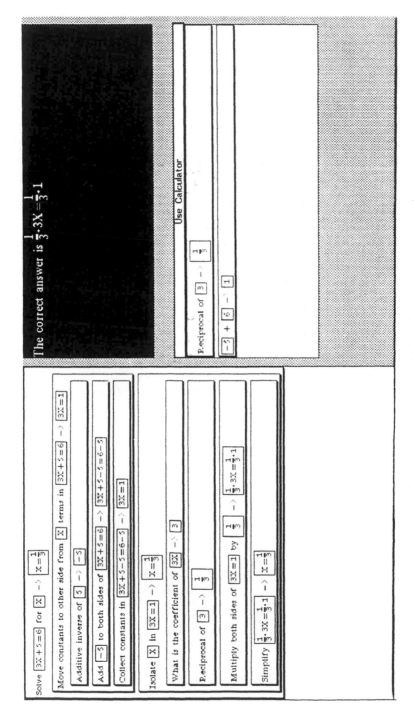

FIG. 3.2.   A screen image of the Algebra Tutor interface.

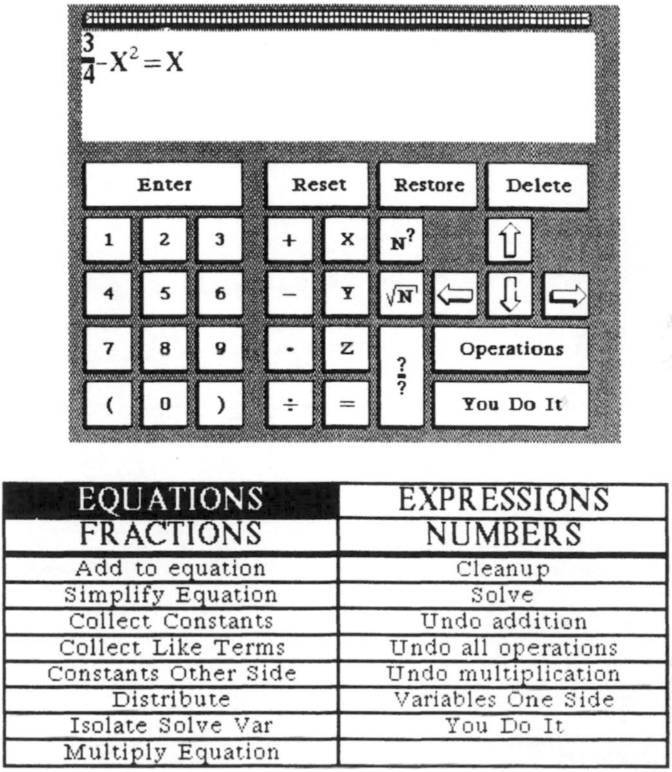

$$\frac{3}{4}-X^2 = X$$

| Enter | Reset | Restore | Delete |

1	2	3	+	X	$N^?$	⇧
4	5	6	−	Y	$\sqrt{N}$	⇦ ⇩ ⇨
7	8	9	.	Z	$\frac{?}{?}$	Operations
(	0	)	÷	=		You Do It

EQUATIONS	EXPRESSIONS
FRACTIONS	NUMBERS
Add to equation	Cleanup
Simplify Equation	Solve
Collect Constants	Undo addition
Collect Like Terms	Undo all operations
Constants Other Side	Undo multiplication
Distribute	Variables One Side
Isolate Solve Var	You Do It
Multiply Equation	

FIG. 3.3.   The screen-presented keypad that is moused to enter results to the system.

Finally, the interface provides the student with a calculator facility. The student, at any time, can activate the calculation window, select an operator and arguments and have the interface perform the evaluation. The calculator is limited to operators that have been previously mastered by the student. In our curriculum this is initially restricted to operations on unsigned numbers and is expanded to include operations on fractions and integers after sufficient student progress. Fig. 3.5 shows the calculation window after a student has used the interface to compute the product of 12 and 17.

The ideal algebra tutor interface should be as usable as paper and pencil, and yet structure the student's work. The design and implementation of an interface that tries to attain such ideals is a difficult software engineering task. Based on our observation of student/tutor interactions, we have redesigned and changed the interface over the course of our evaluation studies. The interface design process is not completed. We are running additional studies to test techniques and features that may improve the interface.

```
 1(G)  "Move Variable Terms"        14(G)  "Add"
 2(A)  X                            15(A)  -3X
 3(A)  18-3X=X                      16(A)  3X
 4(G)  "Additive Inverse"          17(R)  0
 5(A)  -3X                          18(G)  "Add"
 6(A)  3X                           19(A)  X
 7(G)  "Add To Equation"           20(A)  3X
 8(A)  3X                           21(R)  4X
 9(A)  18-3X=X                      22(E)  Mouse the result box of the
10(R)  18-3X+3X=X+3X                       "Collect Like Terms" step.
11(G)  "Collect Like Terms"        23(R)  18=4X
12(A)  X                            24(E)  Mouse the result box of the
13(A)  18-3X+3X=X+3X                       "Move Variable Terms" step.
                                    25(R)  18=4X


(G) Goal Input                     (R) Result Input
(A) Argument Input                 (E) End of Algorithm Input
```

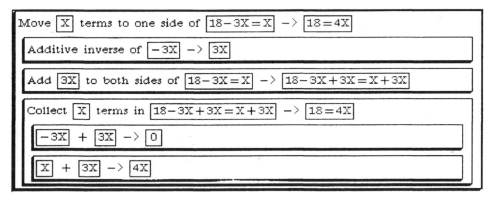

FIG. 3.4.   An example set of interactions with the system.

THE STUDENT MODEL

An essential component of a model-tutoring system is a computer simulation of a student's problem-solving ability. The student model is used by the tutor to diagnose student behavior. The tutor compares the student input against both the correct rules that the ideal model is considering and the associated buggy rules relevant to the current state in the problem solution. When the student is correct, the tutor remains quiet. Errors will cause the tutor to interrupt. If the error matches a known bug, then the tutor will respond with a specific error message; otherwise the tutor will respond with a generic error message.

The fundamental ACT guideline for student modeling is to represent the target skill as a set of productions. Problem solving is treated as the application of rules to generate information and to set further goals. Analogously, the computer simulation of the student model is implemented as a rule-based production system. Each rule is represented by a production

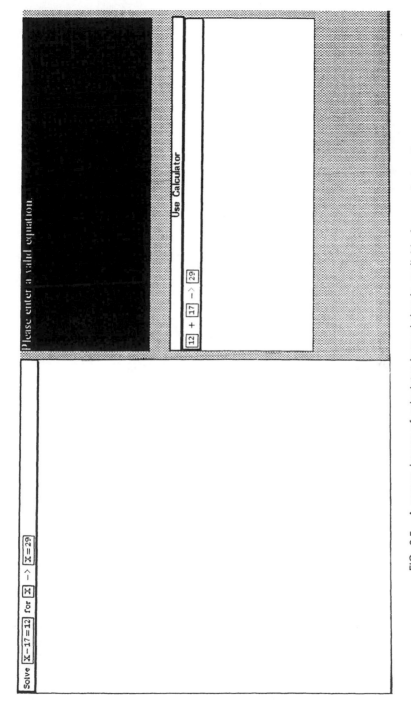

FIG. 3.5. A screen image of calculator keypad that is available for use during the tutor interactions to find partial results.

that specifies a certain set of actions given the current operator goal and its arguments. Here is an example of an algebraic production that is used to solve linear equations.

IF
the goal is to solve a linear equation

THEN
Clean up the equation by distributing, collecting like terms, and simplifying.

Move all the variable terms to one side of the equation.

Move all the constant terms to the other side of the equation.

Isolate the variable by multiplying both sides of the equation by the reciprocal of the variables coefficient and simplifying.

There is a caveat in the application of our modeling paradigm to tutoring. Even though a production system can be used to model student behavior accurately, it does not follow that rules are the only things that students need to be taught. A human student must be exposed to other kinds of information. Just teaching explicit rules of manipulation often has an unfortunate result: The student treats algebraic problem solving as a task of changing symbol strings into other strings according to a set of seemingly arbitrary rules prescribed by the teacher. The student needs to be taught the semantic justifications of these rules first. The student should derive the symbol manipulation rules from these semantic representations through practice (Anderson et al., in press).

The production rules used to model student problem-solving skills have to reflect human approaches to problem solving. Human beings solve problems differently from equivalent, yet faster, computer algorithms. As an example, consider the solution of a system of linear equations. Compared with an efficient matrix-based computer algorithm a human solution would have a more complicated control structure that avoids a large number of numerical computations. Human problem solving involves a diverse number of hierarchically structured goals. In the domain of algebra, for instance, people utilize strategic rules to guide the application of axiomatic knowledge about numbers and equations (Bundy, 1983). Furthermore, the problem-solving productions utilized by a novice have a finer grain-size than those used by an expert, that is, a novice proceeds toward a solution in smaller, more detailed steps. The algebra tutor's student model adheres to both of these guidelines. Our simulation explicitly represents strategic goals and given a single problem will generate several solutions of varying grain-size.

During problem solving and learning students will often make slips and develop misconceptions. Therefore, along with correct problem-solving procedures, the student model should simulate student errors. The error model is instantiated by adding buggy rules and corresponding remediation messages to the production simulation of the skill. The buggy rules predict the errors committed by students under various circumstances. The associated error messages help the student to reject incorrect rules and to learn the appropriate ones. An example of a buggy rule is:

IF
    the goal is to add two fractions,

$$\frac{N_1}{N_2} + \frac{N_3}{N_4}$$

THEN
    give the answer as,

$$\frac{N_1 + N_3}{N_2 + N_4}$$

The message associated with the bug given herein informs the student that one does not add fractions by adding their numerators and denominators and gives a review of the correct method for adding fractions.

There are two ways to generate the buggy rules associated with a tutor's domain. The straightforward, though arduous, method is to monitor many students during the solution of many problems and to catalog the students' mistakes. The more sophisticated approach consists of formalizing a theory of domain errors, applying this theory to the set of rules that define the domain skill, and generating a set of buggy rules for that domain (see Brown & VanLehn, 1980, for a discussion of errors and a generative theory). As an example of the latter approach, consider the observation that students will prematurely terminate iterative algebraic and arithmetical procedures. This observation can be translated into the following bugs:

- Unfinished distribution: Distribute $\{3\ (X + 2)\} \rightarrow 3\ X + 2$
- Incorrect Greatest Common Factor: GCF $\{24, 36\} \rightarrow 4$
- Failure to reduce a fraction fully: Reduce $\{24/36\} \rightarrow 6/9$

A usable theory of generated bugs has to predict most of the bugs generated by students without predicting implausible errors that an actual student would never commit. All ACT tutors, including the Algebra Tutor, obtain their buggy rules by observing students. A formal theory of errors for the domains of LISP programming, geometry, or algebra does not yet exist, but such a theory is a current research goal.

In addition to buggy production rules, the Algebra Tutor recognizes a class of student mistakes that are not simulated by the student model production system. Students make mistakes that can be analyzed on the basis of interface characteristics. Students will try to enter operator arguments in reverse order, setting, for example, a goal to "Solve X for the variable $3X + 2 = 11$." In another frequent interface error, the student forgets that he or she is currently supposed to provide an argument or an answer to a suboperator, and instead inputs the answer to the overall problem. Students can become confused about the tutor's scheme of operator nesting and select goals they have already evaluated or goals that will have to be evaluated at a later stage of the current problem. Observation of students has yielded about 10 different categories of interface errors that involve inputting goals, arguments, and results. An error from any of these categories will cause the Tutor to display a message that explains to the student why the student's latest input was inappropriate.

Implementation of the student model is the aspect of the tutor design process that requires the greatest emphasis on AI and theoretical computer science techniques. Our current simulation of one variable linear equation algebra skill utilizes about 300 correct and 100 buggy rules. More rules will be added as the tutor's curriculum grows. The rules are instantiated in a production system that has to do intensive string matching and yet maintains a reasonable level of performance. Using the finest grain-size, a difficult equation will require more than 100 steps for its solution and requires approximately .5 seconds for every step. So instead, we generate ahead of time a state space representing all operations that a student might perform. Rather than dynamically trying to fire productions, the tutor uses this derived state space to interpret the student.

THE TUTORING STRATEGY

Practice is essential for learning: This is the fundamental insight regarding human skill acquisition. The utility of an intelligent tutoring system lies in its ability to maximize the learning gains of practice. Consequently, the Algebra Tutor instantiates the following principles in its tutorial strategy:

- Allow the student to solve the problem as independently as possible.
- Vary the grain-size of instruction.
- Provide immediate feedback upon errors, in the context of the current problem.
- Prevent floundering by giving help.

Allowing the student to practice independently means that the Tutor should not intervene as long as the student generates correct solution steps.

In such circumstances, the tutoring system should appear as nothing more than a structured editor for the generation of problem solutions. Therefore, the ACT tutors intervene only when the student makes an error or asks for help.

The Algebra Tutor begins the problem-solving session by presenting the student with an unevaluated operator. The student must use the interface to solve the problem. As detailed in the Interface Section, he or she can give the answer immediately, evaluate a number of suboperators, and/or use the calculation window. If the student avoids giving incorrect input, he or she can go through an entire problem without triggering a single tutoring message.

As students progress in expertise they will begin to group their problem-solving knowledge into larger units. This process is called knowledge composition. In terms of tutoring interactions, knowledge composition manifests itself as the desire of the student to skip steps. Therefore, the Tutor must be able to recognize skipped steps and adjust its grain-size of instruction to the level appropriate to the current level of student ability.

The Algebra Tutor has three mechanisms to adjust the grain-size of instruction. First, the only time a student must decompose operators into their component substeps is when he is unable to generate the answer mentally. Thus the level of operator nesting is up to the individual student. Figs. 3.6 and 3.7 illustrate the solution of the same problem with different levels of operator decomposition. Secondly, when a student must perform a sequence of operations he or she can skip over an arbitrary number of intermediate steps. Figs. 3.7 and 3.8 illustrate this feature. The tutor screen in Fig. 3.7 shows all four steps necessary to evaluate the "Move variable terms to one side" operation. The screen in Fig. 3.8 shows the work trace of a student who avoided the first three substeps of the "Move variable terms"operation and skipped to the last "Collect Like Terms" suboperation. The third adjustable grain-size feature allows the student to terminate prematurely a sequence of operators by giving the answer to a supergoal. This "pop-out" feature is illustrated by Fig. 3.9 where the student stops

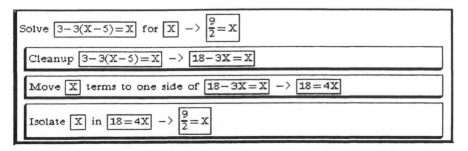

FIG. 3.6.   Solution of an equation with one level of decomposition.

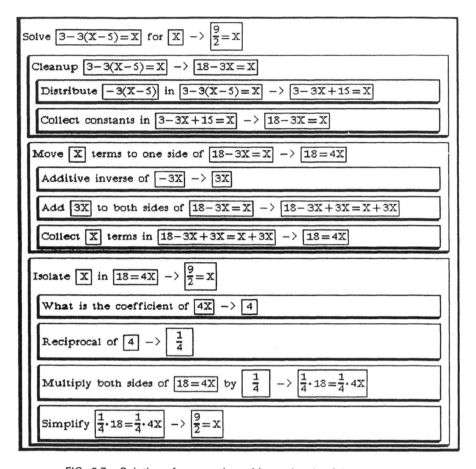

FIG. 3.7. Solution of an equation with two levels of decomposition.

short in an evaluation of the "Move variable terms to one side" operation and gives the correct answer to the "Solve equation goal." The adjustable grain-size features of the Algebra Tutor makes the system more effective because the student can avoid unnecessary and frustrating interface interactions.

ACT tutoring methodology specifies that the student should be given immediate feedback on errors. There are two arguments that support this strategy. Allowing the student to generate erroneous steps can lead to floundering. Tracking down the source of errors can be difficult for a novice and can interfere with the learning of the target skill by diverting attention from the problem solution to the task of analyzing previous work. Furthermore, students are more likely to debug their knowledge correctly upon immediate feedback, because the rules they used to commit the error are still active in memory and thus more successfully modified than when memory search is required to find the responsible rule.

There are criticisms of the immediate feedback strategy that rest upon the pedagogical utility of having the student locate his or her errors. By tracking down errors, the student practices debugging and self-diagnosis skills (McArthur, Stasz, & Hotta, 1987). In defense of the immediate feedback strategy there exists empirical evidence for its effectiveness (Lewis & Anderson, 1985). We feel that in as much as debugging and self-analysis are important skills, they should be taught and tutored explicitly.

The Algebra Tutor always gives the student immediate feedback on errors. At the very minimum, the system communicates to the student that his or her latest action is incorrect and does not allow the student to pursue the consequences of the error. When a student error can be analyzed the tutor will also offer an explanation of why the student's answer was the error. As well as having pedagogical utility, the immediate feedback strategy simplilfies the design of the interface and the design of the tutoring

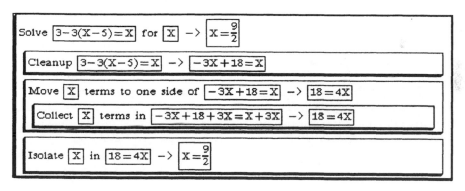

FIG. 3.8.   Solution of an equation with skipped steps.

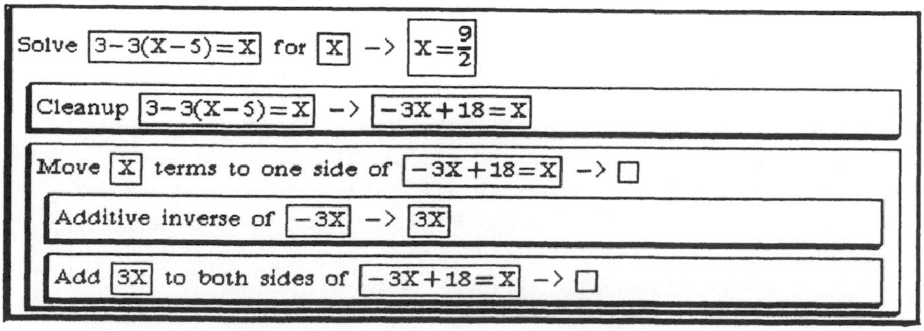

FIG. 3.9.   Solution of an equation with the final goals left uncompleted. The student "popped out" of the problem-solving process to input the correct solution.

strategy. The interface does not have to implement and communicate to the student a backtracking mechanism and is therefore easier to use and understand. A tutoring strategy that allowed the student to pursue errors would have to determine at what point to intervene and where to set the student back on the right track.

When the student is not able to proceed with the problem solution, the tutoring system must be able to provide help. The simplest way to offer help is to indicate the next step in the solution. From the learning-by-doing theory of skill acquisition comes the corollary: Make the student do as much of the work as possible. Hence, the amount of information given away should be small. Giving away too much information will teach the student to rely on the help feature and will fail to give practice with the actual skill. Nonetheless, the tutor should not allow a student to be stuck at one point of the problem solving indefinitely. A minimum of "pushing along" should be used to get the student through the problem.

The Algebra Tutor has two features that ensure the student will get through every problem. At any point the student may ask for help by selecting the "You Do It" option (Fig. 3.3). The wording of this label implies that the student can request the computer to generate the next correct step. If the student can't provide the next goal or argument and asks for help, then the Tutor will select a correct answer for the student. If the student selects "You Do It" when the result to a primitive operation is required, the Tutor will fill in the answer for the student. If the student wants help with the result of a nonprimitive operation then the Tutor will ask the student to decompose the current goal into its substeps. Help is, of course, available for the selection of these substeps. Furthermore, the Tutor prevents floundering by limiting the student to two incorrect actions before intervening. Intervention after two mistakes is identical to the intervention after a help request; that is, the Tutor either gives away the answer or forces the student to decompose the current operator into suboperators. Thus, the Algebra Tutor's strategy of intervention is minimal, but guarantees that a student will get to the end of any problem in a finite amount of time.

Our ideal for the design of the Algebra Tutor's pedagogical strategy is the one-on-one human tutor. Compared with a human tutor, the computer tutor falls short on many accounts. The human tutor has access to the expressive power of natural language and is better able to understand and interpret the behavior of the student. However, we hope to have captured an essential advantage that a private tutor can offer to a student: The Algebra Tutor allows the student to learn mathematical skills through guided practice that is individualized to that student's strengths and weaknesses.

EXTENDING THE ALGEBRA TUTOR
TO OTHER DOMAINS

The implementation of an intelligent tutoring system is a time-intensive task. One of the goals of the Algebra Tutor project is to design a system architecture that can be used in a variety of mathematical domains. The Algebra Tutor represents problem solving as the nested application of operators. This representation suffices for all algebra-like domains, that is, domains where the solution is reached by repeated transformations of formulas. This is appropriate for problem-solving domains such as algebra and introductory calculus, where the problem-solving procedure can be described as a deterministic algorithm, but not for domains such as geometry, where there is a lot of opportunistic search required to find the solution.

The pedagogical strategy implemented by the Algebra Tutor has no domain-dependent expertise built into it. The design of the tutoring strategy is concerned with:

1. What productions can apply in the student model, not the internal semantics of the productions.
2. What responses the student generates and whether these responses match what the productions would generate, not what these responses mean.
3. What tutorial dialogue templates are attached to the error productions, not what these dialogues mean.

Therefore, a different set of rules and bugs would not necessitate changing the system's tutorial strategy.

The interface-related error catcher does not need to vary with domain expertise, either. Regardless of the tutoring domain, students will have to set goals, provide arguments, give results, and will make attendant interface errors. A typical goal-related error involves trying to set a previously evaluated goal. In order to predict and describe such errors, the system needs to know what goals have been previously evaluated, but the system does not need to know the role these goals had in the problem solution. The situation is the same for other classes of interface related errors; the tutoring architecture automatically sets up their detection and limited remediation, regardless of the domain in question.

Therefore, the rule-based student model is the only tutor component that has to be changed from domain to domain. Three steps are required to implement a student model for a new domain.

1. A production system simulation of the domain skills must be written.

2. The labels and printing templates of the new problem-solving operators must be entered into the system.

3. Typical buggy rules must be collected/generated in order to implement the error model.

In terms of time, step (3) is the costliest, because it entails running a study on a tutor without the error model and extracting the domain bugs from the resulting protocols. Nonetheless, the process of extending the tutor to other algebraic domains does not require an intense programming effort and can probably be accomplished in the time span of several months, compared with the several years it takes to build a completely new tutor.

EVALUATION OF THE ALGEBRA TUTOR

We have run three evaluation studies of the Algebra Tutor. We use the studies to guide our design choices, to test various features of the system, and to collect typical student errors. The third and most recent study utilizes a curriculum of prealgebra through linear equation solving. The subjects are 24 local public and private school students who have completed a Prealgebra course but had not had a class in algebra. Each student had approximately 1 hour of individual instruction on the use of the system and regarding fundamentals of algebra such as variables and equations. The students used the tutoring system at their own pace and took from 25 to 58 hours with a mean of 31 hours to complete the course of study. Two types of pre- and poststudy assessments were given: The first test assessed overall math ability, the second assessed equation-solving skills. All students showed improvement on the first test with an average improvement of 32% of correct answers. Twenty-three students showed improvement in their equation-solving skills with the remaining student unable to solve equations before or after the experiment. The second test asked the student to solve 18 equations of varying complexity. The mean pre- and posttest scores for the equation test were 7 and 13 correct answers respectively, indicating a 33% improvement.[1] The conclusion is that the computer tutor can be used to improve mathematical ability. Also, given that the students in the study had no formal coursework in general equation solving and showed a significant improvement in that skill, we can conclude that the Algebra tutor can be an effective aid in teaching students how to solve equations.

Another interesting result of the study is data on the use of tutor-based

---

[1] The equation evaluation test contained some very simple equations, solvable by inspection, and some students had been introduced to simple equations in their prealgebra course.

error messages. Half of the students in the study received no remedial elaboration when they made a mistake; the tutor simply told them they were wrong. The other students were given remedial messages when the tutor was able to diagnose their mistake. While using the tutor, the students who were exposed to remedial messages required fewer overall interactions with the system, made fewer mistakes, and made fewer requests for help. Posttest data, however, do not show a difference in the mean scores of students with and without error messages. These observations seem to indicate that the effectiveness of remedial error messages lies primarily in increasing the usability of the system by students. Fundamental skill improvement, on the other hand, seems to be largely a matter of practice; regardless of error messages all students solved the same number of problems and therefore showed improvement in math ability.

ACKNOWLEDGMENT

This work is supported by grant MDR 8470337 from the Science and Engineering Education division of the National Science Foundation. The research reported here has benefited directly and indirectly from interactions with many individuals: Richard Wertheimer, Margaret Shields, Dr. John R. Young, and Dr. Paul G. LeMahieu of the Pittsburgh city schools and to the members of the algebra-tutoring group: William Barnes, Donnalynne Buterbaugh, Julie Epelboim, Don Hoffman, Kevin Singley, and Ik Yoo. We also thank the Board of Education of Pittsburgh for their ongoing generosity and cooperation in helping us carry out out research.

REFERENCES

Anderson, J. R. (1983). *The architecture of cognition.* Cambridge, MA: Harvard University Press.

Anderson, J. S., Boyle, C. F., Corbett, A. T., & Lewis, M. W. (in press). Cognitive modeling and intelligent tutoring. *Artificial Intelligence Journal,* .

Anderson, J. R., Boyle, C. F., & Yost, G. (1985). The geometry tutor. In *Proceedings of the International Joint Conference on Artificial Intelligence.* Los Altos, CA: Morgan Kaufmann.

Anderson, J. R., & Reiser, B. J. (1985, April). The LISP tutor. *Byte,* 159–175.

Bloom, B. S. (1984). The 2 Sigma Problem: The search for methods of group instruction as effective as one-to-one tutoring. *Educational Researcher, 13*(6), 4–16.

Brown, J. S., & VanLehn, K. (1980). Repair theory: A generative theory of bugs in procedural skills. *Cognitive Science, 4*(4), 379–426.

Bundy, A. (1983). *The computer modelling of mathematical reasoning.* London: Academic Press.

Lewis, M. W., & Anderson, J. R. (1985). Discrimination of operator schemata in problem solving. *Cognitive Psychology, 17,* 26–65.

McArthur, D., Stasz, C., & Hotta, J. Y. (1987). Learning problem-solving skills in algebra. *Journal of Educational Technology Systems, 15*(3), 303–324.

4 A Theory of Graph Comprehension

Steven Pinker
Massachusetts Institute of Technology

A striking fact about human cognition is that we like to process quantitative information in graphic form. One only has to look at the number of ways in which information is depicted in pictorial form—line, bar, and pie graphs, Venn diagrams, flow charts, tree structures, node networks, to name just a few—or to the great lengths that computer companies go to advertise the graphic capabilities of their products, to see that charts and graphs have enormous appeal to people. All of this is true despite the fact that in virtually every case, the same information can be communicated by nonpictorial means: tables of numbers, lists of propositions cross-referenced by global variables, labeled bracketings, and so on. Perhaps pictorial displays are simply pleasing to the eye, but both introspection and experimental evidence (Carter, 1947; Culbertson & Powers, 1959; Schutz, 1961a, 1961b; Washburne, 1927) suggest that, in fact, graphic formats present information in a way that is easier for people to perceive and reason about. However, it is hard to think of a theory or principle in contemporary cognitive science that explains why this should be so; why, for example, people should differ so strikingly from computers in regard to the optimal input format for quantitative information.

The goal of this chapter is to address this unexplained phenomenon in a systematic way. In particular, I propose a theory of what a person knows when he or she knows how to read a graph, and which cognitive operations a person executes in the actual process of reading the graph. This theory will be used to generate predictions about what makes a person better or worse at reading graphs, and what makes a graph better or worse at conveying a given type of information to a reader. In pursuing these goals, one must recognize a very pervasive constraint. Comprehending a graph (unlike, say, seeing in depth, uttering a sentence, or reaching for a target) is not something that anyone could argue is accomplished by a special-purpose mental faculty. Graphs are a recent invention and if they are an especially effective method of communication, it must be because they exploit general cognitive and perceptual mechanisms effectively. Any theory that hopes to explain the process of graph comprehension will have to identify the psychological mechanisms used in interpreting a graph, and which operating principles of each mechanism contribute to the overall ease or difficulty of the graph-reading process. Thus, any theory of graph comprehension will draw heavily on general cognitive and perceptual theory, and where our knowledge of cognitive and perceptual mechanisms is sketchy, we can expect corresponding gaps in our ability to explain the understanding of graphs.

I. WHAT IS A GRAPH?

There is a bewildering variety of graphs in current use, ranging from the line and bar graphs common in scientific journals, to drawings in popular magazines in which the thickness of two boxer's arms might represent the missile strength of the U. S. and Soviet Union, or in which the lengths of the rays of light emanating from a yellow disk might represent the price of gold in different months. Nonetheless, all graphs can be given a common characterization. Each graph tries to communicate to the reader a set of n-tuples of values on n mathematical scales, using objects whose visual dimensions (i.e., length, position, lightness, shape, etc.) correspond to the respective scales, and whose values on each dimension (i.e., an object's *particular* length, position, and so on) correlate with the values on the corresponding scales. The pairing is accomplished by virtue of the fact that any seen object can be described simultaneously by its values along a number of visual dimensions. For example, Fig. 4.1 represents a pairing of values on a nominal scale (countries) with values on a ratio scale (GNP) using objects (bars) whose horizontal position (a visual dimension) corresponds to a value on the first scale, and whose height (another visual dimension) corresponds to a value on the second scale.

Fig. 4.2 represents a pairing of values on an ordinal scale (months) with values on an interval scale (temperature) using objects (wedges) whose radial position represents the month, and whose darkness represents the temperature. This characterization, which can be applied to every graph I have seen, was first pointed out by Bertin (1967) in his seminal treatment of charts, graphs, and maps.

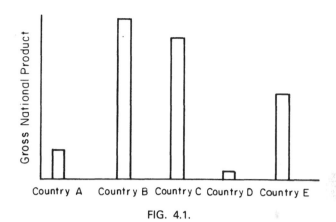

FIG. 4.1.

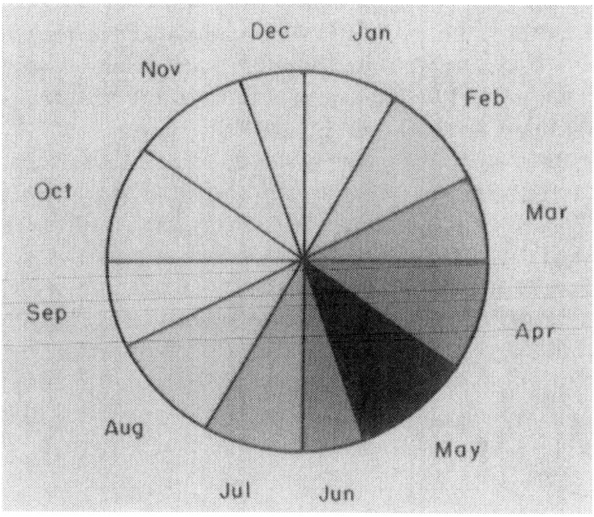

FIG. 4.2.

As Bertin points out, this characterization implies that a graph reader must do three things: (1) Identify, via alphanumeric labels, the conceptual or real-world referents that the graph is conveying information about (Bertin calls this "external identification"); (2) Identify the relevant dimensions of variation in the graph's pictorial content, and determine which visual dimensions corresponds to which conceptual variable or scale (Bertin's "internal identification"); and (3) Use the particular levels of each visual dimension to draw conclusions about the particular levels of each conceptual scale (Bertin's "perception of correspondence").

This simple observation implies that a graph reader must do two things. First, the reader must mentally represent the objects in the graph in only a certain way. In the case of Fig. 4.1, he or she must think of the bars in terms of their heights and their positions along the x-axis, but not necessarily in terms of the jagged contour formed by the tops of the bars, their distance from the edge of the page, and so on. Second, the graph reader must remember or deduce which aspects of the visual constituents of the graph stand for which of the mathematical scales that the graph is trying to communicate. In the theory to be described here, these two forms of knowledge are embodied in two types of mental representation: the *visual description*, which encodes the marks depicted on the page in terms of their physical dimensions, and the *graph schema*, which spells out how the physical dimensions will be mapped onto the appropriate mathematical scales. In using these structures to interpret a graph, a reader may obtain different sorts of information from it: the exact value of some scale paired with a given value on another scale, the rate of change of values on one scale within a range of values on another, a difference between the scale values of two entities, and so on. I will use the term *conceptual question* to refer to the particular sort of information that a reader wishes to extract from a graph, and *conceptual message* to refer to the information that the reader, in fact, takes away from it (cf. Bertin, 1967).

In the rest of the chapter, I characterize each of these representations explicitly, propose ways in which they are constructed and transformed in the course of reading a graph, and attempt to garner principles from perceptual and cognitive research dictating which aspects of these mental processes and representations affect the ease of extracting a message from a graph. These proposals will be justified by reference to concrete instances of graphs and other visual displays whose degree of intuitive difficulty is explained by the proposals, and to a number of experiments designed to test the proposals. Finally, a framework for further theoretical and applied research on graph comprehension will be outlined.

II. THE VISUAL ARRAY

The information in a graph arrives at the nervous system as a two-dimensional pattern of intensities on the retinas. I will use the term *visual array* to refer loosely to those early visual representations that depict the input in a relatively unprocessed, pictorial format (cf. the "primal sketch" and "2½ dimensional sketch" of Marr & Nishihara, 1978, and the "surface array" of Kosslyn, Pinker, Smith, & Shwartz, 1979). Information in this form is, of course, far too raw to serve as a basis for comprehending the meaning of the graph. For that, we need a representational format that can interface easily with the memory representations embodying knowledge of what the visual marks of the graph signify. Such memory representations cannot be stated in terms of specific distributions of light and dark (or even lines and edges) as would be represented in the visual array, because vastly different intensity distributions (differing in size, orientation, color, shape, lightness, etc.) could all be equivalent exemplars of a given type of graph. Thus, the representation that makes contact with stored knowledge of graphs must be more abstract than a visual array.

III. THE VISUAL DESCRIPTION

A fundamental insight into visual cognition is that the output of the mechanisms of visual perception is a symbolic representation or "structural description" of the scene, specifying the identity of its parts and the relations among them (see Winston, 1975; Marr & Nishihara, 1977; Palmer, 1975, Pylyshyn, 1973). In this description, the various aspects of the scene, such as its constituent elements, and their size, shape, location, color, texture, and so on, together with the spatial relations among them, will be factored apart into separate symbols. As a result, each higher-level cognitive process need only refer to the symbols representing the aspect of the scene that is relevant to its own computations. I will use the term *visual description* to refer to the structural description representing a graph, and *visual encoding processes* to refer to the mechanism that creates a visual description from a visual array pattern.

Many such "languages" for visual descriptions have been proposed (Hinton, 1979; Marr & Nishihara, 1977; Miller & Johnson–Laird, 1976; Palmer, 1975; Winston, 1975). Most of them describe a scene using propositions, whose *variables* stand for perceived entities or objects, and in which *predicates* specify attributes of and relations among the entities. It is assumed that the visual encoding mechanisms can detect the presence of each of these predicates in the visual array (see Ullman, 1984, for explicit proposals covering the sorts of mechanisms that are necessary to accomplish this). For example, one-place predicates specify a simple property of an object, such as *Circle* (x) (i.e., "x is a circle"), *Convex* (x), *Curve* (x), *Flat* (x), *Horizontal* (x), *Linear* (x), *Small* (x), and so on. Two-place predicates specify the relations between two objects, such as *Above* (x, y) (i.e., "x is above y"), *Adjacent* (x, y), *Below* (x, y), *Higher* (x, y), *Included-in* (x, y), *Points-toward* (x, y), *Parallel* (x, y), *Part* (x, y), *Near* (x, y), *Similar* (x, y) *Top* (x, y), and so on. Three and higher-place predicates indicate relations among groups of objects, such as *Between* (x, y, z) (i.e., "x is between y and z"), *In-line* (x, y, z), and so on. Parameterized predicates take a number of variables and a number of quantitative constants, such as *Area* (x, α) (i.e., "x has area α"), *Width* (x, α), *Location* (x, α, β), *Lightness* (x, α), *Orientation* (x, α), and so on. These predicates may also be appropriate for specifying continuous multidimensional attributes of

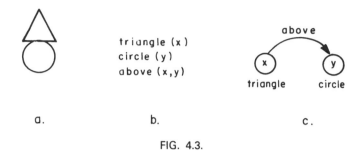

FIG. 4.3.

objects. For example, any member of a class of shapes ranging from a
flattened horizontal ellipse through a circle to a flattened vertical ellipse
can be specified by two parameters, representing the lengths of the major
and minor axes of the ellipse, thus: *Ellipse* (x, α, β).

As is fitting for a discussion of graphs, I will use a graphic notation for
visual descriptions. Each variable in a description will be represented by
a small circle or *node* in which the variable name is inscribed (for simplicity's
sake, I usually omit the variable name in these diagrams); each one-place
predicate will simply be printed next to the nodes representing the variables
that they are true of; and each two-place predicate will be printed alongside
an arrow linking the two nodes representing the predicate's two arguments.
Thus, a particular scene represented as the visual array in Fig. 4.3a will
be represented as the visual description in Fig. 4.3b, or its graphic counterpart in Fig. 4.3c.

Constraining the Visual Description

If, as argued, a visual array representation is unsuitable for the computations involved in extracting information from a graph, an unconstrained
visual description is not much better. Since any visual array can be described
in an infinite number of ways, a theory that allowed any visual description
to be built from a visual array would be unable to predict what would
happen when a given individual faced a given graph. For example, the
array in Fig. 4.4a can give rise not only to the visual description in Fig.
4.4c, but to the descriptions in Fig. 4.4b as well.

Clearly, if it is not to be vacuous, the theory must specify *which* visual
description is likely to be constructed in a given situation, based on our
knowledge of how the human visual system works. Of course, these constraints are simply the totality of our knowledge on perception. In the
following section, I select four broad principles, each grounded in basic
perceptual research, which constrain the form of visual descriptions in ways
that are relevant to graph comprehension. These principles will bear a
large explanatory burden in the theory to be outlined here, since later I

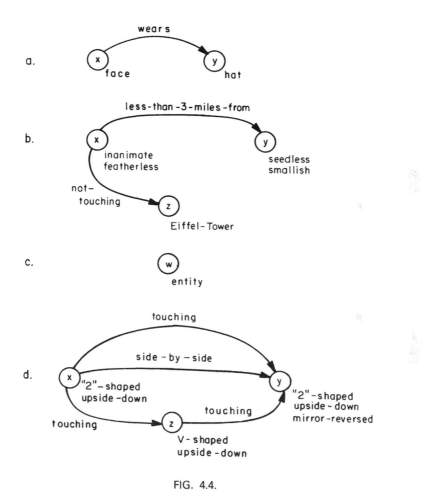

FIG. 4.4.

claim that a prime determinant of the difficulty of a graph will be whether the visual description specifies explicitly the visual dimensions and groupings that the graph maker recruited to symbolize the mathematical scales involved in the message of the graph.

A. The Indispensability of Space

It has long been known that an object's spatial location has a different perceptual status than its color, lightness, texture, or shape. Kubovy (1981) has addressed this issue systematically, and calls the two spatial dimensions of vision (plus the time dimension) *indispensable attributes*, analogous to the dimensions of pitch and time in audition. He defines the term "indispensable attribute" as an attribute with the following properties:

1. Perceptual Numerosity.   The first constraint on a visual description must be on what is to count as a variable or node. Variables should stand for perceptual units of some sort, and not for any arbitrary subset of the light reflected from a scene (e.g., the set of all light patches whose dominant wavelength is divisible by 100). Kubovy points out that our perceptual systems pick out a "unit" or an "object" in a visual scene as any set of light patches that share the same spatial position, but *not* as a set of light patches that share some other attribute such as wavelength, intensity, or texture. Thus, Fig. 4.5a will give rise to the visual description in Fig. 4.5b, which partitions the array into three variables according to spatial location, rather than that in Fig. 4.5c, which partitions the array into two variables according to surface markings.

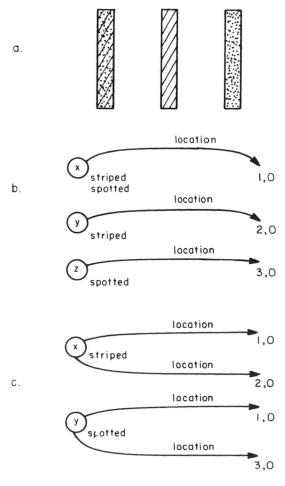

FIG. 4.5.

a.

b.

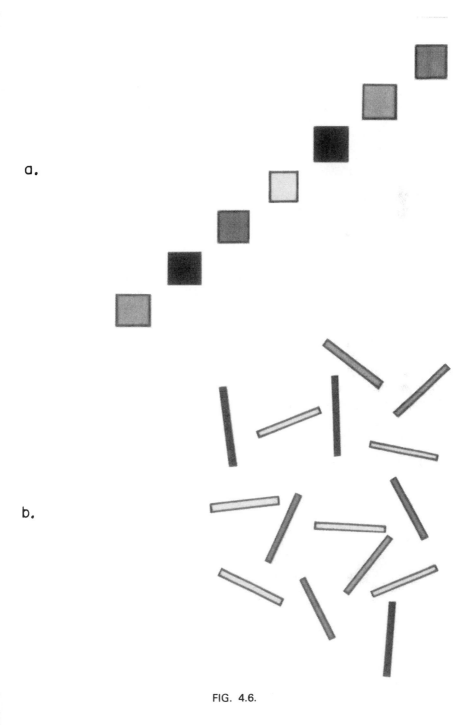

FIG. 4.6.

2. Configural Properties.   The second constraint on a visual scene is the choice of predicates available in assembling a visual description. Naturally, there will be predicates corresponding to all perceptible physical dimensions (e.g., *bright* (x), *red* (x), *shiny* (x), *lightness* (x, α); in addition, there will be "configural" or "pattern" predicates corresponding to higher-order functions defined over the physical dimensions. Kubovy points out that most configural properties in a sensory modality are defined over the indispensable attributes, which in the case of static visual objects are the two spatial dimensions. As a consequence, there exist many predicates for spatial shapes (each of which can be defined by certain well-defined changes in relative horizontal and relative vertical positions in a pattern), but few for nonspatial "shapes" defined by analogous well-defined changes in other dimensions. For example, the array in Fig. 4.6a contains elements whose heights increase with their horizontal position (lightness varying randomly); the array in Fig. 4.6b contains elements whose lightnesses increase with their orientations (position varying randomly). However, the increase is immediately noticeable only in Fig. 4.6a, where the increase is of one spatial dimension with respect to another, not in Fig. 4.6b. Correspondingly, there exists a predicate *diagonal* (x) that can be used to describe the scene in Fig. 4.6a, but nothing analogous for describing the scene in Fig. 4.6b, whose elements would probably be specified individually. Note that as long as one member of a pair of related dimensions is spatial, there may be configural predicates available; when neither member is spatial, con-

FIG. 4.7.

figural predicates are unlikely. Thus, the elements in Fig. 4.7 get darker with height, a change that, unlike that in Fig. 4.6b, is quickly noticeable, and may be captured by a single predicate (e.g., *lightness-gradient* (x)).

3. Discriminability and Linearity. It has been known for a century that physical variables are not in general perceived linearly, nor are small differences between values of a physical variable always noticed. In the visual description, this corresponds to numerical variables [e.g., *height* $(x, 17)$] being distorted with respect to the real-world entities they represent, or to distinct numerical variables sharing the same value when the represented entities in fact differ [e.g., *lightness* $(x, 17)$; *lightness* $(y, 17)$ for two boxes differing slightly in lightness]. Kubovy remarks that indispensable attributes afford finer discriminations and more linear mappings then dispensable attributes, and indeed, the Weber fraction for spatial extent is 0.04, and the Stevens exponent is 1.0, both indicating greater accuracy for the representation of spatial extent than for the representation of other physical variables used in graphs.

4. Selective Attention. As a consequence of (1), each variable may have associated with it a unique pair of coordinates representing its location. This means that location could serve as an *index* or accessing system for visual information. This is a form of selective attention, and Kubovy summarizes evidence supporting the hypotheses that attention is more selective for indispensable attributes (two-dimensional location in vision) than for other visual attributes (see also Ullman, 1984). For example, one cannot easily attend to any visible object with a given shape, regardless of location (see Posner, Snyder, & Davidson, 1980). In the theory outlined in this chapter, selective attention according to location will consist of a mechanism that activates various encoding mechanisms to process a given spatial region of the visual array, in order to encode more predicates into the visual description or to verify whether a given predicate is true of the entity at that location. As we shall see, these mechanisms will play an important role in the "question-driven" or "top–down" processing of graphs.

B. Gestalt Laws of Grouping

The principles associated with the indispensability of space in vision place constraints on the parts of an array that variables may stand for, on how numerical variables represent physical continua, and on how predicates are encoded or verified with respect to the visual array. What is needed in addition is a set of principles governing how variables representing visual entities will be related to one another in visual descriptions, that is, how the atomic perceptual units will be integrated into a coherent percept. A notable set of such principles is the Gestalt Laws of Perceptual Organization (Wertheimer, 1938). These laws dictate that distinct static perceptual elements will be seen as belonging to a single configuration if they are near one another ("proximity"), similar in terms of one or more visual dimensions ("similarity"), smooth continuations of one another ("good continuation"), or parallel ("common fate") in the 2D plane. In terms of the

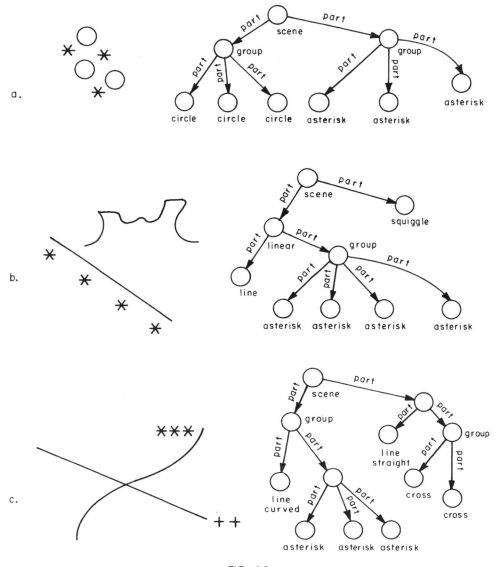

FIG. 4.8.

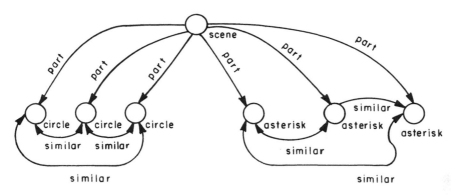

FIG. 4.9.

visual description, these principles will determine how variables are linked via the "part" relation in structures like those in Fig. 4.8a (where the law of similarity links asterisks to asterisks and circles to circles), Fig. 4.8b (where common fate links the asterisks to the line, and similarity links the asterisks to one another), and Fig. 4.8c (where good continuation keeps the straight and curved lines distinct, proximity links the asterisks and crosses to their respective lines, and similarity links asterisks to asterisks and crosses to crosses). Fig. 4.8 also shows how each collection of objects would be represented in a visual description.

There is another way of indicating the effects of grouping within visual descriptions. That is to link each member of a group to every other member using either the relation that gave rise to the grouping, or simply the relation "associated with." Thus, the visual array in Fig. 4.8a could also be represented as in Fig. 4.9: This notation can be used to indicate that the variables are grouped together perceptually, but not so strongly as to be a distinct perceptual unit. In the rest of this chapter, I use both notations for grouping, though no theoretical distinction need be implied by the choice.

C. Representation of Magnitude

Implicit in the earlier discussion of the psychophysics of visual dimensions was the assumption that these dimensions are represented by continuous interval scales in visual descriptions. Though the fine discriminations and smooth magnitude estimation functions found in psychophysical experiments strongly warrant this assumption, there is reason to believe that quantity can be mentally represented in other ways as well. First, there is evidence from experiments on the absolute identification of values on perceptual continua that people cannot remember verbal labels for more than about seven distinct levels of a perceptual continuum (Miller, 1956), and that in making rapid comparisons between remembered objects, subjects' reaction times are insensitive to the precise values of objects belonging to distinct, well-learned categories (Kosslyn, Murphy, Bemesderfer & Feinstein, 1977). Findings such as these suggest that quantity can also be represented (indeed, in memory *must* be represented, in certain circumstances) by one of a set of seven or so discrete symbols each specifying a portion of the range of quantities. These symbols could be signified by the Roman numerals I through VII.

Second, it is useful to distinguish between ratio values, where quantity is represented continuously but the units are arbitrary, and *absolute* values, where the units are well defined. The perception of pitch is a notorious example where a precise mental representation of a dimension is possible, but where for a majority of people, no absolute units can be assigned to the stimuli. Length, on the other hand, is an example of a continuum which people can judge either in ratio terms (e.g., one object being 1.7 times as long as another), or in terms of the well-known inches–feet–yards scale (e.g., Gibson, Bergman & Purdy, 1955). Indeed, whether subjects in magnitude estimation experiments are asked to use a well-learned versus their own arbitrarily selected modulus for estimated magnitude apparently affects their judgments (Stevens, 1961). Thus, interval descriptions must discriminate between these two forms of magnitude, which I will refer to an "interval-value" and "absolute-value," though ordinarily, visual descriptions will only contain "interval-value" propositions.

Finally, as every commercial sign maker can attest, values on a continuum that are extreme in comparison with values of that continuum for other objects in a scene are very likely to be perceptually encoded (as opposed to less extreme values, which are apt to be encoded only if attended to). To account for this salience principle, relatively extreme values will be represented redundantly in visual descriptions: in ordinary propositions such as *height* (x, α), as before, and also by special one-place predicates indicating the extremeness of the value along the particular dimension, such as *tall* (x), *bright* (x), *short* (x), and so on. When capacity limitations of visual descriptions are discussed later, it will be assumed that these special predicates have a very high probability of being encoded in the visual description.

D. Coordinate Systems

To express a unidimensional quality like lightness, one need specify in advance only the origin and the units of the scale to be used. However, for objects that vary along a number of continua, such as the position of an object on a two-dimensional piece of paper, or rectangles in a set varying in height and width, one has to specify how the variation will be partitioned into dimensions and how each dimension will be represented. This is the issue of which *coordinate system* is appropriate to represent an object in a set varying along several dimensions. This involves questions about whether a polar or a rectangular coordinate system is used, whether there is a single or multiple origins, and so on. In their influential paper on shape recognition, Marr and Nishihara (1978) proposed that memory representations of shape are specified with respect to object-centered cylindrical coordinate systems. Furthermore, the coordinate systems are *distributed*: Instead of there being a global coordinate system with a single origin and set of axes, there is a cylindrical coordinate system centered on the principal axis of the object (e.g., in the case of an animal, its torso), in which are specified the origins and axes of secondary coordinate systems each centered on a part of the object attached to the principal axis (e.g., the animal's head and limbs). These secondary coordinate systems are, in turn, used to specify the origins and axes of smaller coordinate systems centered on the constituent or attached parts of the secondary part (e.g., the thigh, shin, and foot of the leg), and so on. I will adopt here the following aspects of Marr and Nishihara's theory: (1) Shapes and positions are mentally represented principally in polar or rectangular coordinates (the former is just a slice of a cylindrical coordinate system orthogonal to its axis; the latter is just a slice of a cylindrical coordinate system including its axis). (2) The locations of the different elements of a scene are represented in separate, local coordinate systems centered upon other parts of the scene, not in a single, global coordinate system. This means that in the visual description, the specification of locations (and also of directions and of parameterized shapes) of objects will be broken down into two propositions, one specifying the object upon which the coordinate system will be centered, the other specifying the extent or value of the object within the coordinate system, as in Fig. 4.10.

In fact, it is generally more perspicuous to indicate the extent along each dimension, and the location of the axis of the coordinate system corresponding to that dimension, separately, as in Fig. 4.11.

The important question of which objects may serve as the coordinate system for which other objects is only beginning to be answered in the vision literature, but the following condition seems to be a plausible first approximation: A spatial property of object *a* will be mentally specified

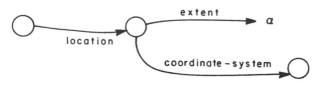

FIG. 4.10.

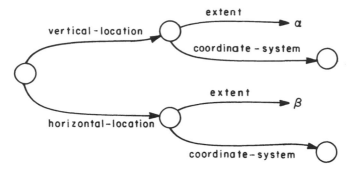

FIG. 4.11.

in a coordinate system centered on object *b* when: (1) *b* is larger than *a*, and (2) *a* and *b* are perceptually grouped according to one or more of the Gestalt laws.

IV. PROCESSING CONSTRAINTS ON VISUAL DESCRIPTIONS

Since, with deliberate effort, people can probably encode an unlimited number of properties (e.g., the angle formed by imaginary lines connecting a standing person's right thumbnail, navel, and right kneecap), visual descriptions can, in principle, be arbitrarily large. In practice, however, two factors will limit the size of visual descriptions:

1. Processing Capacity.   Most models of cognitive processing have restrictions on the processing capacity used to maintain the activation of nodes in a short-term visual description (Anderson & Bower, 1973; Newell & Simon, 1973). Specifically, it is claimed that between four and nine nodes may be kept active at one time, fewer if processing resources are being devoted to some concurrent task. This limitation reflects the well-known finiteness on human immediate memory and processing capacity (Miller, 1956).

2. Default Encoding Likelihood and Automaticity.   As mentioned, any predicate in a persons's visual repertoire can be added to a visual description in response to higher-level processes testing for the presence of a particular predicate applied to a particular variable (e.g., "is *x* a square?"). However, before these top–down processes come into play, a number of predicates will be assembled into a visual description, because they are "just noticed." Different predicates have different probabilities of being encoded under these "default" circumstances. Presumably, some predicates innately have a high default encoding likelihood [e.g., *enormous* (*x*), *dazzling* (*x*)], whereas the default encoding likelihood of others is determined by familiarity and learned importance. Shiffrin and Schneider (1977) and Schneider and Shiffrin (1977) propose that when a person frequently assigns a visual pattern into a single category, he or she will come to make that classification "automatically," that is, without the conscious application of attentional or processing capacity. Translated into the present vocabulary, this means that frequently encoded predicates will have a high *default encoding likelihood*. A number of experiments applying Shiffrin and Schneider's proposals to the learning of visual patterns confirm that the recognition of patterns becomes rapid, error-free, and relatively insensitive to other attentional demands as the patterns become increasingly well practiced.

Therefore, it is important to distinguish among several sizes of visual descriptions. A description that is assembled automatically by purely data-driven (as opposed to top–down or conceptually driven) encoding processes will be called the "default visual description." Its composition will be determined by the relative "default encoding likelihoods" of the various predicates satisfied by the visual array. In contrast, a description that is shaped by conceptual processes testing for the presence of visual predicates at particular locations in the array will be called an "elaborated visual description." Visual descriptions can also be classified in terms of whether short-term memory limitations are assumed to be in effect. A small visual description such as can be activated at a given instant will be called the "reduced visual description"; a visual description that includes all the predicates whose default encoding likelihood are above a certain minimum, plus all the predicates that are successfully tested for by top–down processes, will be called the "complete visual description." The complete visual description will correspond to the description encoded by a hypothetical graph reader with unlimited short-term memory, or to the description integrating the successive reduced descriptions encoded by a normal graph reader over a long viewing period. One way to think quantitatively of the size of the default visual description that a person will encode is to suppose that the probability of a given true predicate's entering into a visual description is a function of its default encoding likelihood multiplied by a constant between zero and one corresponding to the amount of capacity available (i.e., not devoted to other concurrent tasks). When the constant is one, the resulting description will be a "complete" visual description; as the constant decreases with decreasing available processing capacity, the size of the description will be reduced accordingly. I adopt the final assumption that the level of activation of a node begins to decrease steadily as soon as it is activated, but that the reader can repeatedly re-encode the description by reattending to the graph (this simply corresponds to the process of decay and rehearsal in short-term memory, see Crowder, 1976). Since encoding is probabilistic, the description will differ in composition somewhat from one encoding to the next.

V. AN EXAMPLE

Now that we have some constraints on the size and composition of visual descriptions, we can examine how the visual appearance of a particular graph might be described mentally. This will be the first step in working through an example of how a graph is understood according to the current theory. The example, shown in Fig. 4.12, is a bar graph plotting the price per ounce of a precious metal called "graphium" over a 6-month period. A complete "default" visual description is shown in Fig. 4.13. (Dotted lines represent propositions, omitted for the sake of clarity, that may be deduced from nearby propositions for similar parts).

Most aspects of this visual description are motivated by the constraints outlined in the previous section. The scene is parsed into subscenes, each occupying a distinct location in the visual array (though for readability's sake, the locations for the subscene nodes will not always be printed in subsequent examples). This parse is done according to the Gestalt principles, yielding separate nodes for the "L"-shaped framework and for the group of bars. By those same principles, the framework is connected by the "part" predicate to nodes representing its vertical and horizontal segments, and each of these is linked by "near" predicates to nodes representing the conceptual meaning of that text. Of course, the meaning of

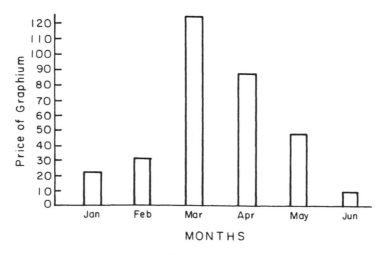

FIG. 4.12.

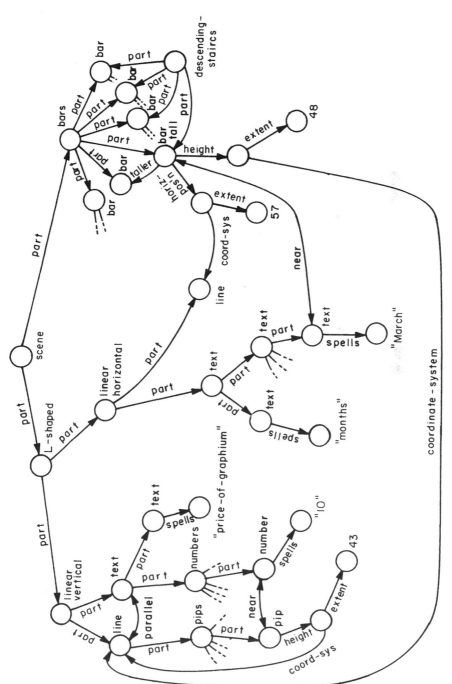

FIG. 4.13.

91

expressions such as "price of graphium" is, in all likelihood, mentally represented by an assembly of nodes linked in complex ways to the nodes representing the visual appearance of the text, but since the process of reading text is not of concern here, this simplified notation will suffice (the predicate associated with these "meaning" nodes will be replaced within quotation marks to indicate that they are not in fact unitary predicates). Predicates for the "bar" shape are attached to each bar node; the "tall" predicate is attached to the salient tallest bar; a pair of particularly discrepant bars is connected by the predicate "taller-than"; and the set of four progressively shorter bars is grouped together under its own node with its own shape predicate "descending-staircase." Finally, the height and horizontal position of each bar is specified with respect to a coordinate system centered on the appropriate framework segment, due to the framework's being larger than the bars and associated with them by proximity and common fate.

VI. CONCEPTUAL MESSAGES, CONCEPTUAL QUESTIONS

We now have an example of the immediate input to the graph comprehension process. Before specifying the process, it would be helpful to know what its output is as well. One can get a good idea of what that output must be simply by looking at a graph and observing what one remembers from it in the first few moments of seeing it or after it has just been removed from view. In the case of the graph in Fig. 4.12, one might notice things like the following: (1) the price of graphium was very high in March; (2) the price was higher in March than in the preceding month; (3) the price steadily declined from March to June; (4) the price was \$20/ounce in January; (5) the price in June was x (where x is a mental quantity about half of that for January, about a fifth of that for May, etc.). Basically, we have a set of paired observations here, where the first member can be a particular value of the independent variable (e.g., "March"), a pair of values (e.g., "March vs. February"), or a range of values (e.g., "the last 4 months"). The second number of each pair can be a ratio value (e.g., a value x along some mental ratio scale), an absolute value (e.g., "\$20/ounce"), a difference (e.g., "larger"), a trend (e.g., "decreasing"), or a level (e.g., "high"). (See Bertin, 1967, for a taxonomy of such questions). This information can be expressed in a representation consisting of a list of numbered entries, each specifying a pair (or, for more complex graphs, an n-tuple) of variables, the extent or type of each independent variable (e.g., ratio-value, pair, range), and the value (or difference or trend) of the corresponding dependent variable. Thus, the conceptual message representing the information which we are assuming has been extracted from the graph in Fig. 4.12 will look like this (the intuitive meaning of each entry can be made clearer by assuming the entry is a sentence beginning with the word *when*):

1: V_1 absolute-value = March, V_2 level = high

2: V_1 pair = March & February, V_2 difference = higher

3: V_1 range = March–June, V_2 trend = decreasing

4: V_1 absolute-value = January, V_2 absolute-value = \$20/oz.

5: V_1 absolute-value = June, V_2 ratio-value = x.

In general, conceptual messages will be of the following form:

i: V_a ratio-value   = α, V_b ratio-value   = β, . . .
                     or   or
                absolute-value   absolute-value
                     or   or
                    pair   pair
                     or   or
                    range   range

i designates the ith of an arbitrary number of entries (in principle), V_a designates the ath of an arbitrary number of variables, and α designates a specific value in a form appropriate to the entry (e.g., a "higher" or "lower" primitive symbol if the entry specifies a difference between values of the second variable corresponding to a pair of values of the first).[1] Note that the variables are differentiated by subscripts instead of being named by their real-world referents (e.g., month); this was done in recognition of people's ability to extract a great deal of quantitative and qualitative information (indeed, virtually the same information) when a graph has no labels at all, leaving the referents of the variables unknown. When the referents are known, the conceptual message can indicate this with entries such as the following:

6:     V_1 = months, V_2 = price-of-graphium.

Presumably, when the reader has integrated all the information he or she wishes to extract from the graph, he or she can make the message representation more economical by replacing each V_i by its associated referent symbol.

---

[1] It is possible to have several equations in an entry refer to the same variable, e.g.: 17: V_1 absolute-value = 14, V_1 ratio-value = 132, V_1 level = high, V_2 level = low.

From here, it is a simple matter to devise a notation for conceptual questions. (Recall that a conceptual question is a piece of information that the reader desires to extract from a graph). One can simply replace the α or β in the generalized entry by the "?" symbol, indicating that that is the unknown but desired information. Thus, if a person wishes to learn the price of graphium during the month of April, we posit that he or she has activated the representation

7: V_1 absolute-value = April, $\qquad$ V_2 absolute value = ?.

If the reader wishes to learn the trend of graphium prices during the first 2 months, he or she sets up the representation

8: V_1 range = January-February, $\qquad$ V_2 trend = ?.

If the reader wishes to learn the month in which graphium prices were low, he or she activates.

9: V_1 absolute-value = ?, $\qquad$ V_2 level = low,

and so on.

VII. THE GRAPH SCHEMA

So far, the theory has implicated the information flow diagram in Fig. 4.14.

Now, one must specify the unknown component labeled with a "?." From the flow chart, we can see what this component must do: (1) It must specify how to translate the information found in the visual description into the conceptual message, and (2) It must specify how to translate the request found in a conceptual question into a process that accesses the relevant parts of the visual description (culminating as before in one or more entries in the conceptual message). Furthermore, since (1) and (2) will involve different sorts of translations for different types of graphs (e.g., for line graphs versus bar graphs), the unknown component will also have to: (3) Recognize which type of graph is currently being viewed. The structure that accomplishes these three tasks will be called a *graph schema*, and it, together with the processes that work over it, will be discussed in this section.

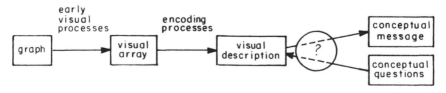

FIG. 4.14.

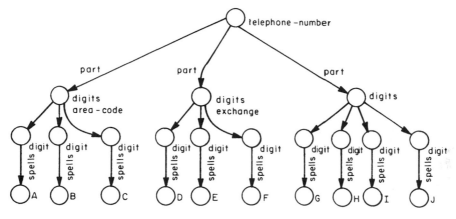

FIG. 4.15.

A. Schemas

I take a "schema" to be a memory representation embodying knowledge in some domain, consisting of a description which contains "slots" or parameters for as yet unknown information. Thus, a schema can specify both the information that must be true of some represented object of a given class, and the sorts of information that will vary from one exemplar of the class to another (see Minsky, 1975; Winston, 1975; Norman & Rumelhart, 1975; Bregman, 1977; Schank & Abelson, 1977). To take a simple example unrelated to graphs, Fig. 4.15 could be a schema for telephone numbers, specifying the number and grouping of the digits for any number but not the identity of the digits for any particular number, these being represented by the parameters *A-J*.[2]

This schema can be *instantiated* for a given person, becoming a representation of his or her telephone number, by replacing the parameters labeling the lowermost nodes by actual numerical predicates. In doing so, one is using the schema to *recognize* a candidate character string as a telephone number, by matching the schema against a visual description of the candidate string. The visual description of an as yet unrecognized number will be identical to the schema, except that it lacks the conceptual nodes such as "area code" and "exchange," and that it contains constants in place of parameters. Once the schema is instantiated by the visual description, one can use it to *retrieve* desired information about the telephone number using a node-by-node net searching procedure (i.e., one can quickly

---

[2] These uppercase parameters, which stand for unknown predicates, should not be confused with lowercase variables, which stand for perceptual entities and correspond to nodes in the visual description (although usually, the variable itself is omitted and only the node is depicted).

find "the first digit of the exchange" without searching the entire string, by starting at the top node and following the appropriate arrows down until the bottom node labeled by the desired number is reached). The double labeling of nodes is what allows schemas to be used both for recognition and for searching: a visual description of a to-be-recognized pattern will contain labels such as "digit," but not "area code," so the "digit" labels in the schema are necessary for recognizing the object. However, the search procedures will be accessing conceptual labels such as "area code," so these are necessary, too.

B. Graph Schemas: A Fragment

It seems, then, that a schema of this sort for graphs might fulfill two of our three requirements for graph knowledge structures: recognizing specific types of graphs, and directing the search for desired pieces of information in a graph. What we now need is some device to *translate* visual information into the quantitative information of the type found in the conceptual message. These devices, which I will call *message flags*, consist of conceptual message equations, usually containing a schema parameter, which are appended to predicates (nodes or arrows) in the graph schema. When such a node or arrow is instantiated by a particular visual description for a

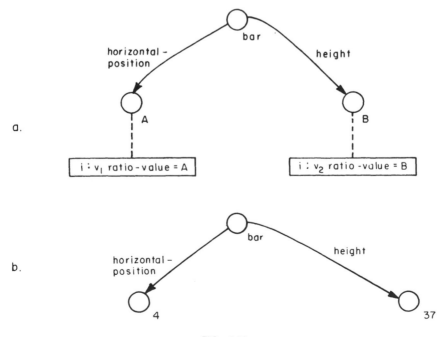

FIG. 4.16.

graph, the parameters in the message flag are replaced by the corresponding value in the instantiated schema, and the equation is added to the conceptual message. Fig. 4.16a illustrates equation flags for a fragment of a bar graph schema (the flags are enclosed in rectangles and are attached to the nodes they flag by dotted lines).

When a reader encounters the graph represented by the fragment of a visual description in Fig. 4.16b (the numbers representing values along a mental ratio scale with arbitrary units), he or she can instantiate the schema (i.e., replace the parameters A and B by the values 4 and 37), and add an entry to the conceptual message. All equations sharing a given i prefix are merged into a single entry, and each i is replaced by a unique integer when the entry is added to the conceptual message. Thus, the following entry is created:

$$1: V_1 \text{ ratio-value} = 4, V_2 \text{ ratio-value} = 37$$

This informal sketch should give the reader a general idea of how the graph schema is used in conjunction with the visual description to produce a conceptual message. In the sections following, I present a comprehensive bar graph schema and define more explicitly the processes that use it.

C. A Bar Graph Schema

Fig. 4.17 presents a substantial chunk of a schema for interpreting bar graphs. It is, intentionally, quite similar to the visual description for a bar graph in Fig. 4.13. The graph is divided into its L-shaped framework and its pictorial content, in this case, the bars. The framework is divided into the abscissa and the ordinate, and each of these is subdivided into the actual line and the text printed alongside it. In addition, the pips cross-hatching the ordinate, together with the numbers associated with them, are listed explicitly. The height and horizontal position of each bar are specified with respect to coordinate systems centered on the respective axes of the framework, and each bar is linked to a node representing its nearby text. An asterisk followed by a letter inside a node indicates that the node, together with its connection to other nodes, can be duplicated any number of times in the visual description. The letter itself indicates that each duplication of the node is to be assigned a distinct number, which will appear within the message flags attached to that instance of the node.

The message flags specify the conceptual information that is to be "read off" the instantiated graph schema. They specify that each bar will contribute an entry to the conceptual message. Each entry will equate the ratio value of the first variable (referred to in the description as "IV," for Independent Variable) with the horizontal position of the bar with respect to the abscissa, and will equate the ratio value of the second variable (the

98

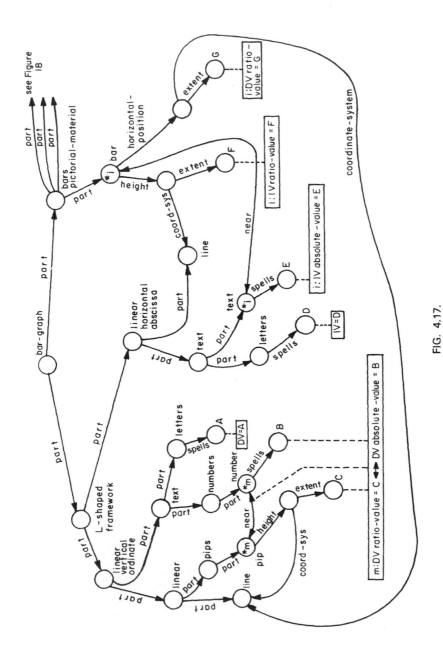

FIG. 4.17.

"DV" or Dependent Variable) with the bar's height with respect to the ordinate. In addition, the absolute value of the independent variable for an entry will be equated with the meaning of whatever label is printed below it along the abscissa. Finally, the referents of each variable will be equated with the meaning of the text printed alongside its respective axis.

In devising these formalisms, I was at one point distressed that there was no straightforward way to derive absolute values for the dependent variable. The ratio value of each bar, corresponding to its height, could easily be specified, but since the absolute values are specified in equal increments along the ordinate, far from most of the bars, and specific to none of them, no simple substitution process will do. However, a simple glance at a bar graph should convince the reader, as it convinced me, that this is not a liability but an asset. The absolute value of the dependent variable at a given level of the independent variable is indeed *not* immediately available from a bar graph. Instead, one seems to assess the height of a bar in terms of some arbitrary perceptual or cognitive scale, and then search for the pip along the ordinate whose vertical position is closest to that height or mentally extrapolate a horizontal line until it hits the ordinate (see Finke & Pinker, 1983). The number printed next to the nearest pip, or a number interpolated between the numbers printed next to the two nearest pips, is deduced to be its absolute value. In contrast, the absolute value of a given level of the independent variable (i.e., which month it is), or the relative values of the dependent variable (e.g., its maximum and minimum values, its trends, or differences between adjacent values) seem available with far less mental effort. The most natural mechanism for representing absolute values of the dependent variable within the bar graph schema, and the one that happens to be in accord with the actual difficulty of perceiving these values, is to add to the conceptual message special entries asserting an equivalence between a certain level of the referent's absolute value and a certain level of the referent's ratio value, each entry derived from a labeled pip on the ordinate. The leftmost message flag in Fig. 4.17 sets up these entries; the symbol " = " indicates that the two equations are equivalent. Presumably, higher-level inferential processes, unspecified here, can use these equivalence entries to convert ratio values to absolute value within other entries in the conceptual message, calculating interpolated values when necessary.[3]

Earlier, we mentioned that the visual system can encode predicates that

---

[3] The schema presented here perhaps unfairly anticipates that the bar-graph example will have individual labels for each bar along the absicssa and a graduated scale along the ordinate. In fact, graduated scales often appear along the abscissas of bar graphs as well. In a more realistic bar-graph schema, the subschemas for the pips of a graduated scale would be appended to the abscissa as well as to the ordinate.

stand for well-defined groups of objects, and also that conceptual messages can contain entries specifying a trend of one variable over the range of another. An implication of the theory, then, is that graph readers (or at least experienced graph readers) should be able to translate directly a higher-order perceptual pattern, such as a group of bars comprising a staircase, into the quantitative trend that it symbolizes, without having to compute the trend by successively examining each element. Furthermore, the difference in height between a pair of adjacent bars might be encodable into a single predicate, which should be directly translatable into an entry expressing a difference in the symbolized values. Also, a salient perceptual entity might be encoded as extreme (independently of the encoding of its precise extent on a ratio scale), and this should be directly translatable into an entry expressing the extremeness of its corresponding variable value, again without the mediation of ratio scale values. These direct trans-

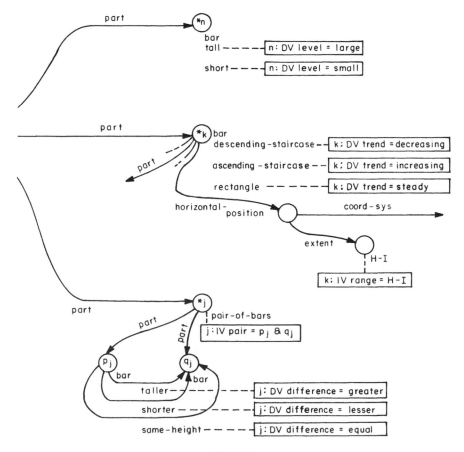

FIG. 4.18.

lations at several levels of globality, we shall see, play an important role in predicting the difficulty of a graph or the effectiveness of a graph reader. In the theory, the translations are accomplished by the message flags in Fig. 4.18 (which should actually be part of Fig. 4.17, but is depicted separately for the sake of clarity). Fig. 4.18 shows that bars in a graph can be described not only in terms of their heights and horizontal positions, but also in terms of being extremely tall or short, in terms of differences between the heights of adjacent pairs, or in terms of groups that constitute a perceptual whole. In each case the appropriate equation is attached to the predicate which encodes the attribute. Two additional notational conventions are introduced in the figure: the location of a pattern that occupies an extended region of the array is specified by its endpoints along a ratio scale (i.e., $H-I$), both in the visual description and in the conceptual message. In addition, one of the equation flags for a pair of bars makes reference to nodes standing for the bars themselves, p_j and q_j, rather than for an attribute like horizontal position. It is assumed that when a pair of bars is encoded as a pair, some information about each bar is encoded as well. This information, be it ratio value, absolute value, or level, can then be linked with or substituted for appropriate symbols for the bars (p_j or q_j) within the entry for the pair.

VIII. PROCESSES

In the account so far, I have relied upon the intelligence and cooperativeness of the reader to deduce how the various structures are manipulated and read during graph comprehension. In order to use the theory to make predictions, it will be necessary to define explicitly the procedures that access the structures representing graphic information. Four procedures will be defined: a *MATCH* process that recognizes individual graphs as belonging to a particular type, a *message assembly* process that creates a conceptual message out of the instantiated graph schema, an *interrogation* process that retrieves or encodes new information on the basis of conceptual questions, and a set of *inferential processes* that apply mathematical and logical inference rules to the entries of the conceptual message.

A. The MATCH Process

The term is borrowed from Anderson and Bower's (1973) theory of long-term memory. This process compares a visual description in parallel with every memory schema for a visual scene, computes a goodness-of-fit measure for each schema (perhaps the ratio or difference between the number of matching nodes and predicates and the number of mismatching nodes and predicates), and selects the schema with the highest goodness-of-fit measure. This schema, or rather, the subset of the schema that the limited capacity processes can keep activated, is then instantiated (i.e., the parameters in the schema are replaced by the appropriate constants found in the visual description). This is the procedure, alluded to in vague terms before, that uses the graph schema to recognize a graph as being of a certain type (e.g., bar graph, pie graph).[4]

B. Message Assembly

This process accomplishes the translation from visual information to conceptual information, also alluded to in previous sections. It searches over the instantiated graph schema, and when it encounters a message flag, it adds the message it contains to the conceptual message, combining into a single entry all equations sharing a given prefix (i.e., all those beginning with the same i:). It is assumed that at the time that the MATCH process instantiated the parameters of the graph schema, the parameters within the message flags were instantiated as well.

Memory and processing limitations imply that not every message flag in the graph schema is converted into an entry into the conceptual message. Some may not be instantiated because the visual description was reduced or because the default encoding likelihood of the predicate was low; some may not be instantiated because of noise in the MATCH process; and some may be skipped over or lost because of noise in the message assembly process. For these reasons, we need a process that adds information to the conceptual message in response to higher-level demands.

C. Interrogation

This process is called into play when the reader needs some piece of information that is not currently in the conceptual message (e.g., the difference between two values of the dependent variable corresponding to a

---

[4] This process has been oversimplified in several ways, in accordance with certain oversimplifications in the graph schema itself. For one thing, conceptual labels such as "abscissa" do not appear in visual descriptions, and so should not count in the goodness of fit calculations. This could be accomplished by distinguishing the conceptual or graph-specific predicates from the rest, perhaps by listing them, too, as message flags, which are "read off" the schema, but not used to instantiate it. The second complication is that different nodes and predicates should count differently in the recognition process. Some might be mandatory, some might be mandatorily absent, some might be characteristic to various degrees, some might occur in sets from which one member must occur, and so on. There are several ways of accomplishing this, such as the introduction of logical operators into schemas, or the use of a Bayesian recognition procedure, but limited space prevents me from outlining them here (see Anderson, 1976; Anderson & Bower, 1973; Minsky, 1975; Smith, Shoben, & Rips, 1974; Winston, 1974).

given pair of independent variable values). As mentioned, each such request can be expressed as a conceptual message entry with a "?" replacing one of the equation values. The interrogation process works as follows: The message flag within the graph schema that matches the conceptual question (i.e., is identical to it except for a constant or parameter in the place of the "?") is activated. If it already contains a constant (i.e., if the equation it contains is instantiated, and thus, complete), the equation is simply added to the conceptual message. If it contains a parameter (i.e., is incomplete), the part of the visual description that corresponds to that branch of the schema is checked to see if it contains the desired constant (e.g., if a certain ratio-value of the dependent variable is desired, the visual description is checked for the presence of a constant attached to the node representing the bar's height). If this constant is absent from the visual description, the encoding process for the relevant predicate (e.g., the process that encodes height) is commanded to retrieve the desired information for the relevant part in the visual array. It can do so by using the retinal coordinates attached to the node for the part, which are assumed to be present in the visual description (though they have been omitted from the diagrams in this chapter). Often, however, these coordinates will have decayed, and the coordinates of an associated part together with the degree and direction of the association will be used to direct the encoding process to the correct location in the visual array. In other words, the conceptual question can initiate a top–down search for the desired part or part parameter in the array. Once the desired information is encoded into the visual description, it can be instantiated in the schema and its message flags, and the instantiated equation within the flag can be added to the conceptual message.

D. Inferential Processes

Human intelligence consists of more than the ability to read graphs. In the category *inferential processes*, I include the ability to perform arithmetic operations on the quantitative information listed in the conceptual message (e.g., calculating the rate of increase of a variable by subtracting one value from another value and dividing by a third value), to infer from the context of the graph (e.g., the paragraph in which it is embedded) what information should be extracted from the graph, to draw qualitative conclusions relevant to some domain of knowledge based on the information in the graph, and so on. Naturally, I have little to say about these abilities here; they are part of the study of cognition in general and not the study of graph comprehensions. However, I mention them here because many types of information can be obtained either directly from a conceptual message or indirectly from inferential processes operating on the conceptual message.

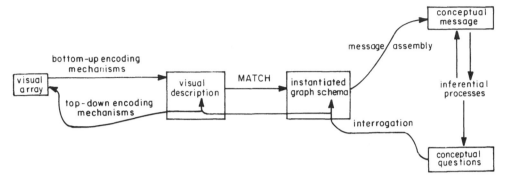

FIG. 4.19.

Which method is used, we shall see, affects the difficulty of a graph and the efficiency of a graph reader.

The flow of information specified by the current theory is summarized in Fig. 4.19, where blocks represent information structures and arrows represent processes that transfer information among them.

IX.   WHERE DO GRAPH SCHEMAS COME FROM?

The graph schema discussed so far embodies knowledge of bar graphs (in fact, a subset of bar graphs). Clearly, the theory must also account for people's ability to read other common types of graphs (line graphs, pie graphs, pictograms, etc.) and to understand completely novel forms of graphs as well (e.g., one in which the length of a ray of light emitted from a disk represents the price of gold in a given month). I propose that people create schemas for specific types of graphs using a *general graph schema*, embodying their knowledge of what graphs are for and how they are interpreted in general. A plausible general graph schema is shown in Fig. 4.20. There are three key pieces of information contained in the schema. First, some objects, or parts of objects (i.e., a display's pictorial content) are described in terms of several visual attributes. Each visual attribute symbolizes a conceptual variable, and the set of values of the n visual attributes encoded for an object or object part corresponds to a particular n-tuple of associated values of the respective conceptual variables for a given conceptual entity. Second, the ratio magnitudes of attributes are usually to be specified in terms of a coordinate system centered upon a part of the graph framework. Third, textual material perceptually grouped with an object specifies the absolute value of the object; textual material perceptually grouped with the framework specifies the real-world referent of the attribute that the coordinate system centered on the framework helps to specify; textual material associated with specific local regions of the framework specifies pairings of absolute and ratio values of the attribute specified by the associated coordinate system. Note that for maximum generality, text is linked to perceptual entities by the predicate "associated," which can symbolize proximity, similarity, continuity, and so on. This helps to encompass graphs with parts directly labeled and graphs exploiting common colors or shapes in keys and legends. Similarly, the predicate "attribute" is meant to encompass length, width, orientation, lightness, color, and so on. However, the indispensability of visual space motivates "geometric shapes" as opposed to arbitrary visual predicates being specified as typical frameworks, and spatially localizable "parts" being specified as the units over which attributes are defined.

In encountering a certain type of graph for the first time, a reader will generate a specific graph schema for it using the general graph schema. The reader will have to replace the predicates "pictorial content," "associated," "attribute," "geometric figure," and so on, by the actual visual predicates found in the visual description of the novel graph. This will be possible when the visual description has a structure similar to that of the general graph schema, with objects described in terms of attributes defined with respect to a framework, and textual labels associated with each. In addition, an astute graph reader will add to the new specific graph schema higher-order predicates (e.g., "descending-staircase") that can be taken to symbolize global trends (e.g., a decrease in the dependent variable). However, the availability of these higher-order predicates, and how transparently they symbolize their trends, will differ arbitrarily from graph type to graph type, and so these predicates cannot be included in any simple way within the general graph schema but must be created case by case. This process will be discussed in more detail in the section describing what makes a graph reader efficient.

Pushing the question back a step, we may ask, "Where does the general graph schema come from?" This question is more profound, and the answer to it is correspondingly murkier. In one sense, one could answer that people are explicitly taught how to read certain types of graphs. But, this still leads one to wonder how people can generalize from the small set of graph types that they are exposed to in school (basically, bar graphs, line graphs, pie graphs, and pictograms) to the myriad exotic forms that are created and easily understood in popular magazines or areas of expertise. This is especially problematic given that formal instruction in graph reading does not teach the abstract concepts such as "attribute," "extent," "ratio value," and so forth, that in fact define what all graphs have in common. A deeper answer to this question is that a great many abstract concepts seem to be mentally represented by structures originally dedicated to the representation of space and the movement of objects within it, a phenomenon that

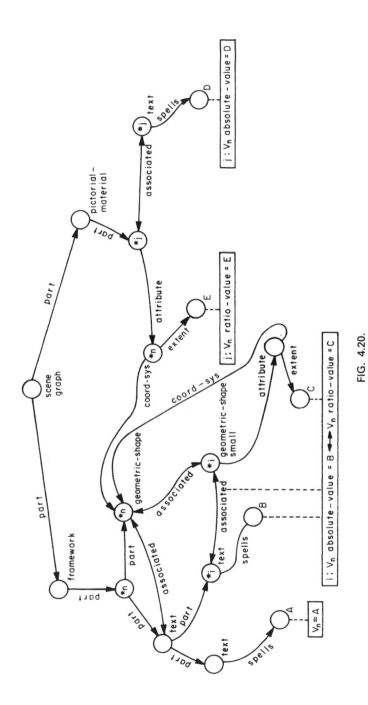

FIG. 4.20.

manifests itself in language in many ways (see Clark, 1973; Cooper & Ross, 1975; Jackendoff, 1978; Lakoff & Johnson, 1980; Talmy, 1978). In particular, abstract quantities seem to be treated mentally as if they were locations on a spatially extended scale (as can be seen in expressions such as *The temperature is rising, John weighed in at 200 lbs.*, and many others), or more generally, as corresponding to virtually any other abstract continuum as long as the "positive" and "negative" ends of the two continua are put into correspondence (see Cooper & Ross, 1975; Pinker & Birdsong, 1979). Thus, the use of continuous spatial predicates to represent abstract variables is part of a larger cognitive pattern of using spatial properties to symbolize nonspatial ones; beyond this informal observation there is, unfortunately, little that can be added with any precision.

X. THE DIFFICULTY OF COMPREHENDING A GRAPH

In this section, I consider what makes different types of graphs easy or difficult when particular types of information have to be extracted (by "type of information," I am referring to different conceptual questions, such as ones referring to ratio values vs. differences vs. trends).

Aside from the limitations of the peripheral encoding mechanisms (i.e., limits on detectability, discriminability, and the accuracy of encoding magnitudes), the structures and processes described here permit *any* quantitative information whatsoever to be extractable in principle from a graph. This is because no information is necessarily lost from the visual description "upward" and there are no constraints on what the inferential processes can do with the information in the conceptual message.

In practice, though, limits on short-term memory and on processing resources will make specific sorts of information easier or more difficult to extract. I have assumed that the visual description that is encoded is, in fact, a small subset of the complete visual description, and that noise in the MATCH and message assembly processes causes only a subset of that reduced visual description to be translated into conceptual message information. The remaining conceptual message entries will contain the information that is "easily extracted" from a graph, since a simple look-up procedure suffices to retrieve the information. On the other hand, if the desired information is not already in the conceptual message, it will have to be generated either by the top–down interrogation process, which adds entries to the conceptual message, or by the inferential processes, which perform computations on existing entries. Each of these processes can involve a chain of (presumably) capacity-limited computations, and each process properly includes the look-up of information from the conceptual message. Therefore, they are necessarily more time consuming and memory consuming (since the results of intermediate computations must be temporarily stored) than the look-up of existing information in the conceptual message. And, in a limited-capacity, noisy system such as the human mind, greater time and memory requirements imply increased chances of errors or breakdowns, hence, increased difficulty. This conclusion can be called the *Graph Difficulty Principle*: A particular type of information will be harder to extract from a given graph to the extent that inferential processes and top–down encoding processes, as opposed to conceptual message look-up, must be used.

There will, in turn, be two factors influencing whether a desired type of information (i.e., the answer to a given conceptual question) will be present in a conceptual message. First, a message entry will be assembled only if there are message flags specific to that entry appended to the graph schema. That, in turn, will depend on whether the visual system encodes a single visual predicate that corresponds to that quantitative information. For example, I have assumed that because of the nature of visual encoding, a bar graph schema appends message flags to predicates for height, horizontal position, extremeness in height, extreme differences in height between adjacent objects, and extended increases or decreases in height. This respectively makes ratio values of the dependent and independent variables, extremeness in value, extreme differences in values, and global trends easily extractable. On the other hand, our visual systems do not supply a visual predicate for an object being a given number of ordinate scale units high, or for one bar's height to be a precise ratio of the height of another, or for the leftmost and rightmost bars to be of the same height, and so on. Therefore, there can be message flags and no conceptual message entries for the absolute value of the dependent variable, the exact ratio of dependent variable values corresponding to successive values of the independent variable, or the equality of dependent variable values corresponding to the most extreme independent variable values. If a reader wishes the graph to answer these conceptual questions, he or she can expect more difficulty than for the conceptual questions discussed previously.

The second factor influencing whether a conceptual message entry will be assembled is the encoding likelihoods of the predicates attached to the corresponding equation flags in the graph schema. In the example we have been using, if the predicate "descending-staircase" has a very low default-encoding likelihood, and hence is absent from the visual description on most occasions, the entry specifying a decreasing trend will not find its way into the conceptual message until interrogated explicitly. Incidentally, apart from innateness and automaticity factors, it is conceivable that the encoding likelihood of a predicate is also influenced by "priming": When a graph schema is activated (i.e., when the graph is recognized as being of a particular type), the encoding likelihoods of the visual predicates may be temporarily enhanced or "primed" (see Morton, 1969). In other words, when a graph is recognized on the basis of partial recognition, the schema may make the rest of the information more likely to be encoded for as long as the schema is activated.

As simple as the Graph Difficulty Principle is, it helps to explain a wide variety of phenomena concerning the appropriateness of different types of graphs for conveying different types of information. Consider Cartesian line graphs, for example. The English language has a variety of words to describe the shapes of lines: straight, curved, wiggly, V-shaped, bent, steep, flat, jagged, scalloped, convex, smooth, and many more. It also has words to describe pairs of lines: parallel, intersecting, converging, diverging, intertwined, touching, X-shaped, and so on. It is safe to assume that the diverse vocabulary reflects an equally or more diverse mental vocabulary of visual predicates for lines, especially since the indispensability of visual space (see Section IIIA) implies that predicates for configural spatial properties such as shape should be readily available. The availability of these predicates affords the possibility of a line graph schema with a rich set of message flags for trends. For example, if "x" and "y" are nodes representing lines on a graph, with V_1 the abscissa, V_2 the ordinate, and V_3 the parameter, the propositions on the left side of Table 4.1 can be flagged with the conceptual message equations on the right side of the table: This makes line graphs especially suited to representing functions of one variable over a range of a second, the covariation versus independence of two variables, and the additive versus interactive effects of two variables on a third, and so on. In contrast, the mental vocabulary for the shapes implicit in the tops of a set of grouped bars is poor, perhaps confined to "ascending-staircase," "descending staircase," and "rectangular," as implied in Fig.

TABLE 4.1
Some Quantitative Trends Associated With Visual Patterns

Predicate	Equation Flag
Flat (x)	V_2 trend = unchanging
Steep (x)	V_2 trend = increasing rapidly
Inverted U-shape (x)	V_2 trend = quadratic
U-shape (x)	V_2 trend = quadratic
Jagged (x)	V_2 trend = random
Undulating (x)	V_2 trend = fluctuating
Straight (x)	V_2 trend = linear
S-shape (x)	V_2 trend = cubic
Rectilinear (x)	V_2 trend = abruptly changing
Not flat (x)	V_1 affects V_2
Parallel (x, y)	V_1, V_3 additively affects V_2
Converging (x, y)	V_1, V_3 interactively affects V_2

TABLE 4.2
**Data Illustrating the Relative Efficacy of Reading Trends From Tables, Line Graphs,
and Bar Graphs**

V_1:		V_2:				
		1	2	3	4	5
V_3:	A	30.0	35.0	45.0	60.0	80.0
	B	20.0	32.0	45.0	57.5	70.0

4.18. Correspondingly, there will be fewer possibilities for specifying trends in a schema for bar graphs, and less likelihood of assembling specific "trend" and "affects" entries in the conceptual message when a bar graph is processed. And the predicates for a *pair* of shapes implicit in the respective tops of two integrated *groups* of bars will be even scarcer, preventing "additively affects" and "interactively affects" entries from being encoded. Small wonder, then, that line graphs are the preferred method of displaying multidimensional scientific data, where cause-and-effect relations, quantitative trends, and interactions among variables are at stake. To convince yourself of the appropriateness of line graphs for these purposes, try to determine the nature of the trend of V_2 over the range of V_1, and the nature of the interaction of V_1 and V_3 (a variable with two levels, A and B) on V_2, from Table 4.2, Fig. 4.21a and Fig. 4.21b. It should be easy to see from the line graph in Fig. 4.21b that at level A of Variable 3, Variable 2 is increasing and positively accelerating, whereas at B, it is increasing linearly. Similarly, one can see that Variables 1 and 3 interact in their effects on Variable 2. This is because the "straight" and "concave-up predicates, corresponding to "linear" and "positively accelerating" trends are readily encodable. In contrast, the like-colored bars in Fig. 4.21a do not form a group where relative heights can be described by a single predicate, and so inferring the trend necessitates a top–down, bar-by-bar height comparison, a difficult chore because it is hard to keep the heights of all the bars in mind (i.e., activated in the visual description) at once. It is even more difficult to extract the trends from the table, because not only is a number-by-number comparison necessary, but the process of encoding a multidigit numeral's magnitude seems to be intuitively slower and more effortful than the encoding of a bar's height.[5]

---

[5] Incidentally, though a line graph is better than other forms of data presentation for illustrating trends, typically only one way of constructing the line graph will illustrate a given trend optimally. For example, a line graph that used Variable 3 (i.e., A vs. B) as the abscissa and Variable 1 as the parameter would not illustrate the linear and accelerating trends as transparently as the graph in Fig. 4.21b, since these trends no longer correspond to single attributes of a distinct perceptual entity, but must be inferred from the successive intervals separating the left end points of the five lines and those separating the right end points of those lines, respectively.

However, try to answer the following question by examining the table, bar graph, and line graph just considered: What is the exact value of Variable 2 at level B of Variable 3 and level 4 of Variable 1? Most people I have asked find the question easiest to answer with reference to Table 4.1, a bit harder with reference to the bar graph, and hardest of all with reference to the line graph. This illustrates the purpose-specificity of graphs, which has frequently been noted in the graph comprehension literature, and which is an inescapable consequence of the present theory: Different types of graphs are not easier or more difficult across the board, but are easier or more difficult depending on the particular class of information that is to be extracted. In this case, we have already seen that absolute values of the dependent variable in a bar graph cannot be directly entered into the conceptual message since there are no visual predicates that correspond to them. Rather, specific ratio values of the dependent variables can be encoded, as can pairings between arbitrary absolute values and ratio values (from the numbers printed along the ordinate), but the absolute value of a particular entry must be computed by effortful inferential processes using these two kinds of information. The line graph is harder still, because the Gestalt principles cause each entire line to be encoded as a single node rather than being broken up into a set of nodes, each corresponding to a level of Variable 1. Thus, when the conceptual question addresses the absolute value of Variable 2 corresponding to a particular value of Variable 1, there is no visual description node specific to the part of the line signifying that value, and one must be created by a top–down encoding process focused on a perceptually arbitrary point along the line.

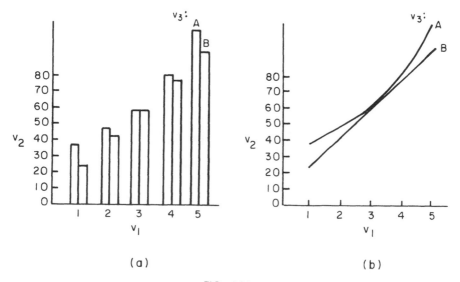

FIG. 4.21.

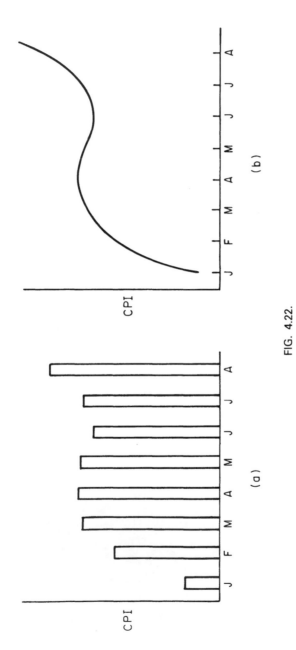

FIG. 4.22.

That is also why it is sometimes easier to use a bar graph than a line graph to determine the difference between two levels of one variable corresponding to a pair of values on another (e.g., whether the Consumer Price Index is higher for March or June in Figs. 4.22a and 4.22b).

In sum, we have seen that extracting information from a graph is easiest when the visual description contains predicates linked to message flags displaying equations that answer the conceptual question (less technically, when the information is conveyed by an easily perceivable visual pattern in the graph and when the reader knows that that pattern encodes desired information). As a consequence, (a) Line graphs should be best for illustrating trends and interactions (since there exist many visual predicates for line shapes); (b) Tables should be best for illustrating absolute values of the dependent variable (since there is no way to specify absolute values for particular levels of the independent variable in line or bar graph visual descriptions and graph schemas); and (c) Bar graphs may be better than line graphs or tables for illustrating differences between dependent variable values corresponding to specific independent variable values (since the desired values are specified individually in the bar but not the line graph, and since it seems to be easier to encode a bar's height than to read a multidigit number). It is comforting to know that these three conclusions have been borne out many times in the empirical literature on graph comprehension (Carter, 1947; Culbertson & Powers, 1959; Schutz, 1961a, 1961b; Washburne, 1927), scanty though that literature is (see Wainer & Thissen, 1981).

Some Further Determinants of Graph difficulty

In general, a graph maker will do best if he or she designs the graph so that the visual system parses it into units whose attributes correspond to the quantitative information that he or she wishes to communicate. In the previous section, we saw how this principle favors either line graphs, bar graphs, or tables, depending on the type of question the reader is to answer. Of course, these are not the only choices that face a graph designer. In this section, I briefly show how often design choices might be resolved by the Graph Difficulty Principle.

1. One Graph with Two Lines or Two Graphs with One Line? As mentioned, the visual system has predicates describing groups of nearby lines (e.g., *Parallel (x, y)*, *Fan-shaped (x, y, z)*, *Intersecting (x, y)*, etc.). These correspond to specific types of interactions between variables (e.g., additive, multiplicative, inversely multiplicative, etc.). Thus, questions about interactions can be answered quickly if the lines are in close enough proximity to the predicate describing them as a group to be encoded. However, if the lines are in different graphs, they will be encoded as units and their interactions must be extracted by interrogating their slopes separately and inferring the interaction from these slopes. Thus, when interactions are of interest, lines should be plotted on a single graph (unless, of course, the number of overlapping lines is large, which may lead to spurious groupings of line segments belonging to different lines). Schutz (1961b) indeed found that graphs with multiple lines were easier to understand than multiple graphs, if the number of lines is small.

2. Legends or Labeled Lines?   As noted earlier, the visual system groups stimuli that are in close proximity. A graph schema can exploit this fact by specifying that a label near a graph element signals the absolute value of a variable for the conceptual message entry specified by that element (e.g., in the bar graph schema we examined previously). If the correspondence is specified instead in an insert or legend (i.e., with a label next to a small patch sharing the color, shading, or internal cross-hatching or stippling of the lines or bars), that correspondence must be extracted by the inferential processes, using one entry specifying the distinguishing feature of the bar or line in the graph, and a second entry linking that distinguishing feature to the appropriate absolute value, based on the legend or insert. Therefore, labeled lines should be better (again, assuming the number of elements is not so large that spurious groupings arise).

In fact, Parkin (1983) has conducted an experiment deliberately designed to test this prediction of the theory. He composed five methods of labeling for line graphs that exploited varying numbers of Gestalt principles to associate lines with their labels. He had each label next to its corresponding line somewhere along its length (proximity), next to each line and aligned with its end (proximity, good continuation), aligned with the end of each line but separated from it by white space (good continuation), in a legend (no Gestalt principle) or in the caption (no Gestalt principle). In addition, lines and labels were sometimes printed in the same respective colors (similarity) and sometimes not. As expected, the greater the number of Gestalt principles associating lines with labels (and the fewer the number of principles leading to a competing organization of labels with labels), the faster subjects were able to answer questions about relative heights and slopes of the different lines at given points on the X-axis. As expected, this effect interacted with geometric complexity as measured by the number of times the lines crossed over one another. For simple graphs, labels close to the lines fostered quicker answers than labels next to and aligned to the ends of lines, which in turn were quicker to read than labels simply aligned with line ends. However, the three labeling methods were equally difficult for complex graphs. Similarly, captions and legends were much harder than labeled lines for simple graphs, but only somewhat harder for complex graphs. Finally, Parkin found that associating lines with their labels via a common color led to quicker responding. Thus, the experiments stand as a confirmation of the prediction that the processes used by the visual system to associate objects with one another exert effects on how quickly graph elements can be associated with their labels, and of the prediction that these effects might be weakened or nullified when the graph displays complex patterns of line intersection.

XI. THE EFFICIENCY OF A GRAPH READER

Though I have referred to a single idealized "graph reader," flesh-and-blood graph readers will differ from one another in significant ways. For example, some people may have swifter elementary information processes, or a larger short-term memory capacity, or more powerful inferential processes. Though these factors may spell extreme differences in how easily different people comprehend graphs, they are not specific to graph comprehension, and I will not discuss them further. Instead, I will focus on possible differences among people in their abilities to read graphs per se.

A natural way of determining what makes a person good at reading graphs is to examine what makes the graph-reading process more or less easy (i.e., the considerations in the preceding section) and to predict that individual differences in the nature of the structures and processes involved will spell differences in the general ease with which individuals read graphs.

Recall that in the last section I predicted that a given type of information was easy to extract from a given type of graph if there were message flags in the graph schema specific to that information, and if the visual predicates to which the flag was attached were presented in the activated visual description of the graph. Each factor allows for individual differences. First, a person's graph schema may lack important message flags. Thus, he or she may not know that parallel lines in a line graph signal the additivity of the effects of two variables on a third. When pressed to determine whether additivity holds in a certain graph, such a person would have to resort to costly inferential processes operating on a set of entries for ratio or absolute values. In general, the theory predicts that the presence or absence of message flags in a person's schema will have dramatic effects on how easily that person can extract the information specified by the flag. Second, the predicates that trigger the process whereby message flags are assembled into conceptual message entries may be more or less likely to appear in the visual descriptions of different people. The needed predicates, because of lack of practice at encoding them, may not yet be automatic, and hence may have low default encoding likelihoods. Furthermore, the links between those predicates and the rest of the graph schema may be weak, dissipating the "priming effect" which assists the encoding of missing predicates once a graph has been recognized.

Of course, this begs the questions of what in fact determines whether people have the necessary equation flags in their schemas, and whether the encoding likelihoods and links among predicates in a schema will be sufficiently strong. As to the first question, there are probably three routes to enriching graph schemas with useful flags:

1. *Being told.* It is common for formal instruction in mathematics and science to spell out what to look for in a graph when faced with a particular question. For example, students learning statistical procedures such as the Analysis of Variance are usually told that nonflat lines indicate main effects, nonparallel sets of lines indicate interactions, U-shaped lines indicate quadratic trends, and so on.

2. *Induction.* An insightful reader or graph maker might notice that quantitative trends of a given sort always come out as graphs with particular visual attributes (e.g., quadratic functions yield U-shaped lines). He or she could then append the message flag expressing the trend to the predicate symbolizing the visual attribute in the graph schema.

3. *Deduction.* Still more insightful readers could infer that owing to the nature of the mapping between quantitative scales and visual dimensions in a given type of graph, a certain quantitative trend *must* translate to a certain visual property. For example, a person could realize that the successive doublings of a variable by a particular exponential function must lead to a curve that becomes increasingly steep from left to right.

Taken together, these principles suggest that improvements in the ability to read graphs of a given sort will come (a) With explicit instructions concerning the equivalences holding between quantitative trends and visual attributes (so as to enrich the graph schema); (b) With instruction as how to "see" the graph (i.e., how to parse it perceptually into the right units, yielding the appropriate visual description), and with practice at doing so (making the encoding process automatic and thereby increasing the encoding likelihoods and associative strengths of the relevant visual predicates); and (c) With experience at physically plotting different quantitative relationships on graph paper (affording opportunities for the induction and deduction of further correspondences between visual attributes and quantitative trends, to be added as message flags to the graph schema).

XII. EMPIRICAL TESTS OF THE THEORY

As Wainer and Thissen (1981) note, there has been very little systematic research on the psychology of graph comprehension. Experiments cited herein on the relative ease of extracting information from line graphs, bar graphs, and tables are consistent with the general claim that graph readers can translate visual patterns directly into trend information when possible (via message flags appended to visual predicates in graph schemas), that readers require that the visual marks signifying values or pairs of values form good Gestalts, and that absolute value information cannot be perceived directly from a graph. However, these data alone are not optimal tests of the theory, or even of parts of the theory. First, in most cases, we have no independent evidence for the perceptual phenomena that figure into the explanations of graph-reading difficulty. For example, we do not in fact know that the shape of a line is easier to perceive than the shape implicit in the tops of a set of upright rectangles, or that a segment within a smooth curve is harder to isolate perceptually than a closed rectangle in the set of stimuli used in these experiments. Without independent evidence concerning the perceptual properties of the display, the theory's explanations risk becoming circular. Second, whenever familiar graph formats are used, there is a risk that subjects' explicit training with that format prior to entering the lab may influence their responses in a way that may undermine attempts to interpret their responses in terms of perceptual factors. For example, graphic style manuals advise designers to use line graphs to convey trends. If designers heed this advice, they may on the average use line graphs more often in contexts demanding the extraction of trends, giving readers more practice reading trends from line graphs. In turn, they may come to execute the sequence of mental operations necessary to verify trend information from line graphs more quickly, even if the operations themselves were at first intrinsically difficult, the style manuals notwithstanding.

There are a small number of experiments that I and my collaborators have performed which are explicitly designed to test the theory proposed here while avoiding the problems described. In Pinker (1983), I report three experiments which tested the hypotheses that graph readers have knowledge of the correspondences between trends and visual patterns when these visual patterns are readily encodable, and that they are then able to translate the perceived pattern into the desired trend directly without having to examine more local units one by one. A novel graph format was invented, consisting of a chain of line segments joined end to end corresponding to the months of the year. The length of a segment (greater than or less than an inch) represented the rainfall for that month relative to a

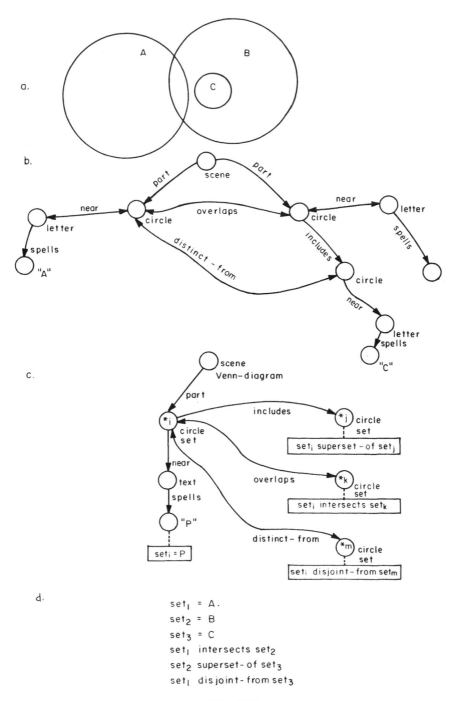

a.

b.

c.

d.

set$_1$ = A.
set$_2$ = B
set$_3$ = C
set$_1$ intersects set$_2$
set$_2$ superset-of set$_3$
set$_1$ disjoint-from set$_3$

FIG. 4.23.

reference level, and its angle with respect to the previous segment (greater or less than 180°) represented its temperature relative to a reference level (or vice versa). It was expected that single values for temperature or rainfall would be easier to extract when encoded as segment length than when encoded as segment angle, because the perception of segment angle requires attention to a pair of segments and normalization of the orientation of the first (since we must mentally rotate a pattern into a standard orientation in order to determine its handedness—corresponding here to the sign of its angle; Cooper & Shepard, 1973, 1975). In contrast, the detection of whether temperature or rainfall was consistently above or below the reference level, versus sometimes being above it and sometimes below, and a similar discrimination involving the detection of alternation, were predicted to be easier when the variable was encoded by segment angle. This is because for the angle variable, consistent years yield uniformly convex curves and inconsistent years yield curves with a concave region, a discrimination our visual systems are adept at making (Hoffman & Richards, 1985), whereas the length variable does not yield curves with recognizable shape differences contingent on the consistency or alternation of the variable. Thus, subjects should be able to create a graph schema in which there are message flags signifying consistency of one of the dependent variables appended to the predicate for convexity and message flags signifying inconsistency appended to the predicates for concave regions. With no such shape predicates for length, there can be no message flags for consistency of the other dependent variable.

In the first experiment, subjects were shown the stimuli described as visual patterns, not as graphs, and answered questions about the lengths and angles of particular segments or the consistency and alternation of the lengths or angles of the entire sequence. As predicted, single lengths were recognized more quickly and accurately than single angles, but consistent sequences of lengths were recognized more slowly and less accurately than consistent sequences of angles. Presumably, this was because consistency of angle translated into convexity, and convexity is an easily encodable visual predicate. Thus, the subjects did not have to encode the angle of each pair of line segments individually, and as a result, they took less time (rather than more) to verify the consistency of the entire sequence of angles than to verify a single angle. This provides independent motivation for predictions about graph-reading difficulty in two subsequent experiments. In the second experiment, the stimuli were introduced as graphs and subjects were told how segment angle and length conveyed information about temperature and rainfall, and were also told that consistency of the variable conveyed by angle translated into convexity and alternation into zigzags (i.e., I tried to induce them to form a graph schema with the right message flags by telling them about the appropriate trend–shape correspondences directly. As a control for attention differences, they were also told how consistency and alternation of the other variable translated into patterns of lengths, though based on the results of the first experiment it is unlikely that visual predicates exist for consistently long or short sequences of line segments). When answering questions about rainfall and temperature, subjects showed the same pattern of reaction times as did their counterparts in the first experiment when answering questions about the corresponding geometric properties of the stimulus. That is, they were faster and more accurate at detecting single values of the variable conveyed by length than of the variable conveyed by angle, but showed the reverse pattern when detecting the consistency of the global sequence. This indicates that the subjects, as predicted, were able to exploit the correspondences between trends and shapes that would be encoded explicitly in a graph schema, allowing them to recognize trends directly without examining individual point values.

In a third experiment, subjects were only told how the graphs conveyed information about temperature and rainfall for individual months, not about how shapes translated into trends. Nonetheless they, too, showed the interaction found in the first experiment. (However, they did show the interaction less strongly, suggesting that being told about shape–trend correspondences for a graph may facilitate the extraction of those trends, as predicted by the discussion in Section XI.) In general, then, these experiments confirm that a given sort of conceptual information is easily extractable from a graph to the extent that the graph encodes the desired conceptual information as an easily perceivable visual predicate and to the extent that the correspondence between the two is represented in the mind of the reader.

Simcox (1983) reports three experiments that are more narrowly addressed to the application of these principles to the issue of line versus bar graphs per se. Specifically, Simcox wanted to see whether there is independent perceptual evidence that in the default case we are more likely to encode a line in terms of its slope and overall height, whereas we are likely to encode pairs of bars into the individual height of each one (this putative perceptual phenomenon is at the heart of my account of the respective superiority of line and bar graphs at displaying trend and point information). He reasoned that whatever attributes we do encode by default should be available in "pure" form to discrimination processes and irrelevant information should not interfere with such judgments. In contrast, if we have to discriminate stimuli on the basis of some attribute that is not part of the default encoding, then the discrimination would require an internal transformation of the encoded information into the desired attributes, which should result in more time and errors, and in interference from values of irrelevant attributes conflated with the desired one in the default encoding.

In his first experiment, Simcox found that people could sort a deck of cards with bar graph-type stimuli into two piles on the basis of the height of one of the bars, and their sorting times were not significantly affected by whether the height of the other bar was constant or varied randomly. However, when asked to sort the deck into two piles on the basis of the slope or average height defined by the two bars, they were significantly slower when the irrelevant attribute (average height or slope) varied randomly than when it was held constant. These two patterns are diagnostic of "separable" and "integral" stimuli, respectively (Garner, 1974) and indicate that people naturally encode pairs of bars into a representation in which the height of each one is stated explicitly; overall height or slope must be inferred from that representation. Precisely the opposite pattern was found when subjects sorted analogous decks of cards depicting line graph-like stimuli. When sorting according to the height of one of the endpoints of the lines, the subjects were slowed down when the height of the other endpoint varied randomly compared with when it was constant. However, when sorting according to the slope of the line or its overall height, the irrelevant attribute (overall height or slope, respectively) did not affect the sorting speed. Thus, a line segment depicted within an L-shaped framework is easily encoded into a representation in which its overall height and slope are stated explicit; the height of individual endpoints must be inferred from that representation or encoded in a second look at the stimulus.

In a second experiment, Simcox found that when subjects are simply asked to classify the overall height, height of one point, or slope of a line or pair of bars, they were faster at classifying the height of bars than the height of one of a line's endpoints, but faster at classifying the slope or overall height of a line than those defined by a pair of bar heights. Finally, in a third experiment involving the speeded sorting of a graph-like stimulus with two lines, Simcox found that sorting by either height or by slope was slowed down when the irrelevant factor (slope or height, respectively) varied randomly and when the variation of that irrelevant factor yielded intersecting versus nonintersecting lines. However, when the stimuli were varied so that intersection was not a concomitant of varying the slope or height, each of the two attributes could be attended to selectively without interference from the other. This suggests that the global property of line intersection finds its way directly into the default encoding of a pair of lines, rather than it being a property derived from heights and slopes of the component lines.

Taken together, the Pinker and Simcox studies offer strong support for the hypothesis that is at the core of the present theory: that graphs will be easy to comprehend when the visual system naturally encodes the geometric features of the graph with visual predicates that stand in one-to-one correspondence (via the graph schema) with the conceptual message that the reader is seeking. The Pinker (1983) study showed that readers indeed can infer global quantitative trends directly from global geometric features representing them so long as those global features are ones that our visual systems perceive easily. Simcox (1983) showed in particular that this sort of explanation can account for the widely observed superiority of line graphs at conveying trends and of bar graphs at conveying point values. He did so by showing that, as the theory would require, uninterpreted stimuli resembling line graphs are more naturally encoded in terms of the overall height, slope, and intersection of lines, whereas uninterpreted stimuli resembling bar graphs are more naturally encoded in terms of the heights of the individual bars.

XIII. EXTENSION OF THE THEORY TO CHARTS AND DIAGRAMS

Quantitative information is not the only kind that is transmitted by visual displays, and it would be surprising if the charts and diagrams used to express qualitative information were comprehended according to principles radically different from those governing graph comprehension. In fact, the theory described in these pages can be extended virtually intact to the domain of charts and diagrams. Again, a visual description of the diagram would be encoded, obeying the principles of grouping, the indispensability of space, and so on, and again, there would be a "chart schema" for a particular species of chart, which specified (a) The constituents of the visual description that identify the graph as being of the appropriate sort (e.g., a flow chart vs. a Venn diagram); and (b) The correspondences between visual predicates and conceptual message entries. The conceptual message entries would be of a form appropriate to the qualitative information represented, and conceptual questions would consist of conceptual message entries with the "?" symbol replacing one of the constants. The MATCH, message assembly, interrogation, and inferential processes would play the same roles as before. Charts would be easier or more difficult depending on whether the visual system encoded them into units corresponding to important chunks of conceptual information, and chart readers would be more fluent to the extent that their chart schemas specified useful correspondences between conceptual information and visual attributes, and to the extent that those visual attributes were encoded reliably. A brief example follows.

Venn diagrams, used in set theory, consist of interlocking circles, each of which represents a mathematical set. Presumably, they are effective because the visual system can easily encode patterns of overlap (which will translate into set intersection), inclusion (translating into the subset–

superset relation), nonoverlap (translating into disjointness), and so on (see Ullman, 1984, for a discussion of how some of these patterns might be recognized). Simplified Visual Array, Visual Description, Chart Schema, and Conceptual Message representations specific to Venn diagrams appear in Figs. 4.23a through 4.23d.

Even from these simplified examples, one can see that, as before, the difficulty of retrieving a given type of information will depend on what is in the visual description and graph schema and not simply what is on the page. For example, here the reader would have to infer the fact that Set C is a subset of Set B from the conceptual message entry stating that Set B is a superset of Set C. A more efficient diagram reader might have a richer schema, containing the predicate "included-in" together with a message flag stating that one set is a subset of the other. This would spare that reader from having to rely on inferential processes.

Other sorts of diagrams and charts use other visual predicates to convey their messages efficiently: For example, flow charts use shape predicates to signify the type of operation (e.g., action vs. test), they use the contiguity of shapes with lines to indicate the flow of control, and they use the orientation of arrowheads to indicate the direction of that flow. The linguist's tree diagrams for the phrase structure of sentences use horizontal position to signify precedence relations among constituents, proximity to common line segments to signify dominance (inclusion) relations, and above/below predicates to signify the direction of the dominance relations. For each type of diagram, there would be a specific schema spelling out the correspondence between visual predicates and conceptual messages.

XIV. CONCLUSIONS

This chapter began with a warning that our understanding of graph comprehension would advance in proportion to our degree of understanding of general perceptual and cognitive faculties. As we have seen, the theory outlined here indeed borrows heavily from perceptual and cognitive theory, adopting, among others, the following assumptions: the importance of propositional or structural descriptions at certain levels of representation; the indispensability of space as it relates to visual predicates, selective attention, creation of perceptual units, and accuracy of encoding; the limited capacity of short-term visual representations; the use of distributed coordinate systems for encoding shape and position; the use of schemas to mediate between perception and memory; the effects of physical salience on encoding likelihood; conceptually driven or top–down encoding of visual attributes; a MATCH process for recognition; "priming" of visual predicates; and strengthening of associative links with practice. I hope that this enterprise is not totally parasitic, though, since in developing the theory, significant gaps in our knowledge of visual cognition came to light; for example, the exact constraints on which physical attributes can serve as visual predicates, the determinants of their likelihood of being encoded, the relative strengths of the Gestalt principles, the format in which the groupings they impose should be represented in structural descriptions, the constraints that determine how message flags can be appended to predicates in schemas, the ways that descriptions can guide top–down encoding processes, and how general the information in a general schema (like the general graph schema) can be. Perhaps the most salient conclusion of this exposition, then, is that our understanding of basic cognitive processes will be the rate-limiting step in our understanding of applied cognitive domains, and that unexplained but pervasive phenomena in applied domains can be very effective diagnostics of important gaps in that basic knowledge.

ACKNOWLEDGMENTS

This research was supported by NSF grants BN5 80–24337, 81–14916, 82–16546, 82–09450, 85–18774, and NIE grant 400–79–006. I thank Stephen Kosslyn, Bill Simcox, Michael Kubovy, and Barbara Tversky for helpful discussion. An earlier draft appeared as Technical Report No. 10 in the MIT Center for Cognitive Science Occasional Paper Series in 1981.

REFERENCES

Anderson, J. R. (1976). *Language memory and thought.* Hillsdale, NJ: Lawrence Erlbaum Associates.
Anderson, J. R., & Bower, G. H. (1973). *Human associative memory.* New York: V. H. Winston.
Bertin, J. (1967). *Semiologie graphique: Les diagrammes—les reseaux–les cartes.* The Hague: Mouton.
Bregman, A. S. (1977). Perception and behavior as compositions of ideals. *Cognitive Psychology, 9,* 250–292.
Carter, L. F. (1947). The relative effectiveness of presenting numerical data by the use of tables and graphs. In P. F. Fitts (Ed.), *Psychological research on equipment design.* Washington, DC: U. S. Government Printing Office.
Clark, H. H. (1973). Space, time, semantics, and the child. In T. E. Moore (Ed.), *Cognitive development and the acquisition of language.* New York: Academic Press.
Cooper, L. A., & Shepard, R. N. (1973). Chronometric studies of the rotation of mental images. In W. G. Chase (Ed.), *Visual information processing.* New York: Academic Press.
Cooper, L. A., & Shepard, R. N. (1975). Mental transformations in the identification of right and left hands. *Journal of Experimental Psychology: Human Perception and Performance, 1,* 48–56.
Cooper, W. E., & Ross, J. R. (1975). *World order.* Notes from the Parasession on func-

tionalism. Chicago: Chicago Linguistics Society.

Crowder, R. G. (1976). *Principles of learning and memory*. Hillsdale, NJ: Lawrence Erlbaum Associates.

Culbertson, H. M., & Powers, R. D. (1959). A study of graph comprehension difficulties. *Audio Visual Communication Review*, 7, 97–100.

Finke, R. A., & Pinker, S. (1983). Directed scanning of remembered visual patterns. *Journal of Experimental Psychology: Learning, Memory, and Cognition*, 8, 142–147.

Garner, W. P. (1974). *The processing of information and structure*. Hillsdale, NJ: Lawrence Erlbaum Associates.

Gibson, E. J., Bergman, R., & Purdy, J. (1955). The effect of prior training with a scale of distance on absolute and relative judgements of distance over ground. *Journal of Experimental Psychology*, 50, 97–104.

Hinton, G. E. (1979). Some demonstrations of the effects of structural descriptions in mental imagery. *Cognitive Science*, 3, 231–250.

Hoffman, D. D., & Richards, W. (1984). Parts of recognition. In S. Pinker (Ed.), *Visual cognition*. Cambridge, MA: MIT Press.

Jackendoff, R. (1978). Grammar as evidence for conceptual structure. In M. Halle, J. Bresnan, & G. Miller (Eds.), *Linguistic theory and psychological reality*. Cambridge, MA: MIT Press.

Kosslyn, S. M., Murphy, G. L., Bemesderfer, M. E., & Feinstein, K. J. (1977). Category and continuum in mental comparisons. *Journal of Experimental Psychology: General, 106*, 341–375.

Kosslyn, S. M., Pinker, S., Smith, G. E., & Shwartz, S. P. (1979). On the demystification of mental imagery. *Behavioral and Brain Sciences*, 2, 535–548.

Kubovy, M. (1981). Concurrent pitch segregation and the theory of indispensable attributes. In M. Kubovy & J. Pomerantz, (Eds.), *Perceptual organization*. Hillsdale, NJ: Lawrence Erlbaum Associates.

Lakoff, G., & Johnson, M. (1980). *Metaphors we live by*. Chicago: University of Chicago Press.

Marr, D., & Nishihara, H. K. (1978). Representation and recognition of the spatial organization of three dimensional shapes. *Proceedings of the Royal Society*, 200, 269–294.

Miller, G. A. (1956). The magical number seven, plus or minus two: Some limits on our capacity for processing information. *Psychological Review*, 63, 81–97.

Miller, G. A., & Johnson–Laird, P. (1976). *Language and perception*. Cambridge, MA: Harvard University Press.

Minsky, M. (1975). A framework for representing knowledge. In P. H. Winston (Ed.), *The psychology of computer vision*. New York: McGraw–Hill.

Morton, J. (1969). Interaction of information in word recognition. *Psychological Review, 76*, 165–178.

Newell, A., & Simon, H. (1973). *Human problem solving*. Englewood Cliffs, NJ: Prentice–Hall.

Norman, D. A., & Rumelhart, D. E. (1975). (Eds.), *Explorations in cognition*. San Francisco: W. H. Freeman.

Palmer, S. E. (1975). The effects of contextual scenes on the identification of objects. *Memory and Cognition*, 3, 519–527.

Parkin, L. (1983). *A comparison of various graph labelling methods in the context of gestalt organizing principles*. Unpublished manuscript, Consulting Statisticians, Inc., Wellesley, MA.

Pinker, S., Birdsong, D. (1979). Speakers' sensitivity to rules of frozen word order. *Journal of Verbal Learning and Verbal Behavior*, 18, 497–508.

Pinker, S. (1983). *Pattern perception and the comprehension of graphs*. Unpublished manuscript.

Posner, M. I., Snyder, C. R., & Davidson, B. S. (1980). Attention and the detection of signals. *Journal of Experimental Psychology: General, 109,* 160–174.

Pylyshyn, Z. (1973). What the mind's eye tells the mind's brain: A critique of mental imagery. *Psychological Bulletin, 80,* 1–24.

Schank, R. A., & Abelson, P. E. (1977). *Scripts, plans, goals and understanding.* Hillsdale, NJ: Lawrence Erlbaum Associates.

Schneider, W., & Shiffrin, R. M. (1977). Controlled and automatic human information processing: I. Detection, search, and attention. *Psychological Review, 84,* 1–66.

Schutz, H. (1961a). An evaluation of formats for graphic trend displays: Experiment II. *Human Factors, 3,* 237–246.

Schutz, H. (1961b). An evaluation of methods for presentation of graphic multiple trends: Experiment III. *Human Factors, 3,* 108–119.

Shiffrin, R. M., & Schneider, W. (1977). Controlled and automatic human information processing: II. Perceptual learning, automatic attending, and a general theory. *Psychological Review, 84,* 127–190.

Simcox, W. A. (1983). *A perceptual analysis of graphic information processing.* Unpublished doctoral dissertation, Tufts University, Medford, MA.

Smith, E. E., Shoben, E. J., & Rips, L. J. (1974). Structure and process in semantic memory: A featural model for semantic decision. *Psychological Review, 81,* 214–241.

Stevens, S. S. (1961). To honor Fechner and repeal his law. *Science, 133,* 80–86.

Talmy, L. (1978). The relation of grammar to cognition—A synopsis. In D. Waltz, (Ed.), *Proceedings of TINLAP–II* (Theoretical Issues in Natural Language Processing). Urbana: University of Illinois Press.

Ullman, S. (1984). Visual routines. In S. Pinker (Ed.), *Visual Cognition.* Cambridge, MA: MIT Press.

Wainer, H., & Thissen, D. (1981). Graphical data analysis. *Annual Review of Psychology, 32,* 191–241.

Washburne, J. N. (1927). An experimental study of various graphic, tabular, and textual methods of presenting quantitative materials. *Journal of Educational Psychology, 18,* 361–376, 465–476.

Wertheimer, M. (1938). Laws of organization in perceptual forms. In W. D. Ellis (Ed.), *A source book of Gestalt psychology.* London: Routledge & Kegan Paul.

Winston, P. H. (1975). Learning structural descriptions from examples. In D. H. Winston (Ed.), *The psychology of computer vision.* New York: McGraw–Hill.

5 What Computers Can See: A Sketch of Accomplishments in Computer Vision, With Speculations on its Use in Educational Testing

Leslie Kitchen
Computer Science Department
University of Western Australia

1. VISION AND INTELLIGENCE: ARTIFICIAL AND NATURAL

There is an apocryphal story that some 20 years ago a professor of artificial intelligence assigned the "vision problem" as a student's summer project. It has not turned out to be quite so easy a problem. Needless to say, the vision problem was not solved then, nor has it been solved completely yet. Still, like many other areas of artificial intelligence, computer vision has entered a phase of maturity. Many problems, perhaps the hardest, remain unsolved, but much progress has been made. A rich repertoire of techniques, and even some theory, has been built up; some practical applications have been realized, and many more seem to be just around the corner.

Computer vision occupies a unique position in artificial intelligence. In no other established area of the field are numeric measurements, geometric structure, and vast quantities of input data such important considerations. (For example, a color video image can be estimated to carry something like three-quarters of a million bytes of information, and in a video sequence such images arrive at a rate of 30 per second.)

Sometimes the question is raised whether computer vision truly is part of artificial intelligence, since its quantitative aspects seem far removed from the symbolic processing of much traditional artificial intelligence. However, a practitioner of computer vision might facetiously agree with the claim that computer vision is not part of artificial intelligence, averring that in fact artificial intelligence is just a part of computer vision. And there would be some truth to this: Most of the classic problems of artificial intelligence, such as representation of knowledge, control of processing (including search), and dealing with uncertainty, appear in some form in computer vision. Furthermore, as artificial intelligence is applied nowadays to more and more realistic problems, it becomes necessary to deal more often with quantitative data in other areas, making the experience gained in vision more valuable to artificial intelligence in general.

Another aspect of this relationship between computer vision and artificial intelligence is the apparent, as opposed to the actual, difficulty of the problems tackled. Most of the obvious early successes in artificial intelligence have been in problems that people readily appreciated as difficult, whose solution was regarded as requiring "intellectual" effort: chess playing at a competitive level, manipulation of complex algebraic formulae, expert systems for solving problems in highly specialized domains. However, we can instantly recognize the face of a friend, and discern subtleties of expression, or drive a car through busy streets, without any sense of great intellectual effort.

Attempts to mechanize such processes have had only limited success, and have revealed these tasks to be of tremendous difficulty. Even a child can effortlessly perform visual tasks that go far beyond the capabilities of any computer vision system realized to date. It seems that something like 60% of the human cerebral cortex is involved in some way in visual processing. With such awesome computational power available, it is no surprise that people can perform difficult tasks of visual perception with so little apparent effort. Similar remarks could be made about other human abilities that artificial intelligence attempts to duplicate, such as language (both spoken and written). But these are very much cultural behaviors, part of a human intellectual tradition; even simple animals have a remarkable ability to perceive the world around them through senses (such as vision), and respond appropriately.

My purpose in making these remarks is twofold: to indicate briefly the relationship between computer vision and the rest of artificial intelligence, and to touch on the relationship between human visual and intellectual ability. Any account of human intellectual capabilities must consider our visual abilities; no attempt to test our intellectual capabilities can afford to ignore vision. (By visual ability I mean the capacity to form and deal with complex visual perceptions, not merely visual acuity as might be measured say by an optometrist's eye chart.)

Following on from this, there are two reasons why computer vision might be of interest to those on the field of educational testing. One is the potential application of the technology, as will be discussed; the other that testing must deal with people, who are chiefly visual creatures. Computer vision can provide insights into visual processes, insights which could be used in designing tests able to measure some of people's visual ability.

In the rest of this chapter I will try first to outline the current state of the art in computer vision, mentioning also those achievements that may not be obvious to someone outside the field. I will then go on to speculate about how techniques of computer vision could conceivably be used in educational testing. I will not try to define computer vision (it is too dynamic a field for that), but I will try to give something of its flavor. I might say that it is the endeavor to equip computers with a sense of sight, but until our own human visual abilities are better understood, such a definition cannot be made usefully precise. A good general introduction to computer vision can be found in Ballard and Brown, (1982).

Before proceeding, I should make two points clear. First is that I write this from a point of view of what might be called "engineering science," rather than cognitive science. That is, I treat computer vision as a business of uncovering scientific principles by which we might engineer visual abilities for machines. My aim is not to use computers as a means for modeling computational theories of human perception. Much excellent work is done along these lines, and it contributes greatly to the storehouse of knowledge that can be used for engineering machine vision. However, its intent is subtly different from mine, which is as I said, one of engineering science. The second point is that within this chapter, I am not advocating any particular methods for computer vision.

2. LANDSCAPE OF COMPUTER VISION

For convenience, I will divide computer vision processing into three levels: low, middle, and high. While this breakdown is often used, it should be borne in mind that it is somewhat arbitrary and something of a simplification, like dividing the earth into tropical, temperate, and arctic zones. There is no sharp boundary where one zone ends and another begins; one shades gradually into the next. On top of a high peak in the tropics, one might well find snow. But the divisions are useful nonetheless, if only to let us talk about the subject in some reasonable order.

2.1. Low-level Vision

Low-level vision is concerned with the initial processing of a visual signal as an image, and with the extraction and representation of elementary (or primitive) visual events (tokens). The sorts of processing that might be done on an image include enhancement, restoration, and rectification. Enhancement is used to bring out more clearly certain visual properties of an image: An example would be the "stretching" of the contrast of an image in order to make details more readily visible. Restoration is used to reconstruct what an image is supposed to have looked like before some process of degradation. For example, such processing could be used, with some success, to remove the "snow" from a poor television picture, or to remove the blurring of an image caused by motion of the camera during exposure. Rectification is used to correct for geometric distortions of an image, as may be caused by optical aberrations within the camera. Note that enhancement, restoration and rectification are not three techniques; rather they represent three whole classes of image-processing techniques with similar uses.

Image processing is not an exclusive preserve of computer vision; it is used in many other fields, such as medicine and remote sensing, in order to convert images into a form more suitable for human inspection and interpretation. In computer vision, however, image-processing techniques are used to prepare raw visual input for later automatic processing.

The later stage of low-level vision has to do with the extraction and representation of primitive visual events, such as the local fragment of an edge, or a small patch of uniform color. An edge fragment may be declared to exist at a point in an image at which there is a consistent change in some visual property such as brightness or color (the change being a clue that there is a perceptible visual boundary between one object and another in the world). Typically, such events are prepresented by "tokens," which describe useful properties of the visual event, and are stored in some sort of a data base for retrieval during later stages of processing at the middle and high levels. For an edge fragment, the corresponding token may describe its position in the image, what property is changing (say color or brightness), and by how much, and in what direction the edge appears to be oriented in the image.

2.2. Midlevel Vision

During midlevel vision, two kinds of processing take place: perceptual organization, and inference of physical parameters of the world from the visual data.

Perceptual organization is the grouping together of primitive visual tokens into greater, coherent wholes, and its complement, the perceptual segregation, or separation, of tokens that belong together away from tokens they do not belong with. For example, a string of edge fragments which all consistently line up would be regarded as forming an extended, whole edge; a new, higher-level, composite token would be formed to represent this more complex percept. If the extended edge looped around and joined itself to form a closed curve, then the area enclosed by the curve would form a perceptual token of another kind, which would be separated from its background. Research at this level of computer vision is currently affected significantly by the work of the Gestalt psychologists. Its vocabulary includes such terms as regions, lines, curves, two-dimensional shape, and two-dimensional spatial relations.

The other part of midlevel vision has to do with the inference of physical parameters of the world from visual data. The pattern of light shading over a surface gives clues to the three-dimensional shape of that surface. (This is used to great effect by visual artists such as painters to create the illusion of a solid surface in the flat surface of a painting.) The parallax between the slightly different views of the world obtained by our two eyes gives us a means of estimating the location of objects in three-dimensional space around us. Similarly, the difference in apparent motion of objects gives us clues as to their distance. (Traveling in a train or car, you would have noticed that nearby objects appear to whizz past rapidly, while far away objects seem to drift more slowly across the field of view.)

All of these processes whereby people infer physical properties of the world from vision can be analysed mathematically and geometrically. Many have been implemented, with some degree of success, in a number of computer vision systems.

2.3. High-level Vision

High-level vision has to do with the semantic interpretation of perceptions, that is, a meaning should be ascribed to the visual data. Exactly what this meaning is will depend on the intended application of the system, but it is generally taken to mean that the objects appearing in the image should be identified (named), as well as being located in space and described physically. In moving images of dynamic scenes (such as a street busy with traffic), it may be necessary to make predictions about the future motions of objects.

To achieve this requires a complex orchestration of low-level and mid-level processing. It also requires representation and use of knowledge about the world (though this has only been achieved in limited domains).

As a vision system is often seen as part of some larger intelligent system (such as an autonomous robot vehicle), interaction with the rest of the system may be needed. This is also regarded as part of high-level vision. A two-way interaction is necessary: to respond to queries or commands from the rest of the system (say to look for some specific object such as an important landmark needed for navigation by a robot), and to spontaneously report significant events back to the rest of the system (say the robot was about to run into a ditch).

Results in high-level vision are perhaps most accessible to someone outside the field: An image goes in, and (perhaps after many hours of processing on today's machines) out comes a semantic interpretation of the image. However, this final result is built on top of intermediate results produced at all levels of processing.

3. THE GENERAL STATE OF THE ART

The general state of the art in computer vision may be summarized as follows: In realistic (but limited) domains, with considerable investment of effort and a lot of computation, reasonable (though fragile) performance is achievable.

The domains include eye-level color images of rural road scenes (Draper et al., 1987) and suburban house scenes (Weymouth, 1986), aerial photographs of suburban houses (Nagao & Matsuyama, 1980), road networks and airports (McKeown, Harvey, & McDermott, 1985). The effort required is usually that of a graduate student working full time at a Ph.D. over a number of years, typically with the support of a fair-sized research group. The processing will often take many hours on a midi computer. The results obtained are reasonable in that the system will usually achieve a high success rate in recognizing the objects represented in its knowledge base. But the results are fragile in that the system will only "know about" a small number of objects (from a handful to a few dozen); that achieving this level of performance will require considerable tuning of the system by its implementor; and that, presented with any unexpected input (such as an image from a different domain, or an image containing an unknown object), the system will fail badly to make any sense out of it all.

4. VISION AND TESTING: SPECULATIONS

In this section I will indulge in some speculations as to how the technology of computer vision might be of use in educational testing. Possible applications such as the reading of handwritten text, or the testing of people's abilities in visual or spatial reasoning, would be a feasible extrapolations from current research. A completely automated robot examiner is at the limit of what can be conceived of for the future.

4.1. Reading Handwritten Text

The "reading" of text by computer is a well established area of research, and nowadays of commercial application. By "reading" is meant only the visual identification of the letters, numerals, and punctuation signs in a piece of text. The determination of the meaning of the text after the characters have been spelled out is the business of natural-language processing, not of computer vision.

This is not to say that the two can be entirely separated: Achieving best performance requires integrating the two. For example, suppose that a computer system for reading text has analysed a printed word and determined that its first letter is "b", its second letter "e", and fourth letter "t." However, perhaps because of poor print quality, it cannot determine unambiguously on purely visual properties whether the third letter is "c," "e," or "s." Thus the three possible readings of this word are "bect," "beet," and "best." Determining the correct reading would have to use additional, nonvisual knowledge. For example, by consulting a dictionary, it could be found that no such word as "bect" occurs in English, and so the first alternative could be ruled out. If the word in question were preceded by "my" and followed by "friend," then semantic analysis could suggest that "my best friend" was a far more plausible reading than "my beet friend." (Note that neither of these techniques is foolproof. "Bect" might be an obscure foreign or technical term; it is conceivable that the phrase "my beet friend" could be used in some unusual circumstances— as it is being used here.)

To date, some systems have used dictionary look-up as an aid to recognition of text, or similar approaches, like statistics of the occurrence of letter combinations. Constraints from grammar or semantics have been little used in reading text (one exception being Brady & Wielinga, 1978, who used the grammar of the programming language FORTRAN to guide the reading of programmers' handprinted coding sheets), although they have been heavily used in the related problem of speech recognition, the automatic interpretation of spoken utterances (Lesser & Erman, 1977).

There is a spectrum of difficulty in reading text by computer. Simplest is single-font optical character recognition (OCR). Such systems are commercially available, and can recognize properly aligned, cleanly machine-printed characters out of a single font (type style and size), with recognition rates as high as 99.99% of characters recognized correctly. Almost all errors are the explicit rejection of a character as being unrecognizable, rather than the undetected misrecognition of one character as another. The details of commercial systems are proprietary, but it is likely that they function by direct comparison of the input character with a number of prestored, fixed templates, one for every character in the font, and by choosing the template most similar to the input character.

Next in difficulty is omnifont OCR, and the similar problem of reading neat, handprinted text. For this, the characters must still be cleanly printed and properly aligned (for handprinting, preprinted guide lines and guide boxes may be necessary), but can be of any reasonable style or size. Doing this requires structural knowledge of the shapes of characters, not merely fixed templates. At the time of writing, only one or two such systems had been commercially released. Recognition rates reported in the literature for experimental systems run as high as 98%. Good surveys of this literature can be found in Kahan, Pavlidis, and Baird (1987) and Suen, Berthod, and Mori (1980).

Most challenging is the reading of cursive handwriting. The difficulty here is that not only is there extreme variation in the shapes of individual letters, but also that it is by no means simple to determine where one letter ends and the next begins. To date, only a few experimental systems have been developed, such as (Hayes, 1980).

It is conceivable that a computer vision system could read handwritten examination answers, and convert them into a form suitable for semantic analysis by a system for natural-language understanding. However, as can be seen from this discussion, no established technology exists for reading even normal handwriting (let alone the scrawl likely to be produced under pressure of examinations). The recognition of neatly handprinted answers is probably feasible, but whether this is a reasonable restriction to put on answers would have to be determined.

As suggested by Roy Freedle of ETS, it would be possible to combine computer vision with speech recognition in inputting examination answers. That is, the computer could analyse simultaneously the visual, written form of the answers by computer vision techniques and a spoken form as read aloud by a human reader. Since it is unlikely that the written and spoken versions of the text would show the same ambiguities in interpretation at the same time, the two types of analysis would complement each other, producing better performance than could be achieved with either alone. However, the proper integration of visual text recognition with speech recognition is an open research problem, and (on the practical side) it would have to be determined whether such a combined system would be more cost-effective than, say, having a skilled typist key in the text.

4.2. Visual and Spatial Reasoning

While it is not a direct application of a computer vision system, an area in which many computer vision techniques could be used is in testing people's ability to perform visual and spatial reasoning.

One can imagine an examinee set at a workstation with a display, which shows an image of a room with furniture and ball in it. The examinee is engaged in a computer dialogue: Requests and questions are put up on the display screen, and the examinee types in responses on a keyboard. A request might be to describe where the ball is in the pictured room. Unless the examinee's responses are to be limited to multiple-choice alternatives, the problem arises that the same position of the ball could be described in many different ways. For a certain arrangement of the room, "just to the right of the sofa," "just to the left of the armchair," "between the armchair and the sofa," and "behind the coffee table" may all be perfectly good ways to describe where the ball is. In addition to a natural-language component to parse the input, such an examination system would need to have its own representation of the spatial layout of the room, and its own mechanism for performing spatial and visual reasoning, in order to judge the appropriateness of a response.

This would not be a computer vision system as such, since the system would not perform any analysis itself of the image. However, many techniques used within computer vision systems for representing and reasoning about the location of objects in space, and the spatial relations between them could be adapted for use here.

Such an examination system could be set up to generate automatically many different room layouts, by computer graphic techniques to produce images of views of these rooms, and then to generate an appropriate set of questions about the spatial layout of the objects in the room. Some work has been done on the generation of natural language to describe spatial relationships, particularly using prepositions (Kender, Allen, & Boult, 1987). Another possibility is to show two images and ask whether they are two different views of the same room.

4.3. The Robot Examiner

Going far beyond the type of limited automatic examination station just described is what might be called the "Robot Examiner." One can imagine a vision system that would watch and evaluate someone performing a physical or manual task. The system could possibly interact with the examinee through automatic speech recognition and generation, and through the use of a robot manipulator to set up problems and give demonstrations.

The basis for this speculation is some work on visual understanding of human body posture and motion (Herman, 1980; O'Rourke & Badler, 1980). However, the practical realization of the Robot Examiner would require major advances in all areas of artificial intelligence, not just in computer vision and robotics. Even so, at this stage it would be interesting to develop some limited, small-scale experimental prototype.

5. RECOMMENDATIONS

Some computer vision systems may be useful in educational testing in 5 to 10 years. This is particularly true for automatic reading of handwritten examination answers. Indeed, if certain restrictions are made, say to hand-printed text, usable technology probably exists already. In addition, some of the internal machinery used by computer vision (representations for spatial concepts, etc.) may also be applicable in testing. However, since computer vision (and artificial intelligence in general) is such a volatile field, it would be advisable to track future developments and assess their usefulness.

REFERENCES

Ballard, D. H., & Brown, C. M. (1982). *Computer vision.* Englewoods Cliffs, NJ: Prentice-Hall.

Brady, J. M., & Wielinga, B. J. (1978). Reading the writing on the wall. In A. R. Hanson & E. M. Riseman (Eds.), *Computer vision systems.* New York: Academic Press.

Draper, B. A., Collins, R. T., Brolio, J., Griffith, J., Hanson, A. R., & Riseman, E. M. (1987). Tools and experiments in the knowledge-directed interpretation of road scenes. In *Proceedings of DARPA Image Understanding Workshop* (pp. 178–193). Los Angeles.

Hayes, K. C., Jr. (1980). Reading handwritten words using hierarchical relaxation. *Computer Graphics and Image Processing, 14,* 344–364.

Herman, M. (1980). Computer interpretation of human stick figures. In *Proceedings of The First Annual National Conference on Artificial Intelligence* (pp. 174–177). Stanford, CA.

Kahan, S., Pavlidis, T., & Baird, H. S. (1987). On the recognition of printed characters of any font and size. *IEEE Transactions on Pattern Analysis and Machine Intelligence, PAMI-9,* pp. 274–288.

Kender, J. R., Allen, P. K., & Boult, T. E. (1987). Image understanding and robotics research at Columbia University. In *Proceedings of the DARPA Image Understanding Workshop* (pp. 71–77). Los Angeles.

Lesser, V. R., & Erman, L. D. (1977). A retrospective view of the HEARSAY–II architecture. In *Proceedings of The International Joint Conference on Artificial Intelligence* (pp. 790–800). Cambridge, MA.

McKeown, D. M., Harvey, W. A., & McDermott, J. (1985). Rule based interpretation of aerial imagery. *IEEE Transactions on Pattern Analysis and Machine Intelligence, PAMI-7,* pp. 570–585.

Nagao, M., & Matsuyama, T. (1980). *A structural analysis of complex aerial photographs.* New York: Plenum Press.

O'Rourke, J., & Badler, N. I. (1980). Model-based image analysis of human motion using constraint propagation. *IEEE Tarnsactions on Pattern Analysis and Machine Intelligence, PAMI-2,* 522–536.

Suen, C. Y., Berthod, M., & Mori, S. (1980). Automatic recognition of handprinted characters—The state of the art. *Proceedings of IEEE, 68,* 469–487.

Weymouth, T. E. (1986). *Using object descriptions in a schema network for machine vision* (Tech. Rep. 86–24). Amherst, MA: University of Massachusetts, Computer and Information Science Department.

6 Issues for a Theory of Analogical Learning

Mark Burstein
BBN Laboratories

Beth Adelson
Tufts University

1. INTRODUCTION

Researchers in artificial intelligence and cognitive psychology have recently begun to focus more attention on the study of analogical reasoning and its role in learning and problem solving. Much of this work has focused on studies of the mapping process (Burstein, 1986; Carbonell, 1986; Falkenhainer, 1987; Gentner, 1983; Thagard & Holyoak, 1985; Winston, 1982). These theories of analogical reasoning all take as central that an underlying conceptual model from a familiar source or base domain is mapped to an unfamiliar target domain. The mapping places objects (concepts) and relations between objects in the source into correspondence with counterparts in the target. Learning then occurs when the mapping supports the construction of new relations between target objects, or suggests that additional objects are involved.

Motivating our research is the observation that mapping is a central process in analogical learning; what can be derived from any given analogical example is limited by what has been mapped. Because mapping is a foundation of analogical learning, analogical learning theories need to specify the mapping process in detail.

Our approach to specifying mapping is based on the fact that one typically knows a large amount about a familiar domain, and, as a result, what is mapped is constrained by the purpose of the analogy (Burstein, 1983, 1985; Burstein & Adelson, 1987; Kedar–Cabelli, 1985; Holyoak, 1985; Winston, 1983). The aspects of the target domain that need to be explained are those that are relevant to the current situation; the problem currently needing to be solved strongly motivates and constrains the use of a particular analogy.

In addition to specifying the mapping process, theories of analogically based learning must also account for the use of multiple analogical models. Descriptions of scientific and technical systems typically consist of a number of different parts, each of which focuses on a particular aspect of the system to be described. Details of purpose, behavior, mechanism, physical and functional topology, and structural composition may all be required to explain, in full, what is going on. Typically, these different aspects are described separately, and the student is expected to integrate them to achieve a full understanding (Burstein, 1986; Collins & Gentner, 1983; Spiro, Feltovich, Coulson, & Anderson, 1988; Stevens & Collins, 1980; Stevens & Steinberg, 1981).

Complex systems tend to be analogous only in certain respects. However, because analogies are such useful pedagogical devices, they are used quite frequently. This means that students trying to learn about a new system often need to relate partial analogical models from several source domains. The analogies involved may be of different types, or contribute to the target model at varying levels of abstraction (Adelson, 1984; Burstein, 1983; Collins, 1985; Collins & Gentner, 1983; Coulson, Feltovich, & Spiro, 1986; Sternberg & Adelson, 1978). For example, Collins and Gentner found that untutored subjects used as many as three analogical models at a time to answer questions about evaporation (Collins & Gentner, 1982, 1983, 1987). Different kinds of models were used to answer different kinds of questions and frequently several models were used together.

We are developing a theory of analogical learning that accounts for this kind of mental model development. The theory has two main parts. First, we have a model of purpose-guided analogical mapping that details how explanatory mental models of different types can be created by an analogy when different kinds of questions need to be answered. Second, we are developing a theory that explains how these different types of models are integrated when solving problems in the target domain.

In order to motivate our current work, this chapter starts with a review of some of the work on analogical reasoning and learning that has gone on over the last 20 years by researchers in the fields of artificial intelligence and cognitive psychology. The review is by no means exhaustive. Our main purpose is to highlight and motivate the problems that we feel need to be addressed in developing a theory of learning by analogy.

2. BACKGROUND RESEARCH

2.1. Evans' ANALOGY Program

The first significant work on analogical reasoning in AI was Evans's ANALOGY program (Evans, 1968), which solved geometrical analogy problems typical of those found on standardized IQ tests. A sample problem ANAL-

OGY could solve is shown in Fig. 6.1. Two pictures containing geometric figures are presented, labeled A and B. A third figure, C, is then presented along with five possible choices for a best D such that "the rule by which Figure A has been changed to make Figure B" also transforms C into D.

To solve one of these problems, ANALOGY first developed representations of transformations that could describe how Figure A was changed to form Figure B and then separately how Figure C could be transformed into each candidate answer. To do so, it identified corresponding objects in Figures A and B when they could be put into correspondence by simple geometrical transformations. Other objects were then noted as deleted or added in going from Figure A to Figure B. The most important step was the determination of all of the spatial relationships between the objects in each figure, using predicates such as INSIDE, ABOVE, and LEFT-OF. The combined result of these steps was a characterization of the between-object relationships that had changed in going from A to B. The transformation that had occurred was captured by "before and after" representations of the spatial relationships between objects, and the notation of added and deleted objects. In problems where there were multiple ways of mapping objects onto objects, ANALOGY developed multiple sets of transformations taking A into B.

Once ANALOGY had computed the set of all transformations that could take A into B, it searched for a transformation of C to an answer (i) most like one of those it had found for A→B. The technique used for this transformation developed generalizations of the transformations of A→B that were also generalizations of some transformation of C to some i. The figure ANALOGY chose as the final answer was the target figure in the most specific generalized transformation, as ranked by a complexity metric based on the number of features in a transformation.

ANALOGY's generalization technique involved placing the objects in A and B into correspondence with those in C, and then using those object

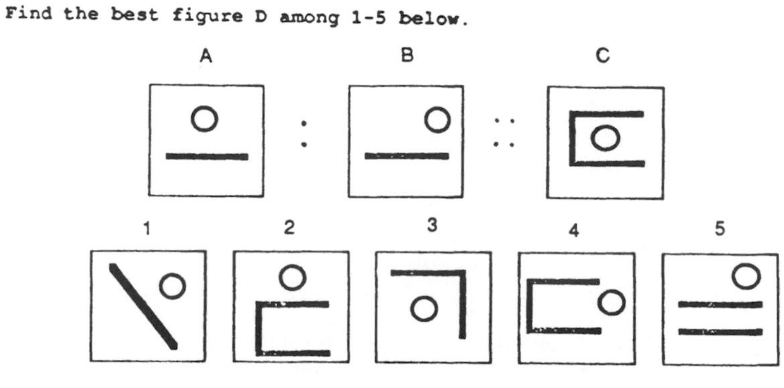

Find the best figure D among 1-5 below.

FIG. 6.1. A typical ANALOGY problem.

correspondences to compare the statements about added and deleted objects, and spatial relations in the before and after parts of the compared transformations. The generalization that resulted was essentially the intersection of those sets of relations shared by both transformations.

Evans's system displayed a number of important characteristics found in most later models of analogical reasoning. Its transformations between figures were based on representations of objects, spatial relationships between the objects in a figure, and transformations between two temporally ordered figures. The best analogy was chosen by finding a best mapping between transformations, essentially by finding how much they matched. The match was described by a set of object correspondences between the objects in A and C, and a generalized transformation that represented the set of relationships and changes that occurred in both pairs of figures.

Although Evans's program illustrated many things that are consistent with current theories of analogy, the strategy that ANALOGY employed to come up with solutions does not extend well to the needs of a model of learning. The representations developed by ANALOGY for individual figures did contain enough information to do a large class of geometrical analogy problems. However, the candidate-elimination technique ANALOGY used to choose an answer can only be used when one is given a set of answers to choose from. When learning by analogy, one doesn't have answers to choose from. Instead, the goal is to find out what it is about a known, familiar situation that can help you in a new, unfamiliar one. This is precisely what students must do when a teacher uses an analogy to explain something about an unfamiliar new domain. Given a description of some action or "transformation" that the student knows occurs in the familiar case, the student must find a generalization of that event that can be used to interpret or predict features of the new situation.

To use analogies in this way, one must also be able to represent or generalize the actions or transformations involved more flexibly than ANALOGY could. To illustrate this further, consider an example (Fig. 6.2) that ANALOGY could not handle by the method described above, but that most people have no trouble with.

ANALOGY's primary technique for choosing an answer couldn't find one in this case[1] because it could not adequately represent the generalized transformation involved. In ANALOGY's representation of the situation, the predicate used to relate the objects in figures A and B was the ABOVE. That is, ANALOGY knew only that the square was ABOVE the triangle beforehand (in A) and the triangle was ABOVE the square afterward (in

---

[1] A secondary, backup strategy involving predicate substitutions before generalization was successful in finding the answer, but that somewhat ad hoc strategy is not relevant here.

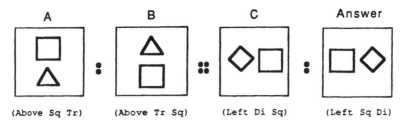

FIG. 6.2.   A problematic example.

B). It had no way of describing the fact that the spatial relationship between the triangle and the square was reversed in going from A to B. Without this characterization of the transformation, the program could not detect any similarity between A→B and C→D because the spatial relationship between the diamond and the square in C and D was that one was always to the LEFT of the other. As ANALOGY's generalization technique removed properties of the transformation of A→B, until it applied to C→D, an empty generalized transformation was formed. It was therefore forced to conclude that figures A→B had nothing in common with the transformation from C to D.

What is interesting about this particular analogy problem is that many people have no difficulty predicting the answer D given only A, B, and C as has been pictured. People quickly detect symmetries such as the role reversal involved in going from A to B. By assuming that the same transformation must be involved in going from C to D, the LEFT relation can then be identified with the ABOVE relation in figure C, and thus predict D without ever seeing that answer among several choices. Evans's system was, in principle, incapable of finding the generalization underlying this analogy because it did not have a vocabulary of abstract transformations on relations. Without such a vocabulary, it could not represent the role reversal that this example used. Evans's system was also incapable of predicting answers because it had no strategy for guessing which generalized transformation was most appropriate for mapping. Indeed, for geometrical analogies there are few reasons to prefer one kind of transformation over another. This is not true of analogies used in problem solving, where there is usually a point or purpose to using an analogy for the task at hand.

It is certainly true that "guessing" the generalization underlying an analogy is a risky business. But we are forced to do just that all the time. When learning about a new domain, we make predictions from what little we know and how closely that resembles more familiar situations. In such cases, one needs to be able to project the important or relevant rules from a familiar situation onto the unfamiliar one. As we will see, this means sometimes making mistakes as well.

2.2. Winston's Analogical Matching System

Another model of the process of analogy formation was developed at MIT by Winston (Winston, 1980, 1982). The initial focus in this work was not on analogical problem solving, but on the discovery of analogical similarities between stories. The stories tested were typically presummarized descriptions of Shakespearian plots. Later, the system's matcher was incorporated into a system for learning generalized rules from comparisons of analogical precedents and new examples (Winston, 1982).

The heart of Winston's model was a pattern matcher that, in essence, tried every possible pairing of objects in its representations of two stories, and then rated the "goodness" of the match produced by those pairings. The representations that the matcher compared were semantic relational networks, described using the frame language FRL (Roberts & Goldstein, 1977). Stories were presented to the system in a restricted pseudo-English that translated more or less directly into FRL's semantic predicate notation. The networks developed from these inputs were augmented by "demons" that inserted CAUSE and PREVENT (and CAUSED-BY and PRE-VENTED-BY) links when actions using predicates such as PERSUADE were mentioned. A typical, slightly shortened, example appears in Fig. 6.3.

The matcher's rating of pairs was obtained by counting the number of identical object classes, attributes, and relations between corresponding nodes in the networks compared. The program treated each matching attribute and relational link as adding one to the match score, although

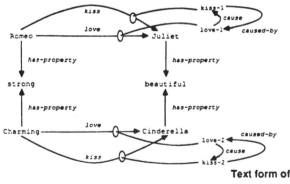

This match produces a score of 6. Two properties match, two corresponding relations between people match, and two causal links match.

Text form of Input

Charming job entertaining -- has-property brave strong -- love Cinderella -- kiss Cinderella Cinderella job cleaning -- has-property beautiful

Romeo job fighting cleaning -- has-property strong -- love Juliet -- kiss Juliet Juliet has-property beautiful

FIG. 6.3. A typical story match by Winston's matcher.

Winston recognized that some measure of importance might ultimately be required in the scoring system. Since the algorithm required that corresponding objects of the two stories were at least tentatively identified, finding a best match required exhaustive consideration of the match scores for all possible pairings of object-nodes between the compared story representations. The system then chose as the "best" match the object correspondence that produced the highest match score.

Winston's matcher rated similarity on the basis of all of the available information about all of the objects in each story. For example, since Macbeth was a-kind-of KING, and KING was a-kind-of MAN, and MAN was a-kind-of ANIMAL, and so on, objects placed into correspondence with Macbeth were also compared as to whether they were kings, men, and so on. Since the matcher counted all of two potentially paired objects' superordinate classes, the system tended to emphasize object similarity over relational similarity. Winston hoped this matching technique would not only account for within-domain or literally similar comparisons but also for cross-domain or analogically similar comparisons, since even in so-called cross-domain analogies, one sometimes finds literally similar objects being placed in correspondence.

Unfortunately, this conflicts with the results of some psychological studies by Gentner and her colleagues (Gentner, 1980, 1988; Gentner & Toupin, 1986) which strongly suggest that for analogical similarity, relational correspondences are considered by adults to be a more important metric than are object attribute correspondences, even though surface similarity seems to be a stronger guide for the retrieval of analogs from long-term memory.

Another more general problem with theories of analogy based principally on the matching of descriptions, such as Evans's and Winston's models, is that a detailed conceptual representation of a situation may contain many objects not taking part in analogies to that situation. Furthermore, the number of such unmatched objects tends to grow as the complexity of the descriptions increases. These extraneous objects can increase the computational cost of finding a good match, especially when all possible pairings of objects in two situations are considered, as in Winston's initial computer model. Winston admits that this particular problem was explicitly ignored in his implemented matcher, with which at most only about 100 pairings of objects could be reasonably considered, or about 5 objects per compared situation.

Other, more recent models have also relied on matching techniques with many of the same properties as Winston's matcher, but using various space–time tradeoffs to effectively consider all possible pairings in parallel (Falkenhainer, Forbes, & Gentner, 1986; Holyoak & Thagard, 1988). As we will discuss in more detail later, we believe that models of this type, relying on network matching algorithms, must be further controlled by some mechanism that preselects the relevant kinds of relationships to be compared in the source and target representations.

Winston suggested that to get out of this bind would, in general, require a method for constraining the number of object pairings considered. For example, he suggested it might be appropriate in some cases to compare only men with men, and women with women. Unfortunately, universal use of such a strategy would lead to missing some generalizations that were independent of the sexes of the characters involved. In general, he claimed, what was required was knowledge of what was important among each objects' classes, features, associated actions and other relations in a given situation. To this end, he suggested that attention to important relations, such as those connected by causal links, can reduce the computational complexity of the matching process to some degree. To demonstrate the role of this match constraint, the matcher was constructed so that, by setting a switch, it would only count relations that were explicitly marked as important or were related by causal links. This indeed reduced the cost of finding a match without changing the basic result.

Correspondences between causal relationships are often critically important in good analogies. For this reason, matching and mapping strategies that use causal links as a guide or focus have been suggested a number of times (see, for example, Gentner, 1980; Burstein, 1986). However, it is also the case that "causal" representations can occur at many different levels of detail. Systems may be composed of subsystems that can be expanded to introduce greater and greater levels of detail (Collins & Gentner, 1983; deKleer & Brown, 1981), thereby introducing new objects and relationships which, although useful, may not play roles in the analogy. As the number of objects and relationships in such representations grows, the computational complexity of matching descriptions grows enormously. Computationally, algorithms such as Winston's become intractably slow, even when focusing primarily on causal relations, unless the level of detail at which the comparisons are made is somehow limited.

Although a fairly simple, early demonstration, Winston intended the matching system he outlined to play a central role in a general model of analogical reasoning and learning. In (Winston, 1982), the matcher was used to demonstrate how causal rules could be learned from examples and precedents. There, Winston described how his revised program could predict or confirm the (plausibility of) new or missing relations between objects in a target example using correspondences between the target exercise and a precedent. When the program was asked about a missing target relationship, it would search for the missing relation and any causal support in the precedent. It would then try to establish the relation that provided causal support in the target exercise.

When learning from precedents, Winston was relying heavily on the causal structure of the precedent in choosing what to carry over to the target. Indeed, similar schemes combining matching and carryover in related ways are used in a number of other current computational models of the analogy process (Burstein, 1986; Falkenhainer, 1987; Falkenhainer et al., 1986; Holyoak & Thagard, 1988; Thagard & Holyoak, 1985). However, the problem of focusing or constraining the representations of the situations compared remains. Two types of mechanisms need to be developed. First, general mechanisms for preselecting relevant parts of a base domain representation are needed in order to constrain what is considered for matching and/or mapping at any given time. Second, mechanisms to make the matching process itself more sensitive to pragmatic and goal-driven concerns need to be developed. Addressing these issues is vital if a model of analogical learning is to be developed.

The complexity of the analogical learning process becomes clearer when considering what happens when teacher's present analogies to students as a means of explaining something. The point of presenting an analogy to a student is to aid in the construction or elaboration of his or her understanding of a target situation; or to correct problems in a prior understanding. That is, the information to be learned from the analogies is not part of what matched, but rather what didn't. Thus, there must be a mechanism that focuses attention on particular parts of an analogical situation, even if it does not correspond to a part of the student's representation of the target situation.

2.3.   Learning by Structure Mapping

Another important model of analogical reasoning and learning has been developed by Dedre Gentner and her colleagues (Gentner, 1980, 1982, 1983, 1988; Gentner & Gentner, 1983). Gentner initially suggested a theoretical framework for describing scientific or "explanatory" analogies and how one learns from them. By explanatory analogies, Gentner was primarily referring to a general class of analogies of which those used to describe models of scientific concepts are typical. Examples included:

The hydrogen atom is like the solar system.

Electricity flows through a wire like water flows through a pipe.

Gentner claimed that such analogies were best defined as structure-mappings between different domains, where relations, or, more generally, predicates involving several objects or concepts, were preserved. She stated that "such analogies are fundamentally assertions that partly identical relational structures apply to dissimilar objects across different domains"

(Gentner, 1982). This model, while similar to Winston's in some respects, was explicitly designed to account for what people learn from analogies like those given. Also, she was concerned primarily with cross-domain analogies, where the objects involved in the analogous situations were very different.

Gentner's model is perhaps most easily illustrated using her example of the analogy "The hydrogen atom is like the solar system" (see Fig. 6.4).

By the algorithm she described, objects-nodes in the base domain (sun, planets) are mapped onto object-nodes in the target domain (nucleus, electrons). This may be done by external suggestion or a structural match. In either case, relations in the base domain are mapped to apply to corresponding objects in the target unchanged. Thus, it is predicted that there is a force ATTRACTing the electrons to the nucleus, the electrons REVOLVE around the nucleus, the nucleus is MORE-MASSIVE-THAN the electrons, and so on. The attributes of the objects in the base domain are not mapped, except when they appear as relative relations (e.g., BIGGER-THAN).

In the diagram of Fig. 6.4, the sun is related to each planet by the predicate HOTTER-THAN, as well as ATTRACTS MORE-MASSIVE and REVOLVES-AROUND. The problem Gentner noticed was that the HOTTER-THAN relation does not seem to be mapped to the atomic model. That is, people don't generally believe that the analogy implies that the nucleus of an atom must be hotter than its surrounding electrons. This is a potentially large problem, since many other "attribute comparisons," such as BRIGHTER-THAN, YELLOWER-THAN, and so on, could also be part of a description of the solar system and those relations should not be mapped either.

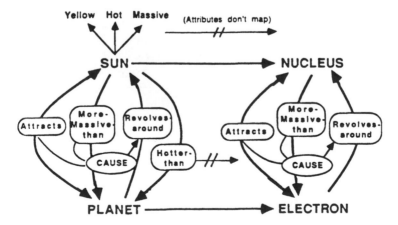

FIG. 6.4. Gentner's representation of Rutherford's atomic model.

The explanation provided by Gentner for this phenomenon was in terms of a general condition on the mapping process, which she called the systematicity principle. Basically, this principle states that people prefer to map connected systems of relations, that is relations governed by higher-order relations, such as CAUSE, rather than isolated relations that didn't have any explanatory value (most possible attribute comparisons would not have any value in this respect). For example, if causal links connected the MORE-MASSIVE relation to the ATTRACTS and REVOLVES-AROUND relation, then those three relations and their causal connections would be mapped, while the attribute comparison relation HOTTER-THAN would tend not to be mapped.

Gentner's theory of structure-mapping explicity ignores object similarity. In her formal model, object similarity is described by correspondences between attributes of corresponding objects, where attributes are represented as one-place predicates. Examples in which similarities between objects are important she classifies as statements of "literal similarity." A typical example of a literal similarity statement is "The X12 star system in the Andromeda nebula is like our solar system." This feature of Gentner's model was supported by experiments (Gentner, 1980, 1988; Gentner & Stuart, 1983), in which adults emphasized relational commonalities in their interpretations of analogies, whenever possible. Other studies she has conducted have suggested that there is a developmental shift toward relational interpretations and away from attributional or "literal similarity" ones (Gentner & Stuart, 1983; Gentner & Toupin, 1986). The latter study (Gentner & Toupin, 1986) suggested that both 5- and 8-year-old children's performance in an analogical transfer task was improved when corresponding objects were similar, but only the 8-year-old children improved when the base domain story had a systematic underlying structure. Another study (Gentner & Landers, 1985) showed that adults preferred analogies where there was a common system of connected relations to those where there were isolated relations in common, but no corresponding systems.

A computer model of structure mapping, the Structure-Mapping Engine (SME) was implemented by Brian Falkenhainer (Falkenhainer et al., 1986). In some sense, it can be considered an efficient tool for the kind of matching that Winston had envisioned. In fact, it is a "tool-kit" in which many variants of Gentner's mapping criteria can be described and tested (Skorstad, Falkenhainer, and Gentner, 1987).

In a recent paper (1988), Gentner noted that the structure-mapping principles are intended to characterize a range of conditions from pure matching to pure carryover. In the former, much like the early examples of Winston, the only activity is establishing correspondences between objects based on the alignment of corresponding relations of two well-understood situations. In the latter, the systematicity principle is used to suggest which first-order relations (and the higher-order relations that tie some of those first-order relations together into a system) should be mapped. In the situation where a teacher suggests an analogy and specifies what objects should be assumed to correspond we see a clear example of how the systematicity principle would function. In general, of course, we are somewhere in between these two extremes, since we usually know something, but not everything about the target domain.

Gentner's structure-mapping theory has many attractive features, taken broadly. Perhaps the most important feature with respect to learning is the systematicity principle, which suggests one important way in which the set of relations considered for mapping can be constrained, other than by matching to corresponding relations in the target. Gentner's theory suggests some guidelines to follow when little is known about the target or when an analogy is used to suggest an alternative system of relations exists between the objects in the target. At this time, there is fairly broad agreement among analogy researchers that the basic processes of analogical reasoning involve some combination of matching and mapping of relational predicates (Burstein, 1986; Burstein & Adelson, 1987; Carbonell, 1986; Collins & Burstein, 1988; Gentner, 1988; Indurkhya, 1985; Kedar–Cabelli, 1985; Reed, 1987; Rumelhart & Norman, 1981; VanLehn & Brown, 1980; Verbrugge & McCarrell, 1977; Winston, 1982). However, there is still a variety of views and disagreements about how and whether causality, goals and purposes, and other contextual and pragmatic factors affect the choice of what to match or map. The systematicity principle is a point of relative agreement in this debate.

There are also several problems with the details of Gentner's description of structure mapping. The distinction made between one and two place predicates is more properly a distinction between semantic attributes of objects (e.g., COLOR), as opposed to relations between objects (e.g., CAUSES). Also, Gentner includes as two-place relations all comparative relations on object attributes (e.g., HOTTER-THAN). The issue of how to include this class of two-place relations in the representation of a system is tricky, because there can be arbitrarily many comparisons made between objects' attributes in representations of any given situation. However, and perhaps this is what is essential about systematicity, one thing that analogies can do is signal when there is a reason for comparing the attributes of two objects in the target. For example, the Rutherford analogy might have suggested to scientists that they try to find and compare the masses of an electron and the nucleus of an atom.

Another problem with Gentner's model was her claim that all relations are mapped "identically" between analogous situations. While this might be true in analogies between purely spatial descriptions of situations, including standard geometrical analogies and some scientific analogies, this is much too strong a claim in general.

In her representation of the analogy "Electricity flows through wires like water flows through pipes," the relation "flows-through" is used to describe the motion of both electricity "in" a wire, and water in a pipe. Yet, it is not intuitively clear that the same relation applies here. We seem to be stretching our notion of containment when we talk about electricity being "inside" a solid wire. The problem is even worse when physical analogs are suggested for abstract concepts. In Burstein's example of teaching programming students about assignment (Burstein, 1981, 1985, 1986), students are told that numbers go "in" variables the way that objects go in boxes. Clearly, these notions of containment are related, but they are not identical.

The real issue here is the level of abstraction at which the analogy is meant to apply. Corresponding relations in different domains may be "similar," but have somewhat different entailments. Depending on how much is known about the target domain when the analogy is presented, it may or may not be reasonable to map a relation exactly from one domain to another. Often, some, but not all of the inferences associated with a mapped relation will apply in the new domain. Burstein (1985), described a model of cross-domain mapping for relations that created new relations sharing some of the properties of the old one, but not others, just as an analogy comparing two well-understood domains may suggest a mapping between two clearly nonidentical predicates or objects.

2.4. Pragmatic Analogical Transfer in Planning and Problem Solving

Planning, like learning, is an extremely important use of analogical reasoning. In this area, an important contribution has been made by Holyoak and his colleagues (Gick & Holyoak, 1980; Holyoak, 1985; Holyoak & Thagard, 1988). Their work has been primarily concerned with characterizing the circumstances under which people are able to notice analogies to things they have seen before in different circumstances, and then put them to use in their problem solving.

Most of their work has centered around psychological experiments and computational models of problems like Duncker's ray problem (Duncker, 1945):

> Suppose you are a doctor faced with a patient who has a malignant tumor in his stomach. It is impossible to operate on the patient, but unless the tumor is destroyed the patient will die. There is a kind of ray that at a

sufficiently high intensity can destroy the tumor. Unfortunately, at this intensity, the healthy tissue that the rays pass through on the way to the tumor will also be destroyed. At lower intensities, the rays are harmless to healthy tissue, but will not affect the tumor either. How can the rays be used to destroy the tumor without injuring the healthy tissue?

Gick and Holyoak's initial experiments (Gick & Holyoak, 1980) were intended to test the extent to which subjects could apply the solution of an analogous problem to the ray problem when a hint was given that the analogous problem was relevant.

Subjects first read one of several versions of a story about the predicament of a general who wished to capture a fortress located in the center of a country. In all versions of the story many roads radiated outward from the fortress, but these were mined so that although small groups could pass over them safely, any large group would detonate the mines. Additionally, the general needed to get his entire army to the fortress in order to launch a successful attack.

One group of subjects saw a version in which the general's problem was solved when a road was discovered without mines. These subjects were likely to suggest using an "open passage" solution when later presented with the ray problem. For example, one subject suggested that the esophagus was used to get the rays to the tumor. Another group of subjects saw a version in which the general divided his men into small groups and sent them down all of the converging roads. These subjects were likely to suggest a "convergence" solution to the ray problem, directing multiple weak rays onto the tumor from different directions.

Based on these results, Holyoak (Holyoak, 1985) concurred with Gentner and others that for interdomain analogies, the perceived similarity of the source and target is determined primarily by relational similarity. However, Holyoak further suggested that the mapping and carryover processes were heavily guided by pragmatic context. For analogies used in problem solving, this meant that "the initial mapping will typically involve detection of an abstract similarity between corresponding goals, constraints, object descriptions, or operators, which constitute the implicit schema common to the two analogs." Any of these could serve as retrieval cues to access relevant source analogs, and initiate the mapping process. In extending a mapping (the carryover process), differences in the target and source would be allowed as long as they were structure preserving with respect to some specified goal. For example, in the military story, the general could simply tell his men to "divide up" and achieve his objective. For the ray problem, subjects often introduced multiple "ray machines," where there was no explicit counterpart for these in the source. Here there was a breakdown of the analogy in the methods for establishing the multiple converging lines of rays.

Holyoak pointed out that one problem with Gentner's structure-mapping theory was that a strict interpretation of the systematicity principle would lead to a prediction that a given base domain would always produce the same structural mapping, when, in fact, differing (problem-solving) goals could lead to different mappings from the same source analog.[2]

Holyoak's central claim is that pragmatic contextual factors influence the uses of analogies. Aspects of the source transferred to the target might be affected by such diverse factors as (1) knowledge of what was conventionally taken to be important (Winston, 1980) or salient (Ortony, 1979), (2) the apparent goal in using the analogy (e.g., what aspects of the target need to be explained), (3) the causal relations known to be central in the source (Burstein, 1983; Gentner, 1980; Hesse, 1966; Winston, 1980), and (4) those aspects that can be mapped without generating structure-violating differences.

All of these factors must somehow be weighed together in deciding what to map or carry over from a source to a target. An important open question, then, is whether these pragmatic factors that were mentioned are disjoint, or whether some of them, in fact, are aspects of a consistent picture. One of the goals of this chapter is to present the initial outlines of a theory that takes many of these factors into account.

2.5. Carbonell's Transformational and Derivational Analogical Problem Solving

Another example where an emphasis on the role of analogy in problem solving leads to a more goal-directed model of analogy can be found in the work of Carbonell (Carbonell, 1983, 1986), who has explored several approaches to automating analogical problem solving. Carbonell defines analogical problem solving as the process of reusing solutions to previously solved problems in the solution of new ones. In this, he was strongly influenced by Schank's theory of memory organization (Schank, 1982) and his characterization of the role that reminding plays in human reasoning processes. Carbonell began with the premise: "When encountering a new situation, people are reminded of past situations bearing strong similarities to the present problem (at different levels of abstraction)." These re-

---

[2] In (Gentner, 1988) Gentner rebuts this by saying that systematicity should be modeled as a preference for structure. Correspondence with the target is not ignored. Holyoak's point may nonetheless be valid, since some explanatory or problem-solving goal may be required to override apparent base-target correspondence.

mindings can be useful. They indicate that people can and do retrieve plans that were appropriate at earlier times and which may be appropriate, or adapted to be appropriate, in new situations.[3] These principles were vital in explaining how a variety of related scenarios were retrieved and used, when appropriate, to help interpret and "flesh out" an analogical model that could explain and predict the consequences of a variety of target domain events.

Carbonell's work was primarily on the problem of adapting recalled problem solutions to the demands of new problems. His initial approach to this problem was to extend the traditional means–ends analysis paradigm (Newell & Simon, 1972). He proposed two different methodologies by which previous problem solutions could be used to help solve new problems, one called transformational analogy, and one called derivational analogy.

In transformational analogy (Carbonell, 1983), the reminding process was modeled by a difference function[4] whose results were used to index into a space of previously seen solutions to problems. The difference function measured differences among the initial and final states of the new and prior problems, and also differences in what he called path constraints, which did things like reject plans that reused operators too many times in the course of solving a problem. It also took into account the proportion of operator preconditions that were satisfied for the new problem by the solution to the old problem.

The core of the Carbonell's transformational analogy proposal was his mechanism for adapting retrieved solutions to fit the needs of new problems. Here, Carbonell suggested that the adaptation process itself be viewed as a problem-solving process, only this time working in an analogy transform problem space (T-space). Essentially, the idea was to invoke the means–ends problem solver on the problem of adjusting a sequence of steps known to solve an old problem into another set of steps to solve the new problem. Thus, in this problem space, the initial and final states (and all intermediate ones) were sequences of actions that would solve different problems. The starting state was a sequence of actions that solved an old problem, and the final state was a sequence to solve the new problem. An operator in the T-space mapped one action sequence into another action

---

[3] Burstein (Burstein, 1985, 1986), whose work we will consider shortly, also makes explicit use of a number of these same principles of memory organization and retrieval, specifically, those developed by Lebowitz and Kolodner who also work in the Schank paradigm (Kolodner, 1980; Lebowitz, 1980).

[4] In means/ends problem solvers, the selection of the next problem solving operator to apply is based on the result of a difference function applied to the current and goal states of the problem being solved.

sequence, hopefully converging on a set of steps that would solve the problem at hand. T-space operators performed operations such as splicing actions in and out of an action sequence, substituting different actions to achieve the same subgoal, adding steps at the beginning or end of a subgoal sequence, and so on.

While it seems clear that the T-space operators that Carbonell listed (Carbonell, 1983) would indeed be quite useful in transforming old problem-solving sequences to the demands of new problems, the problem of deciding when to use those T-space operations remained largely unsolved. The problem is that it is difficult to modify a plan to solve problem X so that it solves problem Y without considering why steps in X were done, and whether they are relevant to the solution of problem Y. In (Carbonell, 1986), Carbonell acknowledged these problems and described a new method, derivational analogical reasoning which addressed many of the problems raised by the earlier approach. Carbonell argued that the earlier approach was flawed primarily in that it was a method for solving problems by mapping and modifying finalized sequences of plan steps. In many situations, it would be easier to develop a solution to the new problem if the planner also had access to the more abstract plans or derivational traces of the reasoning that went into the process of solving the original problem. By mapping the results of these more abstract plans and reasoning choices first, much of the motivational information that was obscured in the final problem-solving sequence could be applied to keep the reasoning about the new problem on track. The intuition behind this can be seen from the following example (Carbonell, 1986): A programmer who had written a sorting routine in PASCAL might easily be able to write a sorting routine in LISP, using the abstract model of that routine he had developed early in the process of solving the original problem. On the other hand, this same programmer might find it difficult or impossible to do a direct translation of a PASCAL sorting program into a LISP sorting program, given no information other than a program listing with no comments.

Carbonell's alternative model, derivational analogical reasoning, makes use of the derivational histories (traces of the original problem-solving process) for the plans developed in the base domain, when solving new, analogically related problems. The advantage of working from derivational histories is that they contain a record of the hierarchical expansions of the original plans, including the causal justifications recorded for individual steps and subplans. They also include the causal constraints used in finalizing the temporal ordering of steps in each level of the plan developed. In addition to the reasons for the choice of particular plans or subplans, derivational histories list the alternative subplans considered and the reasons why those alternatives were discarded. This information is potentially useful since some constraints on the target domain problem may be different, making the discarded subplans preferable in the new solution to ones used in the old plan.

Whenever the derivational analogical reasoner started to solve the new problem, it checked to see whether the first few steps taken to solve that problem were the same or similar to the set of initial steps taken in solving some previous problem. If a match was found, the rest of the old problem's solution trace was retrieved, and the problem solver switched to its analogical planning mode. In this mode, problem solving proceeded by retracing the development of the original problem solution, at each step checking whether the same conditions held for the new problem as held when the original problem was being solved. As long as those conditions held, the step that was used in solving the old problem was repeated for the new one.[5]

When the constraints of the solution to the target problem were inconsistent with the justifications for planning decisions made in the retrieved problem solution, several things could occur: The original planning decision might be rejustified for the target problem by reasoning from other assumptions in the target domain, or the same subgoal might be achieved by one of several kinds of replanning. One method of replanning discussed was to use a subplan which was considered and rejected during the solution of the original problem, but which might not have the same failings with respect to the new problem. Another approach was to initiate a subgoal in the target domain that established some missing preconditions for using the subplan mapped originally. A third was to search for an independent means of achieving the subgoal in the target domain.

In some senses, the transformational and derivational approaches to analogical problem solving illustrate two extremes of a spectrum when it comes to approaches to analogical problem solving. The transformational analogy approach represents an approach to analogical problem solving that relates the old and new problems by taking advantage of the superficial similarities of the solutions to each problem. That is, it works well if simple changes to the old solution produce a useful new solution. The problem is figuring out what to change. The derivational analogical reasoning approach represents the other extreme. There, it is the underlying goal and plan structures that are related. The power of this approach is that the new

---

[5] It was not clear from the description whether there was a mapping process that would allow for the substitution of similar but unequal terms in this process. Almost certainly, the objects being acted upon would not be the same in the old and new examples, but analogies often deal with correspondences between properties as well as between objects. In Carbonell's case, this was left unclear, probably because he tended to deal with analogies that were within a single domain, such as algebra problems, for which the object/object and relational mappings were always simple.

solution that is found is just as principled, explainable, "debuggable" as one derived from first principles, but without much of the searching that would normally be required. The disadvantage is the potentially large amount of information that must be saved in traces of the old solutions.

2.6. Learning from Multiple Analogical Models

Our own prior work (Adelson, 1984; Burstein 1981, 1983, 1985, 1986; Burstein & Adelson, 1987) has focused on how new mental models are learned for the programming domain, by a combination of analogical reasoning and problem solving. Burstein conducted a series of protocol studies of tutorial learning (Burstein, 1981), that led to the development of CARL (Burstein, 1983, 1985, 1986), a computer model of the cognitive processes involved in learning about basic programming-language constructs. CARL learns by reasoning from several analogies presented by a teacher. The program was an attempt to model the behavior found in recorded protocols of several students who were tutored on the programming language BASIC. The model suggested how analogical hypotheses could first be developed and later debugged or modified to model the target domain correctly when some but not all of the predictions derived from analogies turned out to be true.

CARL developed a working knowledge of the use of programming variables and assignment statements in the programming language BASIC by combining hypotheses from three separate analogies that were used in the protocol studies. One analogy suggested a physical model for variables and assignment, by describing assignment as being like "putting things in boxes." Another analogy related assignment statements to algebraic equalities, and the third analogy related computer behavior to human behavior, in particular relating computer memory to human memory, and the computer's ability to respond to commands to a similar human ability. It was by combining these three models that CARL was able to learn about assignment.

In the collected protocols, students learning about BASIC generated a number of plausible, though sometimes incorrect, explanations when asked to predict the effects of examples or solve simple problems using what they had been told about the programming domain. Their answers were plausible in the sense that they were based on scenarios for events in one of the analogical base domains that they had been told of. The "errors," which occurred even when analyzing extremely simple assignment statements, were produced by mapping detailed predictions from the source domain to the target, beyond the point where the two domains were actually in correspondence. For example, after having been told that variables were like boxes, statements like "$X = Y$" were sometimes misinterpreted as indicating that the variable Y was to be "Placed inside" the variable X. Actually, the statement "$X = Y$" makes the value of X the same as the value of Y. The erroneous prediction can be seen as a mapping of the plausible scenario that one box can be placed inside another box.

Though these errors were not the intended effects of the teacher who presented the analogy, they shed light upon the process of analogical reasoning and were included in the data to be accounted for by the process model developed. Indeed they were often the most crucial examples; the subjects generating them clearly did not know enough about the target domain to revise their mapped hypotheses before discussing them, therefore these examples allow us to look at the mapping process separately from the process that then debugs what has been mapped.

Since students must be prepared to modify or debug their analogically generated models, sources of alternate hypotheses are needed. At such times, additional analogies are often introduced, since they can be used to invoke alternative models quite rapidly, and this simplifies the debugging process. The following protocols with one subject (Perry, age 10) illustrate this point quite clearly. Not long after reading a paragraph containing the box analogy, quoted from a textbook, the dialogue in Fig. 6.5 occurred. This example shows one way in which having several analogies can be more helpful than having just one. Here, the tutor was illustrating a point about transferring values from one variable to another. The tutor typed '$P = 10$' and then '$Q = P$'. Fig. 6.5 shows what happened.

At first, Perry clearly seems to have made the inference that if "$Q = P$" was analogous to moving an object from one box to another, then the number that had been in P must now be in Q. Since objects, when moved, are no longer at their original location, P must now be "empty." When

```
Tutor:  So, what's in P now?
Perry:  Oh. Nothing.
Tutor:  Nothing?
Perry:  10! and then Q is also.
Tutor:  What do you think it is?  Is it nothing or 10?
Perry:  Let's find out. First let's see...
Tutor:  Well, what do you think is?
Perry:  If you have two boxes, and you moved...
        You moved or it equals to?  You moved
        what's in P to Q so there's nothing in it,
        or did you only put the same number in Q
        that's in P? I think it's 10.
Tutor:  You think it's 10?
Perry:  Because you don't say that, um, move P at all...
        take P out.  You only said that Q equals the
        same as P.  So if it equals, it has to be 10,
        because if there's no 10 in it, Q wouldn't be
        equal to it.
```

FIG. 6.5. Two analogies making conflicting predictions.

pressed, Perry's uncertainty about this conclusion caused him to come up with an alternate answer, based on an entirely different line of reasoning involving another analogy. If typing "$Q = P$" is treated as a statement to the computer that the two variables have equal values, then, by this algebraic interpretation, from the fact that P was originally 10, the computer may conclude that Q is also 10, while P's value must stay the same.

It is interesting to note that Perry's use of algebra knowledge in forming his second model of the example did not stop him from further use of the box analogy. He continued to use both models in analyzing new situations. It was simply the case that algebra provided what seemed like a more satisfactory answer to this particular problem.

Protocols such as the one in Fig. 6.5 were used to guide the development of CARL. CARL learns semantic representations for most common types of assignment statement, using analogies and other "hints" from a human tutor. It also learns some basic syntactic and semantic interpretation rules for those statements, and causal inference rules that can be used to predict the logical results of their execution. In the process, it makes a number of the mistakes observed in the protocols of people learning the same material. CARL was able to simulate these errors by a structure-mapping process that produced generalized causal representations of the actions involved in different assignment statements from similar causal representations about situations in the source domains of the analogies it was given.

Fig. 6.6 is the English equivalent of one part of a dialogue that CARL engages in (The "tutor's" inputs are the lines preceded by >>. Actual inputs were in an extended version of Conceptual Dependency Representation [Schank & Abelson, 1977]).

By repeatedly mapping causal structures from the base domains of the analogies it worked with, CARL eventually formed a working model of a number of different kinds of assignment statements, making some "plausible mistakes" along the way. The box analogy was initially used to suggest that the statement "$X = 5$" be interpreted as "putting" the number 5 in a variable called X. Based on this description, CARL mapped a causal model of "putting something in a box" to form a model of assignment containing the prediction that the number 5 was "in" the variable. Subsequent mappings from the box domain for another example ("$X = Y$") led CARL to generate the predictions that variables could be placed in other variables, and that "$X = Y$" would leave Y "empty," as Perry had predicted.

As suggested by Gentner's work, CARL did not map attributes of objects unless they were implicated in the causal structure. In fact, objects were not made to correspond directly at all. Instead, CARL mapped generalized object placeholders called role variables, denoting the roles of each object in the causal model. That is, the structures CARL mapped

```
>> The computer remembers a number by putting it in a variable.
>> A variable is like a box.
>> To put the number 5 in the variable named X, type 'X=5'.
>> How do you get the computer to remember the number 9?
CARL: Type 'X = 9'
>> Suppose I then type 'X=6'.
>> Now what's in the variable X?
CARL: 6 is in X and  9 is in X
>> No, the 6 replaces the 9 in X.
CARL: OK
>> Suppose I type 'Y=5' and then 'X=Y'.
>> Now what's in the variable X?
CARL: Y is in X
>> No, it means put the number in Y into X.
CARL: OK
>> Now what's in the variable Y?
CARL: Nothing.
>> Guess again.
CARL: 5 is in Y (by analogy to equality)
>> Correct.
CARL: OK
```

FIG. 6.6.   A dialogue with CARL.

were generalized, domain-specific, causal models, retrieved from memory of the box domain in the way a natural-language-understanding system might do so in order to interpret statements about boxes.

2.6.1 Using Multiple Models through a Merging Process.   CARL's structure mapping engine worked well with descriptions of causal structures. However, structures other than causal ones can be mapped by analogy and the mapping process for these structures needs to be modeled as well. For example, the analogy between algebraic equalities and assignments is a behavioral analogy in the sense that it suggests that the computer infers values for variables using rules of algebra when assignment statements are presented. That is, the computer performs some unspecified set of operations leading to the achievement of an implicit goal, namely, the discovery of a value for a variable.[6] This behavioral model of assignment can also be used to predict behavior in the target domain.

CARL made some of its behavioral target domain predictions by relating its model of algebra to its causal model for assignment based on the box analogy. That is, it mapped behavioral predictions (values for the variables appearing to the left of the equal sign) from its algebra model onto its mechanistic causal model. This mapping was possible because the result

---

[6] We refer to this analogy as a behavioral one for two reasons. First, in the analogy a goal is attained without mention of the mechanism or operations that enabled its attainment. Second analyses of the protocols indicate that this analogy is taken as a behavioral, not a causal one; it does not lead to mappings of causal explanations of the computer's behavior.

predicted by both models matched (X took on the value 5). In forming the mapping between the behavioral and causal result, the behavioral action (inferring the relation HAS-VALUE between a variable and a number) and the causal action ("putting" a number "in" a variable) were placed in analogical correspondence. These initial analogical correspondences between two very different models for assignment were subsequently used by CARL to map and merge predictions developed using rules of algebra with its other means of interpreting assignments.

Although CARL successfully related these two models of assignment, it did so only because it was dealing with very simple causal and behavioral models. Simple models are easily compared. CARL's only mechanism for merging the two models was to be able to do a match between the two models on the basis of their structure, much the same way that Winston (and more recently Falkenhainer) have done it. That is, the success of the merging process was dependent on an analogical structure-matching process that was designed to compare causal systems of actions and results. CARL's matcher was extended by relaxing the match process to allow the relation IMPLIES to be placed in correspondence with the relation CAUSES. Only through this relaxation, could CARL merge the representations of the two analogies.

We would now like to argue that more general knowledge about how behavioral models are related to causal models would allow these two models to be related in a principled way that is more robust than the relaxation method described herein. If the causal model involved had had more than one result, or the algebraic solution process had been represented more completely, the purely structural-matching process that CARL used would have failed to find the correct correspondence between these two models. However, full representations of behavioral models explicitly identify what their principal outputs are, and this information can be used to relate them to causal models, even when the causation is complex. This point motivates our current work on developing rules of mapping that explain how models of different types are related.

3. PURPOSE-GUIDED LEARNING AND PROBLEM SOLVING

Our current research is aimed at developing a theory covering the two related issues of mapping and integrating partial mental models.[7] Specifically, we are addressing the questions of: (1) how analogically based models of different types are mapped to a new domain, and (2) how these different kinds of partial models are integrated in a target domain.

---

[7] We call them partial models because they are representations of a specific aspect of the full mental model, addressing one of the levels of description listed in our taxonomy of types.

Both the mapping and integration components of our theory are being developed around a taxonomy of partial model types. The research presented in the remainder of this chapter is part of a series of experiments by which we hope to produce a detailed account of the process that maps and integrates partial models of various types. The protocols we have collected are being used to identify the kinds of relations that are (and are not) included in target models developed by mapping partial models of a given type. We have found that models of different types are distinguished by the different kinds relations that they contain, and thus models of a given type map to form new models of the same type (i.e., models containing the same relation). By making the distinction between model types explicit in our theory of analogical learning, we hope to provide an account of analogical mapping that has explicit pragmatic constraints on the amount and type of information mapped at one time from a base domain.

Integrating multiple models is an important part of the learning process, since there are many situations that can only be explained by a combination of inferences from several different partial models. As we will explain just below, we foresee that two kinds of integration processes may be used for combining partial analogical models. First, there is a reasoning process that functions to relate newly acquired partial models within a domain.[8] This process is based on principles about how, in general, partial models are interrelated. A second kind of integration process may be used when adapting partial models from an already active analogical source domain. In this case, information about how partial models are related in the source domain, can be used to avoid reasoning from first principles in the target domain. Since an understanding of the integration process is dependent on an understanding of the mapping process, we have chosen to focus first on the mapping process.

3.1. A Taxonomy of Explanatory Model Types

Our investigations of both the mapping and integration processes depend heavily on a well-defined taxonomy of model types. For our initial experiments, we have developed a working taxonomy which we expect will capture a broad set of models used in analogical learning (Fig. 6.7). In developing our taxonomy of models for analogical learning, we have revised a taxonomy developed initially to categorize explanations of complex physical systems (Collins, 1985; Stevens & Collins, 1980; Stevens & Steinberg, 1981). The taxonomy was formulated during the development of the STEAMER ICAI system (Williams, Hollan, & Stevens, 1981).

The data presented here are being used to develop a model of the

---

[8] This process is general to learning in that it functions whether the models have been acquired by analogy, or directly observation or instruction in the target domain.

- **Structural models** are used to describe systems in a time-invariant manner. Structural models include:

    1. **Componential models** simply list components.

    2. **Topological models** specify configurations where the logical or functional connections between components are preserved.

    3. **Geometric models** preserve the quantitative, spatial relations between components.

- **Dynamic models** describe changes that occur in a system over time. Dynamic models include:

    1. **Functional/Behavioral models** describe a system as a "black box", in terms of inputs and outputs.

    2. **Internal Structure models** break the system down into interactions between various components. These models include:

        - **Mechanistic Causal models** describe unique behaviors for each component and break events into causal chains. These include *Action Flow* models, where some substance or energy flows through the system and more abstract *Information Flow* models, where information is described as passing between components. These models typically dictate how the outputs of individual components cause state changes in other, topologically connected components, leading to an account of the behavior of the system as a whole.

        - **Aggregate models** describe systems where the components behave in a uniform manner, subject to global constraints. In these models, components are represented prototypically, in terms of general behavioral characteristics of the group. Individual features of components are represented by distributions of values.

        - **Synchronous models** describe causal systems where events or forces occur synchronously.

FIG. 6.7. A taxomony of model types.

analogical mapping process. Our theory suggests that a learner or problem solver has a purpose that highly constrains the type of model required and that this, in turn, affects the selection of base domain features and relationships for mapping during model construction.

As we have mentioned, different models, can be shown to be based on different structural relations (causal relations, function/goal relations, spatial, or topological relations, etc.). For example, within mechanistic causal models, temporal/causal relationships are used to relate the behaviors of a connected set of components, in order to explain a system's overall behavior. However, in aggregate models, local constraints are replaced by global constraints (e.g., conservation laws), and individual components give way to representative or prototypical entities with properties characterized as distributions.

3.2. Protocols of Mapping by Model Type

Our theory suggests that the type of model selected and mapped during learning is constrained by the aspect of the target situation made salient by the learning task. This prediction generates the following hypothesis:

When explaining a given aspect of a target domain, subjects should map only a subset of the base domain and that subset should be coherent[9] and reflective of the purpose of the learning task.

The following situation was used to provide a test of this hypothesis: Subjects with varying levels of programming expertise were provided with an analogical model of a computer-programming construct. The subjects were all näive to the target construct and familiar with its base domain analog. Subjects were then asked to answer a set of questions about various aspects of the initially unfamiliar target domain concept. This procedure was then repeated until subjects had been taught about the three constructs used in this study: queues, stacks, and sorting. As an example, Fig. 6.8 shows the texts used in teaching the concept of queues and the questions that subjects received following the texts.[10]

Our hypothesis that purpose constrains selection and mapping in a way that results in a coherent and appropriate partial mental model will be supported if subjects who have a complete base domain model map only the part of the base domain model that is relevant to the question they are answering.

In order to see whether subjects were selecting and mapping partial models, we constructed behavioral and causal representations for each of the concepts that the subjects had been taught (queues, stacks, and sorting). As an example, a sketch of our behavioral and causal representations for queues, in both the base and target domains, is given in Fig. 6.9. The representations can be thought of as vertical behavioral or causal chains, read from top to bottom.

The answers to each behavioral and causal question for each subject were recorded and analyzed to see how clearly they corresponded to our behavioral and causal representations of the concept. The number of times that elements from the causal or behavioral representations occurred was counted for both the behavioral and causal questions.

In answering behavioral questions about queues, stacks, and sorting, subjects made, on the average, 2.0 references to behavioral elements and no references to parts of the causal models that were not also part of the behavioral model. That is, all references to components of the causal models were references to elements that appeared in our representations of both

---

[9] In the sense suggested by Gentner's systematicity principle (Gentner, 1983).

[10] The full design of the study is not presented here. We selected behavioral and causal models as a subset of the taxonomy to work with in the pilot study. Text type was crossed with question type and order of presentation was counterbalanced over the full set of protocols; subjects received only one written description of the base domain situation which stressed either behavioral, causal or behavioral and causal aspects of the already familiar base domain situation. This was followed by a causal question, a behavioral question and a question about the relationship between behavior and causality. Differences in the written descriptions of the already familiar base domain did not have a discernible effect on the results described below.

Behavioral Analogy:

Frequently, at Mary Chung's (restaurant) there are people waiting to be seated. Mary keeps track of who to seat in such a way that the first person to be seated next is always the person who, among those currently waiting, came in first.

In sending files to the printer the same situation often occurs; several files need to be printed but only one can be printed at a time. In this case the computer resolves the problem in the same way that Mary does.

Causal Analogy:

Frequently at Mary Chung's, Mary has a list of people who are waiting to be seated and served. Whenever a person enters Mary puts their name at the bottom of the list. Whenever a table becomes vacant Mary calls the name at the top of the list, gives that person a table and then crosses that name off the list.

In sending files to the printer the same situation often occurs; several files need to be printed but only one can be printed at a time. In this case the computer resolves the problem in the same way that Mary does.

Behavioral Question: If Karen and then Janet and then Amy and then Karen all typed print commands one right after the other, in that order, what would the computer do?

Causal Question: Describe what you would do if you were the computer keeping track of print requests.

Behavioral/Causal Integration Question: Explain why/how the computer's method of keeping track of print requests produces the correct result? That is, what is the relationship between what gets done and how it gets accomplished?

FIG. 6.8. Presented versions of an analogy to queues.

the behavioral and the causal representation (Fig. 6.9), because they referred to the goal and starting states in those representations. No references were made to parts of the causal model that were purely descriptions of mechanism.

In answering causal questions about queues, stacks, and sorting, subjects made, on the average, 5.8 references to causal elements and on the average, .9 references to elements that were in both the causal and behavioral representations. Again, all of the behavioral elements that appeared in subjects' answers to causal questions were elements referring to the start and goal in those representations. This implies that a causal account of how something works is, in some sense, not coherent unless some goal- or purpose-oriented statement is included regarding why the mechanism is needed (Adelson, 1984).

It seems that, as our theory predicts, subjects are mapping coherent, purpose-oriented partial models from the target to the base domain, sufficiently to answer the questions asked.[11] The models are coherent in that

---

[11] We cannot, from these experiments, tell directly if more is mapped than is required to answer a question. However, a theory suggesting that more was mapped would have to explain why this information would be derived and then suppressed in answering the question asked.

Behavioral Model

Target		Base
Scene 1:		*Scene 1:*
Print file command issued.	[B1]	Patron enters restaurant.
	then	
	[B2]	Mary takes person's name.
	and	
File 'queued' for printing	[B3]	Patron waits till called.
	then	
(when print request is	[B4](when Patron is first among	
first among those remaining)		those waiting to arrive)
	then	
File is printed.	[B5] Patron is seated.	
	= Goal State	

Causal Model

Target		Base
Scene 1:		*Scene 1:*
Print file command issued.	[C1]	Patron enters restaurant.
	and	
Printer not free.	[C2]	All tables full.
	initiates	
	[C3]	Mary takes person's name.
	enables	
Request put on end of queue.	[C4]	Mary puts name on bottom of list.
	results	
File in queue	[C5]	Name on list
Scene 2:		*Scene 2:*
Printer free.	[C6]	Table empty.
	and	
File is on top of Queue	[C7]	Patron name is on top of list
	enables	
Queue pointer incremented	[C8]	Mary crosses out Patron's name.
	and	
File is Removed from Queue	[C9]	Mary calls Patron's name.
	enables	
	[C10]	Patron hears name
	initiates	
	[C11]	Patron goes to Mary
	enables	
File passed to Printer	[C12]	Patron follows Mary to table
	enables	
File is printed.	[C13]	Patron sits at table.
	= Goal State	

FIG. 6.9.   Base and target domain models of queues.

they provide an adequate basis for responding to questions of a given type. (This can be seen in the excerpts from the protocols that are to be presented.) The models are partial in that they do not provide a complete account of the system being examined.

If our result suggests that purpose, as characterized by the type of model, does constrain selection and mapping, it also confirms that there are interesting and intuitively plausible interdependencies between the kinds of information mapped with each type of model. Earlier we mentioned that any learning theory needed to include an account of how partial models were integrated. Our subjects' responses to behavioral and causal questions suggest that the initial and goal states that occur in both types of models can be used to provide a bridge between the two. This is an example of the kind of knowledge that is required for our postulated model integration process. That is, a behavioral and causal model of a given construct can be related by their shared start and goal states. Other types of models will need similar kinds of overlapping to be related to or integrated with each other. Since these criteria are not domain but model-type specific, the integration process should be applicable whether the models have been acquired through analogy or learned directly.

In the remainder of this section, we present excerpts from the protocols that motivate some central issues for theories of analogical learning.

Subject J[12] received the behavioral version of the analogy. She was then asked a behavioral question, as shown in Fig. 6.10.

J's last response, ("It's just like the thing you get when you call AAA,") is interesting because it brings up the issue of our theory's justification process in which newly mapped models are tested and debugged. After mapping the behavioral model, J is reminded of a recent situation where a computer-like machine was performing the kind of behavior she had just been told that computers use for print queues. That is, by our theory, when J mapped the behavioral model of first-come-first-serve from the Mary Chung (base) scenario to the computer (target) domain, she appropriately placed a computer in the "agent" role that Mary had played. This new behavioral description in the target domain then triggered a reminding of a similar behavioral model, where the agent, a machine similar to a computer, achieved the same goal (Schank, 1982). Recalling the behavior of the AAA phone system can be seen as an attempt by J to justify or test the adequacy of her newly formed behavioral model of a queue by comparing it with a similar, already-known behavioral model.

The fact that J could have mapped a causal model when answering the behavioral question, but did not do so seems clear when her response to the behavioral question is compared with her response to the causal question that followed (see Fig. 6.11).

J clearly has pieces of the causal mechanism, rather than a coherent causal model, since she is able to answer the causal question, but in a bit-by-bit rather than an all-of-a-piece manner. We attribute this to the fact that she did not receive an explicit description of a causal mode when first given the analogy.

---

[12] J is a researcher in music cognition and a self-taught (LOGO) programmer.

E: (*Behavioral Question:*) If Karen and then Janet and then Amy
       and then Karen all typed print commands, one right after the other,
       in that order, what would the computer do?

J: Give me the order again.

E: Karen, Janet, Amy, Karen.

J: All at the same moment?

E: One right after the other. So not exactly a tie.

J: Ok, well it would say that Karen is first...
       and, uh, it's just like, for me it's just like the thing
       you get when you call AAA and they tell you "Don't
       hang up, your calls are being taken in order."

FIG. 6.10.   A behavioral response to a behavioral question.

Another subject, K (Fig. 6.12), received the causal version of the analogy and then was asked a causal question.[13] K's answer is interesting because, for a nonprogrammer, she develops a surprisingly good causal model. She does this by using the analogically related causal description she had been given. As suggested above, in order to produce a well-motivated and coherent description, she includes the related behavioral goal in her mapping from the base domain.

After confirming that the computer could store a list, K correctly described the mechanism of the queue, by mapping the steps that pull requests off the front of the list and add new ones at the end (statements 2 and 4 respectively). K's description of this mechanism is a clear-cut example of a causal analogical mapping from an explicitly described base domain causal mechanism. It can be contrasted with subject L[14] (Fig. 6.13), who received the behavioral version of the analogy and was asked to describe the queue's causal mechanism.

Although we see in statement 2 that L clearly understood the function of a queue and her description of a mechanism satisfied that function, L's response to the causal question is interesting because it draws heavily on her knowledge of a base domain mechanism rather than a target domain mechanism. L chose to map a causal model by analogy from the base domain, despite the fact that she was not explicitly given a causal model

---

[13] K is an antique book dealer. She has used several PC-based software packages, but she does not program.
[14] L is a theater technician who does some programming as part of her technical work. L has approximately 2 years coursework experience with programming in Pascal and LISP.

E: (*Causal Question*:) Describe what you would do if you were
    the computer keeping track of print requests.

J: Label them, I suppose, or put them if you want to think of it
    spatially.

E: If you want to draw it ...

J: OK, you've got a potential for something like this...
                              (draws a row of boxes or 'slots')
    and you can *shove* things into these slots ...
    and Karen calls first
    so that becomes Karen,   *(writes Karen in 1st slot)*
    and Janet..
    and then Amy and then Karen   *(writes each name in a successive slot)*
    and I assume it's the same Karen. But, but, this (slot)
    is probably assigned some label like '1' and so she (Karen)
    will be '4' here and '1' there.
    So Karen is 4, or whatever,
    and when that is finished   *(points to the first slot)*
    this becomes '1'.   *(points to the second slot)*

    When that is finished   *(points to the second slot)*
    this becomes '1'.   *(points to the third slot)*

FIG. 6.11. A causal response to a causal question.

E: (*Causal Question*:) If Mark and Annie and Beth had typed requests
    to the computer, one after another, how would it (the computer)
    keep track of that?

K: Can the computer work like a calculator that has a memory?

E: Yes, it can. That's right, you can have told the computer in advance.

K: It can take all of these names, put it in the memory, and then
    pull the first one out.

E: Exactly right.

K: So that would be virtually the same thing. So as it's printed,
    it won't be in the memory anymore?

E: That's right. Let's say at this point Mark's stuff has been
    printed, and scratched off and Annies stuff and my stuff are
    waiting to be printed. Then Glenn down the hall, has something to
    be printed, where would the computer put that request, in order
    to keep track in just the same way Mary Chung kept track?

K: Well, it would have to have a program that would put that at the
    end of the list.

E: (*Behavioral Question:*) So what....describes how Mark
    got to be first?

K: First come first serve.

FIG. 6.12. K's responses.

E: Frequently at Mary Chung's there are people waiting to be seated.
Mary keeps track of who to see in such a way that the first person
to be seated next is always the person who among those currently waiting
came in first. Ok, so that's the analogy is that the next guy who is
going to get a seat is the one who ...

L: ... came in the longest period of time ago.

E: Yes, ok, now, in sending files to the printer the same situation
often occurs.. if you are not working on a personal computer. It is
that several files need to be printed, but only one can be printed at
a time. And in this case, the computer resolves the problem in the
same way that Mary does.

E: (Causal question:) Describe what you would do if you were the
computer keeping track of the print requests and you have a bunch
of requests at a particular time, and you can only print one at once,
and they came in at different times. Ok, so can you describe to me
how you would make this decision using the Mary Chung analogy.

L: I would give them all a number. And then whoever has the
lowest number gets seated next. Then I take that number and
throw it out. And so I don't have to worry about ever having to
start over again at number 1 and seating the last person who came
in out of order, because I am juggling my numbers as I go.
... I also used to work in a restaurants a lot.

FIG. 6.13. L's response.

of that domain and, could have generated a correct solution directly, rather than by analogy.[15]

L's generation of a causal model by analogy, using her knowledge of the restaurant (base) domain, rather than relying directly on her knowledge of programming suggests that domain-specific solutions to problems are not always preferred. Furthermore, the causal model that L retrieved was from a base domain situation that was not the one provided by the experimenter, but was instead familiar as a result of direct experience working in restaurants. This suggests that the base domain retrieval process, as well as the mapping process is quite complex. We suggest that it may be guided by a combination of factors: the type of explanation required; the problem-solving goal; and the currently salient attributes of the base domain model presented during learning. Holyoak (Holyoak, 1985) has also suggested a

---

[15] Evidence that L could describe a purely target domain solution to the problem was gathered in a follow-up session several weeks after this protocol was collected. In that session, L was asked to describe an implementation for a queue directly rather than by analogy. She first repeated her earlier answer, but when she was asked if the numbers were necessary, she responded that the ordering of the list was sufficient, and proceeded to describe the set of steps involved in using an ordered list to implement the queue; adding new entries to the end and removing the "next" item from the front.

model like this, although his model would not predict that an analogical solution might dominate an existing target domain solution. While our model also cannot account precisely for L's preference of a base-domain solution to the problem, the protocol clearly suggests that a full theory of analogical reasoning will need to include a fairly sophisticated account of the use of base domain features in the retrieval stage of the analogical reasoning process.

4. SUMMARY

In this chapter we have taken the position that analogical reasoning takes place within a context of learning and problem solving and that for a theory of analogy to be sufficient it must be developed within this context.

There is widespread agreement that the mapping process is a central part of analogical reasoning. Therefore theories of analogical reasoning need to account for this process in detail. However, the mapping process is complex. Developing a full and coherent model of a domain requires the use of many analogies, typically from more than one source domain. We suggest that two kinds of mechanisms are needed to address this issue. First, we believe that it is necessary to specify a mapping mechanism that is capable of relating models of a given type in different domains. To a lesser extent, this mechanism should be capable of relating the differing types of models that arise during learning. For complex systems, a second mechanism is needed to integrate widely different types of models, one that is sufficiently structured to preserve the contributions of each partial model, while building "bridges" to allow the different partial models to be used effectively together for problem solving.

The source domain models that provide good analogical examples for problem solving are also complex. Therefore, mechanisms are needed to constrain what is retrieved and mapped from a source domain. We have put forward the hypothesis, supported in part by our initial set of protocol experiments, that the goal or problem-solving purpose driving the analysis of the target problem strongly constrains this retrieval and mapping. For scientific analogies, the constraint appears to be based on the selection of a class of partial mental model best supporting the information requirements of the current problem-solving goal.

ACKNOWLEDGMENT

This work was supported in part by grants from ARI and NSF.

REFERENCES

Adelson, B. (1984). When novices surpass experts: How the difficulty of a task may increase with expertise. *Journal of Experimental Psychology: Learning, Memory and Cognition.*

Burstein, M. H. (1981). Concept formation through the interaction of multiple models. In *Proceedings of the 3rd Annual Conference of the Cognitive Science Society.* Hillsdale, NJ: Lawrence Erlbaum Associates.

Burstein, M. H. (1983). Concept Formation by Incremental Analogical Reasoning and Debugging. In Michalski, R. S., Carbonell, J. G. and Mitchel, T. M. (Eds.), *Proceedings of the International Machine Learning Workshop.* Champaign-Urbana, IL: University of Illinois. Also appears in *Machine Learning, 2,* 351–370. Morgan Kaufmann Publishers, Inc., Los Altos, CA.

Burstein, M. H. (1985). *Learning by Reasoning from Multiple Analogies* (doctoral dissertation). Yale University, New Haven, CT.

Burstein, M. H., & Adelson, B. (1987). Analogical learning: Mapping and integrating partial mental models. In *Proceedings of the Conference of the Cognitive Science Society.* University of Washington.

Carbonell, J. G. (1983). Learning by analogy: Formulating and generalizing plans from past experience. In R. S. Michalski, J. G. Carbonell, & T. M. Mitchell (Eds.), *Machine Learning: An Artificial Intelligence Approach.* Palo Alto, CA: Tiaoga.

Carbonell, J. G. (1986). Derivational analogy: A theory of reconstructive problem solving and expertise acquisition. In R. S. Michalski, J. G. Carbonell, & T. M. Mitchell (Eds.), *Machine Learning, 2.* Los Altos, CA: Morgan Kaufman.

Collins, A. (1985). Component models of physical systems. In *Proceedings of the 7th Annual Conference of the Cognitive Science Society.* Hillsdale, NJ: Lawrence Erlbaum Associates.

Collins, A., & Burstein, M. H. (1988). A framework for a theory of mapping. In S. Vosniadou & A. Ortony (Eds.), *Similarity and Analogical Reasoning.* New York: Cambridge University Press.

Collins, A., & Gentner, D. (1982). Constructing runnable mental models. In *Proceedings of the 4th Annual Conference of the Cognitive Science Society.* Boulder, CO: Cognitive Science Society.

Collins, A., & Gentner, D. (1983). Multiple models of evaporation processes. In *Proceedings of the 5th Annual Conference of the Cognitive Science Society.* Rochester, NY: Cognitive Science Society.

Collins, A., & Gentner, D. (1987). How people construct mental models. In N. Quinn & D. Holland (Eds.), *Cultural Models in Thought and Language.* Cambridge, England: Cambridge University Press.

Coulson, R., Feltovich, P., & Spiro, R. (1986). *Foundations of a Misunderstanding of the Ultrastructural Basis of Myocardial Failure: A Reciprocating Network of Oversimplifications* (Tech. Rep. No. 1). Southern Illinois University School of Medicine, Conceptual Knowledge Research Project, Springfield.

deKleer, J., & Brown, J. S. (1981). Mental Models of Physical Mechanisms and their Acquisition. In J. R. Anderson (Ed.), *Cognitive Skills and their Acquisition.* Hillsdale, NJ: Lawrence Erlbaum Associates.

Duncker, K. (1945). On problem solving. *Psychological Monographs, 58,* 270.

Evans, T. G. (1968). A program for the solution of geometric analogy intelligence test questions. In M. L. Minsky (Ed.), *Semantic Information Processing.* Cambridge, MA: MIT Press.

Falkenhainer, B. (1987). Scientific theory formation through analogical inference. In *Proceedings of the 4th International Workshop on Machine Learning.* Los Altos, CA: Morgan Kaufmann.

Falkenhainer, B., Forbus, K., & Gentner, D. (1986). The structure-mapping engine. In

Proceedings of AAAI–86. Los Altos, CA: Morgan Kaufman. Also appears as UIUC Tech. Rep. 4–86–1275, Champaign–Urbana, IL.

Gentner, D. (1980). Studies of metaphor and complex analogies: A structure-mapping theory. *Presented at the A.P.A. Symposium on Metaphor as Process.*

Gentner, D. (1982). Structure mapping: A theoretical framework for analogy and similarity. In *Proceedings of the 4th Annual Conference of the Cognitive Science Society.* Hillsdale, NJ: Lawrence Erlbaum Associates.

Gentner, D. (1983). Structure-mapping: A theoretical framework for analogy. *Cognitive Science, 7*(2), 155–170.

Gentner, D. (1988). The mechanisms of analogical learning. In S. Vosniadou & A. Ortony (Eds.), *Similarity and Analogical Reasoning.* New York: Cambridge University Press.

Gentner, D., & Gentner, D. R. (1983). Flowing waters or teeming crowds: Mental models of electricity. In D. Gentner & A. L. Stevens (Eds.), *Mental Models.* Hillsdale, NJ: Lawrence Erlbaum Associates.

Gentner, D., & Landers, R. (1985). Analogical reminding: A good match is hard to find. In *Proceedings of the International Conference on Systems, Man and Cybernetics.* Tucson: University of Arizona.

Gentner, D., & Stuart, P. (1983). *Metaphor as structure-mapping: What develops* (Tech. Rep. No. 5479). Cambridge, MA: Bolt Beranek, & Newman.

Gentner, D., & Toupin, C. (1986). Systematicity and surface similarity in the development of analogy. *Cognitive Science, 10,* 277–300.

Gick, M. L., & Holyoak, K. J. (1980). Analogical problem solving. *Cognitive Psychology, 12,* 306–355.

Hesse, M. B. (1966). *Models and analogies in science.* Notre Dame, In: University of Notre Dame Press.

Holyoak, K. J. (1985). The pragmatics of analogical transfer. In G. H. Bower (Ed.), *The psychology of learning and motivation.* New York: Academic Press.

Holyoak, K. J., & Thagard, P. R. (1988). Rule-based spreading activation and analogical transfer. In A. Prieditis (Ed.), *ANALOGICA: The First Workshop on Analogical Reasoning.* Boston: Pitman.

Indurkhya, B. (1985). *Constrained semantic transference: A formal theory of metaphors* (Tech. Rep. 85/008). Boston University Computer Science.

Kedar–Cabelli, S. (1985). *Analogy from a unified perspective.* (Tech. Rep. ML–TR–3). Laboratory for Computer Science Research, Rutgers University, New Brunswick, NJ.

Kolodner, J. L. (1980). *Retrieval and organizational strategies in conceptual memory: A computer model* (Tech. Rep. No. 187). Yale University, Department of Computer Science, New Haven, CT.

Lebowitz, M. (1980, October). *Generalization and Memory in an Integrated Understanding System.* (Tech. Rep. No. 186). Yale University, Department of Computer Science, New Haven, CT.

Newell, A., & Simon, H. (1972). *Human problem solving.* Englewood Cliffs, NJ: Prentice–Hall.

Ortony, A. (1979). Beyond literal similarity. *Psychological Review, 87,* 161–180.

Reed, S. K. (1987). A structure-mapping model for word problems. *Journal of Experimental Psychology: Learning, Memory and Cognition, 13,* 124–139.

Roberts, B., & Goldstein, I. P. (1977). *The FRL manual* (A. I. Lab. Memo 409). Cambridge, MA: MIT Press.

Rumelhart, D. E., & Norman, D. A. (1981). Analogical processes in learning. In J. R. Anderson (Ed.), *Cognitive skills and their acquisition.* Hillsdale, NJ: Lawrence Erlbaum Associates.

Schank, R. C. (1982). *Dynamic memory: A theory of learning in computers and people.* New York: Cambridge University Press.

Schank, R. C., & Abelson, R. (1977). *Scripts, plans, goals and understanding*. Hillsdale, NJ: Lawrence Erlbaum Associates.

Skorstad, J., Falkenhainer, B., & Gentner, D. (1987). Analogical processing: Simulation and empirical corroboration. In *Proceedings of the 6th National Conference on Artificial Intelligence*. Los Altos, CA: Morgan Kaufmann.

Spiro, R. J., Feltovich, P. J., Coulson, R. L., & Anderson, D. (1988). Multiple analogies for complex concepts: Antidotes for analogy-induced misconception in advanced knowledge acquisition. In S. Vosniadou & A. Ortony (Eds.), *Similarity and analogical reasoning*. New York: Cambridge University Press.

Sternberg, R. J., & Adelson, B. (1978). Changes in cognitive structure via metaphor. In *Annual Meeting of the Psychonomic Society*. San Antonio, TX.

Stevens, A., & Collins, A. (1980). Multiple conceptual models of a complex system. In R. E. Snow, P. Federico, & W. E. Montague (Eds.), *Aptitude, learning, and instruction*. Hillsdale, NJ: Lawrence Erlbaum Associates.

Stevens, A., & Steinberg, C. (1981, March). *A typology of explanations and its application to intelligent computer aided instruction* (Tech. Rep. No. 4626). Cambridge, MA: Bolt, Beranek, & Newman.

Thagard, P., & Holyoak, K. (1985). Discovering the wave theory of sound: Inductive inference in the context of problem solving. In *Proceedings of the 9th IJCAI*. Los Altos, CA: Morgan Kaufman.

VanLehn, K., & Brown, J. (1980). Planning nets: A representation for formalizing analogies and semantic models of procedural skills. In R. E. Snow, P. Federico, & W. E. Montague (Eds.), *Aptitude, learning and instruction, 2*. Hillsdale, NJ: Lawrence Erlbaum, Associates.

Verbrugge, R. R., & McCarrell, N. S. (1977). Metaphoric comprehension: Studies in remaining and resembling. *Cognitive Psychology, 9*, 494–533.

Williams, M., Hollan, J., & Stevens, A. (1981). Human reasoning about a simple physical system. In D. Gentner & A. Stevens (Eds.), *Mental models*. Hillsdale, NJ: Lawrence Erlbaum Associates.

Winston, P. H. (1980, May). *Learning and reasoning by analogy: The details* (Tech. Rep. No. 520). MIT A.I. Memo, Cambridge, MA.

Winston, P. H. (1982). Learning new principles from precedents and exercises. *Artificial Intelligence, 19*, 321–350.

7

The Access and Use of Relevant Information: A Specific Case and General Issues

Brian H. Ross
Department of Psychology
University of Illinois

A central issue in cognition is how people access and use relevant information. To perform any cognitive task, a person has to retrieve some information from memory and apply it to the task. For routine cognitive tasks, such as the text-editing operations used by experts (Card, Moran, & Newell, 1980), the information needed may be readily accessible from the person's representation of the task and the retrieved rules may specify exactly how to perform the task. In many nonroutine situations, however, the access of the needed information may not be easy and any accessed information may require modification before it can be applied. For instance, in solving variations of well-learned problems, the relevant information may be accessible from the representation of the problem, but this information may not be applicable without considerable modification. In learning, a common difficulty even once the procedure for accomplishing a task is known is that learners are not sure of the applicability conditions, that is, when to access the relevant procedure (e.g., Larkin, 1981). An important part of learning is developing ways of encoding tasks so that problem representations will successfully evoke the appropriate task information. In solving novel problems, the representation of the problem may often not access the relevant information and, even when it does, any retrieved information may not be easily applied. Thus, how relevant information is accessed and applied are important general issues for a variety of research in problem solving and learning. In addition to the points mentioned so far, it is likely that accessing and using relevant information will result in a modification of this information so that it may be more easily evoked and applied on subsequent occasions.

A major difficulty in investigating how relevant information is accessed and used is gaining any control over what knowledge a person *could* bring to bear in any particular situation. Not only is this information hard to control but, given the large differences in experiences and learning across individuals, it is not possible to even assess what knowledge could be brought to bear. In my research, I have opted for studying these processes in a very restricted setting by having people learn new cognitive skills for which pre-experimental knowledge is only weakly useful. That is, although prior knowledge can be used to some extent in all problem-solving and learning situations, it is not likely that these learners have specific pre-experimental knowledge that will enable them to accomplish the tasks that are taught. In addition, I further restrict the investigation by focusing on a particular type of relevant information, earlier examples.

The choice of earlier examples has two motivations. First, earlier examples provide a particularly obvious instance of the access and use of relevant information, and thus one that is relatively easy to observe and measure. As will be seen, the superficial aspects that examples include are an especially useful means of assessing the extent to which this type of relevant information is being used. Second, this use of earlier examples in learning is interesting in its own right. Anecdotally, many people report that they often think of earlier examples when trying to solve a problem during learning. That is, current problems often *remind* them of earlier problems and they make use of these earlier examples in solving the current problems. Thus, the remindings of these earlier examples may be a common occurrence in learning. In addition, as will be shown, these remindings can have large effects on performance and affect later performance as well. Remindings and the subsequent use of earlier examples appear to be one means that novices have of solving problems in a new domain and learning about the domain.

In this chapter, I will report research on these remindings that I think addresses some issues of general interest on the access and use of relevant information, as well as some issues of particular interest for testing. The organization is as follows. First, I will present a framework I have been using to guide my research on remindings. The parts of this framework will then be described in more detail using results from psychological experiments. Next, these results will be used to investigate whether there may be individual differences in the conditions and means by which learners make use of earlier examples. Following this examination, I will address some implications of this work for general issues in the access and use of relevant information. Finally, I speculatively consider some implications of these ideas for testing.

REMINDINGS IN PROBLEM SOLVING AND LEARNING

A Framework for Remindings

In an earlier paper (Ross, 1984), I proposed a general framework for considering the retrieval and use of remindings during problem solving. The framework assumes that the retrieval is part of the usual way in which information is retrieved from memory. There is no attempt to model the details of this retrieval (e.g., Ratcliff, 1978), but rather to take the perspective that memory probes are formed, memory is interrogated, and some memory trace or record that at least partly matches this probe is returned (e.g., Norman & Bobrow, 1979). The only distinguishing aspects of any retrieval, then, are what is included in the probe and what is retrieved. The learners are presumed to probe their memory for relevant information, using information gathered from their goal and their representation of the problem. What is retrieved is determined by the match between this probe and the information the learner has in memory. A reminding occurs when the match that results is of an earlier example or experience. Thus, remindings are presumed to be products of the usual retrieval process. They differ from other retrievals only in that they contain information about a particular example or experience. (Note that this captures much of the common use of the term "reminding," but does not include cases in which what is remembered is not episode-specific, as in being reminded of a well-known object. This restriction is not a claim about different processes in the two cases, but just an attempt to delineate the types of remindings that will be covered in this chapter.)

Within this general framework, four processes are assumed to operate when remindings occur and are used: noticing, reconstruction, analogy, and generalization. First, if the matching information retrieved by the probe is an earlier example, the learner is said to *notice* an earlier example (i.e., be reminded). Noticing simply refers to the learner's realization that an earlier example has been thought of. In itself, this noticing does not mean that the earlier example may be used. To make use of the earlier example, it must be remembered and then applied. (As will be seen later, these processes are not meant to occur in a totally serial fashion.) The remembering of the earlier example is assumed to involve *reconstruction*. The application of this earlier example to the current problem is assumed to involve some mapping of the problem aspects, as in analogy. Finally, the framework assumes that this analogical mapping forces some small *generalization* as some of the distinctive parts of the different problems are realized to be unimportant. This generalization will not usually be as general as the principle, but will combine aspects of the two problems from which it arises. In solving later problems, the probe may retrieve this generalization instead of one of the examples, which will result in still further generalization.

One point requiring discussion is whether remindings necessarily involve conscious realization, as I have implied. It is clear that earlier experiences can affect performance without awareness (e.g., Jacoby & Dallas, 1981). In the early research I conducted by collecting protocols of learners thinking aloud, I focused on the conscious (and verbalized) remindings, because of their availability. Much of the research to be reported examines the effects of earlier examples, without distinguishing verbalized from nonverbalized instances (i.e., these are studies that do not involve protocol collections). It is an open question as to what qualitative differences, if any, exist between the remindings I examine and the more implicit uses of earlier experiences.

Method and a Similarity Distribution

The explanation of the results will be facilitated if the reader understands the general method used as well as the distinction between superficial and structural similarity. The method upon which most of the results have been based is a simple one in which learners are first instructed in some new domain that consists of a number of learning units (e.g., editing operations, probability principles) and are then given tasks to solve that require this studied information (e.g., editing tasks, probability problems). The further details are easier to understand if a particular situation is used, so I will use the probability theory domain, which has been the primary one used in my research. The learning phase includes both abstract information about the principle being learned (such as the formula and what the principle is for) as well as an example that illustrates this principle. This example is a typical word problem and learners are required to work it out, being guided by a workbook format. In the test phase, learners are given word problems to solve that require these principles.

The primary manipulation that has allowed me to make inferences about whether and how the earlier example is being used is the similarity between the study example and test problem. I will first illustrate this, using an earlier experiment and I will then contrast the types of similarity that may be involved in remindings.

Ross (1984, Ex. 2) demonstrated that learners' solutions to problems may be affected by what earlier example the current one reminds them of. The design of this study is illustrated schematically in Table 7.1. Each subject learned six principles of probability (e.g., permutations, combinations, waiting time) using the method just described. The word problems

TABLE 7.1
Design of Ross (1984, Experiment 2)

Principle[a]	Word Problem Contents[b]		Condition[c]
	Study	Test	
1	A	A	Appropriate
2	B	B	
3	C	G	Unrelated
4	D	H	
5	E	F	Inappropriate
6	F	E	

Note: Each subject received 2 principles in each condition. Principles and contents were counterbalanced over subjects.

[a] Principles: permutations, combinations waiting time, at least one in t trials, either or both, conditional probability.
[b] Each letter represents a different story content for the word problem.
[c] Conditions refer to the study-test contents. See text for a full description.

that were used to illustrate these principles each used a different story line (e.g., IBM workers, golfers, dance contest). The test problems varied in their similarity to the earlier examples. The story line for these problems was either the same as for the study example that illustrated that principle (appropriate condition), a story line not shown before (unrelated condition), or a story line used with a study example for a different principle (inappropriate condition). The logic behind the experiment was that if the superficial story-line information was influencing which earlier example the learner thought back to and if the earlier examples were used to help solve the test problems, then performance would differ across these conditions. In particular, compared with the unrelated control condition, the appropriate condition should show improved performance, since learners would remember an appropriate study example, while the inappropriate condition should show worse performance. The results were as predicted by this idea of remindings, with proportions correct of .77, .43, and .22 for the appropriate, unrelated, and inappropriate conditions, respectively. Note that the last two conditions involved exactly the same study–test problem pairings, with the only difference being whether the principle paired with it used a similar story line or not. Despite this minor difference, these conditions showed a two-to-one difference in performance as a function of the story lines used in the other principles.

This earlier experiment demonstrates that remindings can have large effects on performance, even if the reminding is based on purely superficial aspects of the problems. In some of the work to be presented, distinctions will be made within and between superficial and structural aspects of problems (aspects are used to refer to features within a single problem, while similarity refers to the relation of these aspects between two problems). This distinction is an important one for much research in the access and use of relevant information (e.g., Holyoak, 1985; Gentner & Landers, 1985). Table 7.2 gives some instances of the examples used in this research. Superficial aspects will be used to refer to those aspects such that changing them would not result in any change in the problem's solution. Thus, story lines and the particular objects used are superficial aspects of the problem. In the example about IBM mechanics, the name of the company could be changed with no change in the problem solution. In addition, the fact that it is cars that are being fixed is unimportant for the solution, as are many of the other specific aspects of the problem. Later, I will make further distinctions about these superficial similarities. Structural aspects are those aspects such that changing them would result in a change in the problem's solution. For instance, in waiting-time problems, if the trials were not independent or if the question was the probability of one success anytime during these trials, the solution would change.

TABLE 7.2
Examples of Word Problems Used in the Experiments

Permutations: The IBM motor pool has to make sure the company cars are serviced. On a particular day there are 11 cars and 8 mechanics. The IBM mechanics randomly choose which car they will work on, but the choice is done by seniority. What is the probability that the 3 most senior mechanics, Al, Bud, and Carl will choose the cars of the Chairman, President and Vice-president, respectively?

Combinations: The Nashville Gnats baseball team has 20 players that are going on a road trip to play in a nearby town. The bus has 25 seats. To avoid arguments, the manager randomly chooses a seat for each of the 20 players. What is the probability that the 6 pitchers get the 6 front seats?

Waiting time: The weather forecast is for snow. On each of the next 6 days, there is a 2/7 chance of snow and a 5/7 chance of no snow. What is the probability that the first snow of the week is on the third day?

At least once: Gino's Pizza Restaurant has 2 types of pizza toppings they are known for, anchovies and salami, 1 of which they put on each pizza. From experience, they know that 1/5 of the people order anchovy and 4/5 order salami. Of 9 pizzas ordered one night, 3 are large. What is the probability that at least one of the large pizzas will have anchovy?

Recent Work on Remindings

In this section, I outline briefly my research on these different aspects of remindings, as well as some of the other research on this issue. The purpose of this review is to bring out ideas that will be useful for understanding the later sections of this chapter. More details of this work may be found in Ross (1984, 1987, 1989a; Ross & Kennedy, 1990; Ross & Sofka, 1986).

Noticing. What makes people think back to particular earlier examples? To understand this noticing, I think it is crucial to understand two points. First, there is nothing special about remindings. That is, remindings are not some special memory retrieval, but simply use the same retrieval process as do all other cases in which memory is probed. Second, the probes that lead to remindings are presumably formulated in the course of problem representation and problem solving. Learners are not trying to remember an earlier example, but rather trying to solve the current problem. Therefore, any probes that lead to reminding must be formulated with this goal in mind. Remindings may be considered incidental in many cases, in the sense that they occur not as a response to some specific memory retrieval attempt aimed at them, but rather in response to a probe for information relevant to solving the current problem. This idea will be discussed more fully later.

These two points about noticing help in understanding some of the results. A number of findings demonstrate how usual memory factors affect retrieval. First, similarity (in this case, between study and test problems) is a crucial determinant of noticing, as it is in almost all views of memory retrieval (e.g., Anderson, 1983; Ratcliff, 1978; Tulving, 1983). As mentioned earlier, similarities between problems may be either superficial or structural. The evidence suggests that both types of similarity affect noticing (e.g., Gentner & Landers, 1985; Holyoak & Koh, 1987; Novick, 1988; Ross, 1984, 1987). Second, it is necessary to view similarity not as some absolute measure between problems, but as a relative measure. That is, the likelihood that a test problem will remind a learner of a particular earlier example is a function of the similarity between these two problems, relative to the similarity between the test problem and all other information in memory (see Ross, 1987, Ex. 2, for an experimental demonstration of this idea). For a given earlier example and test problem, the noticing will depend on whether the learner might have any other information which is also similar to the test problem. This idea will be crucial later in understanding both individual differences and more general issues related to remindings. Third, and further supporting this memory perspective, these remindings show other common memory effects, such as interference (Ross, 1984, Ex. 3).

Reconstruction.   Noticing is not enough to affect performance. This earlier example must be remembered in enough detail to be used and then must be used. The remembering of the earlier example details appears to be very reconstructive in character (Ross & Sofka, 1986). Learners recall fragments of earlier problems and piece them together. Although much of this work with Michael Sofka will not be needed for the later discussions, one point is relevant. Learners who are reminded of an earlier example when presented with a test problem do not have available much higher-level (schematic) knowledge to guide their reconstruction, but they do have available a test problem. What we observed is that learners often used this test problem not only to remind them of an earlier example, but to guide their reconstruction as well. For instance, if they saw that the test problem had two types of objects, that would clue them that the study example probably did too. In this way, the reconstruction made use even of the details of the test problem and provided an interleaving of the memory for the earlier example and how its details were related to the current problem.

Analogy.   How are these remembered examples used? That is, given that remindings are affecting performance, how does this occur? We may distinguish two general ways. (This discussion is elaborated in Ross, 1987, where these results are presented in detail.) One, when learners are reminded of an earlier example, they may think of the formula that it illustrated. Two, learners may make an analogy between the details of the current problem and earlier example. By the first explanation, the remindings serve to cue the appropriate abstract information, such as a formula, while by the second explanation any cuing is simply the beginning of the use of the earlier example, not the end of its use. To contrast these alternatives, one needs a test in which all conditions provide equal cuing, but differ in the usefulness of analogy. The first requirement was met by providing the appropriate formula at test and asking subjects simply to fill in both the variables from the numbers in the word problem. The second requirement was met by varying whether the objects in the study and test problems were the same or not and, if they were, how they corresponded to the use in the earlier example.

To elaborate this second point, if novices are making use of the details of the earlier example it is likely that they are relying on the superficial similarities between the two problems to figure out how to instantiate the variables (e.g., Chi, Feltovich, & Glaser, 1981). If so, when given problems with similar objects these learners would be likely to assign the objects to the same variable roles in the test problem that they were assigned to in the study example. For instance, if the study example had cars being assigned to mechanics, so that for permutations the number of cars would be the total number of items and the number of mechanics would be the number of items selected, the test problem could have the same assignment or it could have mechanics assigned to cars (so that the number of mechanics should now fill the variable used for cars in the first example). Thus, if the correspondence of objects between the study and test problems is varied, we can tell whether subjects are making use of the details of the earlier example. The prediction of the analogy explanation would be that, compared with a baseline of unrelated objects, having objects fill the same variable roles in both problems should lead to improved performance while reversing the variable roles should lead to worse performance. In support of this analogy interpretation, compared with baseline performance of about .55, the same and reversed variable role conditions yielded proportions of correctly instantiated formulas of .74 and .37, respectively. Ross (1989a) shows that this effect does not depend on having similar story lines between study and test problems, just similar objects.

The findings lead to four points, some of which will be elaborated in the section on general issues. First, this study shows that earlier examples are used by analogy. While other research shows that subjects *can* make analogies, at least when they are told to use the information (e.g., Gick & Holyoak, 1980, 1983), in those cases subjects are not explicitly provided with a formula at study and test, so if they were to use the earlier example at all, it had to be by analogy. This experiment demonstrates that even when other information may be provided, subjects will sometimes rely on the detailed correspondences to the earlier problem to make the analogy. Second, it provides some details on how this analogy is made by novices. In particular, it shows that similar objects tend to be assigned to similar variable roles. Third, it shows that superficial similarities not only affect noticing, but may affect the use of the earlier examples as well. Finally, and perhaps most importantly, it points out that novices' understanding of how to use the formula is bound up with the example that was used to illustrate this formula. Dellarosa (1985) and Cheng, Holyoak, Nisbett, and Oliver (1986), among others, suggest that examples are important in showing how abstract concepts are instantiated. An unwanted consequence of this illustration, however, is that the understanding of the principle may be in terms of this example. This idea is an important one for understanding problem-solving behavior and will be discussed in detail later.

Later Effects on Performance. My most recent work addresses how remindings might have effects on later performance. The idea behind this effect, sketched in Ross (1984), is that if learners are thinking back to earlier examples and applying them by analogy to current problems, that they may learn something about problems of this type by this problem-solving behavior. In particular, it is possible that the act of applying the earlier example to the current one makes the learner notice that some aspects of the problems need to be irrelevant for the analogy to work. This proposal is elaborated in Ross and Kennedy (1990), but it is essentially a view in which there is no separate generalization process, but rather the learning occurs as a by-product of the problem solving (see Anderson, 1986; Kolodner, Simpson, & Sycara–Cyranski, 1985; Pirolli & Anderson, 1985, for similar proposals).

My research on this topic has proceeded along two lines. Most closely tied to the work presented so far, I have examined the effects that thinking back to earlier examples has on later performance. Ross and Kennedy (1990) control remindings by explicitly cuing subjects with the appropriate earlier example ("This is like the mechanics and cars problem") or not on the first test. After this test, subjects are provided with the answers. Of interest is how this manipulation affects performance on a second test (which is uncued for both conditions). The experiments show that this cuing on first tests affects second test performance. More specifically, for those principles in which subjects are cued on the first test, second-test performance is improved in two ways. First, cuing on the first test leads to better access of the appropriate formula on the second test. Second, if subjects are provided with the appropriate formula on the second test, they are better able to instantiate the variables for the principles that were cued on the first test. Thus the thinking back to earlier examples affects both the access and use of the appropriate formula.

The second line of research, conducted in collaboration with Susan Perkins and Patricia Tenpenny, is concerned with how this analogical use might affect what is learned in a rather different and simplified setting, categorization. Some models of categorization suggest that people sometimes categorize new items by their similarity to old items (Brooks, 1978; Medin & Schaffer, 1978). By this view, when a new item is presented, learners may think back to an old item that this new item is very similar to and classify it in the same way the earlier item was classified. Clearly, this view is much like the reminding idea presented for problem solving. My current research shows that such use of earlier instances affects what is learned about the category. That is, as predicted by the view presented here, which earlier item is used to categorize a new item affects people's later judgments of the category (Ross, Perkins, & Tenpenny, in press). Thus, the reminding is having an effect on how people view these categories (also see Anderson, 1986, and Medin & Edelson, 1988, for related views).

These two lines of research both show effects of remindings on later performance. Although the theoretical mechanisms by which these effects occur is under investigation, some general comments may be helpful in understanding the significance of these results. The idea is that the problem solving (or categorization) results in learning as an incidental by-product. Because the reminding may be by any similarity, but the learning that results may involve generalizing over the differences, the basis of the reminding may be very different from what is learned by using the reminding. For example, in the problem solving, a similar story line may allow subjects to notice an earlier example, but the details of correspondences will affect what is learned. Speculatively, perhaps this is one means by which novices go from a reliance on superficial aspects toward more of a reliance on structural aspects (Chi et al., 1981).

Summary

This section has summarized some results from my research on the access and use of earlier examples during learning, as well as on the effects of this use on later performance. Although these processes require further elaboration, it is clear that this "simple" case of the access and use of relevant information is quite complex. The learner notices an earlier example on the basis of some (often superficial) similarity. In remembering the earlier example enough to make use of it, the learner relies upon the current problem to guide and stimulate reconstruction. Thus, the reconstruction and analogy are interleaved, since by the time the learner has remembered the earlier problem, many of the correspondences to the current problem have already been established. However, the effects of superficial similarities (such as object correspondences) do not depend on this route. Even if learners are provided with the appropriate formula at test, they make use of the details of the earlier example for understanding how to instantiate this formula. Finally, two lines of recent research were outlined that show effects of this use on later performance, although the exact mechanism by which this effect comes about is not yet clear.

INDIVIDUAL DIFFERENCES IN REMINDINGS

The research just reviewed provides some ideas on how people notice and make use of earlier examples during learning, as well as how they might learn from this use of examples. Given the nature of this volume, it seemed appropriate to examine individual differences in my experiments. How might these ideas help in understanding differences in how people solve problems and learn?

Because my research has not been focusing on individual differences, I do not have subjects take independent tests on which I may assess their abilities. Rather, I usually divide subjects into halves or thirds, based on their overall performance on the test problems. The "individual differences" I will be referring to, then, are between these groups. Clearly, higher performing subjects will have higher performance in most, in fact usually all, conditions. (For brevity in exposition, I will refer to these groups as *high* and *low* subjects.) My use of these groups, however, is to examine differences in the pattern of this performance across the conditions. These differences that I focus on are usually logically independent of overall performance. I do find differences in patterns of performance, but these patterns change with experiments. Can any more general statement be made than that? In this section, I speculate about this possibility. To understand these ideas, it is necessary to understand two types of measures that I use in examining these differences; protocol-based and performance-based measures (see Ross, 1989b, for a lengthier discussion). Protocol-based measures separate tests by whether the learner explicitly mentions an earlier example or does not. This measure allows a comparison between tests in which learners clearly thought of an earlier example with tests in which they were less likely to have thought of an earlier example (they may have thought of an earlier example, but failed to verbalize this thought). Performance-based measures use performance across different conditions to make inferences about the effect of earlier examples. In particular, compared with performance in a condition with unrelated study and test examples, we may use performance in other conditions to gauge the extent to which earlier examples are used. In an appropriate reminding condition (i.e., where the superficial similarity between study and test would lead the learner to make use of an appropriate earlier example as in Table 7.1), any increase in performance over the baseline is presumed to be due to the noticing and use of the superficially similar example. Similarly, any decrease in performance in the inappropriate condition is presumed to be due to the noticing and use of the inappropriate, but superficially similar, example.

As I mentioned, empirically the results are messy. Although there are differences in performance patterns of high and low subjects, these patterns change with experiments. To try and make sense of these changes, I will examine the question of differences by breaking it down into two questions. First, are there differences in *when* high and low subjects make use of earlier examples? Second, are there differences in *how* high and low subjects make use of earlier examples? The means by which I determine these groups require that I consider these results to be speculative. I offer them because I think some of the possibilities are interesting and, if true, may have implications for testing.

Differences in When Earlier Examples are Used

Any problem-solving system that makes use of remindings needs to consider that remindings are just one type of relevant information. A common assumption (e.g., Pirolli and Anderson, 1985; Ross & Moran, 1983) is that people may retrieve earlier examples when no other more directly relevant information is available. That is, if problem solvers have well-learned procedures for accomplishing the task or can readily infer these procedures, earlier examples may not be accessed and used. A slightly different, and perhaps more general, view (e.g., Anderson & Thompson, 1989; Ross, 1984, 1989b) is that remindings are retrieved in the same way as other relevant information. Thus, whether remindings occur before other relevant information is retrieved depends on the usual memory retrieval factors, such as how well learned and understood the different types of relevant information are and how well they match the current memory probe.

The possibility that other information could be used to accomplish the task makes the analysis of individual differences particularly difficult. If no other means of solution were possible other than relying on earlier examples, the subjects who had higher overall performance would be those who were better able to access and make use of earlier examples. We could then analyze the details of their performance to find out what parts of reminding access and use are higher than for the subjects who do not perform as well. The difficulty, however, is that often there do exist other means of solutions and the high subjects are probably more likely to make use of those other means. Thus, if a procedure or principle is explicitly given at learning along with an example to illustrate it (as is true in all my cognitive skill learning experiments), it is likely that some subset of the subjects will be particularly adept, will learn these principles, and do well on the test problems without having to rely extensively on the earlier example. This idea is supported by results showing that high subjects may be more likely to learn (and recall) structural information from a single example (e.g., Krutetskii, 1976; Silver, 1979, 1981).

This idea may be made concrete by using some of the results from Ross and Sofka (1986; this particular breakdown of the data is not included in the paper). In the first two studies of that paper, subjects learned four probability theory principles by being given the principle, an explanation of the principle, and the formula for applying this principle. In addition, the subjects received either one or two examples that illustrated each principle. The idea behind the experiment was that we could use the reminding data during the solution of later test problems (in terms of whether subjects, who were thinking aloud, explicitly mentioned an earlier example or not) to separate out specific (reminding) and schematic effects. (The logic is more complicated than that, but the basic idea is that the cases in which subjects mention an earlier example are more likely to be solved using an earlier example than are cases in which no earlier example is mentioned. The schematic test trials presumably include cases in which other, perhaps schematic, relevant information was used, no relevant information was used, or some small number of times when an earlier example was used but not mentioned.) The two experiments varied whether the test problems had superficial contents that were similar or dissimilar to the learning examples. For our present purposes, the important result is the pattern of performance across the conditions for the high- and low-performing subjects. The overall results are shown in Table 7.3 with the important difference being that between the high and low subjects at each condition. The pattern is very similar across the two experiments. High subjects show substantially higher performance than low subjects for the conditions with two learning examples, with differences in proportion correct of .24 and .28 for the two experiments. For the single learning example with a superficially similar test (A-a), however, the pattern changes dramatically with differences between high and low subjects of .46 for both Experiments 1 and 2. (It is difficult to interpret the differences in the final condition of one learning example with a superficially dissimilar test problem, A-b, because of the poor performance even for high subjects). These differences may be broken down further than in the table, by whether a reminding occurred or not. For the conditions with two learning examples, the difference between high and low subjects was about the same for tests with and without remindings. For condition A-a, however, the difference between high and low subjects changed dramatically. Although the difference for reminding trials is about the same as the differences already considered (.26 in Ex. 1, .34 in Ex. 2), the difference for tests in which no remindings occurred showed a much larger difference for both experiments (.59 and .57, respectively). One interpretation of this finding is that the high subjects are able to extract some structural aspects even with one

TABLE 7.3
Proportions Correct for High and Low
Subjects in Ross and Sofka (1986)

	Conditions			
Expt. 1	AA-a[a]	AB-a	A-a	A-b
High	.58	.55	.66	.31
Low	.35	.31	.20	.05
Difference	.23	.24	.46	.26
Expt. 2	AA-b	AB-c	A-a	A-b
High	.62	.68	.51	.30
Low	.34	.40	.05	.01
Difference	.28	.28	.46	.29

Note: 24 subjects per group (48 per experiment), each contributing one observation per condition.

[a] Capital letters indicate learning examples, lowercase indicate test. The same letter indicates superficially similar examples. Thus, AB-a indicates two superficially unrelated learning examples with a test problem superficially similar to one of them.

learning example. Thus, on the no reminding trials, high subjects had other relevant information that they could make use of while the low subjects did not. This extended discussion of the role of other relevant information serves to highlight the difficulty one has in using simple measures of reminding effects as an indication of ability.

The conjecture to be briefly examined here is that if the tasks being learned are not very difficult to understand and learn procedures for, then the better subjects will learn these tasks and procedures and, thus, show little effect of remindings. The low subjects, however, will often not learn these procedures and, hence, need to rely on earlier examples to solve later problems. If the tasks being learned are very difficult to understand or to learn the procedures for, then both groups of subjects will rely on remindings. In this latter case, however, the relative effects of these remindings in the two groups will probably depend on details of the tests and the extent to which the learners can make use of the remindings (both of which will be discussed shortly).

Although I have no firm evidence favoring this conjecture, Tables 7.4 and 7.5 present data consistent with such an explanation. In Table 7.4, some results of Experiment 1 in Ross (1984) are provided. In this experiment, subjects learned several text-editing operations, with two methods for each operation, each of which was taught with a different text content (e.g., shopping list, restaurant review). At test, subjects were given an editing task, with the text content being similar to one of the earlier contents. The idea was that if subjects were reminded of the earlier text, they would be more likely to use the method taught with that content. For those first tests in which remindings occurred, about 30% of the tests, subjects

TABLE 7.4
Ross (1984, Experiment 1) First Test Results Split by
High and Low Subjects

	Subjects	
	High	*Low*
Average number remindings in first test (out of 8)	1.0	3.75
Average absolute consistency difference	.5	2.25
	Tasks	
	Accomplished on first try	*On which subjects experienced difficulty*
Proportion of occurrence	.70	.30
Probability of reminding	.22	.47

TABLE 7.5
Proportions Correct in Ross
(1984, Experiment 2)

	Subjects	
Condition	High[a]	Low
Appropriate	.83	.61
Unrelated	.25	.17
Inappropriate	.23	.00

$n = 12$ subjects/group. Each subject contributed 2 observations/condition.

[a] Middle third of subjects due to ceiling effects in top third.

chose the method that used the similar text 84% of the time (this is referred to as a *consistency* effect in the paper and the table presented here). Performance in the test task was very high. Subjects almost always accomplished the task, but the results of interest were which method they used. By the conjecture just offered, because this task was easy, high-performing subjects (determined here by time to accomplish the total set of test tasks) should make less use of remindings, presumably because they have been able to learn the procedures. In fact, as can be seen in the table, the slower subjects had almost four times as many remindings as the faster subjects. In addition, they provided a much larger absolute consistency effect. By this same logic, those editing operations that proved most difficult should have the greater number of remindings. In fact, there was a strong correlation of this type, $r(7) = .79$ (this correlation is of the number of remindings and the number of first tests in which subjects had difficulty, across the eight tasks). The bottom half of Table 7.4 shows these data in a slightly different format as well. When subjects had difficulty on an editing task, the probability of a reminding was more than twice what it was when there was no difficulty.

Table 7.5 shows performance for a division into high and low subjects for a probability theory experiment that proved very difficult for subjects (Ross, 1984, Ex. 2, which was discussed earlier and illustrated in Table 7.1). After the usual learning procedure of presenting principles and examples, subjects were given test problems that either were superficially dissimilar (unrelated condition) or superficially similar to one of the earlier examples. If the test was superficially similar, it could be similar either to an example that illustrated the same principle (appropriate) or to an example that illustrated a different principle (inappropriate). Shown in the table are the proportion of correct answers for these three conditions for the middle and lowest thirds of subjects (the highest third had strong ceiling effects so showed only small differences). As can be seen there, the high subjects had larger effects of the appropriate superficial similarity. (Although the difference between the appropriate and unrelated conditions is only .14 greater for the higher performing subjects, it would be quite a bit larger if subjects with floor effects were not excluded from the experiment. Since all subjects had to have at least partial credit on one of the problems to be included, and the appropriate condition was the easiest condition, this criterion probably forces some appropriate-unrelated difference for most subjects). Another interesting point, to be returned to shortly, is that the poorer subjects showed a larger effect of the inappropriate superficial similarly (especially if one takes into account the near-floor performance of these subjects in the unrelated condition and the floor performance in the inappropriate condition).

To conclude this section, the fact that other information may also be used to sole these problems precludes a simple correlation between performance and reminding effects. It is possible, however, that better subjects may show less of an effect when other relevant knowledge can be used and more of an effect when it cannot.

Differences in How High and Low Subjects Make Use of Earlier Examples

In this section, I examine cases in which high and low subjects are making use of earlier examples. How might they differ in this use? Using the framework presented earlier, where might individual differences lie? According to the framework, the access and effects of remindings will depend critically on the information used in the probe and the extent of the learner's understanding of the structural aspects of the problem. There are probably a number of differences one could focus on, but I have chosen one I consider to be particularly important. The main assumption I will be using to predict individual differences in the noticing, use, and learning is that the high subjects are more likely to have knowledge about the structural aspects of the earlier examples and the test problems (see Novick, 1988, for a related idea). The idea is that this extra information will allow better performing subjects to more appropriately notice, remember, use, and learn from examples. This assumption is not an arbitrary one, since some studies have noted this relation between ability and the use of the structural aspects (e.g., Krutetskii, 1976; Silver, 1981). Assuming this difference is true, we may briefly discuss the probable effects on the different processes.

Noticing.   Noticing of earlier examples is largely a function of the relative similarity between the earlier example and the representation of the problem. Both high and low subjects include some superficial aspects in their representation of the earlier example and in their representation of the test problem (e.g., Ross, 1984; Silver, 1981). However, high subjects are more likely to include the structural aspects in their representation of the earlier example and in their characterization of the test problem. If the earlier example and test problem are superficially similar, the additional benefit of the structural aspects may be minor. However, if the earlier example and test problem are superficially unrelated, the structural similarity can have a large effect. Under these conditions (with unrelated superficial similarity of study and test examples), we would expect high subjects to show more appropriate remindings. These predictions are borne out by an analysis of the 215 remindings (150 of which were appropriate, i.e., of an examaple using the same principle as the test problem) from the first two studies in Ross and Sofka (1986), a summary of which is shown in Table 7.6. As can be seen, the high and low subjects did not differ much in their probabilities of accessing an appropriate earlier example that was superficially similar to the test problem (and these probabilities were high). However, if these problems were superficially unrelated, high subjects had a higher proportion of appropriate remindings. These differences are even larger if the analysis is restricted to just the first test.

Another interesting possibility is that high subjects, because of their better understanding of the problem (and problem solving) may analyze the problems in a more systematic way. Both theoretical and empirical research (e.g., Bransford, Franks, Vye, & Sherwood, 1989; Carbonell, 1986) suggest that noticing may occur if the initial analysis of the current problem is very similar to the initial analysis of an earlier problem. Though I have not directly examined this processing similarity idea, Ross and Sofka (1986) provide some examples of remindings that appear to have this characteristic, such as the *difficulty* remindings. (In these cases, subjects are reminded that they had difficulty with this type of problem before. Most interesting, this reminding often leads to a detailed remembering of the earlier example, the mistake, and the correct solution, so that performance on the current problem is often high.)

Reconstruction and Analogy. For reconstruction and analogical use of earlier examples, the use of structural aspects will aid performance considerably for several reasons. First, as mentioned earlier, an important limitation in reconstruction is the lack of structural knowledge to guide the

TABLE 7.6
Ross and Sofka (1986) Data on Remindings for High and
Low Subjects

	High	Low
Proportion of appropriate remindings for:		
Superficially similar tests	.84	.76
Superficially unrelated tests	.72	.52

retrieval. Thus, sometimes subjects may access the appropriate example, but without the structural aspects, be unable to remember enough of it to make use of it (this difficulty is very clear in some of the protocol studies). If structural aspects are available, the reconstruction will be much easier. This idea predicts that high subjects can recall structural aspects of earlier problems better (see Silver, 1981, for supporting evidence). Second, if two examples each have several objects, the number of potential mappings is very large. Any conditions that increase the ease of this mapping can be expected to increase the effects of the remindings. It is clear (Gentner & Toupin, 1986; Ross, 1987, 1989a) that the analogical mapping of learners is heavily influenced by superficial similarities between problems, such as the correspondence of objects. If structural aspects are available for mapping of problems, subjects are less likely to make use of these possibly misleading superficial similarities. Third, if the structural aspects are available, an inappropriately accessed earlier example may be rejected. The data shown earlier in Table 7.5 illustrate this possibility. As I mentioned before, the better subjects showed little difference between the unrelated and inappropriate conditions, although they were able to benefit from appropriate superficial similarity. Clearly, they are not simply using the superficial similarity to access and use the earlier examples. The lack of difference between the unrelated and inappropriate conditions suggests that these high subjects are able to reject using the superficially similar example if it is structurally inappropriate.

Learning. Since the better subjects are more likely to access an appropriate earlier example (or reject an inappropriately accessed one) and more likely to have structural aspects available, their learning may benefit in two ways. First, since they will be more often comparing examples from the same principle, whatever they learn from this mapping will be appropriate. Low learners may often try to make analogies between problems of different types, leading to strange and inappropriate generalizations. Final mastery will not only require appropriate generalizations, but will also need to overcome these inappropriate generalizations. Second, since high subjects may be starting out with some structural aspects, they can use the comparisons to refine their understanding of these structural aspects, while the poorer subjects are still trying to find these structural aspects.

Summary

In this section, I speculated on some possible individual differences in the access and use of earlier examples. First, I conjectured that there may be differences in when high and low subjects make use of earlier examples. In particular, when other relevant information might be available, high subjects are more likely to be able to make us of it and, thus, will show less of an effect of these examples than when the other information is not available. High learners, then, can be seen to *adapt* their learning to the type of information that is available. Second, there is evidence that high subjects are more likely to have available some structural aspects of the problems. From this evidence, I speculated on how such a difference might affect the noticing, reconstruction, analogy, and learning processes that had been discussed earlier. As this discussion indicated, these structural aspects can lead to better use of all these processes. In addition, this difference is likely to grow with (at least a few) later tests, as the high subjects extract further structural similarities, while the low learners may still be trying to make comparisons among appropriate problems.

GENERAL ISSUES ON THE ACCESS AND USE OF RELEVANT INFORMATION

In this part of the chapter, I will use the research presented in the first section to outline some general issues in the access and use of relevant information, as well as in the learning that results from the use of this information. As I suggested in my motivations for studying remindings, I believe that these remindings are just particularly obvious cases of very general occurrences in which people do not retrieve the exact information they are looking for, but rather some other relevant information that they can try to use to accomplish their task.

Before beginning this outline of general issues, it may be helpful to put this research into a broader context of recent work on reasoning and problem solving (see Gick & Holyoak, 1987, for a general discussion of transfer). It has become clear in many situations that people are not using general content-free inference rules in thinking.

An especially interesting case is in deductive reasoning, since the logic is well worked out and has a number of properties that people find desirable. For example, the research on conditional reasoning using the Wason Selection Task[1] (Wason, 1966) shows that people perform poorly on this task (see Johnson–Laird & Wason, 1977, for a full discussion of the dif-

---

[1] In the Wason Selection Task, subjects are given a rule (of the form, "If p than q") and asked which pairings of (p, not-p) crossed with (q, not-q) need to be checked to tell whether the rule is being followed. For example, if shown p, people should (and do) realize that they need to know what goes with it, because q would be consistent with the rule, but not-q would not. When presented with arbitrary materials, people have considerable difficulty, particularly in appreciating that not-q needs to be checked to ensure that p is not paired with it. With meaningful materials, performance is much higher (see Cheng & Holyoak, 1985, for a discussion).

ficulties people have and the remedial procedures that seem like they should help but do not). Clearly, the fact that people do poorly on a task does not mean that they do not have general inference rules, but just that they may not have the appropriate ones, and a number of attempts have been made to specify a psycho-logic that people may use in deduction (e.g., Braine, 1978; Rips, 1983). The real difficulty for these views, however, is that the same formal task may become very easy for these same subjects when the content is changed or the rationale is made clear. Although there is debate about the exact type of knowledge that is used in these cases (see Cheng & Holyoak, 1985), it is clear that the knowledge is at least partly dependent on the content of the situation. Given that this content-dependency occurs in a fairly simple task in which the inference rules can be well specified, it may not be too surprising that other domains may also not be reasoned about with general inference rules.

As a very different example, the work on expert systems (cf. Barr & Feigenbaum, 1981) also suggests that much of the reasoning relies on highly specific, content-dependent knowledge, rather than general inference rules. Researchers in this area have found that to get their systems to perform adequately requires storing a great deal of domain-specific knowledge (usually in the form of production rules) and using a fairly simple general inference engine.

Not only is it likely that people use knowledge much more specific than content-free inference rules in their thinking, but some recent psychological and AI research points to the use of highly specific nonrule knowledge being used in what would usually be assumed to be rule-based situations (see Medin & Ross, 1989, for a more detailed review). Three examples may point out the diversity of this work. First, Schank (1982), as well as some of his colleagues (Kolodner, 1983; Lebowitz, 1983; Riesbeck, 1981), have suggested that people use specific remindings of earlier situations to understand current situations (also see Rau, this volume). Second, the exemplar work on categorization (e.g., Brooks, 1978; Medin & Schaffer, 1978) has proposed that earlier instances might be used in categorizing new instances. Third, some recent work in psychology (e.g., Jacoby & Brooks, 1984; Kolers & Roediger, 1984; see Schacter, 1987, for a review of some of this work) shows that performance on what appear to be highly nonspecific tasks, such as object perception, word recognition, and reading of inverted text, may show large effects of particular earlier episodes. For instance, Jacoby and Brooks found that the time to classify an object as a cup could be affected by its similarity to a cup shown earlier.

The point of these comments is to suggest that examining the access and use of specific earlier examples or episodes may address more general issues than one might at first think. There is a great deal of evidence that much of the information we use is highly specific, not content-free. Thus, an examination of this access and use in a highly controlled setting may be helpful in understanding these more general issues. To outline these general issues, I have used the framework presented earlier to separate them into issues of noticing, use, and learning for ease of exposition, though the boundaries are not always sharp.

Noticing

In the first part of this chapter, I reviewed a number of studies showing that the spontaneous noticing of relevant information can be problematical in learning. Although I believe that novices may have greater difficulties with this noticing than might more knowledgeable people, the problem of spontaneously noticing relevant information is a general one. To illustrate this difficulty, let us adopt the general idea of Gick and Holyoak (1983) that noticing depends on a match of the level of representation of the test problem and the representation of the stored earlier example. By this account, noticing may be a problem not just for novices but for any persons who do not have a fairly deep understanding of the current problem or of the stored relevant information. In addition, these understandings must be similarly represented for noticing to occur. Even if one assumes that people may not be noticing a specific earlier problem, but rather some well-understood and more general information, the noticing depends on some match of the information. Although it might seem that this is fairly straightforward, I will mention several points that make this matching more difficult.

Content-dependence of Stored Knowledge.   One difficulty in matching stored relevant knowledge is that much of what we know appears to be highly content-dependent. Gick and Holyoak (1983) demonstrate that people's understanding of the point of a new story often is represented in terms of the story content. In addition, some work I reviewed earlier (Ross, 1987, 1989a) suggests that novices' representation of how to use a principle may be in terms of the example that was used to illustrate the principle. Again, however, it is not just that novices have this difficulty: A general claim of some recent research is that much of our knowledge is highly specific. The basic argument (along lines of the operationality/generality tradeoff) is that to have knowledge that will be available quickly in the usual situations in which it is used, it is necessary to make it highly restricted in its applicability. Thus, though it may be true that some new knowledge has very general applicability, it is also true that many of the situations in which we might use it are likely to be similar to the situation in which we learned it. If so, it would be a strange system that would disregard the content that might later prove useful in noticing. For instance, Hinsley, Hayes, and Simon (1977) showed that expert algebra word-problem solvers can take advantage of the superficial content of word problems if it is predictive of the solution procedure.

Although this content dependence may be useful at times, in some situations it clearly is not. Weaning away from inappropriate content dependence is a major goal in instruction. A common method to accomplish this broadening of applicability is to present a variety of contents. Gick and Holyoak (1983) suggest that learners need to be forced to compare the stories or examples with different contents to form some more abstract schema. Bassok and Holyoak (1989) point out that domains in which students are given a wide variety of examples, such as mathematics, may result in increasing accessibility of the learned information.

Remembering is not the Same as Spontaneously Noticing. A second general point to make about noticing is that it is not the same as remembering the knowledge. Bransford et al. (1989) make this point very eloquently and use the term "inert" knowledge for knowledge that is relevant to a situation, but which is not accessed. In many situations we may have highly relevant knowledge, but simply fail to make us of it. A common problem is the failure to notice this knowledge spontaneously as being potentially useful (e.g., the Gestalt psychologists cited in Hilgard & Bower, 1966, pp. 252–253; Perfetto, Bransford, & Franks, 1983; Weisberg, DiCamillo, & Phillips, 1978).

As mentioned earlier, it is important to take into account the information used in probing memory during problem solving. A main difference between remembering stored information and spontaneously noticing it during problem solving is the way in which memory might be probed. In remembering some information, the person usually has a partial description of the event or information and is trying to fill in the rest of the description (see Norman & Bobrow, 1979, for a more thorough discussion). However, in situations in which some relevant information might be spontaneously noticed, the exact information being "searched for" is less clear. Rather than trying to retrieve knowledge of a specific event, the problem solver is after knowledge to solve the problem. To improve the likelihood that retrieved knowledge is relevant, it is likely that the probe will include goal-related information. In addition, since the problem is being worked on, it is likely that aspects of the problem will also be included in the probe. Thus, what is retrieved will be affected by both the goal and problem information. However, some very relevant knowledge may not have been stored with this particular goal information (e.g., if it was processed very differently as Bransford et al. suggest) and/or it may not match much of the problem information. Thus, even well-learned and well-understood information may not always be accessible in solving problems.

Bransford et al. (1989), using the idea of transfer-appropriate processing (i.e., a type of study–test matching that focuses on the processing rather than the representations), suggest that this noticing failure is due to the fact that the processing of the problem-solving episode is very different than the processing of the earlier stored information. They claim that if the stored information, when it is learned, is processed in a similar way to the way the problem will be processed, noticing will improve. They illustrate this idea by showing how sentences that provide answers to riddles will be accessed under some conditions but not others. Perfetto et al. (1983) had subjects rate the truthfulness of a number of sentences (e.g., Before any game is played, there is no score.) After a few minutes' delay, these subjects, obstensibly as part of another experiment, had to solve riddles for which these sentences provided the answers (e.g., Uriah Feller, the famous Israeli superpsychic, can tell you the score of any baseball game before the game starts. What is his secret?). Perfetto et al. showed that subjects who were informed of the possible relevance of the earlier sentences did significantly better than subjects who were not informed, but this latter group did not do significantly better than subjects who did not receive the earlier sentences. Thus, this uninformed group had relevant information, but was unable to notice it spontaneously when solving the riddle. In subsequent work, Adams et al. (1988) showed that if these uninformed subjects were shown the sentences in such a way as to try to match the processing they would go through at riddle-solving time (e.g., It is easy to guess the score of any game before it begins [Pause]; the score is 0 to 0), then their performance significantly improved (compared with a group that received this exact sentence without the pause). Lockhart, Lamon, and Gick (1988) present very similar findings and also show that the recall of the earlier sentences does not predict well the likelihood of their being spontaneously noticed and used for solving the riddles.

This difficulty in noticing relevant information is a crucial one in instruction and a number of suggestions have been made for ameliorating this difficulty. For example, Brown (1989) claims that if learners develop an understanding of the information, the difficulties of access may be greatly attenuated. Bransford et al. (1989) hypothesize that much of the difficulty is that we do not learn to attend to the appropriate distinctions. They suggest that contrasts of instances along critical distinctions will help greatly in increasing the accessibility of the relevant information. This difficulty is analogous to the one pointed out by Larkin (1981) that a major difficulty in building production system models of cognition is to get the appropriate applicability conditions. Students often are able to learn how to do the various procedures, but have great difficulty in learning when to do them. For instance, in a statistics course I have taught, students' most common error was the application of some statistical test to a case for which it was inappropriate. Even if some knowledge is not content-dependent, it is often hard to notice spontaneously when it is applicable or to distinguish which of a number of possibilities might be applicable.,

Although most suggestions for improving the access of relevant information focus on the learning of the relevant information, there is good reason to also consider what one might do during problem solving to improve this access. Perhaps the best motivation for this approach is that suggestions to apply at learning require a great deal of effort and may lead to little effect. That is, especially in informal self-learning situations, it is difficult to know how generally applicable each piece of information is so one either has to try to make these estimates or apply the extra learning effort to all that is learned. If possible, it would be advantageous to have procedures that could be done at problem solving to increase the spontaneous noticing of relevant stored information. I know of little work on this possibility. Books on problem-solving heuristics (e.g., Polya, 1945; Wickelgren, 1974) provide some general ideas on how one might find relevant information, such as to focus on the goal. These books often suggest that the problem solver try to think of an analogous problem, or a more general or more specific problem, but provide little help on how to do this. This area seems an important one for future research.

I also wish to briefly point out that this difference between remembering and making use of stored information operates at even greater levels of specificity. In particular, one may think of the difference between remembering some specific event and accessing that information as part of some different goal. I will mention two examples of this difference. First, the current work in psychology on the difference between explicit and implicit memory (e.g., Graf & Schacter, 1985; Schacter, 1987) suggests that the factors that make an event explicitly memorable (i.e., such that people can recall it) may be different from those factors that make an event implicitly usable. Thus, researchers in this area have found that earlier events can affect later processing (such as perceptual identification) even when the explicit memory for the event is little better than chance. A second example of this difference between remembering and accessing is more closely related to work on memory. Anderson (e.g., 1976) had demonstrated across a wide variety of studies that the more facts learned about a concept the slower one is to retrieve any particular fact. This "fan" effect has been attacked along several lines, but the one of current interest is that this fan effect suggests that people who know much about a particular topic (e.g., experts) should retrieve information about this topic slowly (Smith, Adams, & Schorr, 1978). Although this criticism may be answered in several ways, one reply is that in many situations there is no reason to retrieve a particular fact, but rather one needs to answer some question. If one thinks about information retrieval as the accessing of relevant information rather than the remembering of a particular fact, it may be that the fan effect does not operate. As one example, Lynne Reder and I (Reder & Ross, 1983) showed that if subjects simply had to make some more global judgment (e.g., about whether a particular person performed any actions related to a particular theme, such as the beach) the more relevant facts known, the faster the response. Again, the point of this example is to show that remembering information and being able to notice spontaneously or access that same information as relevant to some goal may lead to very different effects.

Competition from Other Information.   A final difficulty in spontaneously noticing relevant information is that it is rarely a matter of having one piece of information that could be relevant and probing memory until it is found or until the problem solver gives up. Rather the usual case is probably one in which other information may appear relevant as well and is competing with the "truly" relevant information for retrieval. (For ease of exposition, I am assuming a simplified case in which only one piece of information that is known is relevant, but the argument does not depend on this.) Thus, even if one has learned the appropriate relevant information and has done so in a way appropriate to the current problem, other information may be retrieved because it better matches the probe. This mistaken retrieval could occur for a number of reasons, but a likely one is that there is a great deal of superficial similarity that the problem solver cannot ignore.

In addition, the idea of other information being potentially applicable helps us to understand why noticing is hard in some cases. For instance, the Perfetto et al. (1983) findings discussed earlier seem very surprising given the high degree of similarity between the sentences and riddles, as well as the obvious relevance of the sentences. But, as readers, we are assessing, not accessing. That is, from the subjects' point of view, this earlier sentence is just one piece of information in their memory and they have no particular reason to believe it might be relevant. Given their processing of the riddle, much other stored information may better match than the earlier sentence.

Use

After relevant information is noticed, it must be used. Assuming that much of our knowledge is content-dependent or highly specific, using it in new problems will usually require some modification. This modification often appears to be analogical. Recently, a number of proposals have been made for how this analogical mapping might work (e.g., Burstein, 1986; Burstein & Adelson, this volume; Carbonell, 1983, 1986; Gentner, 1983; Holyoak, 1985; Winston, 1980). For many of these proposals, a common theme is that the analogy makes use of a detailed understanding of the stored relevant information. The research I have presented earlier often examines cases in which the stored information may not be well understood nor well remembered. As argued earlier, these differences lead to important differences in how the analogy is (or can be) made. Learners are often in the situation of having only a partial understanding of the knowledge they are trying to apply. Because of this, I think that the general issues related to my work on the use of the accessed information are likely to be most important for learning situations or reasoning from only partly understood relevant information.

One final comment is needed before presenting these issues. This comment is a reminder that the extent to which behavior is rule-governed is not always easy to assess. That is, it is possible that much of the behavior that appears to be due to the application of rules may rely on some specific episode or combination of episodes. This idea underlies both the processing specificity views mentioned earlier (Jacoby & Brooks, 1984; Kolers & Roediger, 1984) as well as much of the work on parallel distributed processing (e.g., Rumelhart & McClelland, 1986).

Noticing and Use Are Often Affected Differently. As pointed out in the review of my research, it is often necessary to separate out factors, even superficial ones, that affect noticing and use in different ways. Thus, these studies show that the story line of probability problems has a large effect on noticing, but no effect on the use of the accessed information. As Gentner (1989; Gentner & Landers, 1985) points out, some views of analogy assume the noticing is affected by the same causal information (a view that she calls causal indexing) as is the analogical use. A complete theory of analogy will have to account for these differences in how aspects are affected.

The Use of Relevant Information May Often be Affected by Superficial Similarities as Well. Another view of analogical access and use is that, although the access may be greatly affected by superficial similarities between problems, once an earlier example is accessed, the deeper, structural similarities are the only similarities of importance. The research mentioned earlier (Ross, 1987, 1989a; Gentner & Toupin, 1986) demonstrates that a superficial aspect, such as how the particular objects correspond in the two problems, can have very large effects on the use of the earlier example. Two additional comments may be helpful in understanding the importance of this latter view. First, it suggests that our understanding of how to use a principle may be inextricably bound with the example that was used to illustrate the principle. If so, it seems that superficial similarities are likely to affect use. Second, these superficial effects on use are not just seen with novices. For example, Hinsley et al. (1977) show that the procedure used to solve simple algebra word problems is very different for examples that have superficial contents prototypical of a particular principle compared with examples whose contents are not usually related to a particular principle.

The Use of Relevant Information is Opportunistic. As is common to many analyses of novice problem solving (e.g., Larkin, McDermott, Simon, & Simon, 1980), little of the problem solving is based on a general high-level plan. Rather, using some general strategies, such as working backwards from the goal, the novices are often seen to apply principles fairly randomly until they are able to get rid of all unknowns. In much of my work, novices show a similar opportunistic use of information. That is, they will retrieve some information and in their use of it will retrieve some other information that might start them off on a different type of solution. This opportunistic use of information, however, is not simply a reflection of being a novice. Such use may occur when a person is faced with a task that has many possibilities and for which more systematic approaches are not known, are difficult, or cannot be assured of working. For example, Hayes–Roth and Hayes–Roth (1979) present a very opportunistic model for planning and Williams and Hollan (1981) use related ideas for explaining memory retrieval of the names of high school classmates.

Learning

There is a great deal of evidence that learners rely heavily on examples (e.g., Anderson, Farrell, & Sauers, 1984; Lefevre & Dixon, 1976), so the means by which they do so are crucial for an account of learning. The claim made from my recent work is that using an earlier example to solve a current problem affects later performance as well. I proposed that this effect may be due to a reminding-based generalization that comes from the analogical use. In particular, it was suggested that this generalization mechanism provides one way of learning from examples and might allow remindings to be on superficial aspects while what is learned from the use of the reminding may be more structural. This incremental generalization is clearly very conservative and much less powerful than other possible generalization mechanisms, such as maximal common generalizations. However, the argument is that given the great deal of content-dependence, these other mechanisms may be too powerful to model cognition (see also Anderson, 1986). In working out some ideas about how generalization may occur from these remindings, I have been forced to consider several more general issues, which will be brought up in this section. First, the perspective I have outlined forces one to consider which examples are being compared and how (or why) they are being compared. How might one learn from doing examples? Second, how might the noticing change with growing expertise? Third, over how large a unit might this generalization work? I offer some preliminary speculations about these points.

Before beginning these speculations, it is worthwhile to consider how this approach fits in with other views of learning. One basic problem with the approach outlined here is that it does not make use of any understanding (or top–down information) in learning. It seems to me that there are two approaches to overcoming this difficulty, both of which will probably be necessary. First, one can take this basic view and modify it to allow some influence of more top–down information. For example, Anderson and Thompson (1989) have proposed an analogical mechanism that relies heavily on the function (i.e., goal-related information) for determining the analogy and generalization made. I am currently working on ways in which information such as the relevance of features may have an effect through the remindings and use. Second, one can ask how different learning mechanisms might operate together to allow the learner to take advantage of similarities under some circumstances and explanations under other circumstances (e.g., Lebowitz, 1986). It seems likely that other approaches that make use of understanding (e.g., the explanation-based view advocated by DeJong & Mooney, 1986) are important, but may operate only when the learner has considerable knowledge of the domain.

Learning from Doing. A common belief of many learning researchers (e.g., Anderson, 1986; Anzai & Simon, 1979), especially those using some type of adaptive production system (see Klahr, Langley, & Neches, 1987), is that we learn relevant information about how to solve problems by solving problems. Certainly this view underlies much of the instruction in schools, in which students are required to solve a large number of problems. Recently, Sweller and Cooper (1985) have questioned this assumption and shown cases in which having learners study worked-out examples led to better later performance than having learners solve these examples. From the view presented earlier, although it might seem that remindings during problem solving are crucial, what is really important is that the learners get to compare different examples of a given type. This comparison is probably much more likely in the worked-out example case. In addition, some of Sweller's other work shows that getting learners to think back and remember the examples leads to better later performance than having them solve problems (Sweller, Mawer, & Howe, 1982). I think this research suggests that we need a better idea of how the problem-solving activity relates to what is learned. One argument that Sweller makes is that, to the extent that problem solving activity involves searching via some means–ends analysis, much of the activity cannot be profitably applied to later problems. In particular, he argues that means–ends analysis is so effortful that few resources remain to focus explicitly on the relevant variables (also see Sweller, 1988). From this argument and the earlier view, it appears that it may not be so much whether problem solving is required or not, but rather the extent to which the problem solving activities are relevant to later problem solving.

  An important issue that arises from this controversy for researchers who believe that the comparisons of problems or instances are crucial in learning is to consider the types of comparisons that may be made between problems and whether they might affect learning differently. For instance, comparing problems for different reasons, such as for making an analogy versus comparing worked-out examples, may result in different aspects of the problem type being learned. This issue could help us to understand what might be included in generalizations and the relation between a generalization and the instances from which it arises.

Changes in Noticing with Practice.   As people gain greater experience in a domain, a number of changes occur. One salient change is that of the difference in access. For example, Chi et al. (1981) found that novices often rely on superficial features, such as objects, in the problem to access relevant information, while experts categorize the problem by the principles used to solve the problem. Ross and Sofka's (1986) analysis of a large number of remindings indicated changes in noticing occurred over just three tests. In particular, for tests that had no superficial similarity to earlier examples, the appropriateness of remindings increased (i.e., the proportion of remindings for which the accessed example used the same principle as the test problem). This change could be due to a variety of factors such as the inclusion of structural aspects in later stored examples or the inclusion of structural aspects in the probes from later problems. An important issue is to understand the variety of changes that occur with practice and how they are used together to gain expertise. For instance, there is evidence (e.g., Chase & Simon, 1973) that expertise involves storing a great number of highly specific schemata that can be used for recognizing useful configurations.

Analogy and Learning of Parts Versus Whole.   In my research, I focus on the noticing and use (and, hence, the learning) of the whole earlier example to the current problem. Other investigators (e.g., Carbonell, 1986; Lewis, 1988; Pirolli, & Anderson, 1985) have suggested that parts of the earlier example may be used in the analogy and/or may be generalized. Such partial or fractional (Carbonell, 1986) learning would allow transfer across problem types if they shared some subunits (Elio, 1986) and would greatly increase the importance of this analogical learning.

Although I have focused on cases in which the analogy and generalization is to a whole earlier problem, it seems likely that there are some cases in which parts of the earlier example may be used. As an example, Michael Sofka and I have conducted an experiment in which subjects are taught a large number of commands in a text editor. The purpose of the experiment was to examine the effect of superficial similarity of texts on performance, comparing immediate performance and performance after a 2-day delay. The results of interest for the present purposes, however, are that the effects of superficial similarity were evident only for those tasks that had some unique part of the procedure. The other tasks, whose procedure parts partly overlapped with each of a few other tasks, showed no effect of superficial similarity. More concretely, if the task had some procedure part that occurred in no other task, such as "pasting" (using the letter P) from the buffer for moving some test, repeating a similar text at test led to better performance than testing with a new text. However, if all the procedure parts were shared with other tasks (usually in a family resemblance-like structure), then repeating a similar text at test time had no effect. Our belief is that these overlapping parts were being learned across the different tasks. The possibility that parts of examples or relevant information might be used makes this learning by analogy much more powerful, but also requires the researchers to specify how these parts are accessed and used. Some related suggestions have been made for the use of multiple overlapping analogies when using relevant knowledge from other domains to help learn a new domain (e.g., Norman, 1983; Burstein, 1986; Burstein & Adelson, this volume).

Summary

In this section, I have used the framework of processes presented earlier to try to develop some general issues related to the access and use of relevant information. The most general issues concerned the spontaneous noticing of relevant information. This noticing is difficult both because of the content-dependence of knowledge and because the problem solver does not have available many of the cues that he or she would in trying to remember this information explicitly. The issues concerned with how relevant knowledge is used are primarily of importance for applying only partly understood knowledge. Under these circumstances, which may characterize much of the conditions during learning, the application is often opportunistic and greatly affected by superficial similarities. Although noticing may also be affected by superficial similarities, they are at least sometimes different from the superficial similarities affecting use. For learning, the research presented earlier helps to highlight some general issues about how one might learn from doing, as well as the changes with practice and the distinction about part–whole transfer.

IMPLICATIONS FOR TESTING

The ability to access and use relevant information plays an important role in most cognitive activities, such as understanding, problem solving, reasoning, and learning. In this section, I consider two very general implications for testing that come from the earlier discussions (see Ross, 1989b, for a discussion of some educational implications). First, I examine the testing implications of the general issue of noticing just discussed, focussing on the difference between remembering and accessing information. Second, the section on individual differences is used to generate some possible means of testing the access and use of relevant information. My research has not been concerned with testing. The particular suggestions made are only meant as illustrations of how one may use some of these ideas for testing.

Remembering Versus Spontaneously Noticing Stored Information

As discussed earlier at length (and in Bransford et al., 1989; Perfetto et al., 1983; Lockhart et al., 1988), knowing the relevant information is a necessary, but not a sufficient, condition for accessing it in the appropriate situations. What can be remembered in response to a direct query may not be a good indication of how well the knowledge might be accessed and used when it is relevant in problem solving. Clearly, some of the implications of this idea are already incorporated into test items. For example, some test items do not ask, "What is the circumference of a circle?", but rather provide a circle with a particular radius (or diameter) and ask for the distance around the circle's boundary. The logic behind such items, I suppose, is that the student may well have remembered the formula for the circumference of a circle, but may not realize its relevance to this problem or know how to apply it. An important point of the work by Bransford and his colleagues is that much of the knowledge that we have learned may be "inert" under many circumstances in which it might be profitably applied. To the extent that increased access of what stored information is relevant is an important determinant of problem solving performance, it seems appropriate for some tests to emphasize such access.

The content-dependence of knowledge discussed earlier also provides a possible implication for testing. Not only do people have difficulty accessing relevant information in many problem-solving situations, but this difficulty may be particularly acute when it has been learned in a different context than the one at test. Clearly some tests also make use of this idea, asking for the application of some procedures and principles to new settings.

Implications for Testing of Individual Differences in Remindings

A second general implication I wish to address is how one might use the ideas on individual differences in remindings in testing. To do this, I first consider a general paradigm to assess reasoning skills in a restricted domain that makes use of the idea that learners vary in *when* they might make use of earlier examples. I then separate out the different processes, to review *how* people might differ in their noticing and use of earlier examples and consider testing implications of these differences.

Reasoning within Restricted Domains. I am assuming that there is some restricted domain, or a subset of a larger domain, for which the people being tested have very little knowledge. Ideally, this test might consist of constructing a totally new domain for the testees in which their ability to access and use relevant information can be assessed. The domain would be taught to the people making clear the underlying structure (or not), along with examples that illustrated various principles or procedures within this domain. Test problems would then be given in which the learners would have to reason within the domain.

The basic idea underlying this implication was discussed in the section on individual differences in remindings. Stating it more directly, if learners are given an opportunity to learn nonspecific relevant information, the better learners will be able to use this information on later tests, so will be less affected by superficial similarities between learning examples and test problems. This assessment would not simply depend on overall performance, but could use the pattern of performance (across the appropriate, unrelated, and inappropriate superficial similarity test conditions) to infer what relevant information was being used to respond on the test problems.

If, however, the structural aspects to be learned are very complex or could not be expected to be learned given the instruction, better learners will show a great effect of superficial similarity, particularly for the appropriate test conditions. Taking these two tests together, a pattern of performance for each learner can be determined for cases in which other relevant information is available or not. Although the logic and the details need much further work, it may be useful to have a test that can assess the extent to which a learner can adapt to the circumstances (defined by the available relevant information and the appropriateness of the superficial similarity) of the learning situation. Perhaps such an assessment would be a better predictor of success in novel problem-solving situations than would overall performance on this test task.

Separate Processes and Their Testing Implications. In addition to considering how one might use these individual differences in testing within a new domain, one might also want to consider the testing implications for the individual processes outlined in the framework. That is, the idea just mentioned looks at the pattern of performance across conditions, but does not analyze any part of the task to see where the differences might lie. One might want to perform this analysis to gain a better determination of the strengths and weaknesses of different individuals in their ability to access and use relevant information. I briefly illustrate this possibility here.

First, people may vary in their ability to notice relevant information because of differential use of structural information. To examine these differences, one could imagine varying the superficial and structural similarities (perhaps even orthogonally as in Chi et al., 1981; Hinsley et al., 1977; Silver, 1979) and have subjects sort the problems into groups or find the problem most similar to a standard problem. These procedures will allow a determination of the features used to make the groupings.

Second, better subjects may remember different aspects of earlier examples and use different means to remember. To examine these differences, subjects could be given some examples and then asked to recall them (with or without the cue of a test problem). The ability to assess would be how people make use of the test problem and what aspects (e.g., superficial or structural) of the earlier example are recalled.

Third, learners might differ in their ability to make analogical use of earlier examples. A simple means of testing this process would be to provide one worked-out example and a second problem for which they are required to apply the same procedure (see Lewis, 1988, for the use of this procedure to discriminate among different learning mechanisms). One can assess what aspects of the problems are set in correspondence as a function of various superficial and structural similarity manipulations. For instance, the experiment discussed in the first section on analogy varied the superficial similarities of story line and object correspondence. If these manipulations were made, one might be able to characterize people in terms of what manipulations affected their ability to make the analogy correctly.

Fourth, what is learned from these uses of earlier examples may be assessed. As one possibility, following different example pairs, learners could be given a number of problems to solve, with no feedback, so that their generalization could be assessed. In addition to examining what generalization is made, one can also ask whether this type is consistent over different learning pairs.

Summary

This section includes some speculations about the implications for testing of the ideas presented earlier. First, the differences between spontaneous noticing and remembering (along with the idea of content-dependence of knowledge) support the use of questions that assess spontaneous noticing of relevant information, especially across domains. Second, the earlier examination of individual differences was used to generate two types of tests that might provide information about problem solving and learning ability. One, the pattern of reasoning performance within a new domain may be assessed to determine what information learners are using to solve problems. Two, each of the processes may be investigated separately to determine strengths and weaknesses of individuals. Clearly, these ideas are speculative, but if the access and use of relevant information are essential parts of cognition, their assessment should be an essential part of testing.

CONCLUSIONS

This chapter began by claiming that the access and use of relevant information is a crucial part of cognition and has ended with some implications for testing. A brief review of the organization may help the reader to understand (again) how the sections interrelated. The first section dealt with a restricted instance of this access and use: remindings in problem solving and learning of a new cognitive skill. A framework was provided for these remindings and a variety of experimental results were mentioned to flesh out the details of this framework. The ideas from this research were then used in two ways. First, in the second section, I examined some possible individual differences in when and how people might make use of earlier examples. Second, in the third section, the ideas gained from the research in a more specialized setting were used to return to the original topic of accessing and using relevant information. The final section included suggestions for testing that made use of the framework, the individual difference ideas, and the general issues.

As I hope is clear, much work remains to be conducted on the access and use of relevant information. As two examples, the ideas about how learning might result from this use and how this use of specific knowledge might interact with the high-level knowledge are still being worked out. As we gain a better understanding of how relevant information is accessed and used, however, we should be able to refine our understanding of individual differences and the implications for testing.

ACKNOWLEDGMENT

The research in this chapter was supported by National Science Foundation Grant IST 83-08670. The preparation of this chapter was supported by NSF and Air Force Office of Scientific Research Grant 89–0447. I thank Doug Medin for his very helpful comments.

REFERENCES

Adams, L. T., Kasserman, J. E., Yearwood, A. A., Perfetto, G. A., Bransford, J. D., & Franks, J. J. (1988). Memory access: The effects of fact-oriented versus problem-oriented acquisition. *Memory & Cognition, 16,* 167–175.

Anderson, J. R. (1976). *Language, memory and thought.* Hillsdale, NJ: Lawrence Erlbaum Associates.

Anderson, J. R. (1983). *The architecture of cognition.* Cambridge, MA: Harvard University Press.

Anderson, J. R. (1986). Knowledge compilation: The general learning mechanism. In R. S. Michalski, J. G. Carbonell, & T. M. Mitchell (Eds.), *Machine learning: An artificial intelligence approach* (Vol. 2, pp. 289–310). Los Altos, CA: Morgan Kaufmann.

Anderson, J. R., Farrell, R., & Sauers, R. (1984). Learning to program in LISP. *Cognitive Science, 8,* 87–129.

Anderson, J. R., & Thompson, R. (1989). Use of analogy in a production system architecture. In S. Vosniadou & A. Ortony (Eds.), *Similarity and analogical reasoning,* (pp. 267–296). Cambridge: Cambridge University Press.

Anzai, Y., & Simon, H. A. (1979). The theory of learning by doing. *Psychological Review, 86,* 124–140.

Barr, A., & Feigenbaum, E. (1981). *The handbook of artificial intelligence* (Vol. 1). Los Altos, CA: William Kaufmann.

Bassok, M., & Holyoak, K. J. (1989). Interdomain transfer between isomorphic topics in algebra and physics. *Journal of Experimental Psychology: Learning, Memory and Cognition, 15,* 153–166.

Braine, M. D. S. (1978). On the relation between the natural logic of reasoning and standard logic. *Psychological Review, 85,* 1–21.

Bransford, J. D., Franks, J. J., Vye, N. J., & Sherwood, R. D. (1989). New approaches to instruction: Because wisdom can't be told. In S. Vosniadou & A. Ortony (Eds.), *Similarity and analogical reasoning* (pp. 470–497). Cambridge, England: Cambridge University Press.

Brooks, L. (1978). Nonanalytic concept formation and memory for instances. In E. Rosch & B. B. Lloyd (Eds.), *Cognition and categorization* (pp. 169–211) Hillsdale, NJ: Lawrence Erlbaum Associates.

Brown, A. L. (1989). Analogical learning and transfer: What develops? In S. Vosniadou & A. Ortony (Eds.), *Similarity and analogical reasoning* (pp. 369–412). Cambridge, England: Cambridge University Press.

Burstein, M. H. (1986). Concept formation by incremental analogical reasoning and debugging. In R. S. Michalski, J. G. Carbonell, & T. M. Mitchell (Eds.), *Machine learning: An artificial intelligence approach* (pp. 351–370). Palo Alto, CA: Tioga.

Carbonell, J. G. (1983). Learning by analogy: Formulating and generalizing plans from past experience. In R. S. Michalski, J. G. Carbonell, & T. M. Mitchell (Eds.), *Machine learning: An artificial intelligence approach* (pp. 137–161). Palo Alto: Tioga.

Carbonell, J. G. (1986). Derivational analogy: A theory of reconstructive problem solving and expertise acquisition. In R. S. Michalski, J. G. Carbonell, & T. M. Mitchell (Eds.), *Machine learning: An artificial intelligence approach* (pp. 371–392). Palo Alto, CA: Tioga.

Card, S. K., Moran, T. P., & Newell, A. (1980). Computer text-editing: An information-processing analysis of a routine cognitive skill. *Cognitive Psychology, 12,* 32–74.

Chase, W. G., & Simon, H. A. (1973). The mind's eye in chess. In W. G. Chase (Ed.), *Visual information processing* (pp. 215–282) New York: Academic Press.

Cheng, P.W., & Holyoak, K. J. (1985). Pragmatic reasoning schemas. *Cognitive Psychology, 17,* 391–416.

Cheng, P. W., Holyoak, K. J., Nisbett, R. E., & Oliver, L. M. (1986). Pragmatic versus syntactic approaches to training deductive reasoning. *Cognitive Psychology, 18,* 293–328.

Chi, M. T. H., Feltovich, P. J., & Glaser, R. (1981). Categorization and representation of physics problems by experts and novices. *Cognitive Science, 5,* 121–152.

DeJong, G., & Mooney, R. (1986). Explanation-based learning: An alternative view. *Machine Learning, 1,* 145–176.

Dellarosa, D. (1985). *Abstraction of problem-type schemata through problem comparison* (Report No. 146). Boulder, CO: University of Colorado, Institute of Cognitive Science.

Elio, R. (1986). Representation of similar well-learned cognitive procedures. *Cognitive Science, 10,* 41–73.

Gentner, D. (1983). Structure-mapping: A theoretical framework for analogy. *Cognitive Science, 7,* 155–170.

Gentner, D. (1989). The mechanisms of analogical learning. In S. Vosniadou & A. Ortony (Eds.), *Similarity and analogical reasoning* (pp. 199–241). Cambridge, England: Cambridge University Press.

Gentner, D., & Landers, R. (1985). Analogical reminding: A good match is hard to find. In *Proceedings of the International Conference on Systems, Man, and Cybernetics,* Tucson, AZ.

Gentner, D., & Toupin, C. (1986). Systematicity and surface similarity in the development of analogy. *Cognitive Science, 10,* 277–300.

Gick, M. L., & Holyoak, K. J. (1980). Analogical problem solving. *Cognitive Psychology, 12,* 306–355.

Gick, M. L., & Holyoak, K. J. (1983). Schema induction and analogical transfer. *Cognitive Psychology, 14,* 1–38.

Gick, M. L., & Holyoak, K. J. (1987). The cognitive basis of knowledge transfer. In S. M. Cormier & J. D. Hagman (Eds.), *Transfer of learning: Contemporary research and applications* (pp. 9–45). Orlando, FL: Academic Press.

Graf, P., & Schacter, D. L. (1985). Implicit and explicit memory for new associations in normal and amnesic subjects. *Journal of Experimental Psychology: Learning, Memory and Cognition, 11,* 501–518.

Hayes–Roth, B., & Hayes–Roth, F. (1979). Cognitive processes in planning. *Cognitive Science, 3,* 275–310.

Hilgard, E. R., & Bower, G. H. (1966). *Theories of learning.* (3rd ed.). New York: Appleton–Century–Crofts.

Hinsley, D. A., Hayes, J. R., & Simon, H. A. (1977). From words to equations: Meaning and representation in algebra word problems. In M. A. Just, & P. A. Carpenter (Eds.), *Cognitive processes in comprehension* (pp. 89–105). Hillsdale, NJ: Lawrence Erlbaum Associates.

Holyoak, K. J. (1985). The pragmatics of analogical transfer. In G. H. Bower (Ed.), *The psychology of learning and motivation* (Vol. 19, pp. 59–87). New York: Academic Press.

Holyoak, K. J., & Koh, K. (1987). Surface and structural similarity in analogical transfer. *Memory & Cognition, 15,* 332–340.

Jacoby, L. J., & Brooks, L. R. (1984). Non-analytic cognition: Memory, perception, and concept learning. In G. H. Bower (Ed.), *The psychology of learning and motivation* (Vol. 18, pp. 1–47). New York: Academic Press.

Jacoby, L. L., & Dallas, M. (1981). On the relationship between autobiographical memory and perceptual learning. *Journal of Experimental Psychology: General, 110,* 306–340.

Johnson–Laird, P. N., & Wason, P. C. (1977). *Thinking.* Bath, England: Pittman Press.

Klahr, D., Langley, P., & Neches, R. (1987). *Production system models of learning and development.* Cambridge, MA: MIT Press.

Kolers, P. A., & Roediger, H. L. III. (1984). Procedures of mind. *Journal of Verbal Learning and Verbal Behavior, 23,* 425–449.

Kolodner, J. L. (1983). Reconstructive memory: A computer model. *Cognitive Science, 7,* 281–328.

Kolodner, J. L., Simpson, R. L., & Sycara–Cyranski, K. (1985). A process model of case-based reasoning in problem-solving. *Proceedings of the International Joint Conference on Artificial Intelligence,* Los Angeles.

Krutetskii, V. A. (1976). *The psychology of mathematical abilities in schoolchildren.* Chicago: University of Chicago Press.

Larkin, J. H. (1981). Enriching formal knowledge: A model for learning to solve textbook physics problems. In J. R. Anderson (Ed.), *Cognitive skills and their acquisition.* Hillsdale, NJ: Lawrence Erlbaum Associates.

Larkin, J. H., McDermott, J., Simon, D. P., & Simon, H. A. (1980). Models of competence in solving physics problems. *Cognitive Science, 4,* 317–345.

LeFevre, J. A., & Dixon, P. (1986). Do written instructions need examples? *Cognition and Instruction, 3,* 1–30.

Lebowitz, M. (1983). Generalization from natural language text. *Cognitive Science, 7,* 1–40.

Lebowitz, M. (1986). Concept learning in a rich input domain: Generalization-based memory. In R. S. Michalski, J. G. Carbonell, & T. M. Mitchell (Eds.), *Machine learning: An artificial intelligence approach* (pp. 193–214). Palo Alto, CA: Tioga.

Lewis, C. (1988). Why and how to learn why: Analysis-based generalization of procedures. *Cognitive Science, 12,* 211–256.

Lockhart, R. S., Lamon, M., & Gick, M. L. (1988). Conceptual transfer in simple insight problems. *Memory & Cognition, 16,* 36–44.

Medin, D. L., & Edelson, S. (1988). Problem structure and the use of base rate information from experience. *Journal of Experimental Psychology: General, 117,* 68–85.

Medin, D. L., & Ross, B. H. (1989). The specific character of abstract thought: Categorization, problem solving, and induction. In R. Sternberg (Ed.), *Advances in the psychology of human intelligence* (Vol. 5; pp. 189–223). Hillsdale, NJ: Lawrence Erlbaum Associates.

Medin, D. L., & Schaffer, M. M. (1978). Context theory of classification learning. *Psychological Review, 85,* 207–238.

Norman, D. A. (1983). Some observations on mental models. In D. Gentner & A. L. Stevens (Eds.), *Mental Models* (pp. 7–14). Hillsdale, NJ: Lawrence Erlbaum Associates.

Norman, D. A., & Bobrow, D. G. (1979). Descriptions: An intermediate stage in memory retrieval. *Cognitive Psychology, 1,* 107–123.

Novick, L. R. (1988). Analogical transfer, problem similarity, and expertise. *Journal of Experimental Psychology: Learning, Memory, and Cognition, 14,* 510–520.

Perfetto, G. A., Bransford, J. D., & Franks, J. J. (1983). Constraints on access in a problem solving context. *Memory & Cognition, 11,* 24–31.

Pirolli, P. L., & Anderson, J. R. (1985). The role of learning from examples in the acquisition of recursive programming skills. *Canadian Journal of Psychology, 39,* 240–272.

Polya, G. (1945). *How to solve it.* Princeton, NJ: Princeton University Press.

Ratcliff, R. (1978). A theory of memory retrieval. *Psychological Review, 85,* 59–108.

Reder, L. M., & Ross, B. H. (1983). Integrated knowledge in different tasks: The role of retrieval strategy on fan effects. *Journal of Experimental Psychology: Learning, Memory and Cognition, 9,* 55–72.

Riesbeck, C. K. (1981). Failure-driven reminding for incremental learning. *Proceedings of the Seventh International Joint Conference on Artificial Intelligence,* Vancouver, Canada.

Rips, L. J. (1983). Cognitive processes in propositional reasoning. *Psychological Review, 90,* 38–71.

Ross, B. H. (1984). Remindings and their effects in learning a cognitive skill. *Cognitive Psychology, 16,* 371–416.

Ross, B. H. (1987). This is like that: The use of earlier problems and the separation of similarity effects. *Journal of Experimental Psychology: Learning, Memory, and Cognition, 13,* 629–639.

Ross, B. H. (1989a). Distinguishing types of superficial similarities: Different effects on the access and use of earlier problems. *Journal of Experimental Psychology: Learning, Memory, and Cognition, 15,* 456–468.

Ross, B. H. (1989b). Remindings in learning and instruction. In S. Vosniadou & A. Ortony (Eds.), *Similarity and analogical reasoning* (pp. 438–469). Cambridge: Cambridge University Press.

Ross, B. H., & Kennedy, P. T. (1990). Generalizing from the use of earlier examples in problem solving. *Journal of Experimental Psychology: Learning, Memory, and Cognition, 16,* 42–55.

Ross, B. H., & Moran, T. P. (1983). Remindings in learning a text editor. *Proceedings of CHI'83 Human Factors in Computing Systems* (pp. 222–225).

Ross, B. H., Perkins, S. J., & Tenpenny, T. L. (in press). Reminding-based category learning. *Cognitive Psychology.*

Ross, B. H., & Sofka, M. D. (1986). *Remindings: Noticing, remembering, and using specific knowledge of earlier problems.* Unpublished manuscript.

Rumelhart, D. E., McClelland, J. L., & PDP Research Group. (1986). *Parallel Distributed Processing* (Vol. 7). Cambridge, MA: MIT Press.

Schacter, D. L. (1987). Implicit memory: History and current status. *Journal of Experimental Psychology: Learning, Memory, and Cognition, 13,* 501–518.

Schank, R. C. (1982). *Dynamic memory.* Cambridge, England: Cambridge University Press.

Silver, E. A. (1979). Student perceptions of relatedness among mathematical verbal programs. *Journal for Research in Mathematics Education, 10,* 195–210.

Silver, E. A. (1981). Recall of mathematical information: Solving related problems. *Journal for Research in Mathematics Education, 12,* 54–64.

Smith, E. E., Adams, N., & Schorr, D. (1978). Fact retrieval and the paradox of interference. *Cognitive Psychology, 10,* 438–464.

Sweller, J. (1988). Cognitive load during problem solving: Effects on learning. *Cognitive Science, 12,* 257–286.

Sweller, J., & Cooper, G. A. (1985). The use of worked examples as a substitute for problem solving in learning algebra. *Cognition and Instruction, 2,* 59–89.

Sweller, J., Mawer, R. F., & Howe, W. (1982). Consequences of history-cued and means-end strategies in problem solving. *American Journal of Psychology, 95,* 455–483.

Tulving, E. (1983). *Elements of episodic.* Oxford: Oxford University Press.

Wason, P. C. (1966). Reasoning. In B. Foss (Ed.), *New Horizons in Psychology, I* (pp. 119, 120, 143, 145). Harmonsworth, England: Penguin.

Weisberg, R., DiCamillo, M., & Phillips, D. (1978). Transferring old associations to new situations: A nonautomatic process. *Journal of Verbal Learning and Verbal Behavior, 17,* 219–228.

Wickelgren, W. A. (1974). *How to solve problems: Elements of a theory of problems and problem solving.* San Francisco: W. H. Freeman.

Williams, M., & Hollan, J. D. (1981). The process of retrieval from very long-term memory. *Cognitive Science, 5,* 87–119.

Winston, P. H. (1980). Learning and reasoning by analogy. *Communications of the ACM, 23,* 689–703.

8 Modeling Software Design Within a Problem-Space Architecture

Beth Adelson
Tufts University

INTRODUCTION

In this chapter we describe research on modeling software design skills within the Soar problem-solving architecture (Laird, Newell, & Rosenbloom, 1987; Steier & Kant, 1985). We focus on an analysis of expert designers of communications systems designing an electronic mail system. The research addresses the issues of:

1. Guiding mental simulations of a design-in-progress using learned schemas: When designing a complex piece of software impasses will arise. To resolve these impasses, skilled designers will run mental simulations of their designs-in-progress (Adelson & Soloway, 1985, 1986; Kant & Newell, 1984; Steier & Kant, 1985). However, these simulations can be done from many points of view. For example, the simulations can depict the system as a set of functions, as a set of data objects or as a set of interacting functions and data. We have found that skilled designers have schemas that result in a systematic and effective ordering of the viewpoints taken during a design session.

2. The interaction of general knowledge of design with domain knowledge about the system being designed: As stated the designers choose viewpoints of the system and then simulate their designs-in-progress from those viewpoints. For example, using general knowledge about designing communications systems one designer chose to simulate the system from the viewpoint of the system's concurrent processes. However, in order to carry out the simulation the viewpoint was mapped

into domain knowledge and instantiated as a simulation of multiple users concurrently issuing commands such as send and receive.

3. Progressive deepening of problem representations during problem solving: Progressive deepening occurs when a problem solver retraces steps along a path he or she previously has taken. The retracing is done, however, in light of new information that has been acquired since the previous trip down the path. The phenomenon was first noticed in studies of chess players, but occurs in design as well (de Groot, 1965; Newell & Simon, 1972). It is clear that progressive deepening is needed when a problem is too complex (and novel) to be understood in a single pass. However, an explanation of the phenomenon is needed. This explanation should include an account of the mechanisms that guide the selection and integration of new information with the information gathered in earlier passes. In the research presented here we find that progressive deepening takes the form of repeated simulations of the same set of mail commands at increasingly specific levels of detail. The repeated simulations can be used by designers to increase their understanding, both of the system's mechanism and behavior.

Below we describe currently existing Soar systems, which form the theoretical perspective for the research described here. We then discuss our protocol data on software design. This is followed by a description of the Soar system suggested by the data, and a discussion of the issues relevant to developing an architecture that can support a unified theory of cognition.

SOAR: A GENERAL ARCHITECTURE FOR COGNITION

Ultimately, the Soar architecture is intended to embody a unified theory of cognition; capable of accounting for the entire range of cognitive problems or 'tasks.' Additionally, it is expected to be able to do so by relying on the mechanisms of recursive subgoaling and chunking.

Currently, Soar can solve a wide range of standard AI problems. It can solve most of the "toy" problems, such as the eight puzzle and tower of Hanoi (Laird, Newell, & Rosenbloom, 1986). Toy problems are ones which require goal-oriented action, without requiring knowledge about the problem domain. It can also solve knowledge-intensive, expert system tasks, such as those solved by the VAX configuration system, R1, and the medical diagnosis system, Neomycin. The weak methods such as generate and test, means–ends analysis, and a variety of search strategies have been implemented. Additionally, Soar exhibits learning phenomena such as learning with practice, transfer across tasks, and generalization. Table 8.1 provides a list of the tasks now performed by Soar.

TABLE 8.1
Summary of Tasks Performed by Soar (from Laird, Newell,
& Rosenbloom, 1987)

Small, Knowledge-lean Tasks (a typical AI toy task):
Blocks world, eight puzzle, eight queens, labeling line drawings (constraint satisfaction), magic squares, missionaries and cannibals, monkey and bananas, picnic problem, robot location finding, three wizards problem, tic-tac-toe, Tower of Hanoi, water-jug task
Small Routine Tasks:
Expression unification, root finding, sequence extrapolation, syllogisms, Wason verification task
Knowledge-intensive Expert-system Tasks:
R1-Soar: 3300 rule industrial expert system (25% coverage)
Neomycin: Revision of Mycin (initial version)
Designer: Designs algorithms (initial version)
Miscellaneous AI Tasks:
Dypar – Soar: Natural-language parsing program (small demo)
Version-spaces: Concept information (small demo)
Resolution theorem prover (small demo)
Weak Methods
Generate and test, and/or search, hill climbing (simple and steepest-ascent), means–ends analysis, operator subgoaling, hypothesize and match, breadth-first search, depth-first search, heuristic search, best-first search, A, progressive deepening (simple and modified, B (progressive deepening), minimax (simple and depth-bounded), alpha-beta, iterative deepening, B
Multiple Organizations and Task Representations:
Eight puzzle, picnic problem, R1 – Soar
Learning
Learns on all tasks it performs by a uniform method (chunking). Detailed studies on eight puzzle, R1-Soar, tic-tac-toe, Korf macro-operators
Types of learning:
Improvement with practice, within-task transfer, across-task transfer, strategy acquisition, operator implementation, macro-operators, explanation-based generalization

---

In terms of accounting for tasks that are central for a theory of cognition, research is now being conducted to look at learning by analogy and reasoning with mental models (Golding, 1988; Polk, 1988; Steier & Kant, 1985). The research presented here is intended to be part of this effort to extend the range of Soar's performance to complex cognitive tasks.

THE NATURE OF PROBLEM SOLVING IN SOAR

As to the nature of the theory, Soar grows out of three decades of work by Newell and his colleagues (Card, Moran, & Newell, 1980; Forgy & McDermott, 1977; Newell, 1980; Newell, Shaw, & Simon, 1960; Newell

& Simon, 1972). In this body of research, problem solving is characterized as movement through successive states of knowledge in a problem space in order to achieve a goal. The problem solver starts out in an initial state which contains an incomplete representation of the problem solution and a description of what would constitute a sufficient solution. The description of the solution could be, for example, the desired behavior for the mailer, whereas the solution itself would be a pseudocode specification of the mechanism producing the behavior.

The problem solvers's relevant knowledge is then brought to bear and the initial representation of the problem is transformed in a way that brings it closer to the goal state representation: the problem solution. Relevant knowledge may consist of specific information about the problem domain as well as general problem-solving strategies.

ELEMENTS OF THE ARCHITECTURE

To model problem solving as it is framed above we need to be able to provide accounts of:

1. The representation of the current problem solution at varying stages of completion.
2. The representation of whatever is known about the desired problem solution.
3. Knowledge about how to assess and transform the partial solution with regard to the desired solution.

The above are realized using the following elements of the Soar architecture:

Production Memory (PM)

This encodes long-term knowledge that can be applied during problem solving (point 3). This can include factual knowledge about the problem being solved, strategic knowledge about how to proceed in problems such as the current one and operational knowledge about specific problem-solving moves to be made in a given situation. It is the use of this operational knowledge that transforms the problem solution from an early insufficient version to a desired or goal state version. The productions that contain this type of operational knowledge place operators into working memory.

When these operators are applied (see next section), they transform the solution-in-progress.

Working Memory (WM)

This holds the representations of the current and desired problem solution described in points 1 and 2 above. WM also holds long-term knowledge that has been identified as relevant.

The Decision Cycle

This brings the appropriate knowledge in production memory to bear given the state of things in working memory. The difference between the starting and goal states is reduced through the decision cycle. The decision cycle is made up of two phases:

1. An elaboration phase that causes already known information in production memory, to be added to working memory. Information in production memory is added to working memory if it is relevant to what presently is in working memory. Elaboration is achieved by a matching process: The antecedents of all productions in PM are matched against the contents of WM; all productions that do match "fire" causing the objects described in the productions' consequent to be placed in WM.
2. A decision phase that makes problem-solving decisions based on the information working memory. The decision process begins once the elaboration process has added all that it currently can to working memory.

THE ARCHITECTURE IN ACTION: AN EXAMPLE OF PROBLEM SOLVING IN SOAR

Below we present a description of Soar solving the eight puzzle. It illustrates how the elements of the architecture function in order to move the problem solver through the problem space toward the goal state.

The eight puzzle is a typical AI toy problem, calling for goal-oriented, but knowledge-lean behavior. The problem solver is presented with a board containing nine squares and eight numbered tiles. The goal is to transform the tiles' starting configuration into the goal state configuration (Fig. 8.1). The eight puzzle is chosen here not as a representative cognitive task, but because of its simplicity allows us to focus on the Soar architecture. Issues of Soar systems as cognitive models are dealt with in a later section.

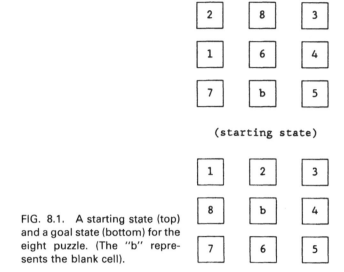

(starting state)

FIG. 8.1. A starting state (top) and a goal state (bottom) for the eight puzzle. (The "b" represents the blank cell).

Soar begins its problem solving by explicitly setting the goal of solving the eight puzzle. In the first decision cycle, "Eight-Puzzle" is proposed and selected as the current problem space, so that only productions relevant to that problem space will fire.

As we can see in line OD of the tile program (Table 8.2), Soar begins its problem solving by setting a top-level goal of solving the problem at hand. In the first decision cycle, "Solve-Eight Puzzle" is proposed and selected as the name of the current problem. Additionally, "Eight-Puzzle" is proposed and selected as the current problem space, so that only productions relevant to that problem space will fire.

As we will see below, problems can be divided into subproblems, each having its own problem space with operators appropriate to the subproblem. During the second decision cycle, the initial and goal board configurations are placed in WM.

The third decision cycle begins, as usual with an elaboration phase; based on the initial configuration, "6 down," "5 left," and "7 right" are all proposed as "operators" (moves). Information is also placed in WM indicating that the down operator is preferable since it will result in moving the 6 into its desired position.

This information about operators and their preferability is placed in WM as a result of productions firing based on the contents of WM. Table 8.3 shows the productions that fired (during the third decision cycle). Instantiate-Operator fired three times, proposing down, left, and right as acceptable operators (line 3.1E in Table 8.2) A-Means-Ends-Analysis-Operator fired next (line 3.2E) marking down as the best operator.

TABLE 8.2
Trace of Decision Cycles for the Eight Puzzle. (From Laird, Newell, & Rosenbloom, 1987)

	Cycle Action
OD	Solve the problem is the current goal
1E	Propose Solve-Eight-Puzzle as the name of the current goal
1E	Propose Eight-Puzzle as the problem space
ID	Select Solve-Eight-Puzzle as the name of the current goal Select Eight-Puzzle as problem space
2E	Place description of goal state board configuration in WM
2E	Place description of current board configuration in WM
2D	Select S1 as the current state (with the initial and goal states in WM)
3.IE	Propose 01 (down)
3.1E	Propose 02 (right)
3.IE	Propose 03 (left)
3.2E	Mark down as best (it moves 6 into its goal position)
3D	Select 01 (down) as operator
4.1E	Propose S2 (swap 6 and blank)
4.2E	Copy the unmodified parts of the board
4D	Select S2 as state
5E	Propose 04 (down)
5E	Propose 05 (right)
5E	Propose 06 (left)
5E	Propose 07 (up)
5E	Mark 7 as worst (it undoes the last move)
5D	Tie impasse, create subgoal

Reading from left to right:
The leftmost column (labeled "Cycle") indicates the decision cycle (D and E stand for decision and elaboration respectively). The next column indicates the action taken in that cycle.

When all of the productions that can fire have fired, elaboration is said to have reached "quiescence"; the decision process begins and down is selected as the best operator in the current situation or "context."[1] This ends the third decision cycle. The fourth decision cycle ends when the down operator is "applied"; the productions relevant to the operator fire (lines 4.1E and 4.2E), a new board configuration results (Fig. 8.2) and a new "current state" is decided upon (line 4D).

Looking at the elaboration phase of the fifth decision cycle in Table 8.3 we see that down, right, left, and up are all placed in WM as acceptable candidate operators. Additionally, up is marked as unacceptable by the Avoid-Undo production (Table 8.3). We also see that after the elaboration phase ends the decision process reaches a "tie impasse" (line 5D); WM contains four candidate operators and all of the information provided in

---

[1] In Soar the current situation is termed the current context and is specified by the value of the current goal, problem-space, state and operator.

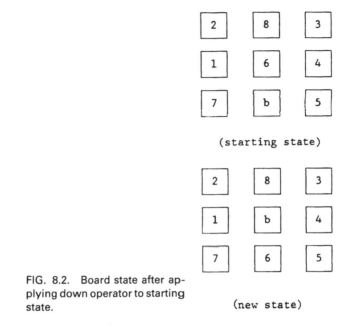

(starting state)

(new state)

FIG. 8.2. Board state after applying down operator to starting
state.

TABLE 8.3
Productions Creating Candidate Operators and Acceptability Values

Production: Instantiate-Operator:
  If:
    the current problem space is 8 puzzle
    & the current board has a tile in a cell adjacent to the blank's cell
  Then:
    place a new operator in WM that will move the tile into the blank's cell
    & place in WM the information that the operator is acceptable.
Production-A-Means-Ends-Analysis-Operator
  If:
    the current problem space is 8 puzzle – and operator will move a tile into its goal
    state position
Then:
    place in WM the information that the operator is the best choice.
Production: Avoid-Undo:
  If:
    the current problem space is 8 puzzle
  Then:
    place in WM the information that the operator to move the tile that was last moved
    is a worst choice.

the elaboration phase says only that three are acceptable. The information in production memory about this problem space is incomplete; it cannot resolve the tie. However, here is where the notion of subgoals and problem spaces comes into play.

SUBGOALING TO RESOLVE IMPASSES

When an impasse is reached, the Soar architecture sets up a subgoal to resolve the impasse.[2] For a tie impasse in the eight puzzle, the subgoal is to "select" an operator from the set of possible ones. This is achieved by moving into the selection problem space. A further subgoal results in which the candidate operators are actually tried out (by moving back into eight puzzle space) and the state that will result from each one is evaluated. For this example (Fig. 8.2, bottom), down is found to be best since it will lead to a follow-up move that will allow the 2 to be moved into place. The other two candidates are found to lead to moves that will move tiles out of their desired spots.

Three points are important here: (1) The detection of the impasse and the setting up of the appropriate type of subgoal is not done by the task specific eight puzzle productions; it is done by the architecture. (2) Once a subgoal is established it is pursued and resolved in the same way as a higher-level goal. A problem space is selected; a current and goal state are defined; and operators are then applied to the current state in order to transform it into the goal state. (3) This subgoaling can occur to an arbitrary depth. These three points lead to some of the appeal that Soar has as a theory. By being able to detect impasses and set up appropriate subgoals, the architecture, the part of Soar which is specified in advance and remains constant across tasks, does a good deal of the problem solving. Additionally, the ability to solve problems in this uniform way (by recursive subgoaling) allows Soar to provide a parsimonious account of complex problem solving.

Turning to software design we will see that organizing the problem solving into problem spaces continues to be useful. We will also look at

---

[2] Here we see a tie impasse, however, no-change, conflict and rejection impasses occur as well (Laird, Newell, & Rosenbloom, 1986). In fact, "no-change" impasses often arise in complex problem solving domains such as (Iosign). A no-change impasse can occur when a problem-solving action is decided on, but how to take the action is not known. (The impasse is called no-change because an action has been decided upon but does not lead to a change in the problem-solver's state). For example, when trying to solve the problem of how to spend lottery winnings a decision may be made to take the action of buying a new car, but how to go about choosing one may not be known. A no change impasse has now occurred. The impasse can be resolved by setting a sub-goal to gather information relevant to making the choice.

the way in which the problem spaces are related and how information from one problem space can further problem solving in another.

MODELING SOFTWARE DESIGN WITHIN SOAR

Method
> Below we present our data on software design.
> *Subjects*
>> Three expert software designers served as subjects. Each of the experts had worked for at least 8 years in commercial settings designing a wide variety of software.[3]
> *Procedure*
>> We presented each of the designers with the following design task to work on.
> *Task:*
>> Design an electronic mail system around the following commands: READ, REPLY, SEND, DELETE, SAVE, EDIT, and LIST-HEADERS. The goal is to get to the level of pseudocode that could be used by professional programmers to produce a running program. The mail system will run on a very large, fast machine, so hardware considerations are not an issue.[4]

This task had several important properties: (1) It was nontrivial, it required close to 2 hours of the subject's time. (2) It was novel; none of the designers had designed a solution to the problem previously. These two properties meant that we would have the opportunity to see not only "routine cognitive skill," but problem solving as well. (3) The problem we chose was similar to the types of problems which the subjects had to deal with professionally. As a result we would be able to see them using the general design skills that they had acquired over time.

ANALYSIS OF THE PROTOCOL DATA

Generally protocol data can be seen as a series of episodes, with each episode reflecting the single, current focus of the subject's attention.

---

[3] The protocols from all three subjects were analyzed. In Appendix 1 we present a long section of the protocol of SI. SI's protocol is representative of the protocols of all three subjects and is focussed on in this chapter.

[4] We have also studied novices designing the same system as well as this group of experts designing and interrupt handler and a data base system (Adelson & Soloway, 1985).

PAIRS OF EPISODES

One striking aspect of the protocol discussed here is that the episodes formed related pairs. The first episode in a pair appears to take place in a general design space and the second episode appears to take place in a space containing knowledge about mail systems. The first four episodes from S1 are representative of this phenomenon.

Episode 1:
S: . . . I'm going to start working here, functions of an electronic mail."
(writes 'Functions' and 'Data' in two separate columns)

Episode 2:
"We must be able to:
Prepare,
Send,
Receive . .
(writes prepare, send, receive under the heading 'Functions')
. . . the system must be able to store them,
the system must be able to handle abnormalities throughout it."
In episode 1, S1 decides to view the system as a set of functions. In episode 2 he goes on to enumerate what those functions would be.
In episode 3, S1 decides to view the system as a set of data objects and in episode 4 he elaborates the features of those objects.

Episode 3:
Let's stop there and take a fresh cut at the data."

Episode 4:
"there must be some data of the users, e.g., the destinations, the addresses;
also data of update formats;
data . . . ,
there must be the message store itself.
The message store would come in several forms:
the store for messages sent but not received,
the store of messages received by some individual,
I think of unix, of the dead letter concept
—the store of messages that we can't do anything with
(what) if we want to store them."
In Table 8.4 we present a summary of episode pairs for the first 10 episodes of S1's protocol. The first episode in each pair establishes the goal of viewing the system from a particular perspective:
View 1. View the system as a set of functions: Episode 1.
View 2. View the system as a set of data objects: Episode 3.
View 3. View the system as a set of concurrent functions: Episode 5.
View 4. View the system as a state machine for states of user: Episode 7.
View 5. View the system as a state machine for messages: Episode 9.

TABLE 8.4
Description of Episodes 1 through 10

Episode 1. View the system as a set of functions.

Episode 2. Simulate the behavior of the system's functions. The commands prepare, send receive and store must be included in specifying the mailer's functionality. Discover that error recovery must be handled gracefully throughout the system.

Episode 3. View the system as a set of data objects.

Episode 4. Elaborate the features of the data objects. In the mailer messages are the data objects. Messages have destinations of senders and receivers. Additionally, messages are grouped together in stores. The stores can have various functions. For example, the mail system needs a store for messages that the user has received but not yet read, as well as a store for messages that have been read but not yet saved or deleted.

Episode 5. View the system as a set of concurrent functions.

Episode 6. Simulate the behavior of a system in which there are concurrent senders and receivers. Discover that the design needs to specify when users should be notified that new mail has arrived (as it arrives, only at log-on, etc.). Also discover that, since mail is both being sent and received, more than one type of processing must be handled and therefore a "dispatch demon" is needed to handle the flow of messages.

Episode 7. View the system as a state machine for the states of a user.

Episode 8. Simulate the behavior of the system as a scenario in which the user logs on and issues a sequence of mail commands. He is notified that he has mail, he lists the headers, he reads a message, he makes some disposition of the message and then is able to begin again (listing headers, etc.). The designer discovers that the postconditions of the commands need to be enumerated both to refine the command definitions and to understand the potential interactions between commands. For example, if READ includes an implicit and immediate DELETE it will prevent the user from being able to save or forward the message.

Episode 9. View the system as a state machine for the states of messages.

Episode 10. Simulate the behavior of the system in terms of the states of the messages. A message is created, sent, received, read and disposed of. These actions described at the level of files and locations within files are sufficient to generate pseudocode.

The second episode instantiates the view as a simulation. Both the content and the ordering of these episode pairs suggest that the designer is using an experience-based schema to direct the design session. It appears that the designer starts off with an incomplete representation or model of the design and then, to attain a finished design, simulates that model from each of these perspectives in order.

Schemas

The design process seems driven by an experience-based schema for two reasons: First, successive episodes do not appear to arise from the context that immediately precedes them; in episodes 3 and 4, the system is viewed as a set of data objects and then in episodes 5 and 6 as a set of concurrent processes. Second, the particular views chosen, such as dealing with concurrency issues, would be ones to develop given these designers' experience with communications system.

The structure of the schema is also interesting; taken in order the five views comprise a set that would be effective in uncovering most of the aspects of the system that need refinement. The first view looks at the commands of the mailer, the second view at the messages themselves. Once the commands have been specified it becomes possible to look at the interactions produced when they, are used in sequence, as they will be by the system's users. This is uncovered by the fourth view which looks at the system as a state machine from the user's perspective. It also becomes possible to look at their concurrent functioning (view 3). The fifth view looks at the interaction of commands and messages; it therefore, is dependent on having specified the commands and messages in the first and second views.

The issue arises as to when during problem solving will this schema be used. It is likely the problem -solver will reuse previous solutions or good analogies whenever possible (Adelson & Soloway, 1985; Burstein & Adelson, 1987; Burstein & Adelson, this volume; Carbonell, 1983, 1986; Kolodner, 1984). However, in the absence of right, or "almost right" (Sussman, 1975) solutions it then becomes likely that the problem solver will turn to a higher level, experience based schemas.

The pairing of the episodes is explained by the schema that was used. The schema suggested views of the system that would lead to refining the design. The first episode in a pair sets up a view and the second episode simulates it.

Interaction of Domain and General Knowledge

In designing a large software system the designers employ three types of knowledge: knowledge of design, knowledge for representing systems as pieces of pseudocode, and knowledge of how mail systems behave. From our perspective, these bodies of knowledge can be seen as three problem spaces; a design space, a pseudocode space and a mail space (see later section of this chapter). In simulating views of the system there has to be a mapping between the designer's high-level problem space for design, in which the schema resides and the domain space where knowledge about the behavior of mailers resides; it is in this domain space design, in which the schema resides and the domain space where knowledge about the behavior of mailers resides; it is in this domain space that the view is instantiated, run, and evaluated. For example, in episode 7 the designer chooses to view the system as a state machine in which the user goes through a sequence of state transitions. This gives rise to episode 8, in which the designer instantiates this state machine by constructing a simulation in which the user logs on, is notified that he has mail, lists the headers, reads a message, makes some disposition of the message and then begins again.

In order to model this piece of problem solving, what needs to be accounted for? The goal to look at the system as a state machine in which a user goes through state transitions needs to be represented. A mapping is then needed in order to instantiate this goal in design space as an executable "reception scenario" in mail space. This means that the user's state transitions need to be put into correspondence with the issuing of commands such as READ or SAVE. Additionally, data objects must be understood to correspond with messages.

In the domain space there needs to be enough knowledge about the behavior of the mail commands to propose and simulate candidate versions of them. The candidate versions then have to be evaluated by comparing their behavior to some representation of the ideal behavior. The candidates can then be modified in accord with the results of the evaluation. The ability to modify a representation of a command in pseudocode space based on the results of a simulation in mail space implies a mapping between mail space and pseudocode space. All of this reasoning is done by the designer in episode 10. The designer simulates SAVE and then realizes that in order to save a message its number must be specified when the command is issued.

> ". . . We can save it somewhere—it goes into some state . . . .
> When we save them off in a file like that are we going to save them as mail objects, or are we going to just append them on so they're not distinguishable.
> I now need to start making some decisions on that.
> "Looking at the (commands) and what they operate on, we're going to assume in many cases that there are some store of messages. We're operating on individual messages themselves.
> So I've got to have some way of identifying where it is within that store . . . .
> . . . Let's just number them (the messages).
> Save is going to take some mail number from his mail store, and move it over to his saved mail."

Progressive Deepening

As we have mentioned, progressive deepening is the retracing of steps along a previously taken problem-solving path. The retracing is done because the first trip down the path was not sufficient; and new, relevant information has been acquired. Both deGroot (1965) and Newell and Simon (1972) found progressive deepening in chess and Newell and Simon suggest that progressive deepening may be one of the hallmarks of complex problem solving. Below we present an example of progressive deepening from our data. This is followed by an explanation of why progressive deepening would occur within Soar.

In the following sequence of episodes we see the progressive deepening of the definition of the store command.

In episode 2 the commands are just written down by the designer as a list of functions to be specified.

> "So I'm going to start working here, functions of an electronic mail, we must be able to prepare, send, receive . . .
> the system must be able to store messages, the system must be able to handle abnormalities through it."

In episode 8 the designer simulates these same commands using each one's output as implicit to the next and discovering that the side-effects of each have to be elaborated. For example, he decides that a user should be able to list all the message headers without being committed to then reading them.

> "Let's look at a reception scenario . . .
> He'll look at all of them in the store . . . .
> (I am) making a conscious decision that he is going to have the option of looking at all the mail items before he jumps in and starts reading them, so he's got a survey capability here.
> That tells me that we've got to start making more design functionality decisions as we go through here . . . .
> (Looking at) this store (of messages) brings him to a new state where he knows what mail he has
> (If, as a result of listing the headers) he reads it, he's got to make a disposition of it, what he's (going) to do with it. Whatever disposition we decide— destroy, store, most of those dispositions are going to get him back to his initial state."

In episode 10 the designer finally simulates the commands at a level sufficient to generate pseudocode. Here he uses language that refers to reading from and writing to files:

> "Each user of the system will have his own mail store, I can save a message into an identified store of messages.
> So I've got to have some way of identifying where it is within that store.
> Let's number the messages in the store.
> So when I store, I want to identify the mail number and the mail store . . . "

Simulation and progressive deepening arise naturally within a Soar architecture. There are two reasons why simulation occurs. The first reason had to do with seeing complex problem solving as occurring in a set of related problem spaces. Problem solvers have different types of representations of the problem solution in different problem spaces. Additionally, the information contained in one type of representation may contribute to the development of another. In design, simulations arise because detailed information about the behavior of a mail command, obtained from a simulation in mail space, can help in developing the representation of the command in pseudocode space.

The second reason for simulation has to do with comparing current and goal states. In designing the mail system, the designers represent the goal state in terms of the desired behavior of the mail system. However, the problem solution is a pseudocode description of the mailer. In order to compare this pseudocode representation to the goal, they need to simulate the pseudocode. The simulations done by the designers need to go through progressive deepening; at the beginning of the design session the designers' representation of the mailer is in terms of the high-level behavior of the system. This is the representation that would be likely for a person who had used, but not actually designed such a system. The representation of the behavior needs to be refined to a degree that allows that behavior to be expressed as pseudocode. But in a task that has a complex solution there are many aspects to the refinement. The use of repeated simulations, from different perspectives, allows the designer to attend to different aspects of the refinement in a systematic way. This allows the designer to bring his or her understanding to the required degree of specificity without overloading working memory.

SKETCH OF THE MAIL DESIGNER-SOAR SYSTEM

Recall that in the context of Soar, problem solving is characterized as movement through successive states of knowledge in order to achieve a goal. The states of knowledge contain representations of the problem at various points in the problem-solving process. Additionally, the different aspects of the problem are regarded as different problem spaces in which different, appropriate, kinds of knowledge are brought to bear.

In order to model the design process within the Soar framework we need to provide accounts of: (1) The initial and goal state representations which form the system's input and output, (2) The problem spaces with their appropriate operators.

As to point 1, the initial state, there is a representation of the desired behavior of the mailer. The goal state would be a pseudocode description of the mailer's commands. On point 2, the problem solving consists of trying first to apply existing knowledge relevant to a pseudocode problem space in order to represent the design as pieces of pseudocode. If existing knowledge is not sufficient to represent the design directly in terms of pseudocode the behavior of the mailer is simulated in mail space. They are repeated, from varying perspectives and in increasing detail until the designer understands the system's behavior at a level that allows it to be expressed as pseudocode. The set of perspectives used in the simulations in pseudocode and mail space are generated by the strategic knowledge in the design problem space. Table 8.5 lists the operators that apply in the "design," the "pseudocode," and the "mail" problem spaces.

The design space operators form a hierarchical tree of perspectives from which to view the system (Fig. 8.3). The perspectives direct simulations of the design-in-progress both in pseudocode and mail space. The tree is traversed in a breadth-first order, this leads to the systematic ordering of the perspectives taken during the design process.

In "pseudocode space" the system is represented as pieces of pseudocode. These pieces are repeatedly executed and defined until the design of the mailer is complete.

TABLE 8.5
Operators in the Design and Mail Spaces

Design Space Operators:
The Operators Causing Differing Views of the System to be Taken
1. Design the system *as a set of functions.
2. Design the system *as a set of data objects.
3. Design the system as sets of concurrent functions.
4. Design a state machine of the states a user goes through (resulting in a focus of attention on interactions between functions).
5. Design a state machine of the states a message goes through (resulting in a focus of attention on interactions between function and data).

Pseudocode and Mail Space Operators:
The Operators to Generate, Run and Evaluate Candidate Versions of the Functions' Mechanisms in Pseudocode Space and the Functions' Behavior in Mail Space
1. Prepare.
2. Send.
3. Receive.
4. List headers.
5. Read.
6. Store.
7. Delete.

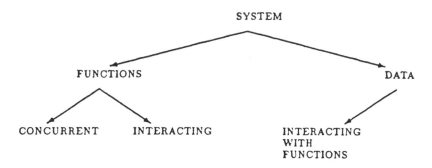

FIG. 8.3.   Hierarchy of design space operators.

CONCLUSIONS

We have described modeling software design within a Soar framework. Using this framework we are to provide accounts for the following:

1. The role of schemas in bringing general knowledge to bear on knowledge about a domain: In the data presented the designer uses a high-level schema in order to create an ordered set of pairs of episodes in which a variety of interdependent aspects of the mailer are considered and refined.

2. The role of simulation: Simulation supports the design process in two ways. It allows the comparison of current and goal states when the current state is represented as a mechanism and the goal state is represented as behavior. Additionally, simulation supports the development of a representation of the mechanism of the system being designed when the system's behaviors are simulated at a level of detail that allows the behaviors to be expressed as mechanisms.

3. The role of progressive deepening: Because a set of simulations from a variety of perspectives are needed to complete the design we find that the same set of commands is simulated repeatedly at increasing levels of refinement.

We are optimistic that a Soar framework will continue to support detailed accounts of the mechanisms that underlie cognitive problem-solving skills.

ACKNOWLEDGMENT

We are grateful to David Steier for his continuing generous help. Also, we would like to thank Minnie Adelson for carefully chewing over earlier drafts. This work was supported by grants from the design, manufacturing and engineering program and the knowledge and data base systems program at NSF.

REFERENCES

Adelson, B., & Soloway, E. (1985). The role of domain expertise in software design. IEEE, TSE.

Adelson, B., & Soloway, E. (1986). A model of software design. *International Journal of Intelligent Systems.*

Burstein, M. (1985). Concept formation by incremental analogy reasoning and debugging. In *Machine Learning.* Los Altos, CA: Morgan Kaufmann.

Burstein, M., & Adelson, B. (1987). Analogical learning: Mapping and integrating partial mental models. *Proceedings of the Cognitive Science Society.*

Card, S., Moran, T., & Newell, A. (1980). Computer test editing. *Cognitive Psychology, 12,* 32–74.

Carbonell, J. (1983). Formulating and generalizing plans from past experience. In R. S. Michalski, J. G. Carbonell, & T. M. Mitchell (Eds.), *Machine learning: An artificial intelligence approach.* Palo Alto, CA: Tioga.

Carbonell, J. (1986). Deprivational analogy: A theory of reconstructive problem solving and expertise acquisition. In R. S. Michalski, J. G. Carbonell, & T. M. Mitchell (Eds.), *Machine learning: An artificial intelligence approach, 2.* Los Altos, CA: Morgan Kaufmann.

de Groot, A. D. (1965). *Thought and choice in chess.* Paris: Mouton.

Forgy, C., & McDermott, J. (1977). OPS, a domain-independent production system language. *Proceedings of the fifth International Joint Computer Conference,* MIT AI Lab, Cambridge, MA.

Golding, A. (1988). *Learning to pronounce names by taking advice.* Thesis proposal, Stanford University, Stanford, CA.

Kant, E., & Newell, A. (1984). Problem solving techniques for the design of algorithms. *Information Processing and Management,* pp. 97–118.

Kolodner, J. (1984). *Retrieval and organizational strategies in conceptual memory: A computer model.* Hillsdale, NJ: Lawrence Erlbaum Associates.

Laird, J., Newell, A., & Rosenbloom, P. (1986). *Soar: An architecture for general intelligence.* CMU CS Tech Report.

Newell, A. (1980). The problem space as a fundamental category. In R. Nickerson (Ed.), *Attention and Performance* (Vol. 8). Hillsdale, NJ: Lawrence Erlbaum Associates.

Newell, A., Shaw, J., & Simon, H. (1960). A report on a general problem-solving program for a computer. *Proceedings of the International Conference on Information Processing,* UNESCO, Paris.

Newell, A., & Simon, H. (1972). *Human problem solving.* Englewood Cliffs, NJ: Prentice–Hall.

Polk, T. (1988). *Fourth annual Soar workshop.* Ann Arbor: University of Michigan.

Schank, R., & Abelson, R. (1977). *Scripts, plans, goals and understanding.* Hillsdale, NJ: Lawrence Erlbaum Associates.

Steier, D. (1986). *Integrating knowledge into an algorithm designer.* Thesis proposal, Carnegie–Mellon University.

Steier, D. (1987). *Proceedings of the 1987 IJCAI Conference.*

Steier, D., & Kant, E. (1985). IEEE, TSE.

Sussman, G. (1975). *A computer model of skill acquisition.* New York: American Elsevier.

APPENDIX 1: EPISODES IN THE PROTOCOL

Episode 1

L1: (writes 'functions') The view I'm going to take as I go through this system,
L2: (writes 'data') keep looking at the data and the information component behind us,

Episode 2

L3: so I'm going to start working here, functions of an electronic mail,
L4: we must be able to prepare,
L5: send,
L6: receive
L6a: (writes prepare, send, receive)
L7: in receiving a number of choices and decisions have to be made
L7a: as to the disposition of it
L8: we'll get into that later;
L9: the system must be able to store them,
L10: the system must be able to handle abnormalities throughout it.

Episode 3

L11: O.K. Let's stop there and take a fresh cut at the functions.
L12: And take a first cut at the data and what would be behind it.
L13: E: Can you say why you stopped at that point?
L14: I feel I've gone as deep as I need for the moment.
L15: I recognize I'm going to go deeper into each of these,
L16: but I'm just taking a top layer of it first of all.
L17: (I'm looking) over here and see if from the data side I can recognize other views that I haven't seen through this approach
L18: and we'll be sure they interact between the two of these approaches, and each time going down more and more in detail.

Episode 4

L19: (begins writing under 'data') For data,
L20: there must be some data of the users,
L21: the destinations,
L22: the addresses;
    (also) data of update formats;
L23: (also) data of update formats;
L24: data . . .
L25: there must be the message store itself.
L26: The message store would come in several forms:
L27: the store for messages sent but not received,

L28: the store of messages received by some individual,
L29: I think of unix of the dead letter concept
L30: — the store of messages that we can't do anything with
L31: (what) if we want to store them.

Episode 5

L32: Throughout the system, it is going to be handling concurrency,
L33: so that is the initial event I need to address.

Episode 6

L34: For the moment, let us break it down.
L35: Concurrency among the senders and receivers.
L36: There must be some function other than senders and receivers, which is periodically monitoring what is happening to our message store;
L37: I think of unix.
L38: We have to make strategy decisions on how we deliver messages to the receiver of it;
L39: whether we deliver when the receiver logs on or when the message is sent,
L40: or whether we deliver through having some continuously running program.
L41: some demon type of program that comes in periodically, looks around and says, 'Can I do anything with the message?'
L42: So there must be some sort of dispatching philosophy.
L43: (writes 'dispatching philosophy')

Episode 7

L44: What's coming to mind is that here we've got,
L45: in fact we can look at the states for our messages,
L46: the states of this whole system,
L47: and take another view as well as the function-data view.
L48: Think of it as a big state machine,
L49: what is happening to it so that we can see that for a while . . .
L50: (paper change, comments about papers)
L51: States:
L52: What are the things we are dealing with?
L52a: Objects, (writes 'Objects) (in) terms of events.
L53: Objects: we've got users,
L54: we've got message mail.
L55: Events, (writes 'events')
L56: new mail ready,
L57: receivers log on.
L58: O.K. Let me start looking at the states of a user first of all. How in the world is this going to be seen from the view of the user?

Episode 8

L59: He starts out, start him out with some state of, let's call it an initial state first of all.

(begins drawing a state diagram)

L60: Let's look at a reception scenario and

L61: through log-on he becomes capable of receiving messages,

L62: receiving mail

L63: — either there is mail or there is not mail.

L64: If there is mail,

L65: and this may be because he gets special messages on,

L66: or because some time later, after he's logged on, he is informed that there is mail and is willing to receive it.

L67: There must be another case where there is mail but not willing.

L68: There is mail *and willing to receive it.

L69: And he starts.

L70: He'll look at all of them in the store,

L71: (I am) making a conscious decision that he is going to have the option of looking at all the mail items before he jumps in and starts reading them, so he's got a survey capability here.

L72: That tells me that we've got to start making more design functionality decisions as we go through here and,

L73: in effect, build up the user's specification over the functional specification of the system as seen by the user.

L74: For the purposes here, this will go into user manuals

L75: — Through the lack of any user input we're going to give it this (survey) capability

L76: That is our decision here.

L77: (Looking at) this store (of messages) brings him to a new state where he knows what mail he has

L78: He can choose at this state to exit and get out to some other place we don't know yet where it is.

L79: Going to read mail,

L80: read monitoring.

L81: When he reads it, it's got to make a disposition of it what he's got to do with it.

L82: Most of those are going to get him back to his initial state.

L83: Whatever disposition we decide — destroy, hold, reply, whatever else will get him back there.

L84: I think it will be very obvious now that I've got to decide what those functions are from the user's point of view before I can continue much farther with this design.

L85: So let me note that. (makes a note)

L86: At this stage, I need the functional specifications.

L87: I'll come back and do that in a little while, time permitting,

L88: and carry on making some other assumptions here.

L89: (Pointing to and looking at each successive command in the drawing of the test case being simulated in the last 5

L90: Store . . .
L91: Read, OK, That's good enough for the user view of it.

Episode 9

L92: Let's look at mail messages.

Episode 10

L93: Any one mail message starts out conceptually as nonexistent and then we create it, prepare it.
L94: So there must be a function of editing mail
L94a: and deciding whether we are going to send it.
L95: Let's hide all of that for the moment and say we prepare and send.
L96: When we say send, there must be some function of routing it.
L97: Prepare and send —
L98: So then that mail message will normally go into a case where it's waiting to be received.
L99: but the receiver may be available immediately, in which case, it would be presented to him.
L100: Let's split apart those two actions into two different states, so it's waiting to be received.
L101: Then there's some command that says, "Read it," — becomes read
L102: Then there's some command that says, "Delete"
L103: and goes back here — (to ready
L104: we can save it somewhere — it goes into some state.
L105: I'm thinking, what is the form of these message.
L106: When we save them off in a file like that are we going to save them as mail objects, or are we going to just append them onto they're not distinguishable. I now need to start making some decisions on that.
L107: Let me look back at my primitives.
       (looks back to previous sheet)
L108: Read, Rely, Send, Delete — I'm going to make an assumption that these primitives are operating on mail themselves — read a mail message as well as to read a line of something. Reply to a mail message, delete a mail message, store, the data view of this system, works in units of mail. messages.
L109: O.K. I don't see here any primitives that will help me in preparing a message. There's an edit primitive which edits an existing message? . . .
L123: Looking at the primitives and what they operate on.
       (begins looking back at primitives)
L124: We're going to assume in many cases that there are some store of messages
L125: We're operating on and individual messages themselves.
L126: For instance "list headers," I can give that an argument that says, list headers in this particular store of messages, and it will list them out.

L127:   I can send *an individual message and the primitive will have enough intelligence to take the addresses within it and dispatch it off to the correct recipient.

L128:   I can save a message into an identified store of messages.

L129:   I can read a message from a store of messages.

L130:   So I've got to have some way of identifying where it is within that store.

L131:   So if I make a mental model of this thing called message store, mail store, which contains mail messages. Let's just number them. The first one is always one, etc. So when I read, I want to identify the mail number and the mail store.

L132:   Each user of the system will have his own mail store, there will be many of them, and the primitive will be able to operate on the appropriate one.

L133:   Reply, and what this does is it presents the mail message to user.

L134:   Delete again deletes a particular mail number from the mail store.

L135:   This will . . . Decision to be made. When we delete, it will be based on a user request, so we are in an interactive session with the user. He's going to have this as his mental model of what's happening with his mail messages. If we delete one of them in the middle, we've got to decide if we change the order of the messages or not.

L136:   My decision is that this delete primitive will make no change in the ordering of messages. The effect of delete takes place at some later time after the session is over.

L137:   Reply, takes from the user and replies to an unidentified mail number in the mail store. So the reply primitive uses this mail message to get the address of the sender of it and replies back to him.

L138:   Whereas Send, more general, send is just a new message, and out of that new message the primitive is able to abstract the destination of addresses.

L139:   Save, save, save, brings us to our two main stores that we have already made up there . . . save state.
        Now we've got our model elaborated on to reveal that there is an addition to each user having its mail store, he's got his saved mail.

L140:   Does he get rid of saved mail? An issue to be decided. (marks it)

L141:   We may need to come back and give him the capability to re-read saved mail and decide what to do with it.
        That grows slightly large.

L142:   Save is going to take some mail, number from his mail store, and move it over to his saved mail.

L143:   Edit. What's going through my mind here is that in giving me these seven primitives is what's helping me and hindering me because you're giving me a constraint that I've got to work with and not letting me construct that I would like to have, and I now find myself working around the seven primitives, trying to build up a system that will work in the presence of these seven primitives.

L144:   This says edit. I've been assuming that a lot of the editing takes place hidden underneath it. I don't know why I would ever want to edit something that is already sitting inside in one of my mail stores. The editing normally takes place at the moment of preparation of the message which I have

identified before, but I don't have primitives to deal with and that phase —
under it. Edit, edit, edit, I'm at a loss as to how to interpret edit right
now. Let's leave it aside for the moment.

L145: List headers is straight forward. List headers by how mail is stored.

L146: The function that's missing from this one (save) would be some form of
pointing to the saved mail instead of the mail store. We would normally
need to save, I'm aware of that.

L147: There might be some copy function, copying saved mail over to mail store,
that is nothing new. We could make some other definitions of these primitives and play on the behavior as to what happens in our model between
mail stored and saved mail.

L148: For instance, it could be that when I log on to a session with the mail
system, I list out the headers and then I go through reading. When I read
one, it is automatically taken out of mail store and then my decision is
whether I delete it or save it. Deleting just discards it; saves it would
automatically move it over to saved mail, as opposed to this primitive of
where we don't move things from the mail store automatically.

L149: So we get more decisions that have to be made to relate to the functionality
as seen by the user. I think I've gone as far as I want to go with that one
for right now.

9

Memory Organization and Retrieval: An Artificial Intelligence Perspective

Lisa F. Rau
General Electric Company

1. INTRODUCTION

Artificial Intelligence has long been trying to gain insight into cognitive processes through the construction of computer models of thought and reason. Perhaps the earliest such work was the pioneering 1963 effort by Feigenbaum to simulate the serial position effect in learning lists of nonsense syllables (Feigenbaum, 1963). However, recent trends in psychology suggest a new emphasis on the study of memory in more natural tasks, as described in a recent book by Neisser (Neisser, 1982). Although Bartlett's early work on reconstructive memory (Bartlett, 1932) took more than 50 years to be implemented in an AI program, an implementation by Kolodner (Kolodner, 1984) leads the way toward a modern study memory organization and retrieval in everyday tasks, drawing from psychology and AI perspectives and methodologies. AI's perspective is a functional, procedural orientation that concentrates on theories and models of cognition that can be implemented on a computer.

The study of memory organization and retrieval may be of interest to the testing community for many reasons. For one, in a traditional testing situation, a tester will be asking a testee to retrieve information, stored in some fashion in their "knowledge bases." How that knowledge might be organized affects the kinds of questions that might be asked, as do the different types of retrieval strategies available to the testee. Different types of questions may be composed to access different kinds of information or to test the efficiency of various kinds of retrieval. The study of memory retrieval and storage may also provide insight into mechanisms to increase the capabilities of computer-aided instruction programs, by tailoring instruction to internal states of knowledge.

In this chapter, the topics of long-term memory organization and retrieval are discussed from an Artificial Intelligence perspective. Only a minimal set of assumptions about an organization of long-term memory is made, and various types of memory retrieval processes that seem functionally distinct are put into a taxonomy.

2. RETRIEVAL

In this section, we taxonomize various types of conceptual retrieval. This taxonomy is based on differences in either the processing that appears to go on in the performance of the different kinds of retrieval, or in the kinds of conceptual items being retrieved. The first distinction that is made is between FORCED (sometimes termed "strategic") versus SPONTANEOUS (sometimes termed "automatic") retrieval. The difference between these two is the difference between trying to remember something and having things pop into one's head unbidden. Schank has argued (Schank, 1982) that the latter kind of reminding is so ubiquitous that for the majority of cases, we don't even know it is occurring. For examaple, when we see a table, in some sense we are "reminded" of a table. Object recognition in this case is a kind of matching between items we see and stored representations that are brought up spontaneously.

Within this broad classification between forced and spontaneous retrieval, further distinctions are made. The following outline illustrates the taxonomy to be discussed in this section.

    2.1. Forced Retrieval
        2.1.1. Direct Recall from Semantic Memory
            A. Explicit Recall
            B. Implicit Recall
        2.1.2. Direct Recall from Episodic Memory
        2.1.3. Reconstructive Recall
            A. Regenerative
            B. Procedural
        2.1.4. Procedural Simulation
    2.2. Spontaneous Recall
        2.2.1. Forced Spontaneous Recall
        2.2.2. Analogous Recall
        2.2.3. Opportunistic Recall

2.1 Types of Retrieval—Forced

Forced retrieval is very much a task-motivated occurrence. In these cases, an individual may pose a question to oneself or someone else may pose a question. This is in contrast to spontaneous retrieval, in which items come to mind without a person's consciously desiring them to do so.

Forced retrieval may appear to be the main kind of retrieval going on in test taking, for example. However, subconscious processes may spontaneously retrieve answers to questions not initially available through any of the kinds of retrieval isolated. Also, important background material necessary to answer a question may rise spontaneously. To answer a question about why India consecrates the cow when many people are hungry might cause images of Indian life to come to mind, potentially useful in formulating alternative hypotheses. To give another example, if an analogous problem previously solved pertaining to why Moslems do not eat pork came to mind, it could then be perturbed to fit this situation.

These examples stand in contrast to trying to retrieve an answer to a more factual question such as "What is the major language spoken in India?" In a case like this, one seems to simply wait for the answer to come to mind. The distinction is simply that in the latter case, one is waiting for something in particular to be retrieved. In the former case, what comes to mind was unplanned. Its relevance to the current task must still be "computed."

In the following sections, we postulate different types of forced retrieval processes. First a description of what characterizes the request for information is given, followed by a discussion of potential mechanisms (from a processing point of view) that seem to account for the phenomena. Whenever possible, discussions are included on the implications for the structure and organization of memory.

2.1.1. Direct Recall from Semantic Memory

There is a great deal of information explicitly present in semantic memory. However, there is probably more information that can be derived from what is in semantic memory. For example, one cannot not only ask if a hammer is a tool (presumably explicitly represented), but one can ask if it is a fish, a state, a person, and so on. Given our minimal assumptions about the organization of memory, we do not assume to have all of this negative information explicitly stored. We store what a hammer is, and from that, we can figure out what it isn't.

It is on the basis of this distinction that direct recall from semantic memory is further classified into recall of explicit information, and recall of implicit information.

A. Explicit Recall.   In direct recall from semantic memory, one is asked (or asks oneself) questions that address knowledge typically thought to reside in semantic memory. Examples of questions that address information believed to be explicitly stored in semantic memory are the following.

1.   Does a canary have wings?

2.   What noise does a duck make?

3.   Is a hammer a tool?

4.   Is an uncle a relative?

Answers to these types of questions are characterized by their speed, the certainty of the answers, and the lack of conscious effort to answer. A model capable of answering these questions should access directly into memory with only the features present in the questions. What seems (from introspection) to be recalled is simply the answer "yes" or "quack" in the cases given. That is, there are no other processes going on that can be illuminated by a protocol analysis.

B. Implicit Recall.   The following questions also address semantic kinds of information. However, the questions address things that require some figuring out before an answer can be given.

1.   Is an uncle a grandfather's son?

2.   Does a duck bark?

3.   Is a dog a cat?

4.   Does a limousine have a rudder?

The last question is interesting in that individuals report imagining a limousine and seeing that there is no rudder to answer the question. This indicates that there may be some higher-level cognitive process that must go on to transform the answer from the form that it is retrieved in (a mental image in this case) to the form suitable to answer the question. It also raises issues of how memory might know what form to have items brought up in. Given that the information that limousines do not have rudders is present in the mental image, it seems clear that the underlying retrieval apparatus is not powerful enough to pick this detail up without some higher-level cognitive processes.

2.1.2.   Direct Recall from Episodic Memory

Direct recall is recall of more event-based, episodic, or autobiographical information from memory. Thus questions that probe this type of memory typically would address more personal experiences, and answers to these questions would differ from person to person. Some examples:

1.   What did you do yesterday for lunch?

2.   Have you even been ice skating?

3.   When was the last time you went to a public library?

The retrieval of answers to this last question sometimes necessitates some of the reconstructive procedures described next.

Aside from the difference in the type of information retrieved, direct retrieval from episodic memory and direct, explicit retrieval from semantic memory appear identical. In both cases it seems the features present in the questions (the cues) are sufficient to retrieve an answer without additional computation.

2.1.3. Reconstructive Recall

Reconstructive recall is characterized by the need to postulate or reconstruct what might have been present in the past or to construct additional contexts as aids in recall. These types of recall are further broken down according to the types of cognitive processes that go on. In models proposed by, for example, Kolodner (Kolodner, 1984) and Reiser (Reiser, 1986), one must first plan a context of search. After an initial context for search is determined, plausible indexes or cues are generated to look around that planned context of search (elaboration strategies).

Reconstructive recall is further broken down into regenerative and procedural recall. The distinction is that in regenerative recall, subjects use different kinds of tactics to find the information asked for. In procedural recall, there are fixed methodologies. The strategies used in procedural recall are intimately related to the conceptual representation of the items being asked for. In regenerative recall, there are many different potentially successful strategies that could be employed.

A. Regenerative. In this type of retrieval, specific and identifiable retrieval strategies are employed to obtain partially forgotten events. Many of these types of questions look like "questions you never thought you would be asked." It is perhaps for this reason that alternate retrieval strategies must be employed to find these events.

Some example questions that can be solved in this manner are:

1. What were you doing two years ago in September?
2. Have you ever gotten someone else's meal at a restaurant?
3. When was the last time you rented a car?
4. Name 20 fruits.

This is the classic kind of reconstructive recall focused on by the model developed by Kolodner (Kolodner, 1984). Note that it is not necessarily restricted to items from episodic memory, as illustrated in example 4. There is a fine line between direct recall from memory and this type of regenerative recall. When one cannot directly recall the information asked for, one must come up with more complex strategies to access the information. However, it is difficult to predict when one must resort to these complex strategies, and the need to do so probably varies with differences in individual memory capacities.

It is interesting to speculate on why certain features of events are directly recallable, and why others must be derived. On the surface, there seems to be no principled answer, aside from the rather simple memory capacity is insufficient to store everything directly." Perhaps the answer to this question lies more in a theory of forgetting than a theory of remembering.

One view of regenerative recall is that the strategies employed by humans are simply compensation for failures in the memory system. From a computational perspective, there is no necessary reason to model human's inadequacies in memory retrieval except as an interesting cognitive model. With a sufficiently large contents-addressable memory, complex reconstructive techniques to retrieve events may be unnecessary.

B. Procedural or Derivative.   In procedural or derivative recall, one comes up with specific problem-solving strategies to aid recall. When mental images are used, this process is called Image Retrieval. A person may use this method of retrieval to answer questions such as: (1) How many windows are in your house? (2) Name the 50 states.

In order to answer the first question, most individuals walk around a "mental map" of their house, keeping an ongoing tally of windows. They walk in some systematic fashion. This mental process is completely accessible through introspection. In the second question, a frequent tactic is to traverse a mental map of the United States, say from east coast to west coast, listing states as one traverses.

These types of processes, like some of the direct semantic questions that have been listed, imply mental spatial representation of a physical object to aid in the recall of that object. However, this approach is only successful if the relevant features of that object are present. In a study done by Nickerson and Adams (1982), subjects were asked to reproduce or recognize all the features on a penny. This study showed that no amount of mental visualization of the object (by drawing potential penny representations) can aid in either the recall or recognition task, as the features in question were simply not accessible in the individual's memory of the object.

This experiment is most remarkable for what it implies about the importance of attention and instantiation of input features. If a feature of an object isn't noticed or used in processing, it will be very unlikely to be remembered. Whether or not this type of processing is necessary to model human abilities on a computer depends on the computer representation chosen to represent things such as houses. If the representation were a visual one as in humans, such a process would be necessary for the computer as well. Unfortunately, it is hard to imagine a computer with enough intelligence to realize that the information desired was present in the image, and construct for itself the "routine" that could answer this question. This raises the question of an appropriate computer representation to allow for recall of information like this, given the need for automatic generation of question-specific recall strategies.

A computer implementation could, however, rattle off the 50 states with no difficulty due to its memory capacity and ability to keep track of a large number of items at once.

2.1.4. Procedural Simulation

Procedural simulation addresses the recall of processes that appear to only be encoded procedurally. Although at one time the knowledge of how to perform the process may have been accessible directly, over time the knowledge may have become procedurally encoded. In this case, the only way to retrieve the answer to questions that address parts of the procedure is to simulate the process: (1) Do you put your left lace over or under your right lace when tying your shoes? (2) Did you lock the car door?

In the second example, one can imagine trying to recall the sequence of actions one took when getting out of the car to verify if one of them was locking the door.

2.2. Types of Retrieval—Spontaneous

2.2.1. Forced

Forced spontaneous recall may seem like a contradiction in terms. However, people often "try and remember" something. For example Meacham and Leiman (1982) make a distinction between prospective remembering and retrospective remembering. An example of the distinction they give is that to deliver a message one must remember the message (retrospective) and also seek out the person for whom the message is intended and deliver the message (prospective).

Remembering to seek out the person for whom the message is intended is an example of forced spontaneous recall. Another example found in Neisser (Neisser, 1982) is trying to remember to bring a book with you to work. This process is called prerecall. The following items are typical things people "try and remember."

1.   Remember to call or write someone.
2.   Remember to bring something with you somewhere.
3.   Remember to tell someone something when you see them.

What happens in these examples is that a decision is made to perform the desired action. Then this decision is essentially "forgotten." One hopes that it will be spontaneously retrieved at an appropriate time to perform the desired action. However, one typically has very little control over whether this spontaneous retrieval will occur or not. Meacham and Leiman (1982) document some of the common ways people compensate for this inability, for example, making lists or leaving things by the door.

2.2.2. Analogous

This type of retrieval is identified by the presence of the preface "that reminds me of . . . ." In analogous retrieval, an event or story input to the system causes one to remember a related event or story. Often casual conversation is composed of long strings of these types of analogous re-mindings, where people relay personal experiences that all illustrate the common theme or point under discussion.

Analogous retrieval can be useful in memory-based or case-based rea-soning situations. For example; suppose John was supposed to meet Mary at "the fountain" at a certain time. John waits for Mary at "the fountain" but Mary never arrives. When they meet up again later, they determine that each was waiting at a different fountain; in fact, there has been two fountains. A few weeks late, John is supposed to meet Mary at "the lobby." When Mary is not on time, John starts to wonder if there might be more than one lobby in the hotel. Analogous reminding can thus be used to make predictions based on events in the past that are similar to current events.

Spontaneous analogous retrieval is on the border between memory recall and memory recognition. A person may recognize a given experience as similar to another experience.

2.2.3. Opportunistic or Serendipitous

Opportunistic recall occurs when something spontaneously comes to mind at an appropriate moment that may help in achieving some goal. Opportunistic recall is typically used in AI planning. In this case, a goal one wants to achieve lies dormant, awaiting some condition to activate it, for example, seeing the pet store reminds you that you have to buy cat food. Another example is when a question previously asked but unan-swered is answered by some incoming stimulus. For example, one might have been wondering exactly how big the United States's federal deficit really was. This "wondering" could have been mere idle speculation be-cause the answer to this question was unknown. However, given an article in a newspaper that mentions this figure, one might spontaneously recall the speculation. This recall could cause you to remember this piece of information better.

Schank (Schank, 1982) believes that spontaneous retrieval is so ubiquitous that most of the time we are unaware that it is happening. Although it is difficult to postulate a type of retrieval that one is unaware is happening, it seems that one must certainly be accessing memories of what one experiences in order to be understanding those experiences. However, these memories do not "come to mind" so they are not included here.

2.3. Remarks

It is interesting to speculate on the relationship between spontaneous recall and recognition. When input items in the environment serve as a trigger to spontaneous recall, those input items cause a kind of recognition procedure to take place in which one recognizes that the input is related or similar to the items spontaneously recalled.

Another issue is the relationship between things that consciously come to mind and things that must have been accessed in memory but that one is unaware of having accessed. This subject also addresses the recognition versus recall issue; in order to recognize an object as a chair, for example, one must access the representation or memory of a chair.

One interesting problem in memory retrieval is the question of what exactly is retrieved. In order to make a processing model of memory retrieval, decisions must be made about not only what conceptual categories are brought into a short-term memory, but what features of those categories might be also included.

Another interesting topic for future research is an investigation into how to characterize questions in terms of the type of retrieval they might require to obtain an answer. With such a characterization, tests could be constructed that would probe different retrieval skills, or access different kinds or memory.

3. MEMORY ORGANIZATION

Many computer and cognitive scientists have come up with theories of the structure of memory (Anderson, 1983; Minsky, 1981; Quillian, 1966; Schank, 1982; Schank & Abelson, 1977) at various levels of conceptualization, from low-level neural models to high-level cognitive "explanatory" theories. In spite of these theories, and the experiments performed by psychologists and cognitive scientists to verify constraints on the structure of memory, few theoretical constructions stand out as essential to a plausible structure of memory. That is, it is very difficult to prove or disprove the validity of any given theory. One reason for this difficulty may be the ease with which one theory may be transformed into another.

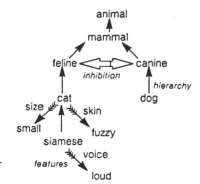

FIG. 9.1.   Overlay of organizations.

Fig. 9.1 illustrates how the features of a given memory organization can be superimposed on any other organization. The different link types represent hierarchical information, features of semantic categories, and mutual exclusion (inhibition) links. These links can be superimposed on other organizations as well. Moreover, a discrete representation such as this can be implemented with a number of lower-level distributed connections, further increasing the ways such a memory can be organized. Within this large space of potential memory organizations, it is difficult to prove that any one is superior to another.

In this section, a small number of plausible assumptions are made about the structure and organization of human memory suitable for direct modeling in a computer system. These assumptions serve to limit the space of possible theories, and provide a framework within which one may construct a new theory. These assumptions are widely acknowledged and accepted as useful constructs for most current-day AI knowledge representation systems.

They are the following:

1.1.   **Hierarchical:** Elements of long-term memory are either organized into a hierarchy, or such a hierarchy can be superimposed on any other organizational structure. The hierarchy may be explicit or may be an emergent property implicit in a distributed representation.

1.2.   **Categorical:** Long-term memory is organized into conceptual, feature-based categories. Features inherit and are refined as they are inherited by more specific categories.

1.3.   **Continuous:** Episodic and semantic memory form a continuum, and episodic memory becomes semantic memory via a process of generalization or abstraction.

1.4.   **Associative:** Memory has an associative organization to it if that is, concepts are defined in terms of other concepts.

1.5. **Procedural:** Part of memory is procedurally stored, in that the knowledge present can only be accessed by performing the action.
1.6. **Distributed:** Items in memory share themselves as components with other memories.

Many of these assumptions, such as the HIERARCHY assumption, are so pervasive in current and past thinking about memory organizations that they may seem hardly worth mentioning, and are difficult to attribute to a specific researcher or research group. However, to be complete, such assumptions are included explicitly. Each of these assumptions is discussed in turn.

3.1. Hierarchical

The HIERARCHICAL assumption states that subsumption information is one type of information present in memory. For example, although it may not be the case that a dog's mammal properties are inherited from a mammal category, the fact that a dog is a mammal is present, as is the fact that a dog shares with other mammals the mammal properties. Thus any memory organization must either be explicitly hierarchically organized with inheritance, superimpose this information on top of any other given organization, or have this knowledge emergent. Moreover, the hierarchy is not a strict hierarchy, in that concepts may be members of more than one conceptual category. Thus a dog is not just a member of the mammal category, but of the pet category.

A hierarchical organization of knowledge is practical in designing easily extensible knowledge bases, in that features inherited from higher-level categories need not be reduplicated upon the addition of a new category member.

3.2. Categorical

The CATEGORICAL assumption asserts the presence of symbolic concepts (called categories) as the fundamental units of memory. Although categories may be represented internally by some kind of distributed representation as described in Hinton (Hinton, McClelland, & Rumelhart, 1986), one can choose to focus on the higher-level symbolic level of representation instead of a subsymbolic representation. Thus, this assumption does not preclude a lower-level distributed representation of concepts.

Symbolic concepts can be thought of as "chunks," as first described by Miller (Miller, 1956). That is, higher-level categories represent information that has been "more chunked." For example, when one thinks of a cat, for example, one is not typically thinking of the fuzziness of the cat, the fact that the cat is a mammal, or even a particular cat. Although this information is present in memory, the generic or prototypical cat one calls to mind is a single "chunked" entity.

Experiences also are chunkable. One can remember a trip to Disneyland without having short-term memory flooded with all the details of that trip. Although all the subevents may be present in memory, and one can zoom in on certain details of those subevents, there are higher-level concepts that can be brought to mind that somehow chunk that experience into a manageable, unitary concept.

As to the number of conceptual categories, there have been suggestions ranging from a small set of primitives as in Conceptual Dependency (Schank, 1975) to a proliferation of conceptual categories, as in the KODIAK knowledge representation language (Wilensky, 1986), and this assumption is neutral with respect to this question.

Categories are also assumed to have features; for example, animals make noises. These features are refined for more particular categories; for example, a cat makes a meow noise. This property is sometimes referred to as "structured inheritance," and is present in such knowledge representation systems as KL–ONE (Brachman & Schmolze, 1985) and KODIAK. This is also illustrated in Fig. 9.1.

3.3. Continuous

In the CONTINUOUS assumption, episodic and semantic memory form a continuum. This presupposes that there are at least two different kinds of items stored in memory. Following Tulving (Tulving, 1983), semantic memory is assumed to consist of items that look like facts about the world. This is in contrast to episodic, experiential, or autobiographical memory, which differs greatly from individual to individual. Episodic memory contains memories for specific, time-dependent experiences.

Schank's theory of dynamic memory (Schank, 1982) implicitly assumes the continuum from episodic (scriptal) memory to semantic (more goal-based) knowledge. In this theory, generalization operates to transform specific experiences into more general "MOPS." A simple example of how one learns from generalization could be the following: Suppose one experiences a cat that often asked to be let in by scratching at a door. If one then later had another cat that scratched at a window to be let in, one might generalize that cats, in general, scratch at entry ways as their means to communicate their desire to enter. This type of feature would be added to one's other general knowledge of cat behavior. Note that there may be any number of intermediate levels of conceptualization. For example, one may believe for a while that only these two cats exhibit this behavior. It is also possible that this generalization may "trickle up" farther to general animal behavior, if one found out that dogs also scratch to be let in.

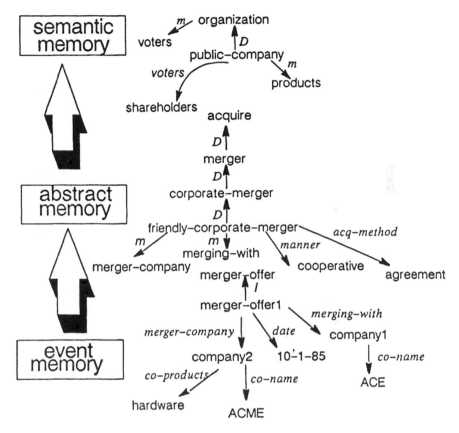

FIG. 9.2. Continuous memory.

The CONTINUOUS assumption does not say that generalization is the only means of acquiring semantic memory. Learning new facts, as in school, adds information directly to semantic memory. This is the difference between learning by being told and learning from experience. However, the learning episode itself is certainly an experience. For example, consider a student who must study for a test by memorizing some facts about geography. Given the sentence "Managua is the capital of Nicaragua," the student has an "experience" of reading this sentence. This experience is stored in episodic memory. A protocol analysis may later retrieve something like "Last night I was studying for my geography test. I was sitting at my desk between 6 and 8 P.M. memorizing facts about Central America. One of those facts was that Managua is the capital of Nicaragua. I was using my class geography text and my notes to study from."

The CONTINUOUS assumption claims that there are not a finite number of "levels" of memory. It claims that there are specific experiences at one end of memory, and general, factual knowledge about the world at the other end, and an infinite number of partial states in between, of knowledge derived from experiences, at various levels of conceptual abstraction. Fig. 9.2 illustrates knowledge at various levels of conceptual abstraction, in a part of a knowledge base about companies and corporate mergers. In this example, a specific instance of a corporate merger offer is shown, along with a generalized concept of a friendly corporate merger, presumably abstracted from multiple experiences of friendly mergers. The very top illustrates knowledge about what a company is.

Continuous memory organizations are not as common in AI systems as, say, hierarchical organizations because few AI programs have the ability to learn effectively from experience. Zernik's RINA program (Zernik, 1987) is one example of a program that learns from experience and has a continuous representation.

3.4. Associative

The ASSOCIATIVE assumption is perhaps the least controversial and most commonly agreed on assumption in memory organization theories. It is hard to imagine a theory in which associations did not form the basis for any representation system. However, within this simple assumption, there is a great deal of variation in theories about what kinds of association are allowable, what associations are primitive, and what associations may have special meaning attached to them. One example of a complete theory of associative memory can be found in the ACT theory by Anderson (Anderson, 1983).

Associations between concepts are typically represented with links in most representational systems. Frequently these links are labeled to represent a particular kind of association, such as an "isa" relation (as in a "cat 'isa' feline") or a "part-of" relation.

3.5. Procedural

The PROCEDURAL assumption simply asserts that there are procedurally encoded pieces of knowledge. These are actions that have at one time been performed so frequently that they become automatic in their execution. Moreover, it is very difficult to recover the individual steps involved in the action without actually performing the action. Tying one's shoes or driving a car are examples of procedurally encoded knowledge. In these cases, the knowledge of the sequence of events is represented in the actual execution of these actions.

The representation of procedural knowledge depends on the particular form of the representation of executable actions in the system.

3.6. Distributed

Finally, in the DISTRIBUTED assumption, it is assumed that concepts participate in multiple experiences and are parts of multiple facts. For example, one may have an experience of one's grandmother baking a cake, and one's grandmother planting flowers. The "grandmother" involved in these experiences is the same. Although there may be philosophical arguments that question the validity of this assumption, it is in general fairly noncontroversial. However, this DISTRIBUTED assumption actually is quite powerful. It is because of the interrelatedness of concepts through their participation in multiple events that a partly (or perhaps completely) contents-addressable knowledge base could be obtained. That is, thinking about one's grandmother actually can serve to "address" all those events involving one's grandmother, at some level.

Within this space of assumptions, many possible organizations of memory are possible. However, not all additional assumptions are reasonable from the viewpoint of cognitive validity. For example, some researchers assume the presence of mutual exclusion links on all categories. This means that it is explicitly represented that members of the "cat" category, for example, cannot also be members of the "dog" category. Although this may make certain computations more efficient, it does not seem easily supportable in theory. When people are asked "Is a fish a dog?" (informal experiment) most subjects seem to think about this. In fact, the more similar the items are, the longer people must think about the answer. It seems that some kind of mental comparison is taking place in response to the question. This contradicts a mutual exclusion link hypothesis, in that if such a link existed, answers to this type of question would be very fast, and not vary with the elements being inquired about.

That is not to say that some of this type of information is not explicitly stored. For example, the fact that black and white are opposites is certainly present in almost everyone's memory. Factual, positive (information adding) information such as that black and white are opposites is perhaps more likely to be explicitly stored than negative information, such as that black is not white.

3.7. Remarks

So far we have concentrated exclusively on the physical organizational structure of a long-term memory. However, any given organization of memory affects the methods of retrieval used. For example, a discrimination net as used in the EPAM model of retrieval (Feigenbaum, 1963) is best suited to retrieval via a series of discriminations of the features in the input cues with features stored as indexes in the discrimination net.

Others have postulated that spreading activation intersection search is an appropriate retrieval technique for items stored in a semantic netlike formalism (Collins & Loftus, 1975). Whatever the organization of memory, it must support retrieval of all kinds of information from memory, such as those described in section 2.

4. INDEXING

One topic that is conspicuously absent from this discussion is the issue of indexing. According to Tulving (Tulving, 1972), episodic memory is indexed in terms of the current context active at the time the experience occurs (encoding specificity). This current context contains knowledge structures that were necessary in the initial understanding and processing of the experience.

Appropriate indexing strategies depend on the desired end organization of knowledge, as they serve to put knowledge into that organization. Understanding the processing mechanisms of retrieval is also a prerequisite to formulating indexing strategies that support those mechanisms. Indexing then is something to be concerned with after memory organization and retrieval mechanisms have been formulated.

5. CONCLUSION

In this chapter we have isolated some of the issues that arise in a representation of human memory, and retrieval processes from such a memory. A small set of plausible assumptions that can be made about an organization of memory were given. These assumptions were that memory was HIERARCHICAL, CATEGORICAL, CONTINUOUS, ASSOCIATIVE, PROCEDURAL, and DISTRIBUTED.

A claim is made that there is a distinction between what is explicitly stored in memory and what can be reconstructed from what exists in memory. Items that need to be reconstructed result from inadequacies in the memory storage capacity. Computer implementations may or may not exhibit these inadequacies.

A taxonomy of retrieval mechanisms was described. This taxonomy was created by differences in either the processing that goes on in the performance of the different kinds of retrieval, or in the kinds of conceptual items being retrieved.

REFERENCES

Anderson, J. R. (1983). *The architecture of cognition*. Cambridge, MA: Harvard University Press.

Bartlett, F. C. (1932). *Remembering*. Cambridge, England: Cambridge University Press.

Brachman, R., & Schmolze, J. (1985). An overview of the KL–ONE knowledge representation system. *Cognitive Science*, *9*, 171–216.

Collins, A. M., & Loftus, E. F (1975). A spreading-activation theory of semantic processing. *Psychological Review*, *82*.

Feigenbaum, E. A. (1963). The simulation of verbal learning behavior. In E. A. Feigenbaum & J. Feldman (Eds.), *Computers and thought*. New York: McGraw–Hill.

Hinton, G., McClelland, J., & Rumelhart, D. (1986). Distributed representations. In D. Rumelhart & J. McClelland (Eds.), *Parallel distributed processing*. Cambridge, MA: MIT Press.

Kolodner, J. (1984). *Retrieval and organizational strategies in conceptual memory: A computer model*. Hillsdale, NJ: Lawrence Erlbaum Associates.

Meacham, J. A., & Leiman, B. (1982). Remembering to perform future actions. In U. Neisser (Ed.), *Memory observed: Remembering in natural contexts*. San Francisco: W. H. Freeman.

Miller, G. A (1956). The magical number seven, plus or minus two: Some limits on our capacity for processing information. *Psychological Review*, *63*, 81–97.

Minsky, M. (1981). K-Lines: A theory of memory. In D. A. Norman (Ed.), *Perspectives in cognitive science*. Norwood, NJ: Ablex.

Neisser, U. (1982). Memory: What are the important questions. In U. Neisser (Ed.), *Memory observed: Remembering in natural contexts*. San Francisco: W. H. Freeman.

Nickerson, R. S., & Adams, M. J. (1982). Long-term memory for a common object. In U. Neisser (Ed.), *Memory observed: Remembering in natural contexts*. San Francisco: W. H. Freeman.

Quillian, M. R. (1966). *Semantic memory*. Cambridge, MA: Bolt, Beranek, & Newman.

Rau, L. F. (1987a). Knowledge organization and access in a conceptual information system. *Information Processing and Management*, *23*, 269–283.

Rau, L. F. (1987b). Spontaneous retrieval in a conceptual information system. In *Proceedings of the 10th International Joint Conference on Artificial Intelligence*, held in Milan, Italy.

Reiser, B. (1986). Autobiographical memories. In J. Kolodner & C. Riesbeck (Eds.), *Experience, memory, and reasoning*. Hillsdale, NJ: Lawrence Erlbaum Associates.

Schank, R. C. (1975). *Conceptual information processing*. New York: American Elsevier.

Schank, R. C. (1982). *Dynamic memory: A theory of reminding and learning in computers and people*. Cambridge, England: Cambridge University Press.

Schank, R. C. & Abelson, R. P. (1977). *Scripts, plans, goals, and understanding*. Hillsdale, NJ: Lawrence Erlbaum Associates.

Tulving, E. (1972). Episodic and semantic memory. In E. Tulving & W. Donaldson (Eds.), *Organization and memory*. New York: Academic Press.

Tulving, E. (1983). *Elements of episodic memory*. New York: Oxford University Press.

Wilensky, R. (1986). Knowledge representation: A critique and a proposal. In J. Kolodner & C. Riesbeck (Eds.), *Experience, memory, and reasoning*. Hillsdale, NJ: Lawrence Erlbaum Associates.

Zernik, U. (1987). *Strategies in language acquisition: Learning phrases from examples in context* (Doctoral dissertation, University of California at Los Angeles). Computer Science Division Report UCLA–AI–87–1.

10 Two Hurdles for Natural Language Systems

Paul S. Jacobs
General Electric Company

1. THE NATURAL LANGUAGE PROBLEM

During the 1960s, scientists investigating natural-language processing were dealt a severe blow by the report of an organization called **ALPAC** (Automated Language Processing Advisory Committee; 1966). The committee reviewed the progress of intensive and costly efforts at automatic machine translation, and concluded that the goals of the projects would never be achieved. In support of this conclusion, among other things, the committee observed that the understanding of language depended on knowledge of the world, and that computers had not yet begun to achieve the level of knowledge required to perform such a task. In many ways, this analysis is indisputable. Yet, while fully automatic machine translation (like many other ethereal goals in Artificial Intelligence) may be little nearer than it was 20 years ago, automated language processing has made some measurable progress.

The recognition of the connection between understanding language and understanding the world was itself an achievement. At the beginning of the machine translation efforts, language processing was modeled largely as the process of manipulating the symbols of a language, rather than as deriving and expressing concepts and intentions. Current research in natural language highlights the encoding of these concepts and intentions in a computational framework as much as it does the formal properties of languages.

Within this newer framework, understanding language may be viewed as the process of translating a spoken or written message in English or other natural language into a computer representation. Language production or generation consists of constructing a natural language message that expresses a particular concept or goal. Both processes are knowledge-intensive, relying not only on an understanding of language but also on an understanding of how language relates to world knowledge. This chapter concentrates on the representation of knowledge for natural language processing and the impact that this representation has on computer programs designed to understand language.

1.1. Natural-language Programs

The mastery of language as a communicative tool is the end goal of natural language research, but individual computer programs tend to emphasize certain aspects of language for particular tasks. One of the difficulties of fully automatic machine translation, mentioned earlier, is that it is difficult to see how the task can be performed well without a complete understanding of the use of language. On the other hand, a program that takes natural language input for an on-line data base may perform effectively with a very limited linguistic capability.

The best areas of application for natural language technology are those where (1) the competition is weak, (2) the end user is inexperienced, or (3) the environment is ill suited to other methods. Each of these application areas will be elaborated on.

Weak competition. This class includes natural language front ends for data bases, where the "competition" is a query language that many computer users find difficult to use. Text-processing systems also fall into this category, as computers simply cannot do very many useful things with extended texts without understanding them. An example of the "competition" here is a keyword-retrieval system, such as those that retrieve documents from legal case histories, given a word or phrase that describes a key legal principle.

Inexperienced users. People who are not skilled at using computers are already experts in using language; thus the motivation is strong for providing computer interfaces that communicate in their users' language. Natural language help facilities (systems that provide conversational capabilities for inexperienced users) fall into this category. Most natural language data base systems are targeted at inexperienced users as well, although the users become more skilled as they gain practice.

Specialized environment. The "normal" means of interacting with a computer is via a keyboard and a terminal screen, but this is not the only way computers will be able to communicate. Speech technology, although still very limited, will continue to improve, and will ultimately increase the need for natural language technology. Interacting with computer systems will make some of the alternatives to natural language communication impractical. For example, if one talks to a computer over the telephone, or is involved in a task where it is not possible to type, the voice medium would be preferred over a menu-driven system or a formal command language, and thus natural language could be essential.

Of the relatively few commercial successes of natural language processing, virtually all products are front ends for data bases. In the research community, programs that skim news stories and perform other intelligent functions have existed in a variety of forms, but this technology has not reached maturity, largely because of some glaring limitations. Some examples of the type of interaction that a user might have with existing natural language programs will follow.

The Data Base Front End

Natural language front ends to data bases translate inputs from the user to a formal data base query, which is then passed on to a large piece of software that interacts with the data base. Such systems give the user flexibility and ease of use because the user does not have to learn the often cryptic query language (Harris, 1984):

> **User:** Give me the names of the women in the western region who are over quota.
> **System:** PRINT THE LAST NAME AND 82 YTD ACT % OF QUOTA OF ALL SALES PEOPLE WITH SEX = FEMALE & REGION = WEST & 82 YTD ACT % QUOTA OVER 100.00 [produce 24 records]

The Intelligent Help Facility

Help facilities provide inexperienced users of computer systems with a last-ditch means of finding an appropriate command. Natural language may be the only way for such a user to pose the question (Kaczmarek, Mark, & Sondheimer, 1983; Wilensky, Arens, & Chin, 1984):

> **User:** Send the message to Jones.
> **System:** Your message has been sent to Jones.

The News Story Skimmer

Programs that scan news stories select articles from a particle domain and extract important information from the articles. This information can then be used to produce summaries (possibly in multiple languages), and answer questions about the texts (DeJong, 1977):

Input text.   A severe earthquake struck northeastern Italy last night, collapsing entire sections of towns northeast of Venice near the Yugoslav border, killing at least 95 persons and injuring at least 1,000, the Italian Interior Ministry reported . . . . The earthquake was recorded at 6.3 on the Richter Scale, which measures ground motion. In populated areas, a quake registering 4 on that scale can cause moderate damage, a reading of 6 can be severe, and a reading of 7 indicates a major earthquake.

System summary.   95 people were killed and 1,000 were injured in a severe earthquake that struck Italy. The quake registered 6.3 on the Richter scale.

1.2.   Limitations of Existing Systems

Experience with natural language systems has shown that robust language processing poses some apparently insurmountable problems. Thus the foregoing programs, as well as others like them, depend on a limited context and a greatly restricted mechanism to appear linguistically capable. The technical papers that describe such programs seldom go into much detail about the examples that they fail to handle. But the following exchanges are taken from real, if generally unpublished, results from the programs:

The Data Base Front End

User: Give me John's address and Mary's phone number.
System: [produces Mary's address and John's phone number as well]
John Smith   112 Millstone Rd.   484-5214
Mary Tyler   5414 Appian Way   323-1492

The Intelligent Help Facility

User: Send the job to the line printer.
System: I'm sorry, I don't understand what you mean.

The News Story Skimmer

Input text: [headline] Pope's Death Shakes the Vatican.
System summary: An earthquake struck Italy today. There was one victim: the Pope.

Examples such as these illustrate the dependence of natural language programs on the limited context in which they operate. The programs tend to rely heavily on context-dependent knowledge to make up for their limited linguistic skills. Thus data base front ends ignore many of the subtleties of the questions they are asked. Help facilities know enough about electronic mail to handle simple requests and questions, but do not know enough about language to comprehend closely related inputs. Text readers start with certain information that is expected in a story, and are easily fooled into finding the information even when it is not present.

The next section defines more clearly two of the problems with existing natural language programs and outlines some promising techniques for a solution to these problems.

2. TWO HURDLES TO OVERCOME

Many gaps in natural language technology account for the problems that have been described. The very limited vocabulary of most systems, the inability of programs to acquire linguistic knowledge from practice, and the lack of much general knowledge about the world are only some of the barriers that stand in the way of computers that really communicate. The following two issues encompass many of these failures, will need to be addressed by the next generation of natural language programs:

Exploiting Core Knowledge about Language. Like the computer programs described herein, people depend heavily on specific domain knowledge in communicating within a specialized context. It is difficult to converse effectively about computers, for example, unless one has practiced doing so. Unlike the programs, however, human beings do not relearn their language for each application. They associate new words and phrases with other similar expressions, and learn to adapt their linguistic knowledge to the domain. Thus "send a message" and "send the job to the printer" have specialized meanings in the world of computers, but any competent English speaker has some idea of what that meaning is. On the other hand, a program that is not specifically told what each expression means will tend not to understand at all.

Integrating Conceptual and Linguistic Processing. Text-processing programs in particular are guided by the information that they are programmed to obtain. This accounts for their inability to detect certain cues that contradict their expectations, as in the earthquake examples. On the other hand, programs that depend primarily on syntactical parsing, or the complete analysis of sentence structure, often produce no useful information at all when confronted with an ungrammatical input or one that, for some reason, cannot be fully processed. Ideally, a natural language program should use its linguistic knowledge as its primary guide and its conceptual expectations to derive as complete an understanding as possible. Neither linguistic nor conceptual knowledge can be sacrificed.

The first hurdle is mainly a problem in knowledge representation: how to give a computer enough basic knowledge about language that it will be adaptable to individual tasks. The second issue is primarily a program design question: How a natural language system can be flexible enough to combine the best of different techniques.

To address the core knowledge hurdle, one must lay out a representation of language and meaning that allows for variations among words and constructs that appear in various uses. Verbs such as send (in the foregoing example), as well as the more common give, take, have, make, get, be, put, and do, must be understood at least in part in a domain-independent fashion, as none of them loses its meaning entirely, even in a specialized domain. Concepts such as possession, distance, direction, and time, as well as the linguistic structures used to express them, should be encoded in such a way that they serve as building blocks for other linguistic knowledge.

The integrated processing hurdle motivates an approach in which the operation of a program does not depend on full knowledge at any level. In other words, the language processor makes use of whatever is available, without being restricted as to what type of information can be derived from what source. For example, if a specific piece of linguistic information tells the program that "send the message" describes electronic mail, then the program will use that knowledge; otherwise the meaning might be inferred from the conceptual context.

The following sections briefly describe an approach to language processing oriented toward extending the capabilities of future natural language systems by concentrating on generic capacities for language instead of specialized mechanisms. The discussion briefly describes a number of natural language systems, which are further presented in (Jacobs, 1986, 1987a, 1987b; Jacobs & Rau, 1985). Section 3 will present a framework for knowledge representation; section 4 will address the application of this framework to the task of understanding language.

3. EXPLOITING CORE KNOWLEDGE ABOUT LANGUAGE

The knowledge required to perform natural language processing includes three classes of information:

1. Conceptual knowledge (e.g., computers are machines), world knowledge useful for understanding and producing language, such as metaphorical and categorial relationships that influence linguistic constructs.
2. Linguistic knowledge (e.g., "send" is a verb), information about the

categorization of words and phrases and about the surface structure of a language, including grammatical knowledge.

3. Linguistic/conceptual associations (e.g., the indirect object of a verb represents the recipient of a transfer), information about the intricate relationships between linguistic structures and world concepts used in understanding and constructing linguistic expressions.

The subsections that follow describe some of the features of a knowledge representation designed for the encoding of core information about language.

3.1. Structured Associations

The knowledge representation framework used here, called Ace (Jacobs & Rau, 1985), is derived from a variety of AI projects (Bobrow & Winograd, 1977; Brachman & Schmolze, 1985; Wilensky, 1986) and applies the fundamental principles of knowledge representation to the representation of linguistic information. The basic unit of the representation is the structured association, a relationship between two entities that can involve roles or attributes of those entities in a variety of ways. One example of a structured association is shown in Fig. 10.1.

Fig. 10.1 shows a simple example of a Dominate association (labeled D), which represents the subcategory relationship between the concept sending and the concept action. Attached to this association is a Role-Play relation (labeled R and P), which indicates that the sender associated with a sending concept "plays the role of" the actor in that concept. This association basically represents the knowledge that what is true of actions is by default true of sending actions, and that the relationship between sending and sender by default derives from the relationship between action and actor.

The motivation for this type of association is that much of the information about expressing actions in general may be applied to expressing sending concepts; for example, a verb is often used to describe the concept, and the subject of the active verb "send" expresses the role of actor or

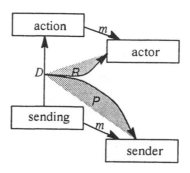

FIG. 10.1. An Ace structured association.

sender. On the other hand, specific information can be attached to sending that is not associated with action, such as the use of the verb "send" itself and the fact that the actor of the sending is also the source of some kind of transfer. A program that understands "John sent Mary a book" thus can make use of knowledge that the subject of an active verb expresses an actor, which in the case of a sending is the sender, which is the source of a transfer, to determine that "John" is the source of the transfer of the book. This process will be described further in section 4.

This hierarchical representation gives a framework in which information, including some facts about linguistic expression, can be represented in a parsimonious way.

3.2. VIEW Associations

Not all relationships between concepts can be arranged as neatly as in the previous example. In many cases, there is no simple relationship between a linguistic expression and a conceptual role, but there are a variety of ways of expressing that concept. For example, in describing a commercial event, one might say "I sold the book to Mary," or "Mary bought the book from me." In this case, the role expressed by the subject of the verb depends on whether the event is being viewed as a buying or a selling action. In a simpler example, a given transfer may be described using either "give" or "take," depending on perspective, and the event need not even be categorized as a transfer. "Frank gave Bill a punch," and "Bill took a punch from Frank" illustrate such metaphorical use of the verbs give and take.

The point is that there are consistent ways of expressing concepts, even metaphorically, and that such expressions must be represented in a manner that is not hierarchical, but which associates analogous concepts. The representation of the actions giving and taking is shown in Fig. 10.2.

In the graphic notation used here, links between concepts are often labeled m (for manifest) to indicate that some relationship exists between a concept and the role. In Fig. 10.2, some of the links are labeled with the name of a role, which indicates an implicit Role-Play relation between the labeled role and another role. The label part, for participant in Fig. 10.2 means that both the source and recipient of a transfer-event play the role of participant in the event.

Giving and taking are represented as explicit Views of the transfer-event concept. This allows a linguistic mechanism to apply knowledge about expressing giving and taking to a variety of concepts that are not necessarily subcategories of these concepts. The combination of Dominate, described earlier, and View, permits the representation of a range of relationships among abstract concepts.

3.3. Linguistic Hierarchies

Like conceptual entities, linguistic structures in Ace are organized hierarchically, with specialized expressions deriving from more general structures. This organization has the benefit of allowing even idiomatic constructs to be represented in terms of more general expressions, as well as making the representation of linguistic knowledge more parsimonious. Domain-specific linguistic entries may be added to the hierarchy more easily than in a nonhierarchical system where such entries would be treated as special cases.

Fig. 10.3 illustrates some of the different types of core linguistic knowledge structures. Fig. 10.3a shows the representation of a prepositional phrase with preposition "by" in conjunction with a passive verb. The motivation for such a linguistic structure is that the object of the preposition "by" in this case expresses the actor of the concept being described, as in "The message sent by Jones."

Fig. 10.3b shows some of the flexibility of a core "lexicon." The lexicon is the dictionary of a natural-language system, but the type of information contained in it can be much richer than the information in a standard dictionary. The linguistic structure represented in (b) is a category that includes verbs used with the particle (or preposition) "back," as in "send the message back" or "give back the result." The reason for this structure is that these expressions implicitly suggest a transfer whose direction is the reverse of the one being described. Thus the sender in "send the message back" probably received the message previously, and a program "giving back" a result received input from the user receiving the result. Since language is consistent in the use of such expressions, the linguistic representation should reflect this consistency.

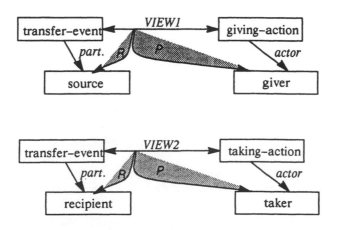

FIG. 10.2. The giving and taking views.

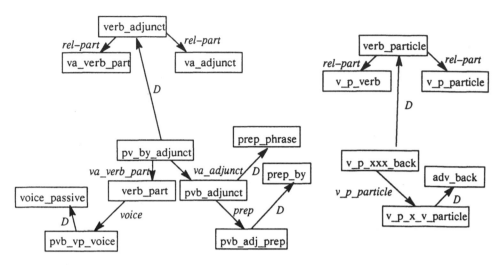

(a) the passive verb with by-adjunct relation   (b) the verb–particle with particle "back"

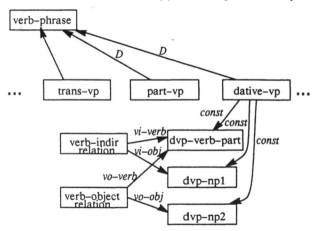

(c) relations attached to syntactic structures

FIG. 10.3. Some linguistic structures.

Linguistic relations, such as those in Figs. 10.3a and 10.3b, can be expressed in a variety of grammatical forms. They are associated with the grammatical structures that determine the order in which words must appear in a sentence and group together linguistic relations. Fig. 10.3c shows a segment of a verb phrase hierarchy in which the dative (or ditransitive) verb phrase dative-up is associated with two relations, verb–indir and verb–object. The verb phrase dictates the surface form, which consists of a complete verb followed by two noun phrases, while the relations are used to associate the roles of the expressed concepts with the surface structure. The flexibility of linguistic expressions such as those in (b) is the motivation for the distinction between relations and grammatical structures; the verb–object relation, for example, can be expressed in several grammatical forms.

3.4. Linguistic/Conceptual Associations

The discussion to this point has shown how the Ace representation allows for the encoding of a variety of linguistic and conceptual structures. The most important associations for natural language processing are those that relate language to meaning. These are represented by an explicit link in the Ace hierarchy called Ref.

Like Dominate and View, Ref is a structured association that relates entities and their roles to other entities and roles. In the case of Ref, however, the relationship is one that ties a linguistic structure to a concept that it expresses. These relationships range from simple entries in a word lexicon to associations between complex linguistic structures and conceptual roles. Some Ref associations are shown in Fig. 10.4.

Fig. 10.4a shows the simple relationship between the lexical category lex_send, which includes the conjugations of the verb "send," and the concept sending. Fig. 10.4b depicts the association between the passive with "by" and the actor of an action.

Fig. 10.4c illustrates the more complex relationship between the object of the preposition "to" and the indirect object of a verb. Superficially, one might conclude that these express the same conceptual role, as "John sent Mary the message" and "John sent the message to Mary" seem to have the same meaning. In general, this is true, but in fact the object of "to" expresses the conceptual role of destination, while the indirect object expresses a recipient. The difference is that a recipient must be an active participant in an event, while a destination can be just a physical location. Thus, "John sent Brazil a message" and "John sent a message to Brazil" actually can have different meanings: The first suggests that John sent a message to the government of Brazil or to some organization designated by Brazil, while in the second the message might have been sent to anyone in Brazil. Similarly, "Reagan sent a walrus to Antarctica" makes more sense to most hearers than "Reagan sent Antarctica a walrus" because Antarctica has no government to receive the walrus.

3.5. Exceptions and Idiosyncratic Metaphors

While the need for such generalized relationships between language and meaning may seem obvious, many natural language systems do not have them. The justification for relying on more specialized knowledge is that

Conceptual Structures   *Linguistic Structures*

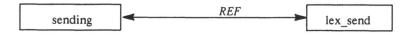

(a) Lexical – conceptual relation expressed with REF

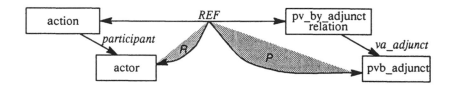

(b) Role relationships between by-adjunct and action

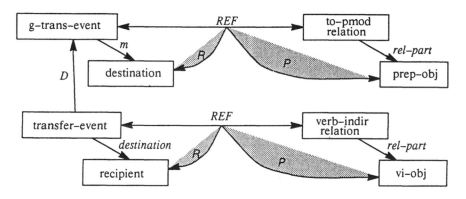

(c) The hierarchical organization of role relationships

FIG. 10.4. Associating language and meaning.

language is idiosyncratic, and it is difficult to handle all the exceptions. For example, in "John charged Mary five dollars for the book," why is Mary the recipient of the "charge" when John is the one getting the money? One who has studied the history of language might know that Mary is receiving the charge because she is receiving the obligation to pay John, but since this explanation does not readily come to mind, it is hard to believe that we use it in understanding.

The field of Artificial Intelligence has devoted much attention to dealing with exceptions. While there is some debate, a good general strategy is to prefer specific knowledge to general knowledge, but to use generalizations wherever they apply. Exceptions, furthermore, may themselves follow some pattern, although they contradict an expectation. A representation of "core" linguistic knowledge cannot ignore the idiosyncrasies of language.

As an indication of some of the method behind specialized expressions, consider the sentence "the command takes three arguments." This is an exception because ordinarily takers are active participants or recipients of unfortunate circumstance (as in "How did John take the news"). But the language is extremely consistent in describing many such events as if they were transfers, as in the following examples:

1. You must give the command three arguments.
2. "Concat" returns the concatenation of two strings.
3. The function gives a sum back for three inputs.
4. The receipe takes three cups of sugar.

While none of these sentences really expresses a giving or taking concept, each of them describes a concept that is conventionally viewed as a giving or taking. Thus exceptions can themselves be clustered into categories, as in Fig. 10.5.

The concept of causal_dual_trans in Fig. 10.5 represents an exchange, roughly corresponding to the meaning of the generalized linguistic category v_part_xxx_back, or a verb used with the particle "back." As transfer events can be described using verbs such as "give" and "take" and

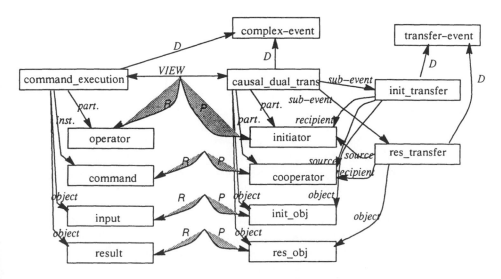

FIG. 10.5. A complex metaphor.

causal_dual_trans events can be expressed using "back" and "return," these expressions are used metaphorically to describe the execution of a command. There are no exceptions to this exception.

This section has covered the basic elements of a hierarchical representation for core linguistic knowledge, showing how basic relationships between language and meaning are encoded. Section 4 describes how this knowledge is applied to the task of understanding language. An equally important topic, the use of core knowledge in producing natural language, was also involved in the design of Ace, but is not covered in detail in this chapter.

4. INTEGRATED LANGUAGE UNDERSTANDING USING ACE

Given the model of linguistic representation that associates even specialized phrases with general knowledge structures, a language processor must make use of a combination of generic and specialized linguistic knowledge in deriving a meaning representation from a linguistic input. Furthermore, it must use domain-specific knowledge to aid in understanding, to disambiguate words, and to interpret expressions in context.

This section describes the language analysis mechanism employed in a program called TRUMP (Jacobs, 1986, 1987b), a language understanding package designed for transportability across domains. The goal of this type of language analysis is to improve robustness by taking advantage of generalizations, even in constrained domains.

4.1. The Language-understanding Process

The language analysis process outlined here embodies three basic elements: (1) a syntactic matching or grammatical mechanism, which combines words into phrases and sentences, checks syntactical constraints, and instantiates linguistic relations, (2) a mapping mechanism, which produces concepts and conceptual relations from linguistic structures, and (3) a concretion mechanism, which combines these bits and pieces of conceptual knowledge into an interpretation of the input. These three mechanisms work from a common set of knowledge representation and manipulation tools that maintain an Ace network, as described in section 3.

The first element that we have described will be referred to here as the parser. This program takes a natural language input and produces a diagram or parse tree consisting of linguistic structures such as nouns and verb phrases. The mapping and concretion elements, items (2) and (3) in the previous paragraph, make up the semantic interpreter, which incrementally builds a meaning representation of the input. Critical information for both the parser and the semantic interpreter is contained in the lexicon, considered earlier.

In order to apply this mechanism to an application, an application program must take the output of TRUMP's semantic interpreter and use it to control an action or response. Since the information needed for an application depends on the application itself, the interface between the semantic interpreter and the application-specific knowledge base is critical. This interface is called the oracle, because it serves as the communication window between the linguistic mechanism and the application program. The concretion process integrates knowledge derived from the parser, the semantic interpreter, and the oracle from the application knowledge.

The operation of the language analyzer on the input "Send Jones the message" is shown in Fig. 10.6. The discussion that follows describes the function of each element of the system in understanding this input.

4.1.1. Syntactical Parsing

The parser, or syntactical matcher, executes the following algorithm: For each word read in, match the syntactical categories started by the word against the linguistic patterns that are currently active. If there is a match, make the new syntactical pattern active. Whenever a pattern is complete, put back onto the active list any patterns of which the completed one is a subpattern.

As an example, consider the sentence "Send Jones the message." At the point where the parser considers the word "send," it goes through the following sequence of operations: (1) It finds in the lexicon that "sent" may be a past tense verb. (2) It looks in its grammar to find that verbs start verb phrases. (3) It matches the verb phrase specification to the position in the parse to determine that a verb phrase fits here as part of an imperative sentence. (4) When the period is read, it determines that the verb phrase is complete, and reduces the verb phrase. This means that the information in the verb phrase, both its structure and its meaning, are complete, and any other linguistic structures that include the verb phrase can be continued. (5) Determining that the imperative sentence can be continued, it puts the sentence pattern, or structure, back onto the list of active constructs. In this case the period immediately terminates the sentence.

There are many complications to the scheme that we have described. Much linguistic knowledge and most semantic knowledge is attached to relations, rather than directly to the patterns. For example, the relationship between a verb and its subject is independent of where the subject and verb fall in a sentence. Also, to avoid making many multiple copies of a pattern that has many possible variations, the system makes a new copy

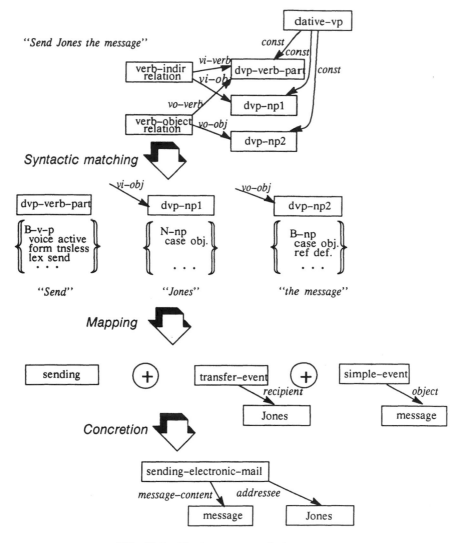

FIG. 10.6. The language analysis process.

of a pattern only when the pattern would otherwise be activated by two conflicting parses simultaneously. For this reason, the details of the pattern-matching algorithm cause complications at the implementation level.

In the case of ambiguity, the parser constructs a chart or data structure that accounts for all valid parses of the input; however, at each point where there is more than one possibility, the possibilities are weighted according to various influences on their likelihood. The chart may then be traversed in such a way as to consider only the most likely interpretation. For example, in the sentence "John sent out the message," TRUMP actually constructs two parses, one in which "sent out" is the operation, the second in which "sent" is the action and "out the message" is the location or direction. The latter parse does not make sense, and will not influence the final meaning selected. TRUMP scores each parse based on syntactical and semantic information and simply chooses the most likely parse.

As the parser completes its processing of each input, it passes information to the semantic interpreter, which determines how the new information influences the interpretation of the meaning of the input. This process is described next.

4.1.2. Mapping

The semantic interpreter takes its input from the parser and incrementally builds a meaning interpretation from the input. Care is taken to keep track of the dependencies between syntactical and conceptual alternatives, and to print out only the interpretation that corresponds to the parse that is printed.

The semantic interpreter makes use of a conceptual hierarchy and a set of mappings between linguistic and conceptual knowledge. The mappings may include metaphorical relationships between concepts as well. Examples of mappings are: (1) the relationship between the word or lexical category "send" and the concept of a sending action; (2) the relationship between the linguistic relation in which a "by" prepositional phrase is used with a passive verb and the actor of an action; (3) the association between command_execution and causal_dual_trans events, in which the operator of the action is viewed as the source of the initiating transfer, as in "The command takes three arguments." Most of this knowledge was shown in the figures in section 3.

Each time a new concept is produced by mapping, the semantic interpreter tries to apply concretion to that concept. This means that it tries to combine the new semantic information with other information that has been derived previously. For example, upon seeing "Jones" in "Send Jones the message," the semantic interpreter uses mapping to derive that Jones plays a recipient role in some transfer-event, but this is combined with the sending concept, as in Fig. 10.6, to find that Jones plays a addressee role. Of course, all these concretions are assumptions made as the text is processed; If the sentence continued "Send Jones the message I sent to Smith," the role of "the message" as object is changed. This is why the process of building a meaning representation as the input is processed is a complicated one. The process of concretion will be described in more detail.

4.1.3. Concretion

A concretion mechanism is one that cements together different pieces of information, possibly derived from a variety of knowledge sources, to determine a meaning representation that is as specific as possible. In other words, the full understanding of a sentence depends on a combination of linguistic, conceptual, and domain knowledge, and it is the role of the concretion mechanism to achieve this combination.

An example of concretion is illustrated in Fig. 10.7. The syntactical matcher determines the linguistic structure of the input, which via mapping results in filling certain generic conceptual roles, such as actor and recipient. Conceptual knowledge determines that sending messages is a particular kind of transfer that is also a communication, unlike "Reagan sent the walrus," which is strictly a physical transfer. Domain knowledge concludes that the message transfer is electronic mail, given that this makes sense in the computer domain.

Because the concretion mechanism is not designed to expect certain types of information from specific sources, the result of this design is to make the program flexible and to allow it to use whatever information is available. If the lexicon is robust enough to suggest a specific interpretation

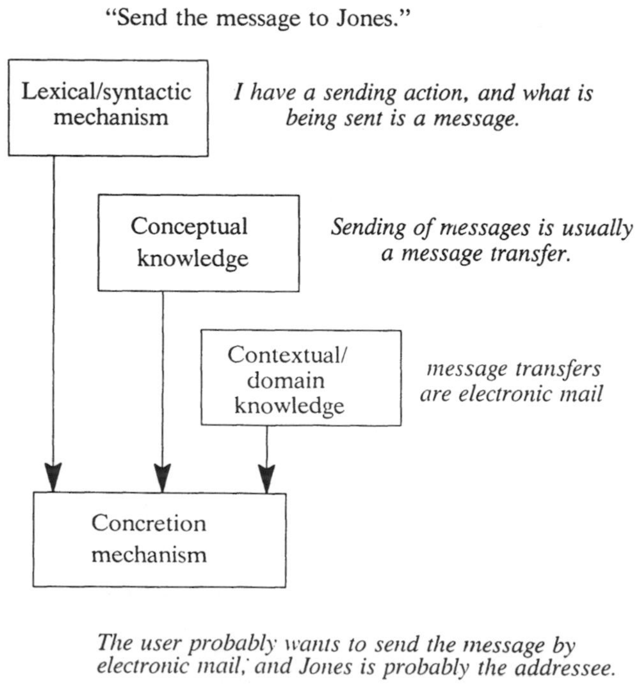

"Send the message to Jones."

| Lexical/syntactic mechanism | *I have a sending action, and what is being sent is a message.* |

| Conceptual knowledge | *Sending of messages is usually a message transfer.* |

| Contextual/ domain knowledge | *message transfers are electronic mail* |

| Concretion mechanism |

The user probably wants to send the message by electronic mail; and Jones is probably the addressee.

FIG. 10.7. How concretion integrates knowledge.

of the input, then it may not need as much help from the domain knowledge, while in other cases the application knowledge will help to derive a specific interpretation even in the absence of certain key words and phrases.

This section has covered one design of a natural-language program that accounts for core linguistic knowledge as described in section 3. While robust interfaces still are not available commercially, it is likely that the next generation of natural language programs will use this type of technology.

5. THE NEXT GENERATION

The current generation of natural language programs includes simple interfaces to specialized applications, such as data bases and spreadsheets, and newer programs that process large quantities of text in particular domains, such as bank telexes and certain types of news stories. The interface programs are greatly restricted, and the text-processing programs are easily fooled. No program can be said to "communicate" or to "understand" in any legitimate way. Nevertheless, computers that process natural language are useful, and their abilities are bound to improve in several ways.

One cause of improvement will be that experience with building previous natural language systems, tricks in reusing technology, and some of the knowledge representation techniques described here will make natural language systems more widely available. This already accounts for the fact that several widely used pieces of software available for personal computers in the $200 range include a natural language interface, albeit a crude one. For each application, a certain amount of domain-specific engineering will be involved, but not so much to prevent the use of natural language in new question-answering-type applications.

A second push toward better natural language systems may come from the availability of text information on-line. Read-only memories and to time-shared textual data bases are increasing the wealth of information available in text form. This information includes on-line encyclopedias, travel information, legal cases, and news and financial reports. Access to the text is done in a crude fashion (usually using single "key" words to search through texts) that makes it difficult to get at the required information. The use of natural language techniques to extract information from text can be motivated by this type of on-line information. While natural language systems will not be able to digest encyclopedias for some time (if at all), there is reason to believe that they can perform at least some useful operations on the texts, such as identifying relevant topics and extracting particular types of information.

Both interface technology and text extraction systems may have a long-term impact on AI in education. Natural language interfaces enable users without computer experience to interact with the machines, and can help make computers explain their operation better to such users. Text-processing systems may serve as aids in research, in reading, and possibly in writing. The tremendous difficulty in building AI systems means that the development work on most natural language technology will be funded by rich sources in high-payoff areas, but the technology will then continue to find its way into inexpensive software for casual computer users. The ALPAC report of 1966 may have been right about the possibility of fully automatic, intelligent language processing, but this certainly does not preclude more automatic, more intelligent language processing.

6. CONCLUSION

To build natural language systems that can effectively understand and produce language in a variety of contexts, it is essential to have a core understanding of language that is independent of domain. While new vocabulary and specialized world knowledge will be needed for many applications, the design of a core knowledge base limits the amount of specialized knowledge that is required and makes the encoding of the specialized knowledge easier. A natural language understander, then, can be flexible in using whatever knowledge is available to produce a specific interpretation of the input.

The impact of this type of mechanism will be to build natural language programs that, like human beings, are versatile in their ability to use language in a variety of applications. This is a major step toward having programs that will communicate, read texts, and answer questions without being both expensive and severely restricted.

REFERENCES

ALPAC. (1966). *Languages and Machines: Computers in Translation and Linguistics*. Report of the Automatic Language Processing Advisory Committee 1416, Division of Behavioral Sciences, National Academy of Sciences, Washington, DC.

Bobrow, D., & Winograd, T. (1977). An overview of KRL, a knowledge representation language. *Cognitive Science*, *1*, 3–46.

Brachman, R., & Schmolze, J. (1985). An overview of the KL–ONE knowledge representation system. *Cognitive Science*, *9*, 171–216.

DeJong, G. (1977). *Skimming Newspaper Stories by Computer*. Research Report 105, Department of Computer Science, Yale University, New Haven, CT.

Harris, L. (1984). Experience with INTELLECT: Artificial intelligence technology transfer. *AI Magazine*, *5*(2).

Jacobs, P. (1986). Language analysis in not-so-limited domains. In *Proceedings of the Fall Joint Computer Conference*, Dallas.

Jacobs, P. (1987a). A knowledge framework for natural language analysis. In *Proceedings of the 10th International Joint Conference on Artificial Intelligence*, Milan, Italy.

Jacobs, P. (1987b). Knowledge-intensive natural language generation. *Artificial Intelligence*, *33*, 325–378.

Jacobs, P., & Rau, L. (1985). Ace: associating language with meaning. In T. O'Shea, (Ed.), *Advances in Artificial Intelligence*, (pp. 295–304). Amsterdam: North Holland.

Kaczmarek, T., Mark, W., & Sondheimer, N. (1983). The consul/cue interface: An integrated interactive environment. In *Proceedings of CHI '83 Human Factors in Computing Systems*.

Wilensky, R. (1986). Knowledge representation—A critique and a proposal. In J. Kolodner & C. Riesbeck (Eds.), *Experience, Memory, and Reasoning* (pp. 15–28). Hillsdale, NJ: Lawrence Erlbaum Associates.

Wilensky, R., Arenas, Y., & Chin, D. (1984). Talking to UNIX in English: An overview of UC. *Communications of the Association for Computing Machinery*, *27*, 574–593.

11 Comments on Artificial Intelligence Research: Related Issues in Education and Testing

Saul Amarel
Rutgers University

I'll make some comments about a few of the papers I heard this morning and based on some of the material that I've received. Then I'll make some comments about what goes on in AI these days and its relationship to education, especially educational testing.

First of all, I'm absolutely delighted to see that ETS is interested in AI. I think it's a very important development. There are many interesting things that are going on in AI that relate to education, but I don't think the area is moving fast enough. It is such a very important area from the point of view of science and from the point of view of social impact; I hope that ETS will keep going along these lines and will move on with research and development in this area.

Concerning the papers I heard this morning, my first impression was the reminder we got, that the first good piece of work on analogy was done roughly 20 years ago by Evans within AI. That was a long time ago. The field of AI has moved a lot since then, especially in the last 10 years or so. The question is, why is the entire field of analogy moving relatively slowly? Actually, in looking back on Evans's work, you find that many, many good ideas were produced a long time ago. There has been an increment in additional good ideas since then, but it's not dramatic. Why is that? Analogy is a very difficult combination of processes as was pointed out [in one of the presentations.] You're given a task. You're asked to find a solution to the problem. Then, the first thing you do is you have to go and search in memory and find something which is similar. [Similar! That's the most difficult concept that you have to play with]. Then, you retrieve from memory experiences with that similar task. You try to transfer those experiences to the problem at hand. You do as much as you can with this transfer. And usually, in most cases, you're just not quite there. You have to repair. You have to patch. You have to change. And then you can solve your problem. But you're not done. Then you have to store that experience. This is now part of the new memory you have. So the next time, when a similar situation occurs, this new memory of the entire process, together with all the other memories, are going to be used and influence the way you are going to handle another similar task. This is a very complex combination of things.

Especially complex is the entire issue of just what we mean by a *similar task*. Very much at the heart of the notion of what is a similar task is the problem of representation—how to represent a thing. Some people believe we represent a thing in a unique way. That's absolute nonsense. More and more we find out that a thing is represented "in our head" in a variety of ways. It's represented structurally. It's represented functionally or behaviorally. Also, it may be represented at different "grains," i.e., at different levels of abstraction or detail. So, we have a variety of ways of representing a memory of a thing or of an event or of a problem-solving episode. We still don't have a good understanding of these various representations and of relationships between them. We don't understand really what it means, to choose "appropriate" representations except we know that the choices of representation are extremely important and critical for all the processes we are talking about—retrieving a similar thing, transferring an experience, and so on.

Several people in the 1960s, including myself, looked into the entire issue of the effect of choosing a representation on problem solving efficiency. Twenty years later, we still are not quite clear how to handle this particular issue of choosing a representation. And after we have chosen, we are not clear how to repair, how to reformulate problems so that we will have better ways of looking at and solving the problems. I believe that what happened in the last few years, in the area of analogical reasoning, is that work in the area provided very good examples that illustrate some of the very difficult issues of choice of representation, of how to handle multiple representations, and of how to use a representation in particular contexts.

The notion of *context* became better understood fairly recently. This notion involves the following: in order to choose among all the various ways in which you are going to think about a similar thing, it is important to know *under what conditions* you are thinking about that thing. What is the particular goal that you have in mind? What is the context? Because, by having a more specific view about what is your goal and context, you can select among various facets of the problem, or various ways in which the problem has been stored in your memory. So, by necessity, you have to look at a choice of representations in context. This is a very old and difficult problem. For what kinds of goals, for what kinds of problems, is one or the other representation appropriate? What conceptual framework is appropriate? What particular grain? All of these issues have to do exactly with the problem of context, i.e., with the particular goal you have in mind.

There is nothing absolute about choosing a representation. In my opinion, choice of representation is a relative thing. It is important that we develop the notion of relativity of representations. This has to do with the context, the goal, the special things you have in mind, concerning the use of the thing to be represented. This is a very important area of research in AI. It is also important for our understanding of human reasoning and human learning.

I want to make a comment about the methodology of work in the field of AI. I believe the field is very difficult and it takes some experience to recognize how difficult it is. The way it is approached is by focusing on problems in a specific domain. For example, we do some work in geometry, or in some particular area of problem solving; we do some work with theorem proving, and so on. I think what we need is a much more disciplined approach to the choice of domain. We shouldn't just choose any topic for study—such as, work on analogy—but to be modest about our business and to start from problems that are *almost* solved. I mean that in the following sense.

Suppose you are designing an artifact. You're designing a piece of machinery. Suppose you have some experience already about what you've done in attaining designs based on sets of given specifications. Now suppose you have a new problem that involves a slight modification of a previous design, a redesign. It's presented to you in terms of specifications that are slightly different from the specifications of some previous problem. The problem of redesigning—not of starting from the beginning the entire design process, but starting by using a previous design experience and modifying it slowly so that you can get a new design—forces us to look into the issue of how to use the previous information about a design in the solution of the current design problem. What representations to use and modify? How to reason with these representations. These are very difficult problems. But I think they are important. Take analogies again. You have to choose the problem that is the base problem, and then you have to transfer things from the base to the target, and then you have to patch up. Here again you say "How do I take something which is almost close to my desired solution and patch up?"

After we understand well the entire problem of redesign, of correcting, of patching something which is almost the solution to our problem we will be in a better position to understand what the concepts, and the ideas of choice of a similar problem are. The "good" similar problem is that similar problem that is amenable to very effective processing in changing its solution to produce a solution to our current problem. We need a good careful methodology in researching this area. In AI, we are a little undisciplined about such matters. But I think it's important to do it.

I hope we can also develop a good methodology in cognitive psychology and test out the same kinds of issues by carefully developing an experimental set of problems where at first the distance between the target problem and the base problem is small, but then slowly the distance is increased; psychologists need to try to understand what is involved in doing this. Maybe in psychology, this is already going on—I don't know. But I don't see that kind of an attitude for such a methodology within AI.

What I have sketched for you is a proposal, or a type of recommendation. You should recognize that these problems are very difficult. There are very difficult issues involved in choosing an appropriate way for representing things. We should recognize that in approaching such problems we have to be very modest in our research objectives and in our choice of experimental tasks. Problems of redesign, probably, are very good candidates for work in this area.

I was very much interested to see that there is more and more work done on case-based reasoning, on the entire question of episodic memories and their use in problem solving, and the entire question of memory organization. We don't have much work in this area. I'd like to see much more work done.

The work I heard about today—although I didn't read about it beforehand—represents a good direction. Actually, what is going on in AI at this point, by considering work of this kind, represents a fairly important shift in point of view, a shift in paradigm.

For example, most of the work in problem solving in the late 1950s and 1960s had been *one episode at a time*. You are given a problem in terms of a present situation and a desired situation. These constitute the conditions of the problem. You are provided with the building material for solutions; for example, you are given a set of operators. You have a controller, and you use the controller to try to build a solution by letting the building materials for solutions establish a bridge that takes you from the present situation to the desired situation. After you have done that, you erase the whole thing. You throw it out. Then a new problem comes in and you start all over again. There was no memory of what you did in the past. Such an approach has continued and continues up to now, including in problems of learning. To my mind, concept (hypothesis) learning is another problem-solving task in which you are given a body of phenomena; you are given a language or a conceptual framework in terms of which a hypothesis is to be developed that describes and binds together the phenomena. Your problem is to find some way to create the hypothesis that explains, is consistent with, those pehnomena. It's a problem-solving activity and it's fairly well defined: Here are the examples, here are the phenomena, that is, here are the things that you have to understand, here is the particular language in terms of which you are going to develop your generalized conceptual descriptions; find appropriate "high-level" descriptions for the phenomena.

But the interesting paradigm shift that I see emerging now is that we're no longer thinking in terms of a single problem-solving episode. We're thinking about a *history of problem-solving episodes*. We're not thinking about an instantaneous agent but a persistent agent. So within AI, we are developing the notion of a persistent agent and, in that sense, we are much closer to the kind of thing that a psychologist might be interested in because human beings are persistent agents. As persistent intelligent agents we have various controlling procedures for handling information, but we also have something which is much more important—a tremendous knowledge base of not only things that already have been constructed, but a tremendous amount of unstructured experience, especially problem-solving experience. We still don't know within AI how to use large repositories of such experiences.

At present, work in the field is starting to put a lot of emphasis on how to acquire, store, and use the traces of problem-solving experience. We have a problem, then another problem, one problem-solving experience, and then another experience. We want to see in what way these things connect to each other. Also consider the problem-solving traces—we have to think how to represent them. At what level of granularity? What concepts do we construct out of those traces? What do we learn from these traces? That's a very important part of the paradigm shift. I think that only a few people within AI are aware that this is happening. I would like to see much more research occur in that direction. It's going to be very useful both from the point of view of AI and from the point of view of cognitive psychology.

Another issue that comes with that is a practical issue. It has to do with the notion of complexity. One of the important things that happened as the field of AI evolved from the 1950s until now is that we became much more interested in moving from so-called toy problems to real-life, complex problems. When we come to situations with very complex problems, we have to deal with questions of scale and size. We have to deal with very large memories. We have to deal with processes of reasoning that have to be done within time constraints This means that we have to think much more about the architecture of the mechanisms that do these things.

Consider for instance the computer architectures in the case of AI. The way in which we organize memories. The way in which we organize procedures in general. This is a nontrivial issue. It's not only an AI problem. It's a problem in computer science. I'm not even talking about the ability to have very fast machines or the ability to have very large memories. We are working on that, What I am saying is something else. It has to do with something we think is very important in computer science. It is the question of computational complexity. It's a question of how the resources needed for computing your problem grow with the size of the problem. Within AI, we usually work with very complex problems, almost intractable, combinatorial problems, meaning that, as the size of the problem goes up, the complexity in time and/or space grows exponentially, or almost exponentially. And the fundamental game that we play within AI—and I'm saying that from a computer scientist's point of view—is to try to fight this war against the combinatorial explosion of complexity. Within AI, we are trying to use the information and knowledge about the problem at hand in a very clever way—so as to reduce the computational complexity that is needed as the size of the problem goes up.

Now, I'm concerned that, by looking at problems where episodic memories are going to be dealt with, where memories will grow, the issues of complexity are going to be a much more important problem for us. We'll have to estimate how long it will take to find a "similar" situation in memory. How many times do we have to reject almost-similar situations that are not right. We are going to have to handle very difficult problems of not having a single "similar" situation or not even 10 "similar" situations, but 10,000 "similar" situations, and try to go through them and find a way of extracting out of them something that really is useful. The decision of how we are going to organize the experiential memory into categories is extremely important. Probably different "personalities" of computing agents are going to arise and might be distinguished by the way in which they organize these various experiences in memory. So, if you talk about differences between individuals or differences in styles of thinking, maybe to a great extent they are going to be related to the way in which an agent, for example, organizes and restructures memories of the past. That's another AI direction in which not much work has been done. I think we're going to have much more work in this area in the next few years.

These are some of the thoughts that were triggered by a few of the things that I heard this morning. I like to give you a sense now of what is the level of activity in AI in this country at present, and what's going on in general.

I think probably about a quarter of all work in computer science in the country is in AI. This happened, to a great extent, not only because of the intellectual excitement of the field, but because in the last 5 to 10 years, it was found that AI ideas may have a practical impact on the work of industry and defense. The entire expert system thrust has produced, say, by now, on the order of 600 or 700 deployable expert systems in the country. It would seem a very promising direction to go. The amount of funding, the amount of support, and the amount of excitement around AI has grown. I might add that the rate at which new ideas occur and good research in AI is done is growing also. But it is not growing at a rate which is higher than that of 5, or 6, or 10 years ago. We need to do much more fundamental work in AI because what's occurring is that we are eating our intellectual capital very, very quickly by directing much of our effort into many specific applications. There is so much more to be done; that's why I was very pleased to hear that interesting stuff is going on in the area of analogical reasoning. In general, case-based reasoning guided by an episodic memory is a direction in which we should be doing much more research.

My feeling is that the best AI work in the country is supported by various government agencies at the level of around $60 million a year. I've been in Washington for one and a half years now and, just within DARPA, the overall support for basic AI is in the order of 40 million out of the total 60. I'm not talking about very large applications (e.g., applied expert systems) but basic work. I think we need to increase the amount of support for basic work in AI. To give you also an idea of distribution, artificial intelligence evolved roughly into three general areas: perception, cognition, and control of action. In perception, we have vision, speech, language. In cognition, we have all sorts of problem-solving issues including learning, but in general we have symbolic manipulation of things. In control of action we have such things as robotic manipulation and real-time control of situations. The relative amount of support for control of action is small. I think we are losing *vis-à-vis* other countries in the robotics area. We should do much more along these lines. Most of the activity, especially within DARPA, has been in the area of support of perceptual tasks. In other words, vision, language, and speech are being supported relatively more than areas of cognition, complex problem solving, planning, and learning. I would like to see this change. I would like to see much more going in the direction of cognitive tasks. Fundamentally, they are much more impactful on many things we are doing. Many of the papers that we heard this morning have to do with cognitive tasks.

I think if you look at the developments in areas of language and speech, which I understand are also of importance for what goes on in this conference, there's some very good work being done at present. What I consider to be an interesting development is that speech and language are coming closer together as an area of research. The notion of handling discourse in general, and dialogue, is becoming important and this is giving a unifying, much more coherent way of looking at problems of speech and language in the large. Rather than looking at small components of the entire enterprise, it's possible to look at bigger kinds of components of the activity—this is an important development.

In the area of AI and education, I think there is not enough support and there is not enough research. There are many things that relate to education, but we are not doing enough. Of course there are a lot of things that are relevant. Almost anything that is going on in AI is relevant to problems of education. I would like to express my own prejudice, that educational testing is only a small part of what we are talking about. Testing of what? What exactly are we testing? Probably, it's going to be much more important to focus at least some resources and some thought on fundamental issues of education, and not necessarily on testing aspects of education. In what way do people learn, in what way do people learn on their own as opposed to being taught? In what way do people learn from reading material in books or from theories? In what way do they learn from practice? I believe that we have to learn much more about *how* people learn from apprenticeship or how people learn from their own experiences of problem solving, which is part of the thing we discussed earlier. The entire question of expertise acquisition either through one's own experiences or by being coached by someone else is extremely important. From the point of view of the laborpower situation in this country as a whole, questions of how to train people, how to shift from one particular area of expertise to another, how to increase the knowhow in a given technical area are becoming increasingly urgent. This is all very important, extremely important.

We are not doing enough to understand the process of training through a variety of formal and informal ways. I think by using some of the methodologies of AI, in modeling those processes, and duplicating them on computers, we are really going to be in a better position to understand what's going on in the area of training people. I think the issue of testing will come as *part* of that, but I don't know how to focus on the issue of testing without understanding the issue of testing what, and testing the processes themselves. So, I would like to stress again the importance of research on the processes of learning and teaching over the entire spectrum. It would be excellent if a place like ETS would participate to some extent in this research.

Another issue that I know arises many times, especially in private corporations, is how much basic research can you do, versus how much development and production. I believe it's important to devote a certain amount of the R&D activity—I don't know what percentage, it depends on the style of the organization, it could be 10% or it could be 50%—to continue basic research in many of the issues we are talking about. It could perhaps be oriented and especially guided by an educational mission or by an educational testing mission. I would very much like to see a combination of both basic research in AI and, of course, exploration of possible uses of AI in educational testing and in other areas of education, as time goes by.

12 Communicative Functions in Interactions in Natural Language and Other Modalities

Aravind K. Joshi
University of Pennsylvania

The interest in language-processing centers around the need to build good interfaces between people and machines. Since language use does not have to be taught early workers sought to exploit it in building better interfaces. Computer implementation of these interfaces has turned out to be quite difficult. But what has turned out is that work in language processing has given insight into some of the communicative functions that exist in any kind of interaction, which are really independent of the language modality. So, some of the work that has come out of the language-processing area will be discussed, especially that involving the building of cooperative interfaces, see, for example, Joshi (1982), Joshi, Weischedel, and Webber (1984), and Finin, Joshi, and Webber (1986).

Some of the communicative functions these facilities support could also be supported in other kinds of modalities. So, when people talk about artificial languages as interfaces, some of the same questions [concerning communicative functions] come up and must be adequately addressed. I can perhaps best illustrate the nature of this problem with an example which I have often used. Early data base systems gave you something like the following kind of performance. Suppose you asked these early systems, say, "How many students in Computer Science 101 in the Fall of 1986 got A's?" the answer might be "nil." If you asked "How many got B's?", the answer might still be "nil." If you asked the system "How many got C's, D's, or failed?", the answer still might be "nil." Then if you asked "Was Computer Science 101 offered in the fall of "86?", the answer could well be "No."

We see in this example that there is a presumption on behalf of the person asking the question that he or she presupposes that the course *was* offered. So the very fact that the person has uttered a sentence of a certain form and in a certain context, means that you could describe the person as having the belief that the presupposition is true. So in asking "How many students got A's in Computer Science 101 in the fall of 1986?", there is an implied presumption that the course was offered. A more helpful interface system would pay attention to such presumptions because if you, the user, assume certain presumptions are true, and if indeed they are false, then the interface system should not go through the foregoing sequence of queries [and answers] but instead should immediately inform the user that "Computer Science was not offered in the fall of 1986." Failing to do this will only confirm the presupposition of the user, which is actually false. This is not cooperative behavior.

By the way, it so happens, in this case at least, that this extra information was available to the systems that actually existed 10 years ago; in other words, in order to answer this first question the system had already made certain computations. One of the computations it made was whether or not Computer Science 101 was offered and had obviously discovered that it was not offered. But the interface system did not take advantage of the fact by informing the person making the inquiries about this situation. This is instructive: The early systems already had the ability to produce that kind of response, but it was not considered a requirement of the systems that they exhibit certain communicative functions, even though such functions are certainly exhibited by a *person* had he or she been asked the initial question.

Considerable work since about 1978 has gone into building more helpful interfaces, which incorporate various kinds of communicative functions such as those involved dealing with different types of presuppositions. Yet some of this work often fails to indicate that the real goal is to pay close attention to these communicative functions, and to produce various kinds of helpful responses, including explanations. [By "explanation" I mean not only to give the response, but to give the user the reason(s) why such a response was given].

Such communicative functions are not necessarily restricted to the use of the English language or any other natural-language interface. These functions would have to be supported even for an artificial [restricted-domain] language; this refers back to the question that was raised during the question-answering part of several of the earlier talks namely what happens if people wanted to use artificial languages because they are skilled in a certain domain—and in some situation why shouldn't we exploit that ability.

As a matter of fact there are certain applications where you might want to play the following game: namely, the user who starts off in English, but once the user gets acquainted with a certain special domain, then he or she can begin to use a more restrictive, domain-dependent language. Such a restricted language is more artificial, but it is much more efficient. But even in this case in spite of the efficiency of the restricted language, the communicative functions involving presuppositions, and so on, would still have to be supported in such restricted domains.

Some of the papers referred to the need for efficiency of language processing. The use of pronouns was referred to as one thing that ought to be exploited in gaining efficiency. Analyzing pronouns is very complicated, as I'm sure everyone knows. Consider the following sentences:

Suppose you have 10 balls. (1) One of the 10 balls is not in the bag. It is under the sofa. (2) Nine of the 10 balls are in the bag. It is under the sofa.

In (1) we know what "it" refers to. There are 10 balls, and there's 1 ball that the "it" refers to which is not in the bag. In (2) we know that there is one ball that is not in the bag, so there is a conceptual entity corresponding to the ball that is not in the bag (and which is under the sofa). However, "it" in (2) cannot refer to this entity because this entity has not been explicitly "evoked" in the preceeding discourse, and therefore cannot be referred to.

Here is an instance where I can combine my comments on various papers. This example [of "it" referring to "the one ball that isn't in the bag" in (2)] points out the fact that the problem of language generation is very hard because it has to pay attention to such things as pronoun reference. While the two discourses [in (1) and (2)] in some sense have the same information, everybody would agree that the second one has some incoherences. In order to know what that incoherence is you need a lot more information about the structure of language, you need to know the structure of discourse and how pronouns are used. So, a point I want to make right now, using this example, is that in language processing, although one might think of understanding and generation as some sort of inverses of each other, the fact is that that is not quite the case. Clearly, in some ideal sense they are inverses of each other, but in practice they are not. Most of the understanding programs exploit the domain information very heavily and quite appropriately, to overcome or to avoid certain problems about the syntax, or semantics, or maybe even some pragmatic aspects because there is so much information known about the domain and for the particular task you have to do, and so on.

When it comes to generation, however, you cannot avoid the problem as Paul Jacobs [this volume] pointed out. What you must generate must not only have the right kind of information, it also must be organized in just the right way so that the resulting output "feels" like sentences of English. Further, the sequence of these sentences has to hang together as text, so all the problems that you could perhaps successfully avoid in comprehension [I'm talking of the practical system here; I'm not saying that for people's comprehension and generation one can make these claims] must be dealt with directly in generation.

When it comes to practical systems, the problem of generation is actually quite hard—it requires you to integrate all the components such as syntax, semantics and, of course, world knowledge in a fairly systematic way. You cannot take easy ways out because you pay the price for it if you want to produce a long, coherent text, which can be comprehended by the user.

The work on generation is therefore bringing together people from different disciplines much closer. The interaction between AI and linguists is going to be even stronger, I think, especially when they pay attention to generation, because the grammatical part has to interface appropriately with the higher-level components. Language interfaces with generation may pay off much earlier and much more effectively than those involving understanding or comprehension. This is so because it might very well be the case that as far as the input is concerned you can use artificial language as your input. But on the output, you want some kind of explanation for the answer and also why certain things went wrong if they did. You want the explanation to appear as a coherent text, because you cannot give a response that is just a sequence of statements in an artificial language [and hope thereby to communicate useful information]. That's where artificial language begins to lose out when the system has to compose longer responses than just one-statement-long responses. A sequence of such statements will be hard to comprehend because it may be textually incoherent. The same information which appears as a coherent English-language text should be much easier to comprehend. So there may very well be applications where the input would be an artificial language, but the output has to be coherent English.

So, I think that the technology that's coming out in language generation might actually find applications much earlier than the language understanding part will.

Let me take another point relevant to several talks where a distinction was made between the core linguistic information and the domain information, and the different ways of integrating these types of information. I think this is a very positive trend. Most systems being developed now are proceeding along those lines.

To motivate this part of my talk let me take an example. If you take some word such as *rent*, then there are various roles or cases to be distinguished. The various roles associated with rent would be the *renter*, the *rentee*, and *what is rented*. If you are talking about the renting of cars then some of the other roles are the *amount of rent paid per day*, the *place where you rent*, and *the place where the car is to be returned*, and so on. It's only the first three that are sort of linguistic in the sense that they are syntactically marked, the word "rent" being subcategorized for those three roles. This is not true for the other roles, that is, they are not roles the verb "rent" is subcategorized for, they are more domain-dependent.

So if you want to divide up your verbs into categories, as some of the speakers were doing, then you would place some roles in the linguistic realm and the others in a category of domain knowledge. Now, this is not often so easy, because there are cases where it's not clear whether the particular role that you are considering should go in the linguistic part or whether it's really domain-dependent.

There's one point about this distinction which I will mention. I don't know to what extent it's directly relevant for this conference, but it's been pointed out recently that in terms of processing by humans, this distinction between roles shows up. If you make an error in assignment of the case role to a certain entity while you are processing, then you are able to recover and get the correct assignments much more easily if those roles refer to the core linguistic roles, as against the ones that are domain roles. This is a claim made by, I believe, Tannenhaus and Greg Carson at Rochester. If the evidence for this distinction holds up, then I think it makes even greater sense to deal with these categories differently. But, as I said, I don't know whether this particular psycholinguistic observation has any direct relevance for testing applications that are of interest to the sponsors of this conference; I would imagine that it should be somehow relevant to testing.

REFERENCES

Finin, T., Joshi, A. K., & Webber, B. (1986). Natural language interfaces for artificial experts. In *Proceedings of the IEEE* (Institute of Electrical and Electronics Engineers).

Joshi, A. K. (1982). Mutual beliefs in question-answer systems. In N. Smith (Ed.), *Mutual beliefs*. New York: Academic Press.

Joshi, A. K., Weischeded, R., & Webber, B. (1984). Preventing false inferences. In *Proceedings of the International Conference on Computational Linguistics, COLING-84*. Stanford, CA.

13

Assessment of an Expert System's Ability to Grade and Diagnose Automatically Student's Constructed Responses to Computer Science Problems

Randy Elliot Bennett
Brian Gong
Roger C. Kershaw
Donald A. Rock
Educational Testing Service

Elliot Soloway
Alex Macalalad
Yale University

Among several recent trends in educational measurement is one toward providing information that more directly benefits individuals as opposed to institutions. One instance of such measurement is diagnostic assessment (e.g., Bejar, 1984; Forehand, 1987), which attempts to offer guidance to teachers and students about the specific problems encountered in learning and how they might be addressed. A second, related instance is constructed-response testing (e.g., Ward, Frederiksen, & Carlson, 1980), in which the test task is closer to that required of students and workers in academic and vocational settings, and therefore of more obvious relevance to the examinee. Both forms of assessment have been practiced for many years; diagnostic assessment has long been a standard, though typically informal, practice of master teachers and constructed response assessment a routine component of classroom tests, graduate school comprehensive exams, and even some standardized testing programs (e.g., the Advanced Placement Program of the College Board).

While these forms of assessment are well established, their use in large-scale testing programs has been hampered by an absence of sound theoretical models upon which to base diagnoses and by practical constraints. With respect to the latter, the primary difficulty has been the subjectivity and high cost associated with scoring; training human readers to achieve acceptable levels of agreement and supporting them while they score thousands of exams could be achieved in only limited ways and by only a very few testing programs.

However, recent advances in cognitive psychology, computer science, and educational measurement have opened up new possibilities for making diagnostic, constructed-response assessment both scientifically defensible and practical. These advances include work on the nature of expertise (Glaser, 1986), the application of expert and novice cognitive models to diagnostic teaching and measurement (Wenger, 1987), the construction of psychometric models for diagnosis (Tatsuoka, 1985), massive decreases in hardware price/performance ratios, and the development of programming methodologies that permit machines to store, access, and apply knowledge in ways that ever more resemble human cognitive functioning (Barr & Feigenbaum, 1981).

These various advances are reflected in different combinations in a growing crop of educationally oriented computer programs being developed under the rubric of "intelligent tutoring," or more generally, "artificial intelligence" (Wenger, 1987). One prototype, MicroPROUST, was used to rate diagnostically and numerically students' free-response solutions to College Board Advanced Placement (AP) Computer Science problems. This chapter describes a study of the level of scoring agreement between MicroPROUST and human readers to determine whether these different graders are interchangeable.

PROCEDURE

Subjects

MicroPROUST.   MicroPROUST, a version of PROUST (Johnson & Soloway, 1985), attempts to find nonsyntactical bugs in Pascal programs. MicroPROUST has knowledge to reason about (1) selected programming problems, (2) stereotypical ways in which subcomponents of these problems are solved in Pascal, and (3) common faulty implementations of these subcomponents.

MicroPROUST's knowledge base contains information about two simple Advanced Placement Computer Science problems (see Appendix A). This information is a coded version of the English text of each problem, which MicroPROUST uses to guide its analysis of student solutions. MicroPROUST's knowledge base divides the first problem into eight subcomponents, for which it has a total of 116 unique solutions, and the second into two subcomponents with 33 solutions. Forty-eight faulty subcomponent implementations are also included. MicroPROUST analyzes solutions subcomponent by subcomponent, looking for templates in its knowledge base that match parts of the student's code. This subcomponent-matching strategy gives it considerable leverage; correct and incorrect implementations can be put together in different combinations to handle the variety of responses generated by novice programmers.

MicroPROUST's analysis produces a summative score on the 0–9 scale used by the AP program (where 9 represents a perfect solution), and, where appropriate, a diagnostic comment. Diagnostic comments identify the location of a conceptual error, describe the error's nature, and sometimes guide the student toward a reasonable correction (see Appendix B).

For the current study, subcomponent solutions and faulty implementations were based on an analysis of student papers selected from AP program files. Because papers can be requested by the institutions from which students are seeking advanced placement and/or course credit, the solutions left in the files may not be fully representative of those produced by the test-taking population. However, the full range of numerical grades assigned by AP readers was represented in the remaining solutions; hence, five papers from each of the nine score levels were drawn randomly to form a sample of 45 solutions for each of the two APCS problems.

After developing the knowledge base, point values were assigned to the faulty implementations to allow the program to produce a numerical score for each solution. Point values were based on the grading criteria used to score the problems operationally in 1984 and 1985.

Next, the solutions used to develop the knowledge base were typed in computer-readable format for analysis by MicroPROUST. As part of the typing process, syntactical errors were corrected, introductory and concluding statements were placed around the solutions associated with one problem to make it a complete program, and other minor changes in form and format were made. Because of their poor conceptual quality, two solutions were not entered for one of the problems, bringing to 88 the total number of solutions submitted to the program.

MicroPROUST runs on an IBM Personal Computer/AT with 4 megabytes of random access memory, a 10-megabyte hard disk, an enhanced graphics adapter, and the Golden Common Lisp environment.

Readers. To organize and coordinate an experimental reading, two individuals were selected based on their central roles in grading past AP Computer Science examinations. These "chief" readers were asked to suggest a list of the most qualified readers from those participating in the 1986 reading. Eight readers were selected and invited to ETS for a 1-day reading.

Of the eight, five were male; six were from secondary schools and two from universities; five were from the Northeast, two from the South, and one from the Midwest.

Method

Two sets of research questions were posed. One set focused on summative scoring and the other on diagnostic comments.

Summative scoring.
1. To what degree do human readers of APCS free-response questions agree among themselves in assigning scores?
2. Is MicroPROUST's level of agreement with human readers as high as the level of agreement of human readers among themselves?

Diagnostic comments.
1. To what degree do human readers of APCS free-response questions agree among themselves in making diagnostic judgments?
2. Is MicroPROUST's level of agreement with human readers as high as the level of agreement of human readers among themselves?
3. How do machine and human diagnoses differ?

To gather the data needed to answer these questions, a balanced incomplete block (BIB) design was used (see Table 13.1). In this design, the eight readers were divided into two equal groups. Without knowledge of the ratings assigned by MicroPROUST, each group read half of the student solutions to each of the two problems, with all four readers in a group reading the same set of solutions. In general, the higher quality solutions were assigned to one set of raters for problem 1 and the other set for problem 2.

Two types of readings were conducted: summative and diagnostic. The summative reading was intended to simulate the readings typically performed by the AP program in scoring the Computer Science Examination. Briefly, these readings involve the initial collaborative development by the chief reader and the table leaders of analytical scoring rubrics for each of the exam's five free-response questions. The rubrics are then introduced to the readers, who, in discussions and practice gradings, refine them. Once operational readings begin, the table leaders reread samples from each reader, and the chief reads samples from each table leader, to check for and resolve instances of significant scoring discrepancy (2 or more points). This entire process is conducted over a 5- to 6-day period.

For the experimental reading, the two chief readers refined the rubrics originally developed for the problems through the operational testing program. MicroPROUST's scoring algorithms were then adjusted to conform with these refined rubrics. At the experimental reading, the rubrics (see Appendix C) were discussed with the readers and a dozen or so practice solutions scored (considerably fewer than in the typical operational read-

TABLE 13.1
Study Design

Type of Reading	Student Paper	1	2	3	4	5	6	7	8
Numerical	1-1	x	x	x	x				
	.	.	.	.	.				
	1-22	x	x	x	x				
	2-1					x	x	x	x
	.					.	.	.	.
	2-21					x	x	x	x
Diagnostic	1-23	x	x	x	x				
	.	.	.	.	.				
	1-45	x	x	x	x				
	2-22					x	x	x	x
	.					.	.	.	.
	2-43					x	x	x	x
Numerical	1-23					x	x	x	x
	.					.	.	.	.
	1-45					x	x	x	x
	2-22	x	x	x	x				
	.	.	.	.	.				
	2-43	x	x	x	x				
Diagnostic	1-1					x	x	x	x
	.					.	.	.	.
	1-22					x	x	x	x
	2-1	x	x	x	x				
	.	.	.	.	.				
	2-21	x	x	x	x				

ing). The chief readers then served as table leaders for each group, responding to questions about the scoring as ones arose. The chiefs did not reread any papers because rereading such a small sample would artificially increase reader agreement to near-perfect levels.

The diagnostic reading was an attempt to simulate the conceptual comments offered by MicroPROUST (such comments are *not* usually made as part of APCS readings). Readers were asked to read student papers and (1) identify the location of any error, (2) describe its nature, and (3) offer a suggestion for improvement, where appropriate. Suggestions for improvement were generally not to give replacement code, but rather point the student toward a correction, and were not to exceed two sentences.

As Table 13.1 indicates, the summative and diagnostic readings were interspersed; that is, after each group of readers summatively rated one-half of a solution set, they made diagnostic comments on the other half.

Summative Analysis Procedures. To assess the level of agreement among readers, the product moment correlation between each pair of readers grading the same sample of papers was computed. For each of the four samples (i.e., two problems each split into two sets), six correlations were computed, transformed via the Fisher r-to-z transformation, and averaged. To take account of situations in which papers are reread, the interrater reliability for papers read by two readers was computed from this average using the Spearman–Brown formula (Stanley, 1971).

To evaluate the level of agreement between MicroPROUST and the readers, the correlation between MicroPROUST and each of the four readers in each sample was computed. These correlations were transformed, averaged, and compared with the average correlation among the readers. The difference between the two averages was tested via a two-tailed t-test of the difference between the mean z-scores, where the standard error of the mean for the readers was $1/[6N-18]^{1/2}$ and for Micro-PROUST $1/[4N-12]^{1/2}$ as per McNemar (1962), and the standard error of the difference was the square root of the sum of the squared standard errors of the means (because the two average correlations are themselves correlated, this is a conservative test). Next, the reliability for two readers was computed to give an estimate of the interrater reliability to be expected when MicroPROUST is used in concert with a human reader whose level of agreement with other humans is equivalent to that of MicroPROUST's.

A second method of comparing the agreement between MicroPROUST and the readers was also used. This method involved computing the mean rating across readers for each paper in a sample, a value conceptually similar to classical test theory's "true" score. These means were then correlated with MicroPROUST's ratings to provide an overall index of agreement and subtracted from MicroPROUST's ratings to identify how disagreements were distributed.

A third method of examining agreement involved computing the distribution of the disagreements among readers for each solution. These disagreements were found by comparing the ratings of each individual with each of the other three readers, resulting in 12 disagreements for each paper. MicroPROUST was then substituted for each of the four readers in turn and its ratings compared with each of the remaining three, again producing 12 contrasts per paper. By this method, MicroPROUST had as many chances to disagree with the readers as they had to disagree among themselves.

Last, the scale levels of ratings assigned by the program and the readers were compared to detect any tendency of the program to assign higher or lower ratings and to examine whether the readers themselves graded on comparable scales. To do this, individual mean ratings within each of the four samples were compared by repeated-measures analysis of variance. For the samples rated by the program, F-tests significant at $p < .05$ were followed by post hoc, Scheffe contrasts (Scheffe, 1953) of the grand mean of the reader ratings with MicroPROUST's mean ratings. Finally, post hoc, paired-sample t-tests among each pair of readers were conducted to identify the sources of score-level differences.

Diagnostic Analysis Procedures. The diagnostic comments of the readers and MicroPROUST were analyzed in several ways. First, the number of solutions commented on were compared for readers and for Micro-PROUST. Next, the correctness of comments was determined by examining the specific code to which each comment referred. This determination resulted in the percentage of correct comments given by MicroPROUST, the percentage of correct comments given by the readers, and the total number of correct comments offered on each solution set by the readers and by MicroPROUST.

Third, comments were classified according to a multistage procedure. In stage one, the readers' comments were grouped into *distinct* comments, comments of the same nature referring to the same piece of program code regardless of the wording used by the reader. For example, comments expressed as "C (the variable name) is uninitialized," "Need to assign C a value before you use it," and "What is the value of C the first time through the loop?" were all coded as dealing with the distinct comment, "Need to initialize variable."

In the second stage, these distinct comments were grouped into general *concepts*. For example, the distinct comments, "should localize loop variable" and "should localize array variable" were organized under the concept "localize variables."

The last stage involved classifying the concepts into one of five *categories*:

Structured programming practices. Structured programming comments dealt with use of structured programming practices, particularly functional decomposition, data abstraction, and information hiding. Examples of such comments included "should break this code into smaller procedures," "need to pass as parameter rather than access as global variable," and "localize this variable initiation to the procedure that manipulates the variable."

Functionality. Program functionality comments indicated that the program did not perform all functions defined in the problem specifications. An example was, "program only reads and prints list of numbers," when the problem was to read the numbers and print them in reverse order.

Algorithm. Algorithm comments pointed out deficiencies in the procedure used to solve a particular problem. Some algorithms could not be implemented in Pascal; others, if implemented, would produce incorrect results. For example, a programmer might write code that rotates all array elements except the last one. A comment might focus on the need to modify the algorithm to take proper account of the last case.

Implementation. Implementation comments dealt with the way the algorithm was carried out. Comments identified mistakes or indicated better or poorer ways of doing some function.

Style. Programming style comments given by readers dealt with making the program easier for a human to understand or use. These comments usually do not affect the output of the program. Examples of comments were "use meaningful variable names" and "provide the user with a prompt when he has to provide input from the keyboard."

Once comments were classified, agreement between readers was calculated for each diagnostic concept. Agreement for each concept was defined as the number of readers giving the same comment (regardless of wording) to the same code in the same program. Reader agreement for all the concepts was calculated as the mean of the reader agreements on each concept. MicroPROUST's agreement with the readers was indicated by the number of readers giving the same diagnostic comment as MicroPROUST for the same code on the same program.

Since no reader could be expected to make every possible comment with respect to the sample of papers read, an attempt was made to characterize the extent to which each reader made all possible comments. This characterization was defined as the number of correct distinct comments made by a single reader divided by the total number of correct distinct comments made by all readers (including MicroPROUST) for that sample. This value indicated how complete the reader was in making his or her diagnoses relative to the combined diagnoses made by the group. The percentage of correct distinct comments made by MicroPROUST was also calculated and compared with the individual reader values.

To identify areas in which MicroPROUST differed from readers in the comments it made, the number of comments was tabulated for each of the five categories. To correct for the fact that four readers commented on each paper, the mean number of comments per reader was compared with the total number of comments made by MicroPROUST for each category. Variation across readers in the types of comments made was considered by looking at the distribution of comments for each individual and by computing the standard deviation across readers of the number of comments made per category.

RESULTS

Summative Scoring

MicroPROUST was able to analyze only 8 of 23 papers in one of the two problem 1 samples and 12 of 22 in one of the two problem 2 samples; in the remaining two samples it analyzed all papers. Mean correlations between the grades awarded by each reader and MicroPROUST's success or failure to analyze papers for the two samples posing difficulty were .57 for problem 1 ($p < .001$, $t = 5.77$, $df = 80$) and .35 for problem 2 ($p < .01$, $t = 3.19$, $df = 76$), indicating that MicroPROUST tended to be more successful with well-developed problem solutions. Because solutions generally were assigned on the basis of quality (better solutions to one set of raters for problem 1 and to the other set for problem 2), MicroPROUST's tendency to be more successful with well-developed solutions helps explain why analysis failures were concentrated in two of the four samples.

Table 13.2 presents results of the summative analysis. As the table indicates, the mean correlations for the readers were .94 and .77 on problem 1, and .83 and .93 on problem 2. Within each problem, the mean correlations were significantly different across reader groups, with the lower values associated with the samples on which MicroPROUST had difficulty.

Mean correlations of MicroPROUST with the readers are only shown for the two samples in which MicroPROUST was able to grade all papers. These correlations are .74 for problem 1, significantly lower than the value for the readers alone, and .95 for problem 2, no different from the reader value.

Table 13.2 also presents reliabilities for two readings. These estimates indicate the level of consistency that might be expected between the average

TABLE 13.2
Comparison of Reader vs. MicroPROUST Ratings

| | Problem 1 | | | |
| | Readers 1–4 | | Readers 5–8 | |
Index	Readers	MicroPROUST	Readers	MicroPROUST
Number of papers	22	22	23	——
Mean correlation	.94	.74*	.77**	——
Reliability for				
2 readers	.97	.85	.87	——
	Problem 2			
Number of papers	22	——	21	21
Mean correlation	.83***	——	.93	.95
Reliability for				
2 readers	.91	——	.97	.97

Note: For readers, the mean correlation is the average of the transformed correlations between each pair of readers. For MicroPROUST, the mean is the average of the transformed correlations of MicroPROUST with each reader.

* $p < .001$, t (two-tailed) $= 7.19$, 190 df; computed against the problem 1 mean for readers 1–4.

** $p < .001$, t (two-tailed) $= 5.61$, 234 df; computed against the problem 1 mean for readers 1–4.

*** $p < .001$, t (two-tailed) $= 3.59$, 222 df; computed against the problem 2 mean for readers 5–8.

ratings of pairs of readers. If MicroPROUST was to be paired with a human reader whose agreement with other humans was similar to Micro-PROUST's, the reliability for problem 1 would be .85, a respectable value. The reliability for two human readers, however, is considerably higher at .97. For problem 2, the reliability for two human readers is equivalent to that for a human paired with MicroPROUST.

The correlation between MicroPROUST's ratings and the average rating

TABLE 13.3
Distribution of Absolute Differences Between MicroPROUST's Ratings and the Mean of the Reader Ratings

Absolute Discrepancy	Frequency	
	Problem 1 Readers 1-4	Problem 2 Readers 5-8
2	2	1
1-1.99	9	0
0-.99	11	20

TABLE 13.4
Distribution of Differences Between 12 Pairs of Readers and 12 MicroPROUST-reader Pairs

	Problem 1			
	Frequency of Absolute Discrepancy			
Absolute Discrepancy	Among Readers 1-4	Between Readers 1-4 and MicroPROUST	Among Readers 5-8	Between Readers 5-8 and MicroPROUST
4			4	——
3			10	——
2		26	68	——
1	38	141	112	——
0	226	97	82	——
Mean	.14	.73	1.07	
	Problem 2			
6	4	——		
5	4	——		
4	4	——		
3	10	——	2	
2	32	——	24	27
1	66	——	68	54
0	144	——	158	171
Mean	.83		.48	.43

TABLE 13.5
Mean Ratings Given by MicroPROUST and Human Readers

		Readers 1–4				
Problem	MicroPROUST	All Readers	Reader 1	Reader 2	Reader 3	Reader 4
1[ab]	8.46	7.85	7.82	7.86	7.82	7.91
2[c]	——	2.73	3.32	2.5	2.86	2.23

[a] $p < .001$, $F = 9.84$, $df = 4,84$ for differences among readers, including Micro-PROUST.
[b] $p < .001$, $t = -6.27$, $df = 84$ for the difference between MicroPROUST and the mean for all readers.
[c] $p < .01$, $F = 5.22$, $df = 3,63$ for differences among readers.

		Readers 5–8				
Problem	MicroPROUST	All Readers	Reader 5	Reader 6	Reader 7	Reader 8
1	——	4.62	4.96	4.61	4.39	4.52
2	6.43	6.53	6.48	6.57	6.38	6.67

for each problem taken across all four raters was also computed. These average ratings can be taken to represent an estimate of classical test theory's "true" score, the examinee's actual standing on the attribute being measured. For problem 1, the correlation with the average rating was .75 whereas for problem 2 it was .96.

In Table 13.3, the distribution of absolute differences between MicroPROUST's ratings and the mean of the reader ratings is presented. For the problem 1 sample rated by MicroPROUST, half of the papers had discrepancies of one or two points. For the problem 2 sample, only one paper had such a difference.

In Table 13.4, the distribution of absolute differences is presented between pairs of readers and between MicroPROUST-reader pairs. As the table indicates, for the problem 1 sample rated by both MicroPROUST and the readers the largest discrepancies are on the order of two points and belong to MicroPROUST. The readers never disagree among themselves by more than one point. For the problem 2 sample rated by both machine and humans, the distributions are very similar to one another, consistent with the correlational results. Finally, the disagreements among readers are far higher for the problem sets that MicroPROUST did not rate than for those that it did. The magnitude of disagreements among readers 5–8 is about twice as great for the former than for the latter problem set; for readers 1–4, it is almost six times larger.

Table 13.5 shows the mean ratings given by each reader. For problem

TABLE 13.6
**Univariate Repeated Measures F-Test for Table
13.5, Mean Ratings Given by MicroPROUST
and by Readers**

Problem 1: Readers 1–4

Source	S.S.	df	M.S.	F	P
Readers	6.51	4	1.63	9.84	.000
Error	13.89	84	0.17		
Total	20.40	88			

Problem 2: Readers 1–4

Source	S.S.	df	M.S.	F	P
Readers	14.73	3	4.91	5.22	.003
Error	59.27	63	0.94		
Total	74.00	66			

1, significant differences among the five individual mean ratings (four readers and MicroPROUST) were detected ($p < .001$, $F = 9.84$, $df = 4,84$). Post hoc contrasts showed MicroPROUST's mean rating to be significantly higher than the mean for all readers ($p < .001$, $t = -6.27$, $df = 84$) and to be higher than each individual reader mean (t range $= 3.20$ to 4.54, p range $< .001$ to $.005$, $df = 21$). No human reader mean, however, was different from any other human reader mean. For the same group of readers (minus MicroPROUST) on problem 2, however, differences in score level did exist ($p < .01$, $F = 5.22$, $df = 3,63$). Paired-samples t-tests showed reader 3 to differ from readers 1 and 4 and reader 2 to differ with reader 4 (t range $= 2.59$ to 3.24, p range $< .005$ to $.02$, $df = 21$).

For readers 5–8, no differences among the individual mean ratings were found on the problem set graded with MicroPROUST ($p = .56$, $F = .765$, $df = 4,80$) or the set graded by the readers only ($p = .28$, $F = 1.30$, $df = 3,66$).

Diagnostic Comments

As noted earlier, MicroPROUST was able to grade only 8 of 23 papers in one of the two problem 1 samples and 12 of 22 in one of the two problem 2 samples. In the two remaining samples, it graded every paper. Even though it was able to grade every paper, it did not comment on every paper it graded. For the samples in which it graded all papers, it commented on 7 of 22 solutions to problem 1 and 18 of 21 for problem 2, the difference between problems being due to the proportion of papers to which MicroPROUST awarded perfect grades (68% for problem 1 and 14% for problem 2; on these perfect papers, it made no commentary). In contrast, every human reader commented on each solution, except one reader who made no comment on two papers. On perfect solutions (i.e., those graded 9 by the *other* group of readers), readers made mostly stylistic comments not included as errors in the scoring rubric.

Over all solutions analyzed by MicroPROUST, approximately 90% of the program's comments were correct. Taken across problems and groups, the human readers averaged 98% of their comments correct; the worst human error rate was 97% correct. The errors committed by the humans and MicroPROUST did not overlap, nor were there patterns among readers or between problems.

Table 13.7 presents the number of correct comments given each solution set by the readers and by MicroPROUST. Several points should be noted. First, within some groups readers varied widely in the number of comments they assigned. For example, on problem 2 reader 1 made almost twice as many comments as reader 4, while on problem 1, reader 1 made nearly twice as many as reader 3. Second, the number of comments varied considerably by group and problem with many more comments assigned to the less adequate solutions (i.e., the ones not analyzed by MicroPROUST). Finally, while readers gave many more comments than MicroPROUST overall, this relationship varied by problem. For problem 1, readers 5-8 gave on average four times as many comments, while for problem 2 the numbers of comments awarded by the program and the readers were comparable with the program equaling or exceeding two of the four readers.

TABLE 13.7
Number of Correct Comments Given by Readers and by MicroPROUST

		Readers 1-4				
Problem	*MicroPROUST*	*Reader Mean*	*Reader 1*	*Reader 2*	*Reader 3*	*Reader 4*
1	——	73	93	78	54	67
2	22	25	32	27	22	18

		Readers 5-8				
Problem	*MicroPROUST*	*Reader Mean*	*Reader 5*	*Reader 6*	*Reader 7*	*Reader 8*
1	10	42	34	43	46	45
2	——	67	69	69	65	65

TABLE 13.8
Percentage of Total Correct Distinct Comments Generated by Group
that Were Also Identified by Individual Readers

		Readers 1–4				
Problem	MicroPROUST	Reader Mean	Reader 1	Reader 2	Reader 3	Reader 4
1	——	59	76	63	44	54
2	52	59	76	64	52	43

		Readers 5–8				
Problem	MicroPROUST	Reader Mean	Reader 5	Reader 6	Reader 7	Reader 8
1	11	46	37	47	51	49
2	——	68	70	70	66	66

When agreement between readers is expressed as the number of readers giving the same comment to the same code in the same program, agreement was moderate, with an average 2.4 readers of a possible four giving each comment (calculated across both reader groups and problems). The readers had high agreement with MicroPROUST on most of the errors it diagnosed. An average 3.2 human readers (out of a possible four) noted each of the 64 errors correctly diagnosed by the program (calculated across all problems analyzed by the program).

Table 13.8 gives the percentage of total correct distinct comments generated by the readers that were identified by individuals. As the table indicates, readers identified, on average, between 59% and 68% of the total number of diagnostic comments identified by their subgroup, indicating a substantial amount of variability in the comments made across individuals. On problem 1, MicroPROUST identified a far smaller proportion of the total (11%) than the readers did. For problem 2, however, its performance, at 52%, was comparable with the readers, at least in terms of the proportion of the domain covered.

How exactly did MicroPROUST differ from the readers in the kinds of comments it made? Table 13.9 shows the number of correct comments made by category for readers and for MicroPROUST. To correct for the fact that four readers (but only one MicroPROUST) commented on each paper, the mean number of comments per reader is presented against the total number of comments for MicroPROUST. As indicated in the table, the distribution of reader comments varied across problems and reader groups. Across problems and groups, readers made multiple comments in each of the five categories. MicroPROUST, in contrast, concentrated its comments on implementation. When compared with readers within problems, the biggest differences between MicroPROUST and the readers were for problem 1, a finding consistent with the correlational analysis. On this problem, MicroPROUST performed comparably with readers on function, algorithm, and implementation, but made no comments on structure and style (readers made 11 and 25, respectively). For problem 2, the numbers of comments were distributed similarly for MicroPROUST and the readers with the possible exception of structure, which readers made more mention of. Finally, it is well to note that reader comments were extensive on the problem sets that MicroPROUST could not analyze completely.

TABLE 13.9
Number of Correct Comments by Concept Category for Readers and MicroPROUST

Concept Category	Readers 1–4 Mean Comments	MicroPROUST Total Comments	Readers 5–8 Mean Comments	MicroPROUST Total Comments
Problem 1				
Structure	13	——	11	0
Function	15	——	1	3
Algorithm	7	——	0	0
Implemen- tation	23	——	5	7
Style	15	——	25	0
Problem 2				
Structure	4	0	13	——
Function	0	0	3	——
Algorithm	9	9	23	——
Implemen- tation	11	13	26	——
Style	1	0	3	——

TABLE 13.10
Number of Correct Comments Made by Individual Readers Within Concept Categories

Concept Category	Reader								
	1	2	3	4	5	6	7	8	Mean (SD)
Structure	22	15	12	18	24	30	29	13	20 (6)
Function	17	16	17	10	5	1	8	2	10 (6)
Algorithm	18	16	14	17	23	21	20	28	20 (4)
Implemen- tation	47	39	28	24	30	33	31	28	33 (6)
Style	21	19	5	16	21	27	23	40	21 (8)

Within groups, there were some striking differences in the categories of errors individual readers chose to comment on (see Table 13.10). For instance, although they read the same programs, reader 1 made style comments over four times as often as reader 3. Similarly, readers 5 and 7 commented on program functionality much more frequently than did readers 6 and 8. Overall, the greatest variability across readers was found for style comments and the least for algorithm comments.

DISCUSSION

This study examined the extent of scoring agreement between a computer program and expert human readers for two constructed response problems taken from the College Board's Advanced Placement Computer Science examination. The results suggest several conclusions. First, MicroPROUST appears unable to grade a significant portion of solutions to a given problem (28% in the current study and 58% in an independent sample). This comes as no surprise, for the program is a prototype running on a personal computer (albeit, a substantially expanded one); the fact that it can analyze *any* substantial portion of solutions is an accomplishment.

MicroPROUST is unable to analyze all solutions because the great variety of correct and incorrect ways of formulating problem solutions requires more knowledge than the program currently has. While its knowledge base can be increased, it is questionable whether the program will ever be able to evaluate the same wide range of responses that humans can. One solution to this shortcoming may be to place constraints on the types of responses students can make. For example, instead of giving students a specification and asking them to write a program to implement it, one might present a faulty program and ask them to write a correct version of it (Braun, 1988). These corrected versions would then be given to MicroPROUST for analysis.

While it is clear that MicroPROUST cannot analyze some significant portion of papers, it is not completely clear whether this failure is related to the quality of the solution. In the current sample, there was a clear tendency for the program to analyze well-formed solutions more frequently than poorly formed ones. However, in a second independent sample for problem 2, analysis failures were *not* associated with reader score level ($r = .16$, $p > .1$, $t = 1.04$, $df = 43$). These contradictory findings may be in part a result of the development process: MicroPROUST's knowledge base was built from the same set of solutions that was used in the study. Hence, an effort was made to include in the knowledge base as many correct program plan subcomponents from the development sample as possible. This effort might be expected to result in the program's being able to analyze a high proportion of well-formed responses. Because poorly formed responses contain many types, levels, and combinations of bugs, it is more difficult to represent them in a knowledge base. Therefore, a smaller proportion of the total number of bugs in the development sample was included in the knowledge base. As a result, for the development sample MicroPROUST was able to handle more well- than ill-formed responses.

Students' development strategies, however, might differ somewhat from sample to sample (there are many ways to solve programming problems correctly and a development sample of 45 solutions probably provides only a small number of these). To the extent this occurs, MicroPROUST might have more trouble analyzing well-formed responses in new samples. In an independent sample, therefore, one might expect MicroPROUST's ability to analyze well-formed solutions to degrade to a level more comparable with its ability to analyze poorly formed ones. Should MicroPROUST's knowledge base be extended, encompassing more and more of the universe of common well-formed solutions, a generalized bias toward analyzing well-formed responses might result.

It is interesting to note that, like MicroPROUST, readers also had more difficulty grading poorer solutions. For both problems, their agreement levels were significantly lower for these solutions than for the better formed ones. In contrast to MicroPROUST, readers assign a grade, albeit a less reliable one than they otherwise generate.

Whereas MicroPROUST could not analyze a significant proportion of responses, its performance on the subset it could analyze was impressive, though not always as good as the readers. For one of the two problems studied, MicroPROUST assigned grades and diagnostic comments that were very similar to those assigned by readers. For the other problem, several important differences were evident: MicroPROUST's level of agreement with the readers for summative scores was lower than the level of agreement for readers among themselves; its grades were, on average, higher; and it gave fewer comments, particularly in matters related to structure and style. Finally, though MicroPROUST was incomplete, compared with readers in the diagnostic comments it assigned, readers agreed more with MicroPROUST on its comments than they did on their own remarks.

Though MicroPROUST disagreed with readers on one problem in assigning summative scores, the magnitude of disagreement was, by most measures, relatively small. For example, the average correlation between MicroPROUST and the readers was in the .70s, which while smaller than the agreement level among readers, indicates a substantial degree of association all the same. Second, whereas MicroPROUST's ratings were higher, they were so by only six tenths of a point on a ten-point scale.

Finally, the program's discrepancy with individual readers reached the level required for resolution in operational readings (2 points) for only 10% of the possible disagreements for the problem.

Disagreement appeared to be more substantial for this problem on the diagnostic analysis, particularly the proportion of the total universe of potential correct remarks covered. While readers were far from perfect, they covered a much greater segment of this universe than the program, indicating that their diagnostic commentary is generally more complete. This indicates that even on those solutions that MicroPROUST can analyze it is apt to miss student errors.

Many of the errors MicroPROUST failed to comment on were related to programming style. Style omissions also would seem to play a considerable role in score disagreements between the program and readers: When solutions are rescored to remove the effect of style, MicroPROUST's agreement with readers increases substantially. For problem 1, the average correlation between MicroPROUST and the readers increases from .74 to .86 and level differences are eliminated ($p = .636$, $F = .639$, $df = 4,84$). Work on incorporating style knowledge in MicroPROUST might, therefore, remove a major source of disagreement with human readers.

Whether solutions are graded by readers or MicroPROUST, the problem and/or adequacy of the solution seems to affect reliability. For example, the same group of readers was able to grade on a common scale for one problem but not the other. Because the adequacy of the solutions across these two problems differed considerably, further investigation of the stability of rater reliability across problems and solution quality seems warranted.

What limitations might have affected this study's outcome? One important limitation was the use of the same sample of solutions for both knowledge base development and evaluation of interrater agreement. To get a rough indication of whether MicroPROUST's performance would generalize to other solution samples, the program was given a set of 45 solutions to problem 2 randomly drawn from AP files. The correlation between MicroPROUST's ratings and the original reader-assigned grades for the 19 solutions the program was able to analyze was .82 ($p < .001$, $t = 5.8$, $df = 17$), a respectable performance. All the same, a more complete cross-validation might provide stronger evidence of the program's power.

A second set of limitations that might have affected the study's outcome is that the experimental reading differed from operational ones in several ways. On the negative side, less time was spent going over and practicing application of the scoring rubric; discussing problems with one's neighbors was discouraged; within groups, papers were more restricted in quality, providing less variety; and the indentations made by students in their solutions were changed inadvertently by the printing program, making the papers somewhat harder to read. On the positive side, the problems presented were the easiest on the Advanced Placement Computer Science Examination, the reading lasted 1 day instead of 6, and all the readers had participated in previous operational readings. Because no other studies of rater reliability for the APCS exam exist, it is impossible to estimate confidently the effect of these differences. The reliabilities observed here, however, are not dramatically different from those found for analytically scored AP exams in other subjects (e.g., physics, mathematics). Consequently, there is little reason to suspect that these differences had any material overall effect.

What does this research suggest for practical uses of MicroPROUST-like systems in scoring constructed response items? First, the data suggest that, given certain constraints, such systems can do as well as readers. This ability is limited to a portion of the solutions that the system encounters, perhaps to the quality of the solutions and/or a particular class of problem, and, with respect to diagnostic commentary, to domains other than style. These limitations make clear that such systems must be used in conjunction with people; depending on the setting, those individuals might be classroom teachers or Advanced Placement readers. For example, in an instructionally based diagnostic system, if the computer cannot analyze a solution it might present a series of multiple-choice or more constrained free-response items. The student's performance on these items might be used either to compute an estimate of the student's ability to solve programming problems or to give it the information needed to analyze successfully the student's original production. Should the computer still be unable to analyze the original solution, that response could be routed to the teacher. Research will need to be conducted on whether and how information gathered from multiple-choice and more constrained free-response item types might facilitate analysis of open-ended items.

In the Advanced Placement setting, a MicroPROUST-like system might also work in conjunction with people. After submitting a validation sample to the program to ensure that it graded on a common scale with the readers, the program could be used as a "first-pass" reader. Solutions the program was unable to grade would be routed to people. Alternatively, the program could be used to help readers stay on scale. Papers could be preread by MicroPROUST between their arrival at ETS and the time they are submitted for grading; or, already-graded papers could be reread by the program during the operational reading. Discrepancies would be resolved by the table leaders and/or chief reader.

Using MicroPROUST-like systems in the classroom presents only temporary implementation problems. Though it is true that such systems require computing resources beyond those currently found in schools, the price of these resources is rapidly decreasing. Consequently, advanced computer systems should eventually be common enough to permit the use of expert assessment systems in educational settings.

Significant implementation problems will, however, need to be addressed before such systems can be used in the Advanced Placement environment. In this setting, the major issues relate to getting solutions into machine-readable form. Students currently submit handwritten solutions in examination booklets. Having these solutions transcribed at ETS might introduce errors in punctuation, spacing, or other subtleties that could affect test score. Therefore, it would seem wise to determine the frequency and effect of errors introduced in transcription if this method is to be considered seriously.

Requiring students to submit their solutions in machine-readable format is an obvious alternative to transcription. However, this alternative also presents problems. Should solutions be entered using only an editor, or are interpreters and compilers permissible? If interpreters and compilers are allowed, those using these tools would have the benefit of programs that locate certain types of programming errors. If all students are advised to use an interpreter or compiler, other inequities are introduced. For example, interpreters permit programs to be developed faster than compilers, giving students more time to produce their solutions. In addition, some tools are more capable than others, providing more help in error prevention and location. How serious these potential inequities are is not clear. Experimental studies should be conducted to elucidate the effects of these different data entry options.

Given that the conversion problem can be solved, significant savings in grading free-response items might be realized if the student solutions that MicroPROUST will not analyze can be predicted. Performance on the multiple-choice section, for example, might predict the program's success in grading free responses. If so, only selected papers would be transcribed; others would be routed to readers as is. Assuming that MicroPROUST could analyze 50% of student responses, only half the current number of graders might be needed (or the same number of graders for half the time).

What general conclusion can be drawn from MicroPROUST's performance? MicroPROUST is an "existence proof" of the fact that a machine is, within certain important limitations, interchangeable with humans in grading complex constructed responses. Our next task is to find practical ways to exploit this capability to improve the grading of AP examinations and, further, to create powerful, individualized learning and assessment environments that advance the way Advanced Placement content is taught and knowledge of it measured.

REFERENCES

Barr, A., & Feigenbaum, E. A. (1981). *The handbook of artificial intelligence* (Vol. 1). Stanford, CA: HeurisTech Press.

Bejar, I. I. (1984). Educational diagnostic assessment. *Journal of Educational Measurement, 21*, 175–189.

Braun, H. I. (1988, February 4). Personal communication.

Forehand, G. A. (1987). Development of a computerized diagnostic testing program. *Collegiate Microcomputer*, 5, 55–59.

Glaser, R. (1986). The integration of instruction and testing. In *The redesign of testing for the 21st century* (Proceedings of the 1985 ETS Invitational Conference). Princeton, NJ: Educational Testing Service.

Johnson, W. L., & Soloway, E. (1985). PROUST: An automatic debugger for Pascal programs. *Byte*, *10*(4), 179–190.

McNemar, Q. (1962). *Psychological statistics*. New York: Wiley.

Scheffe, H. (1953). A method for judging all contrasts in the analysis of variance. *Biometrika*, *40*, 87–104.

Stanley, J. (1971). Reliability. In R. L. Thorndike (Ed.), *Educational measurement*. Washington, DC: American Council on Education.

Tatsuoka, K. K. (1985). *Diagnosing cognitive errors: Statistical pattern classification and recognition approach* (Research Report 85-1-ONR). Urbana–Champaign: University of Illinois.

Ward, W. C., Frederiksen, N., & Carlson, S. B. (1980). Construct validity of free-response and machine scorable forms of a test. *Journal of Educational Measurement*, *17*, 11–29.

Wenger, E. (1987) *Artificial intelligence and tutoring systems: Computational and cognitive approaches to the communication of knowledge*. Los Altos, CA: Morgan Kaufmann.

APPENDIX A: PROGRAMMING PROBLEMS

Problem 1: Write a program to read eight integers from the terminal, display them in reverse order, and display the number of negative integers read. For example, given the input:

$$-4 \quad 3 \quad -2 \quad 1 \quad -18 \quad -20 \quad 5 \quad -7$$

the program should produce the output:

$$-7 \quad 5 \quad -20 \quad -18 \quad 1 \quad -2 \quad 3 \quad -4$$

5 of the integers are negative.

Problem 2: Write a procedure that rotates the elements of an array s with n elements so that when the rotation is completed, the old value of $s[1]$ will be in $s[2]$, the old value of $s[2]$ will be in $s[3]$, . . . , the old value of $s[n - 1]$ will be in $s[n]$, and the old value of $s[n]$ will be in $s[1]$. Your procedure should have s and n as parameters. You may assume that the type *Item* has been declared and s is of type *List* which has been declared as *List* = array[1 . . . *Max*] of *Item*.

APPENDIX B: EXAMPLES OF STUDENT SOLUTIONS AND DIAGNOSTIC COMMENTS FOR PROBLEM 1

```
1.  Program Find(input, output);
2.
3.      Type
4.          ListType = Array[1 . . 8] of Integer;
5.
```

```
6.       Var
7.           List: ListType (* array of eight integers *);
8.           Found: Integer (* holds number of negative numbers found *);
9.
10. procedure RData (List1; ListType);
11.
12.      Var
13.          I: integer (* counter used to move through List1 array *);
14.
15.      Begin
16.          for I := 1 to 8 do
17.              Begin
18.                  Write('Enter number ',I,': ');
19.                  Readln(List1[I]);
20.              End (*end for when I := 8 *);
21.      End (* end procedure RData->ReadData *);
22.
23. procedure DWrite(List1: ListType);
24.
25.      Var
26.          I: integer (* counter used to move through List1 array *);
27.
28.      Begin
29.          for I := 8 downto 1 do
30.              Write(List1[I]:5);
31.          Writeln;
32.      End (* end procedure DWrite->DataDisplay *);
33.
34. procedure Scand(List1: ListType);
35.
36.      var
37.          I: integer (* index to array List1 *);
38.
39.      begin
40.          for I := 1 to 8 do
41.              if List1[I] < 0 then Found := Found + 1;
42.      end (* end Scand->ScanList *);
43.
44.
45. begin (* main program *)
46.      RData(List) (* go input a list of 8 numbers *);
47.      DWrite(List) (* print list in reverse order *);
48.      Found := 0;
49.      Scand(List) (* find all negative integers in list *);
50.      Writeln (Found, ' of the integers are negative.');
51. end.■
```

****

BUG REPORT: On line 10, your array should have been passed
as a variable parameter rather than a value parameter.

```
1. program ReadIntegers(input,output);
2.
3. type
4.      Num = array[1 . . 8] of integer;
5.
6. var
```

```
 7.       Number: Num;
 8.       I, Total: integer;
 9.
10. procedure Enter;
11.
12.       begin
13.           I := 0; Total := 0;
14.           while I < 8 do
15.               begin
16.                   Write ('Enter a Integer ==>');
17.                   readln(Number[I]);
18.                   I := I + 1;
19.                   if I < 0 then Total := Total + 1;
20.                   writeln
21.               end
22.       end;
23.
24. procedure PrintOut;
25.
26.       begin
27.           writeln ('Output ==>');
28.           i := 8;
29.           while I > 0 do
30.               begin
31.                   write(Number[I],' ');
32.                   i := i - 1
33.               end;
34.           writeln;
35.           writeln(Total,' of the integers are negative.');
36.           writeln
37.       end;
38.
39. begin
40.       Enter;
41.       Printout
42. end.■
```

****

BUG REPORT: On line 13, you have used the wrong initial value. It will not be within the bounds of your array.

On line 14, you have used the wrong boundary value. The WHILE loop will exit before you have read in the last number.

On line 19, it appears you have used the wrong variable to test for a negative value.

Grading Rubric — Question #1 1984

Program/Procedure Headers Present and Correct	+1		
Type/Var Declarations Present and Correct	+1		
		max	−1
Negative Counter Initialized Correctly	+1		
Input Loop Present and Correct	+1		
		max	−2
Reads and Stores 8 Integers Correctly (read statement present & correct) (also includes calling a read module if implemented)	+2		
Negative Test Present and Correct (valid if reading of integers present)	+1		
Negative Count Incremented Correctly (valid if reading of integers present)	+1		
		max	−3
Reverse Loop Direction Correct (and consistent with the other loop)	+1		
Displays Negative Count Correctly (including a descriptive string in the output)	+1		
Displays All Integers Present	+1		
		max	−2
Style and Syntax			
		max	−1
user prompt missing	−1		
confusing indentation (formatting)	−1		
redefining standard procedures or using reserved words incorrectly	−1		
improper data structure (8 variables)	−1		
unnecessary or useless code	−1/2		
3 or more syntax errors	−1/2		
[ ] and ( ) confusion	−1/2		

1984 Question #1

Reader # / Booklet #	PROGRAM/ PROCEDURE HEADERS (Max −1) +1	TYPE/VAR DECLARATIONS +1	NEGATIVE COUNTER INITIALIZED (Max −2) +1	INPUT LOOP PRESENT +1	READS 8 INTEGERS +2	NEGATIVE TEST PRESENT/ CORRECT (Max −3) +1	NEGATIVE COUNT INCREMENTED +1	REVERSE LOOP DIRECTION CORRECT +1	DISPLAYS NEGATIVE COUNT (Max −2) +1	DISPLAYS ALL INTEGERS PRESENT +1	SYNTAX & STYLE (Max −1) +1	TOTAL POINTS +9

317

Grading Rubric — Question #1 1985

Procedure Header Error
    Missing VAR   −1
    Missing Parameter   −1
                                            max   −1

Interpretations:
    extra VAR or unnecessary parameter
    in formal parameter list   − 1/2 style

Declaration and Statement Errors
    Type Error   −1
    Missing Declaration   −1
    Incorrect or Missing Loop Initialization   −1
    Incorrect or Missing Loop Conclusion   −1
                                            max   −2

Interpretations:

        initialization/conclusion:
            if consistent w/problem
            temp: = s[N] — OK

            if consistent w/reversed
            rotation solution
            temp: = s[1] — OK

            points are lost for inconsistency
            or incorrect statements

Loop Logic Errors

        Minor Loop Error
        (using max, index out-of-bounds)   −2

        Loop Direction Error
        (single array using 'TO')   −2

        Loop Inconsistency
        (over-writing array elements)   −3
                                     max   −5

Grading Rubric — Question #1 1985 (Cont.)

Interpretations:

Really minor errors:
initialization inside loop   −1

rotation correct except one
element is wrong   −1

Loop Direction/Loop Consistency:

for index: = 2 to n do
  s[index]: = s[index − 1]   {1111} −2 direction
                                                 −3 overwriting

for index: = 2 to n do
  s[index − 1]: = s[index]   {2341} −2 direction

for index: = n downto 2 do
  s[index]: = s[index − 1]   {4123} OK

for index: = n downto 2 do
  s[index − 1]: = s[index]   {4444} −3 overwrite

Style and Syntax
                                                 max   −1

confusing indentation (formatting)   −1

redefining standard procedures or
using reserved words incorrectly   −1

disregard for efficiency (two arrays)   −1

---

unnecessary or useless code   −1/2

3 or more syntax errors   −1/2

[ ] and ( ) confusion   −1/2

1985 Question #1	PROCEDURE HEADER MISSING VAR	PROCEDURE HEADER MISSING PARAMETER	DECLARATION TYPE ERROR	DECLARATION MISSING	INCORRECT/MISSING LOOP INITIALIZATION	INCORRECT/MISSING LOOP TERMINATION	LOOP LOGIC MINOR ERROR	LOOP LOGIC LOOP DIRECTION	LOOP LOGIC LOOP INCONSISTENCY	SYNTAX & STYLE	TOTAL POINTS
Reader #	Max −1			Max −2			Max −5			Max −1	
Booklet #	−1	−1	−1	−1	−1	−1	−2	−2	−3	−1	+9

Author Index

Subject Index

327

Printed and bound by CPI Group (UK) Ltd, Croydon, CR0 4YY

17/10/2024

01775688-0015